The Greatest Proven Seer Since Biblical Times!

In *The Fate of the Nations*, Arthur Prieditis places Nostradamus in the line of the biblical prophets—those visionaries of doom and regeneration. After a brief introduction to clairvoyance, he establishes Nostradamus' credentials by documenting his amazing record of fulfilled predictions. This is preparatory to sifting out the yet unfulfilled prophecies relevant to mankind's immediate and long-range future.

The book becomes a guide to the chronology of that future. Through his analysis of fulfilled predictions, Mr. Prieditis offers patterns and keys useful in interpreting Nostradamus' enigmatic unfulfilled prophecies. He also includes, in full, the prophet's epistles to his son Caesar and King Henry II, both of which offer clues necessary to understanding Nostradamus' own view of his methods and visions. In addition to selecting the relevant quatrains and offering his own analysis, he brings in many other commentators. And in one chapter he presents in detail the differing views of three commentators on Nostradamus' view of the future: E. Ruir, H. Bauder, and G. Gustafsson. This he follows with another containing relevant predictions by prophets other than Nostradamus, including Cayce, Dixon, C. A. Chader, Anton Johansson and others.

By assembling all this material, he guides the reader toward arriving at his *own* conclusions about the future. Because of his background in political economy, his formal studies in the occult, and his fifteen years of research into the topic, the book is more than a guide; it becomes a reference work encyclopedic in scope. But it is broadened by more than scholarship, for the author infuses his treatment with a visionary zeal, and the book becomes a personal testament.

• • •

Mr Prieditis was born in Latvia where he lived until the Second World War. He then lived in Germany and Switzerland for five years before settling in the United States. Having seventeen books to his credit, he has written on Chinese poetry and philosophy and Greek mythology as well as translated from English, French, German, and Russian.

THE FATE OF THE NATIONS

The FATE of the NATIONS

Great Events of the Near Future
as Predicted by Nostradamus and Other Clairvoyants

SECOND ENLARGED EDITION

ARTHUR PRIEDITIS

1982
Llewellyn Publications
St. Paul, Minnesota, 55164-0383, U.S.A.

First Edition 1975
Second Revised and Enlarged Edition 1982
Second Printing, revised, 1982

International Standard Book Number: 0-87542-624-7
Library of congress Catalogue Card Number: 73-20450

Llewellyn Publications
Post Office Box 43383
Saint Paul, Minnesota 55164-0383

Printed in the United States of America

CONTENTS

INTRODUCTION

Can the future be predicted? Does clairvoyance really exist? Many so-called educated people answer these questions with a smile and a superior air. They don't believe in medieval superstitions. They think it beneath them even to investigate such phenomena. They believe only in science. And modern authorities have declared—have they not?—prophecy and similar phenomena to be impossible. Impossibility is the pivot of this question.

Yet the history of science testifies to the realization, by scientific progress, of marvels that were considered impossible by the greatest scientists and thinkers of previous centuries. Only fantastic novels dealt with rocket journeys to the moon, with "television," submarines and similar impossibilities. Sensible men did not read such trash. They classified it, with fairy tales, as juvenile literature.

Many pioneers of science did not fare better. The history of the academies of sciences of London and Paris registers a long list of ignominious slurs and blots. The members of these academies did not believe in steamships nor railroads. They ridiculed the idea that London could ever be illuminated by gas. An outbreak of hilarity was the result of Benjamin Franklin's lecture on his lightning conductor. They refused to print and to publish it. It is a well-known fact that Galvani was derided by his contemporaries. Semmelweiss, the discoverer of puerperal fever, died in a lunatic asylum, and

Robert Mayer, the discoverer of the law of conservation of forces, would have suffered the same fate, had not his strong constitution overcome the maltreatment. Mesmer, the rediscoverer of hypnotism, was declared to be a fantast and impostor by the Paris Academy of Sciences. He did not live to see his theory acknowledged. Louis Pasteur and Rudolf Diesel suffered ridicule and mockery to the end of their days.

Many pages could be filled with similar instances. Authorities, may they be ever so genial men, have always been opposed to any new ideas which did not fit into the then prevailing system. Even scientific opinions, hypotheses, theories and dogmas are subject to fashions and fads. With time they too become antiquated. It happens this way: At first an inconvenient, upsetting theory or an inexplicable phenomenon is ignored, then rejected, but after an immense accumulation of data, it is reluctantly recognized and given a scientific name which serves as a presumptive explication.

For ages science taught that the sun circles around the earth; but today we must be of the opposite opinion to be in accord with science. Today the earth is not flat as a board anymore, but round as a ball. Formerly science taught the conservation of matter; today matter can be transformed into energy without remnant. The chemical elements, which formerly were taught to be stable and indestructible, today "collapse," disintegrate and transmute into other elements. Mesmer died without recognition and a pauper; but today suggestion and hypnotism in an ever higher degree are therapeutically used in medical praxis, although the evoked phenomena to a great extent still remain scientifically inexplicable.

How can we be sure that the truth which today is represented by science, in the future will not turn into something wrong, incorrect, incomplete and false, in other words, into delusion and superstition? It is wrong to surmise superstition in all things not yet scientifically explicable. The so-called scientific explication usually is nothing more than a utilitarian formula and thesis. For instance, the famous doctor of psychiatry, Professor C.G. Jung of the University of Zurich, having ascertained in his praxis of psychiatry the usefulness of astrological characterization of his patients and having seen himself compelled to make his experimental experience concur with his scientific mode of thinking, came forward with the formulation of his famous law of acausal synchronicity. Now, it remains only for another scientist to prove experimentally that planetary movements and human psychical occurrences both depend upon a third, heretofore unknown common factor, and the result will be the reconstitution of causality and the simultaneous recognition of astrology as a science.

In one of his many books Professor C.G. Jung boldly declares: "Although half-educated people still sneer at astrology as a long ago wound-up science, astrology again knocks at the doors of all universities." And Professor A. Einstein in his last book of reminiscences admits that he often had occupied himself with astrology and had found it extremely useful.

After such statements by eminent scientists all modern adherents of the 200-year-old ideas of the "enlightenment" period must be puzzled and ask themselves: What is superstition, and is there anything left for us to turn into ridicule? The answer is: Always and ever, recognized as well as unrecognized ideas and theories have been used to dupe and swindle credulous people, but it is something that has to be deplored and not to be laughed at. The regrettable fact of cheating alone cannot upset any of the misused ideas and confirms only the fact that on this earth there is never shortage of credulous people. Credulity is a shortcut to superstition. We have to be critical of everything, but our criticism should be consistent. It should not stop at the dogmas, hypotheses and theories which happen to be fashionable and in vogue at the given time. Such standstill or sticking fast is what is called bias or prejudice and by it our critical faculties are robbed of objectivity.

* * * * *

The materialistic article of faith recognizes only matter and energy. The laws, discovered as being valid in these two fields, are subsequently applied also to psychical and spiritual occurrences. Clairvoyance, not reconcilable with these laws, is therefore denied by science. And yet the phenomenon of clairvoyance exists and has existed for thousands of years. Such great thinkers as Plato, St. Augustine, Kant and Schopenhauer did not doubt the existence of clairvoyance.

What is this scientifically inexplicable phenomenon, called clairvoyance? The meaning of the French word is "clear-sightedness." It is seeing or vision with an inner, undimmed eye, an insight into the invisible spiritual world, of which the visible material world is only a replica, and in which effects have not yet detached themselves from causes and exist simultaneously with them. Due to this circumstance, the scientifically "impossible" prophecy becomes possible, but only very few people possess this spiritual vision, and still fewer are those who after such "insight" are capable logically and comprehensibly to report what they have seen. It is a very hard task, because such a report is always only a translation, an effort to convey in words things that have not yet been intellectually grasped.

Most people, being devoid of the gift of clairvoyance, make conjectures about the future only from past and present experiences, intellectually following, sequence by sequence, the long, tedious path of logical deductions. Is it the only way? Are all scientific accomplishments and discoveries a product of logic and of intellectual effort? Many scientists have admitted that their greatest findings, discoveries and inventions have been attained not by long, excruciating mental toil, but as if by chance, suddenly, unexpectedly, sometimes even in a dream. To a greater extent, the same applies to works of art. They cannot be regarded as products of intellectual effort. They are seen or heard inwardly. They break forth "like a source from secret depths" (Schiller), they are "unexpected gifts from above" (Goethe). Composer Handel heard the "Hallelujah" section of his oratorio "Messiah" during his sleep, all of a sudden, unexpectedly.

These established facts alone should suffice to confuse the materialist and to disarm him. But no, he is quick at subterfuge with such expressions as hallucination, delusion, imagination, fantasy and so on, with the result that all artistic creation would seem to be derived from abnormal, pathological brain conditions.

The question of clairvoyance can be put on the same footing with artistic vision. Both have their roots in a psychical function called intuition. Nostradamus himself speaks of "fureur poetique" (B.6), which is identical with the poet's artistic vision. Nostradamus also speaks of "heraclian agitation" (A.18) and of "inspiration by the power of God." (A.4)

The scholastic psychology when dealing with intuition and other hidden domains of man's mind, puts them all in one common pot called "subconsciousness." Everything that comes to pass outside of the "wakeful" consciousness, intuition along with the lowest instincts, is lumped and thrown together in a pell-mell jumble. That is very convenient. Further inquiries or investigations are not immediately necessary. A snug formula has been found. With the label of "the subconscious" all this assembled material is qualified as being seemingly less valuable than "the conscious," having been accommodated "under" it. Only lately, due to Professor C.G. Jung's investigations, this

---

1. Letter A refers to Nostradamus' epistle to his son Caesar, and letter B to his epistle to Henry II, king of France.

subconscious material has begun to be appraised and sifted. Much of it has now been rescued from the "Freudian" clutches. It is now evident that there exists a psychical sphere which, being superior to and more estimable than normal consciousness, should rather be classified as "supra-consciousness." If, along with normal consciousness and subconsciousness there exists also a supra-consciousness, it is wrong to regard the results of intellectual efforts and logic as the highest attainments of the human mind.

To supra-consciousness, this highest realm of awareness, belong all intuitional psychical manifestations, including religious cognition, artistic inspiration and prophetic vision, a vision which is unrestrained by limitations of time and space.

It is this last manifestation that we are concerned with in this book. And let us ask ourselves—which is the better, higher achievement: a biography of Napoleon, written after his death; or the prophecy by Nostradamus about Napoleon's life and fate, written even before Napoleon was born? Consider also the prophecy, by Nostradamus, about the fate of the duke of Montmorency, seen clairvoyantly without any mental effort and written down 80 years before the actual occurrence and, in this case again, before the duke's birth.

Some of Nostradamus' predictions are very hard to solve, others on the other hand are so easy to apprehend that the existence and reality of clairvoyance can be proven by Nostradamus' texts alone. Therefore, it is worthwhile to become acquainted with this man's biography and work.

You may say: It is peculiar that there exists only one such man as Nostradamus. No, it is not in the least peculiar, since there is only one Shakespeare, one Beethoven and one Michelangelo. But just as there are many writers and poets less remarkable than Shakespeare, so there are many less remarkable clairvoyants than Nostradamus. Most of the voyants can predict only events in their nearest proximity, in the surroundings of their family and relatives. Less frequently we meet voyants who are capable of predicting events in which they themselves are not directly involved. And there is only one Nostradamus, who could predict the future not only for his own district or province, but also for all of France, and not for his France alone, but for all Europe and the whole world.

Nobody can warrant that all of the not yet fulfilled predictions of Nostradamus will come true. But since so many have come true, we are inclined to accept the fulfillment as very plausible probability. The number of true predictions serves also as a convincing proof of the fact that man can possess the gift of clairvoyance to a surprisingly perfect degree. In this respect Nostradamus is unequaled and must be considered as the greatest psychological problem in the world's history.

1
THE LIFE OF NOSTRADAMUS

The genealogical tree of Nostradamus has been for some time a confused matter. Lately all wanting information has been collected, and with some certainty we can maintain the historical truthfulness of the following genealogical and biographical data.

There is no doubt about the ancestors of Michel de Nostradamus, both parents being of Jewish nationality. So it is safe to say that in the veins of Nostradamus runs Jewish blood, but his ancestors had accepted the Christian faith for several generations. That the Christian conviction of Michel de Nostradamus was true, deep and genuine, is not doubted by anyone who has read his predictions. This book too contains profuse evidence of it.

Michel de Nostredame, known as Nostradamus, was born around noon on Thursday, December 14, 1503, at Saint-Rémy-de-Provence, a small town near Avignon in Provence, Southern France. His father was Jeaumet de Nostre-Dame, notary at the same town, but his mother was Renée de Saint-Rémy, daughter of Jean de Saint-Rémy, doctor of medicine and astrologer at Saint-Rémy de-Provence, We know nothing about Michel's other grandfather, but his father's grandfather was Pierre de Nostredame, a Jewish physician in the service of King René (1409-1480), a romantic, tolerant ruler. This Pierre was the one who with the suggestion or perhaps pressure by the king became converted and baptized in the Christian faith and took on the family name of Nostredame. He was a native of Marseilles and, as a Jew, had called himself Abraham Salomon.

So now we have established as Michel de Nostredame's predecessors on his father's side:

1. Pierre de Nostredame, born as Abraham Salomon, father of
2. ?–(name not identified), father of
3. Jeaumet de Nostredame, notary at Saint-Rémy-de-Provence, father of
4. Michel de Nostredame, known as Nostradamus.

His mother's genealogy is as follows:
1. Jean de Saint-Rémy, descendant of converted Jews, doctor of medicine and astrologer at Saint-Rémy-de-Provence, father of
2. Renée de Saint-Rémy, mother of
3. Michel de Nostredame, known as Nostradamus.

Jeaumet and Renée had the following children:
1. Michel, who became the famous Nostradamus,
2. Jean, solicitor of the parliament of Aix and author of *The Lives of the Ancient Poets of Provence.* He died without children.
3. Bertrand, who remained in Saint-Rémy-de-Provence and married Thonine de Roux of Salon. His descendants existed until the seventeenth century.

It is evident that little Michel could have had reason to be proud of his predecessors, among whom were two eminent physicians: his father's grandfather (not his own grandfather, as some biographers claim) had been private physician of Count René (Renatus), titular-king of Jerusalem and Sicily, and his grandfather on his mother's side had served in the same capacity to Count René's son Jean, Duke of Calabria. And we know too, that Michel's own father was notary in Saint-Rémy-de-Provence, a position which in those times had great importance.

His grandfather on his mother's side, Jean de St. Rémy, was the one who brought little Michel up. This is a very important circumstance, because this man awakened in him at an early age a deep love of natural sciences. Michel's grandfather must have been a famous physician and scientist, otherwise he wouldn't have become the private physician of a duke. But besides being a physician, he was also an astrologer and, as a Jew, did belong to the tribe of Issahar. Some members of this tribe, which had close connections with the temple of Jerusalem, had after the destruction of the city in 70 A.D. emigrated to Provence, taking with them part of the temple's holy scriptures and manuscripts. It is customary to attribute the wisdom of the Jewish members of this tribe in later generations to the possession of these ancient writings. Nostradamus himself mentions the inheritance of manuscripts which he, after perusal, claims to have burned. Probably under the guidance of this wise grandfather little Michel had received also the first instruction in and initiation into astrology, at that period a venerable branch of learning. His grandfather had probably noticed also the boy's innate supersensual perceptivity and given him practical hints how to develop and cultivate this faculty.

After his grandfather's death Michel went to Avignon to study humanistic arts and philosophy, but later continued to study philosophy and medicine at the University of Montpellier, then the most renowned university of the whole cultural world. After graduation at the age of 22, he practiced medicine at Narbonne, Toulouse and Bordeaux, helping as a physician to fight sudden epidemic outbreaks of plague. Four years later he returned to the University of Montpellier, where on October 23, 1529, with the enthusiastic approval and laudation by the whole faculty, he received his doctor's title and doctor's cap.

This is a historically indisputable fact which has to be underscored, because even in our days, some intellectual prigs speak of Nostradamus as an adventurer and quack.

From Montpellier Nostradamus went to Toulouse, but soon shifted his residence to Agen to practice medicine. Here he became acquainted with Jules Caesar Scaliger, one of the greatest humanists of that time. In Agen Michel de Nostredame married a girl of the town's high society. In due time she bore him two children, yet the plague which then ravaged France robbed him in 1533 of his wife and children and left him in great desolation. Crushed by this tragic fate and incapable of finding peace of mind anywhere, he spent ten years traveling in France and Italy. Now and then he returned to his native Provence with the intention to settle down, but restlessness always made him rise anew and start off on another journey. At last, coming from Marseilles, he stayed in Aix and let himself be elected a member of its parliament, which circumstance caused him to remain there for three years. From official documents it can be seen that he lived there from 1544 to 1546. Then he took up his domicile in Salon-de-Craux, a small town at a distance of one day's ride from Aix and midway between Avignon and Marseilles.

Here he, for the second time, got married, on November 11, 1547 to Anna Pontia Gemella, called Anne Ponsard de Salon, the daughter of a patrician. She gave him four sons and four daughters. Son Michel died in 1547. César (1553-1631), historian, poet and painter, married Claire de Grignan and died without descendancy. Charles (1555-1629) died a bachelor. André (1557-1601) died as a capuchin friar. Daughter Jeanne married Pierre Tronc de Codolet, Madeleine married Paul de Chanquin, but Anne and Diane remained unmarried.

Salon now became Michel de Nostredame's constant domicile until his death. During the great plague of 1546 he distinguished himself as a physician so conspicuously that the town of Salon settled on him, as on one who has well deserved of public welfare, an annuity for many years. In Lyons, too, as a physician to plague-stricken patients, he gained the gratitude of the sufferers.

The erudite physician led in Salon a retired life, secluded from the outer world. He did not seek society and society sought him less and less. After a rumor had spread that Nostradamus was not a true Catholic but secretly adhered to Calvinism, he completely forsook the praxis of medicine and dedicated himself entirely to his inner world, which—as he himself stated in the preface to his prophecies—lifted him above the finiteness and showed him the course of history as one continuous, coherent spectacle.

Days and nights he spent in his small study which allowed him the range of vision over the whole horizon of his dwelling place. The house, in which he then lived, still exists and is shown to tourists. Here he composed his prophecies which later made him world renowned.

These prophecies are not the result of astrological calculations. His main gift was that of seership, of second sight, doubtlessly inherited from his ancestors. He himself has said that he received inspired revelations. He used astrology only as an expedient to determine fixed dates for the observed historical visions. In matters of clairvoyance it is important to keep in view the fact that clairvoyants usually are not capable of connecting their visions of the future in a correct sequence. First, these visions do not appear in a chronological order. Second, the more glaring visions they ascribe to the nearest future, which is not always the case. Third, in order to connect in a logical continuity visions which are often inexplicable to themselves, they are in the habit of patching separate visionary fragments together with intellectual images. In such a way all the isolated visionary fragments acquire an epical character, but this story, as a whole, is incorrect. Only separate parts are true.

Astrologers experience difficulties of an entirely opposite kind. They are capable of correct calculations of exact dates or apportioned spaces of time, when in the life of a person or country important events, for the better or the worse, should happen; but that is as far as they can go. They are incapable of describing what exactly will happen. The interpretation is lame, because no precise, true and detailed interpretation is possible without good intuition. The calculation of stellar configurations and aspects requires a well-tempered intellect, but the obtained result is and remains only a mathematical quantity, a numeral character, attained by logarithmic calculations. The interpretation of this cipher or of the relation of several such ciphers requires a deep intuition, and both these gifts, a strong intellect and a high intuition, usually are not found combined in the same person. An expert in advanced mathematics and cosmography as often as not is a person with an inclination to suppress his intuitional faculties, if he possesses them at all. That is the explanation why the forecasts of diverse astrologers so greatly differ one from another, although they are based on the identical result of mathematical calculations.

Nostradamus was one of the few men whose indubitable visionary faculties were combined with a strong, critical intellect. He did not permit himself to be deceived by what he saw and he did not mix the isolated visions one with another. A believer in astrology, he sought confirmation for each vision in stellar configurations, but astrology was and remained for him only an expedient.

He himself has said that he received "arousing stimulations" (A.29). Rendering his nights agreeable by long calculations, he may have found his intellectual brainwork simultaneously supplemented by "arousing stimulations," since in another instance he says that his predictions have been "calculated by celestial movements, in association with emotions handed down to me by my ancient forbears, and which emotion is infused into me at certain hours of loneliness." (B.23) On another occasion he says that he is capable of predicting the future by adjusting and coordinating his natural instinct with long calculations, and by emptying his soul, spirit and courage of all care, solicitude and vexation, in having repose and tranquillity of spirit. (B.12)

In the opinion of Nostradamus, all existence is necessary and indispensable in exactly the way it exists, and all occurrences occur at the time and place and in the manner they necessarily have to occur. Thus each occurrence has been given a definite place in time, space and in cipher, which can be calculated.

Nostradamus wrote his predictions in French prose, but in mystic expressions in dark, confused sentences. He did not wish his predictions to be unveiled and interpreted long before the occurrence of the predicted event, because in his own words: "If I came to reveal what will happen in the future, the leaders of kingdoms, sects, religions and faiths would find it little in accord with what their fancy would like to hear." (A.6) Thereby, his predictions could get lost entirely. He is doubtlessly right in his supposition, because his predictions contain many governmental changes in France and other countries (the great French Revolution, Napoleon's glory and end, world wars and so on).

During the German occupation of France in 1940, Emil Ruir's book *The Great Carnage 1938-1947*, published in 1938, was on the spot prohibited and taken out of circulation, because the author, substantiating his book by Nostradamus' predictions, had warned of the imminent outbreak of war and already then had pronounced the allied invasion in France and the complete defeat of Italian and German armies. In this book we can read, among other things, on page 48: "Both dictatorships (Germany and Italy) will combine their forces and widen their influence, but this alliance, depending on conquest, will cause the outbreak of so horrible a war that all nations will rise against these instigators of bloodshed and war." On the next page we read: "Russia will extend her forces along Eastern Europe up to Pannony (Czechoslovakia, Austria and Hungary)."

It is evident that such a plain language could not be tolerated by German forces of occupation. The book was destroyed wherever found, but the original text of the predictions by Nostradamus has not been lost, because it is written in enigmatical expressions, not to mislead the readers, but for reasons of self-preservation. His book has survived the Great Revolution, Napoleon's dictatorship and other changes of government. A reader, well versed in history and astrology, with good will (and, we have to repeat, with good intuition) will find in it sufficient indications about the time and place of predicted events.

After the first draft Nostradamus once more revised his text, finding it still too plain and easy to decipher. He rendered it into quatrains with rhymes and assembled them by hundreds in "centuries." Even then the seer considered them too openly comprehensible. He was afraid that somebody would decipher them prematurely and all his efforts would be in vain, since he wished his work to be preserved until the "end-time." He hesitated long to publish his centuries and could not make up his mind, but at last, when some of the predicted events (the abdication of Carlos V, king of Spain, the death of Henry II, king of France, and the Huguenot Wars) had to occur in the near future,

Nostradamus took courage and decided to bring out the first centuries. Quatrains, which at first had been arranged chronologically, he disarranged again, throwing them together pell-mell. He published them in 1555.

They had barely come out when already scorn and derision were showered upon them. Without delay Nostradamus was pronounced a cheat and mountebank, who was deceiving simple-minded people with incoherent rubbish. But then some of the predictions began to come true, and his fame revived and grew to such an extent that Catherine de Médicis, consort of King Henry II, invited him to the court. And so it came that on August 15, 1556, Nostradamus was presented to Henry II, king of France, and to Catherine de Médicis. The king offered him the honor of becoming his private physician and astrologer with a big salary. Nostradamus expressed his gratitude, but declined the offer. Then Catherine asked him to cast nativities for her four sons, living in Blois Castle. He truthfully predicted that three of them would become kings, but diplomatically concealed that the coronation of one would be dependent on the death of another. Two of them, François II and Charles IX, later when reigning as kings, repeatedly did ask Nostradamus for advice and became his friends and admirers. The same can be said of their mother, Catherine de Médicis.

Overwhelmed by gold and honor, Nostradamus returned to Salon. Two years later in 1558, Nostradamus published three more centuries with a dedication to King Henry II. He had become so famous that several falsifiers began to publish prophecies under his name. Thereby arose confusion and Nostradamus underwent a new wave of taunts and sneers. The number of his adversaries and enemies grew. They published pamphlets with mockeries and denunciations. Some pamphlets accused him of magical practices, demanding his arraignment before the Holy Inquisition; yet in quatrain I-42 he had sharply condemned spiritistic meetings and had called necromancers "a diabolic assembly searching for the bones of the demon of Psellus." In his quatrains Nostradamus rarely mentions occult questions and only in VII-41 does he speak of a haunted house, which becomes "healthy and inhabited without noise," after, due to a dream, the hidden bones have been found and dug up.

The battle for and against Nostradamus was in full force when suddenly the prediction of the king's death, given in the 35th quatrain of the first century, came to be fulfilled. During the festivities celebrating the double wedding in July, 1559, of Henry II's daughter and sister (daughter Elisabeth married Philip II, king of Spain, and sister Marguerite married Emanuel Philibert, duke of Savoy), the "young lion," Count Gabriel de Montgomery, in a single combat (not in buhurt or tournament) killed the "old" King Henry II. The count's lance pierced the visor of the king's golden helmet and entered his right eye. From this fatal injury the king died on July 10, at the age of forty. The agony was so severe that the king cursed Nostradamus and all his predictions. It appears that the king, who did very much like tournaments and physical contests, had been forewarned of the impending and predicted disaster, but had refused to desist from the contest. Nostradamus' prediction reads as follows (I-35):

Le Lyon ieune le vieux surmontera
En champ bellique par singulier duelle:
Dans caige d'or les yeux lui creuera,
Deux classes vne puis mourir; mort cruelle.

(The young lion will overcome the old one on the battlefield in single combat; in a cage of gold his eyes will be put out, two wounds one, then to die a cruel death.) The prediction is simple and clear. The word "classe" is derived from Greek "klasis," which means "to break" or "to fracture," from which word comes the French substantive "clase" (fracture), now used mainly as a geological term.

The news of the king's death and of Nostradamus' prediction and his malediction spread into all corners of Europe. From that moment nothing could ever darken the fame of Nostradamus. That is confirmed by contemporary literature. All rulers of Europe began to burden Nostradamus with honors and money and with requests of predictions about their own fates.

Later Philibert Emanuel, the duke of Savoy, the late king's brother-in-law, together with his wife Marguerite, came to visit the seer. When Marguerite was pregnant, she invited Nostradamus to Nice and questioned him about the sex of the expected child. He answered that it would be a son, who should be christened Charles and who would become a great military leader. On January 12, 1562, Marguerite gave birth to a son, and Nostradamus cast his nativity, in which it was said that in a certain year he would be wounded, but would not die before nine preceded seven. The prince carefully guarded his horoscope. One day he spoke to Count Garignan about the mysterious and uncertain twilight of predictions and told him that Nostradamus had predicted to him a notable injury for the present year. The count answered that it was not likely that he would get a wound in times of peace, whereupon the prince quickly rose to get the nativity. In great haste he overturned the heavy table which fell on his foot, causing serious injury, which required a long curative treatment. After this, Prince Charles never doubted the fulfillment of the prediction about his death. He anticipated death at the age of 97, but he died when only 69 years of age. It is evident that in this case too nine precedes seven, because 69 is followed by 70. Nostradamus was justified. To be sure, this case and innumerable other similar cases nevertheless prove the great difficulty in interpreting even true predictions, if they are hidden in riddles, charades, allegories and anagrams.

On October 18, 1564, the young king Charles IX with his mother Catherine de Médicis and a great suite came to see and to personally greet Nostradamus in Salon. Among the followers was the young Prince Henry de Béarn-Navarre, who later became king of France (Henry IV). During the visit Charles IX appointed Nostradamus as state counselor and his personal physician and presented him with two hundred gold coins. Catherine added another hundred from her own purse. The seer predicted to Catherine de Médicis that her favorite son, then Duke Henry of Anjou, would ascend the throne. This prediction came true ten years later, when Duke Henry became Henry III, king of France. For the Prince of Navarre Nostradamus too predicted the crown. The prince became Henry IV, king of France, twenty-five years later.

It is evident that Michel de Nostredame did not lack either money nor honors. His fellow citizens of Salon esteemed him highly, because he was a benefactor to the poor and to the ill and, devotedly serving his duty as a physician, never refused his help to patients who could not pay for his services.

This man, citizen of Salon, scientist, seer, prophet, mathematician, astronomer and astrologer, who at the age of twenty-six had received from the University of Montpellier his degree of a doctor of medicine, and who had been the intimate counselor of the kings Henry II, François II and Charles IX and had shined as a luminary of his time, died in Salon on July 2, 1566, in the sixty-third year of his earthly existence, having lived for 62 years, 6 months, and 17 days.

His friend, doctor of the science of law and theology, Jean Aimé Chavigny, tells that he had left the sick-bed of Nostradamus late on the night of July 1, 1566, promising to return at sunrise. The afflicted Nostradamus, who during the last sixteen months had suffered from gout and had eight days before his death partaken of the Lord's Supper, having two days earlier made his will, answered to his friend: "The sunrise will not find me among the living." But seeing him breathe easy, with no indications of his approaching death, everybody left him in order to rest for a few hours. When they returned at daybreak into the sick-room, they found Nostradamus dead on a bench, in a position which clearly proved that he had come to a peaceful end.

Thus in every detail had come true a prediction written by Nostradamus in a quatrain about his own death. This prediction reads as follows:

De retour d'ambassade, don du Roy mis au lieu.
Plus n'en fera, sera allé à Dieu,
Proches parents, amis, fréres du sang
Trouvé tout mort, près du lict et du banc.

(On return from the embassy, the king's gift put in place, will do no more, will be gone to God. Close relatives, friends, brothers by blood, found entirely dead near the bed and bench.)

Indeed, Nostradamus had recently returned from a trip to Arles, where he had met the envoy of King Charles IX and had declined an offer which would have brought him three hundred pieces of gold. His relatives, friends and disciple Aimé de Chavigny found him dead, near the bed, collapsed on the bench where he had been sitting when death overtook him. Moreover, in a letter to Jean Stadius, written in June, 1566, he had included these words in Latin: *Hic prope mors est* (Here death is near).

About Nostradamus' last days his biographer L. Ginon writes: "His testament he wrote on June 17, 1566, in the presence of Joseph Roche, a notary of Salon. After that he confessed his sins to Father Vidal and partook of the Lord's Supper with visible religious fervor, as a good, ardent Christian."

Following the directions of the executioners of his testament, Mark de Châteaunef and Jacques Suffren, he was buried on his day of death in the church of the Franciscan monastery, whose superior was Father Vidal, Nostradamus' confessor. His tomb was soon visited by pilgrims from all over France. Among them were two kings, Louis XIII in 1622 and Louis XIV in 1660. The latter was accompanied by his mother, Anne of Austria, his brother, the duke of Anjou, his cousin, the Mademoiselle d'Orléans, and by Cardinal Mazarin.

On his mausoleum was engraved the following epitaph:

D. M.
Clarissimi ossa
Michaeli Nostradâmi
unjus omnium mortalium judicio digni
cujus pene divino calamo totius orbis
ex astrorum influxu futuri eventus
·conscriberentur.
Vixit annos LXII, menses VI, dies XVII.
Obiit Sallone an. MDLXVI.
Quietem posteri ne invidete.
Anna Pontia Gemella
conjugi opt. v. felicit.

(Here rest the bones of the most illustrious Michel Nostradamus, alone of all mortals judged worthy to describe with his almost divine pen, under the influence of stars, the future events of the whole world. He lived 62 years, 6 months, 17 days and died at Salon in the year 1566. Let the posterity not disturb his rest. Anna Pontia Gemella wishes her husband true happiness.)

During the Revolution in 1791, some rioters from Marseilles, heedless of the protests by the citizens of Salon, broke into the church, opened Nostradamus' tomb and scattered his remains. After the disturbance the citizens of Salon gathered his mortal remains together again and, the monastery church being damaged, transferred them on November 6, 1791, with the approval by the municipal council of Salon, to the Chapel of the Virgin in the collegial church of Saint-Laurent in Salon.

There on his tomb even today quite often flowers of the field can be found, deposited by the citizens of Salon as manifestation of their veneration and acknowledgment of the man who as their physician and their prophet had made the name of Salon renowned not only in France, but far beyond her borders.

Very early the predictions by Nostradamus found commentators. An important work, entitled *The Concordance of the Prophecies of Nostradamus with History* by B. Guynaud, was published in 1693. Book after book followed. Between 1555 and 1867 in France alone eighty editions of Nostradamus' centuries were published. One of the most extensive commentaries of Nostradamus' works is Anatol Le Pelletier's book *Les Oracles de Michel de Nostradame,* published in 1867. It contains also a dictionary of foreign words and expressions. Four hundred years after the death of Nostradamus, the number of books which are yearly published about him does not grow less. The public is taking ever greater interest in him. Dr. Max Kemmerich, a German philosopher, in his book *Prophezeiungen* (Prophecies), published in 1911 in Munich, affirms that Nostradamus "is an authentic prophet, possessor of divinatory gifts within the dimensions of space and time." The American writer Henry Forman in his *The Story of Prophecy,* published in 1936 in New York says:

The most celebrated prophet who has ever appeared in Europe, possibly the most .celebrated outside the Bible, was Michel de Nostradamus. Faust, in his high-vaulted chamber, with the secret-laden book of Nostradamus in his hands, is made by Goethe to exclaim: "Was it then a god who penned these signs?"

In the sixteenth century, that most dazzling century of the Renaissance, perhaps no single human being occupied a more remarkable place than did Nostradamus. It is safe to say that in all European history there was no one who stands out more for the unusual and abnormal gifts of clairvoyance than does this Provençal physical and seer, of Jewish descent, a man who could conquer the great plague of his time, yet was a humble worshiper of God, and also the greatest prophet of his age and all subsequent ages.

So swiftly and amazingly did his fame spread, that in the brief space of some fifteen years all Europe was interested in and curious about him, and kings and queens, to say nothing of lesser personages, both sent for him and made long journeys to his little Provençal town of Salon for a taste of his gifts.

After the Second World War book after book is being published in Europe on Nostradamus and his predictions. The explanation is simple: the number of fulfilled predictions grows ever larger and the number of such predictions that still need interpretation diminishes. Therefore the task of arranging the remaining predictions in a chronological order is getting ever easier. Of 957 quatrains 511 can already be considered fulfilled. About one hundred quatrains are either hard to identify or could be applied to several events. There remain only 346 quatrains, containing unquestionably unfulfilled predictions and the majority of these are dedicated to Muhammedan and Asiatic invasions of Europe. Although Nostradamus in his letter to his son Caesar writes that his predictions reach up to the year 3797, there is reason to believe that the majority of them are applicable to events before 1999.

Commentator Piobb claims to have found in Nostradamus' centuries three astrological clues, the first of which fits the period from 1547 to 1792, the second from 1792 to 1921, and the third from 1921 to 1999. It is not possible to check his assertions, because Piobb does not disclose what these three clues are. Emil Ruir, one of the best of Nostradamus' interpreters, on the other hand, considers the year 2023 as the one which will see the end of the dominant role of the white race and the Christian civilization on the face of this earth.

2
THE WRITINGS OF NOSTRADAMUS AND THEIR INTERPRETATION

A list of the works of Nostradamus:

1. Epistle to his son Caesar Nostredame
2. Epistle to Henry II, king of France
3. Centuries
4. Presages (quatrains and sixains)
5. New editions of earlier works, with several previously unpublished additions.

The first edition of the centuries was published in 1555 in Lyons by Macé Bonhomme with the title *Les Propheties de Me Michel Nostradamus*. This book included the letter to Caesar, to be considered as preface to the book, and only the first seven centuries. The second edition was published by Pierre Rigaud in 1558, but in 1566 Rigaud published an entirely new book, which included the epistle to King Henry II and centuries VIII, IX and X.

After that were published many other reprints, more or less differing one from another, until in 1668 Jean Jansson in Amsterdam published a definitive collected edition of the works of Nostradamus with the title *Les Vrayes Centuries et Propheties de Maistre Michel Nostradamus* (The True Centuries and Prophecies of Master Michel Nostradamus).

This edition is the best known and most widely circulated of Nostradamus' works. It contains:

1. The letter to his son Caesar.
2. The letter to the most Invincible, most Powerful and most Christian Henry II, king of France
3. The centuries, 12 in number, each containing, as the name indicates, a hundred quatrains, except centuries VII, XI and XII, which have only 44, 2 and 11 quatrains respectively.
4. The presages, another collection of 141 quatrains, all particularly dedicated to certain months and years.
5. Sixains, his last "canto," in 58 stanzas.

Everybody who wants earnestly to study the original texts of Nostradamus' predictions has to be reminded that both the first editions of Lyons can be considered as authentic texts, whereas the edition of Amsterdam, although the most complete in contents, was published a hundred years after the author's death and contains revisions and additions, the correctness of which cannot be warranted. As always happens to be the case with similar, hard-to-interpret texts of predictions, ostensible "rectifications," be they ever so diminutive and seemingly immaterial, may alter the whole content of the interpretation. Besides, it has to be taken into consideration that the first edition of the centuries consists of *two* separate books: The first one contains the letter to Caesar and centuries I–VII; the second one contains the letter to Henry II and centuries VII–X. Each book has its own letter, serving as a preface, and the second book must be considered as the continuation or the supplement of the first. This is a very significant circumstance, because both prefaces, written in prose, are themselves so rich with predictions, references and hints, that the procedure of those commentators who are searching in these letters for clues to the whole text of the centuries seems to be very well substantiated.

The genuineness of Nostradamus' "sixains" is a question which today cannot be verified with any degree of certainty. A Vincent Seve of Beaucaire claims to have received these 58 stanzas from the nephew of Nostradamus, Henry Nostradamus, before the death of the latter. These stanzas were published in 1605. Possibly Nostradamus had meant them as the completion of or addition to the incomplete seventh century, since it is known that Nostradamus had the intention of composing one thousand stanzas and of dividing them into ten centuries.

Some uncertainty reigns over the question of the origin of the thirteen quatrains which after the death of Nostradamus were added to different editions of the centuries as the eleventh and twelfth centuries. If they are genuine and have been found among the posthumous papers of the author, they may belong to the incomplete seventh century.

It follows from the preceding remarks that only ten centuries and both prefaces can be considered indubitably as Nostradamus' writings. Only on these have I based my present study. Other prognostications have been used only where they confirm matter that has already been included in the authentic texts.

*   *   *   *   *

As soon as we start to read these texts we stumble upon difficulties. Excepting the letter to Caesar, all of Nostradamus' other writings seem to be disconcerting, chaotic, obscure and unintelligible. The texts are full of ciphers, anagrams, symbolical terms for animals borrowed from the Bible and from astrology, mythological allegories, metaphors, parables, transformed foreign expressions and words whose etymological roots have been taken from the Latin, Italian, Greek, Spanish, Provençal languages. Sentences are curtailed, images abstruse, sense incomprehensible. It is impossible to interpret Nostradamus' texts without frequent reference to dictionaries of symbols and biblical terms, but even that does not always suffice. For instance, how would you translate this quatrain (Presages 5):

O Mars cruel, que tu seras à craindre.
Plus est la Faux avec l'Argent conjoinct.
Classe, copie, vent. L'Ombriche vraindre.
Mer, terre, treve, Lamy à LV s'est joinct.

No literal translation is possible, and all commentators have a great divergence of opinion about this quatrain.

I have already mentioned the reason for such haziness, namely, the wish of Nostradamus to preserve his predictions until the "end of time." If in the meantime somebody would happen to manage a correct deciphering, he would be ridiculed and persecuted, his interpretation would be destroyed, but the original text would not suffer and would be kept safe. This was clearly the case with the already mentioned book by E. Ruir in 1940, during the German occupation of France.

The writings of Nostradamus are different from many other prophetic documents because of the unquestionable fact that hundreds of the predicted events have already been fulfilled with correctly assigned causes and consequences, with accurately mentioned personages and at exactly the place and time shown. To many readers it may sound ridiculous, but it almost looks as if Nostradamus had been called to comment on the prophecies of the Old Testament and of the Apocalypse, in order to prepare humanity for the "end of time."

Is not Nostradamus the last of the prophets, right in the long line of biblical prophets? Prophecy surely is a gift not to be acquired, but only to be received, a fact attested to by the same word "gift." Some theologians, however, maintain that the age of prophecy has ended and that prophets, who are inspired and enraptured by God and compelled by him to prophecy, nowadays don't exist. Is such assertion justified? Is it not in contradistinction to the words of the apostle St. Paul about many kinds of spiritual gifts (1 Cor. 12, also 14–29 and Eph. 4-11)? Karl Rahner, Austrian theologian, professor of dogmatics of the University of Innsbruck, also speaks about this question, in his booklet *Visionen und Prophezeiungen* (Visions and Prophecies), Innsbruck, 1952. Among other things, he writes:

> The possibility of a private revelation through visions and connected auditions is for a Christian in principle a quite certain fact. That historical manifestations of God through created signs exist is attested by Holy Scriptures. There could not be a history of Christianity if we try to exclude prophecy and visions. But if such phenomena have existed as foundations of the revealed religion in times of the Old and the New Testament, then a priori and in principle we cannot deny, that such manifestations *may* occur also *after* the times of Christ. Indeed, they have occurred within the church of the apostolic age and have there been accepted as a gift, connected with possession of the Spirit, thus belonging to and remaining in the church. Consequently, whoever denies the possibility of private revelations, offends against the faith, and whoever contests the possibility of such occurrences after the time of the Apostles, offends against a theologically positive and certain doctrine.

Everybody who earnestly wants to study Nostradamus, must first indispensably acquaint himself with biblical prophecies, because all the most important prognostications of Nostradamus are closely connected with prophecies found in the Bible.

What is a prophet? The word "prophet," from the Greek *pro ephoein* (prophecy—*propheteia*), means simply "to foresee," to be a seer, to see the future. The respective Hebrew word is *roeh,* which again means "seer." If some readers don't like the biblical term "prophet" applied to Nostradamus, they should instead read "seer." Etymologically it is the same thing!

A prophet is one who sees the future. To the charge that it is not possible to see what does not yet exist, Nostradamus replies that the future exists already today, because "all three times (past, present and future) comprise but one eternity" (A.26) and "even the present fact comes from the total eternity which in itself embraces all time." (A.17)

Prophets were all patriarchs from Adam to Moses, but prophet Samuel was the first who exercised this ministry in the restricted sense of the word. Nathan, Elijah, Elias and David were prophets. It is customary to divide the later prophets into two groups: 1. Isaiah, Jeremiah, Ezekiel and Daniel are called the greater prophets; and 2. the rest, twelve in number, are the lesser prophets: Amos, Hosea, Joel, Obadiah, Jonah, Micah, Nahum, Zephariah, Habakkuk, Zachariah, Haggai and Malachi.

The Jews sometimes designated their prophets with the word *rȃbi,* which means "the inspired," because prophets received all prophecies from God in the form of an inspiration, which was communicated to them in three manners: by words, by visions and by dreams. Theologian Karl Rahner says in his already mentioned book:

According to the testimony of the Holy Scriptures, God has spoken to man in manifold ways. The prophet, who has to become God's spokesman to humanity, hears a voice (Ezek. 1:28 etc.), has a vision (Isa. 2:1 etc.), sees God's revelation in images and symbols (Jer.

1:13, 24:1 etc.); to him appear angels, who deliver a heavenly message (Luke 1:11; 26 etc.); the divine communication arrives in a dream (Matt. 1:20, 2:19 etc.); the communication is received, the seer being in a state of ecstasy (Acts 10:10, 11:5, 22:17, 2 Cor. 12:2-5, Apoc. 4:2).

The Old Testament to a great degree consists of prophecies about Jesus Christ. These prophecies have been fulfilled, and we are absolutely certain that they originated before the time of Jesus. In the same manner prophecies were fulfilled about the destiny of the Jewish nation. Like chaff in wind innumerable nations and civilizations have been scattered, dispersed and annihilated. Where are today the Assyrians, Babylonians, Phoenicians and many other nations and states mentioned in the Bible? We find only ruins of immense buildings and remnants of their literature. The nations themselves have become extinct. But the Jewish nation still exists even after what has happened to it during the foregoing thousands of years of its history. The Jews have lived for two-and-a-half-thousand years without a fatherland, without their own country and state; they have been persecuted, hated, despised and massacred. They have lived under host nations, which have disappeared, but the Jews have remained. Today they again have their own state. No prophecy has been fulfilled more miraculously than the Old Testament prophecy concerning the Jewish nation and its destiny.

The New Testament too contains many prophecies. Of prophecies by Jesus, indirectly respecting himself, let us remember words said to Peter (Mark 14:30): "Verily, I say unto thee that this day, even in this night, before the cock crows twice, thou shalt deny me thrice." Speaking about himself, Jesus often refers to the prophets, but speaking about the "end-time" and the end of the world, he mentions

Daniel (Matt. 24:15). Apocalypse, the last book of the New Testament, is an incomprehensible vision of the future, full of symbolical images, symbols and allegories. After Apostle John (exiled to Patmos) had written this book, right away it began to deeply influence the soul and to occupy the mind of everybody who had acquainted himself with it. How many eyes have again and again read and scrutinized the lines of this writing, trying to perceive in them the prescribed course of the historical events of the world. Up to this very day the images of the Apocalypse continue to inspire writers, poets, musicians, painters and philosophers.

To be a prophet means to have been born with a special calling. Who has not been called, cannot become a prophet. But to the chosen one himself this calling often remains unintelligible and even undesirable. Fleeing from his calling, Jonah went to Tarsish and landed in a whale's belly. Jeremiah complained: "Lord, Lord, I am still young." Because of his calling he often had to suffer blows from priests and had to sit in jail. He laments: "The word of the Lord was made a reproach unto me, and a derision, daily." (Jer. 20:8)

Always it has been the case that the reigning secular and clerical powers persecute and deride those who openly and fearlessly presage unpleasant things. On the other hand, various conjurers and soothsayers, who in reality are charlatans, impostors and hypocrites, are overwhelmed with compliments and money, if they predict glory, victory and prosperity. Jeremiah objects: "Ah, Lord God! behold, the prophets say unto them: ye shall not see the sword, neither shall ye have famine, but I will give you assured peace in this place. Then the Lord said unto me: the prophets' prophecy lies in my name. I sent them not, neither have I commanded them, neither spake unto them." (Jer. 14:13-14)

Regardless of ridicule and persecution, the called have spoken, have threatened and warned, but in vain. The course of external events has not changed. It cannot change.

Prophets preach and warn not in order to change the course of history. They warn and preach for the very few people who still are capable of changing their own inner disposition, they warn and preach for that part of humanity which always remains a minority. The decisive battles are fought not on battlefields, but in the innermost depths of man's mind and soul, in the invisible and unexplored world, which is a part of himself. And even for the sake of a single man it is worthwhile to preach and to warn. Man's personal will and freedom of choice do not suffer; they remain safe, but that does not alter or influence the external, historical course of events. If one man heeds the warning and puts off the sword, there will inevitably arise another who picks it up again. The man who did heed the warning is saved; his substitute perishes, because, as the Bible says: "It is impossible but that offenses will come: but woe unto him through whom" (Luke 17:1). The external event has not changed, but in the invisible world there has been fought a great, decisive battle. And that is the world where the "last battle" will come to pass.

Thus we are taught by our Savior's life on earth and by His death. Everything that pertained to His person, His life and death had been, before His coming, predicted by the prophets. And yet the priests of Sanhedrin, whose duty it was to know all these prophecies in detail, did not recognize and acknowledge Him. And even the ignorance of these priests had been predicted. Jesus was put to death in the name of truth, justice and religion. He died in order "that the words of the prophets should be fulfilled."

In spite of His death, man still does not see nor comprehend. In spite of two world wars, man's eyes have not been opened. Man has indeed eyed and explored the whole visible world with the help of telescopes and microscopes. He claims to know and to understand everything. Now he has progressed to a point where he is able to devastate the whole terrestrial globe, with everything on it that can be seen and explored. And evermore man is born, lives and dies without knowing himself and without perceiving the invisible world, in which all the decisive battles are fought for his own sake. The few privileged who indeed are capable of seeing and who therefore are warning the world, are declared by the world to be superstitious simpletons, or raving idiots and maniacs. At the same time the world obediently follows all kinds of political "leaders," instigators of wars and revolutions, men who truly deserve the name of "maniacs." In the end, indeed, they are so called, but always when it is far too late, and when another political, social or sectarian superstition has already been chosen, and in place of the "fallen leader," a new one has risen.

Nostradamus saw it all and understood. He therefore did not accept any of the honors which many rulers conferred on him. He did not choose to move and to live in the court and all appointments given him remained only nominal honorary dignities.

His had been the gift to read from the book of the future. He divined the course of events up until and beyond the "end-time," mentioned by the prophets of the Bible. He did everything to ensure the preservation of his prognostications until the "end-time." He did not write his books to warn his contemporaries. All who attentively have perused both of Nostradamus' letters realize that they were not addressed to his son Caesar nor Henry II, but to the people of the "end-time," i.e., to the people of the twentieth century. His work has been addressed to us, since we live in the "end-time".

What is the end-time or the time of the end? Does it mean end of the world? The Bible tells us about both the end-time and the day of judgment or end of the world, but they are not identical. About the "end-time" or "time of the end" prophets speak and prophesy, but about the Day of Judgment or end of the world Jesus speaks and says that nobody can prophesy about it (Matt. 24:36): "But of that day and hour knoweth no man, no, not the angels of heaven, but my Father only."

About the end-time it is possible to prophesy and about it the prophets and Jesus speak in the already mentioned 24th chapter, which should be read in its entirety. Jesus tells about when the end-time will not be and when it will be. Jesus' warning is worded as follows:

For many shall come in my name, saying, I am Christ; and shall deceive many. And ye shall hear of wars and rumors of wars: see that ye be not troubled, for all these things must come to pass, but the end is not yet. For nation shall rise against nation, and kingdom against kingdom, and there shall be famines and pestilences and earthquakes in diverse places. All these are the beginning of sorrows. Then shall they deliver you up to be afflicted and shall kill you, and ye shall be hated of all nations for my name's sake. And then many shall be offended and shall betray one another and shall hate one another. And many false prophets shall rise and shall deceive many. And because iniquity shall abound, the love of many shall wax cold. And this gospel of the kingdom shall be preached in all the world, for a witness unto all nations: and then shall the end come. When ye therefore shall see the abomination of desolation, spoken of by Daniel the prophet, stand in the holy place . . . then shall be great tribulation, such as was not since the beginning of the world to this time, no, nor ever shall be. Then if any man shall say unto you, lo, here is Christ, or there: believe it not. For there shall arise false Christs and false prophets and shall show great signs and wonders, insomuch that, if it were possible, they shall deceive the very elect. (Matt. 24:5-12, 14-15, 21, 23-24)

One should also read His further admonishment to learn from the fig tree: "When his branch is yet tender and putteth forth leaves, ye know that summer is nigh: so likewise ye, when ye shall see all these things, know, that it is near, even at the doors. Verily, I say unto you: this generation shall not pass until all these things be fulfilled." (Matt. 24:32-34) Jesus is speaking about the generation of the end-time, meaning that all these things will be fulfilled within one generation's time, so quickly that those who saw the beginning of the end-time events would see also the end.

Behold, this is an entirely authentic prophecy concerning the end-time and the Day of Judgment. Very significant is the fact that Jesus mentions the prophet Daniel and his prophecies, thereby confirming Daniel's prophecy as true and authentic. The last verses of Daniel's 11th chapter and the whole 12th chapter are dedicated to the end-time. Speaking about the abomination in the holy place, Jesus refers to Daniel 9:26 where it is written: "And after sixty-two weeks shall Messiah be slain, but not for himself; and the people of the prince, that shall come, shall destroy the city and the sanctuary, and the end thereof shall be with a flood, and after the end of the war the appointed desolation." In Daniel 12:1 we read: "And there shall be a time of trouble, such as never was from the time that nations began even until that time." These words too were repeated by Jesus in his prophecy. In Daniel 12:7 we find the following admonition: "It shall be after a time, two times and half a time, and when the scattering of the holy people shall be accomplished." Apostle Paul in 1 Thess. 2:16 speaks about the destiny of the Jewish nation, saying " . . . for the wrath of God is come upon them to the end," that means, to the end-time. Now, in the twentieth century, after thousands of years spent in exile, the Jewish nation is back in its own land. Apostle Paul's, as well as Daniel's, words about the time when "the scattering of the holy people shall be accomplished" give testimony to the fact that the end-time has come in the twentieth century. The Jews have their own state and country again. We now, today, are living in the time of the end, in the end-time, in the latter days.

Even Isaiah (24:5-6) speaks about the latter days or end-time: "The earth is defiled by the inhabitants thereof, because they have transgressed the laws, changed the ordinance and broken the everlasting covenant. Therefore has the curse devoured the earth and they that dwell therein, are desolate; therefore the inhabitants of the earth are scorched up and few men shall be left." Hitherto the world's population has only grown in number, regardless of devastating wars. The big "scorching up" is still to be expected.

* * * * *

According to Nostradamus' predictions the end of the age (the end-time) began with the First World War (1914-1918), the continuation of which was World War II, (1939-1945). What do Nostradamus' predictions promise for the future? We are interested foremost in the question: Will there be a third World War? Nostradamus answers in the affirmative. He prognosticates also many other future disasters. The first two world wars were occasioned by economic reasons (foreign markets, living space, etc.), but future conflicts and wars will evermore reflect doctrinal, ideological and racial divergences and antagonisms. Two important factors in future wars will be the Arabs and the Jews, to wit, Islam and Judaism, violently fighting each other. A third factor, no less formidable than the two others, will be atheism, which will try to exploit the hate between the Jews and the Arabs, with the intent to dominate both, in order finally to be in a position to vanquish the fourth factor—Christianity. The last phase of the combat will turn into a war between the races. The white race will be under the necessity to defend itself against all other races.

In the past the white race has been dominating other races, conquering, governing and exploiting their territories, and hypocritically coming forward as the bearer and disseminator of a better civilization and culture and a better and more genuine, true religion. But everywhere the white race has played the part of Judas Iscariot, treacherously selling its ideals for silver farthings. Individual persons, truly inspired by ideals, were incapable of changing the general trend. In all colonies the white race has spread vice, venereal diseases, alcoholism, ignominies, infamies, lies and hypocrisy, in the name of Christ slaying all who would not submit to its influence, dominion and power. Such was the case in Africa, Asia, America. The nations and civilizations of Aztecs and Incas were completely exterminated. So ancient and cultural a nation as the Chinese was militarily compelled through two so-called "opium wars" to accept the indulgence of opium, in order that the white race should not lose the profit from the export of opium, which was grown in India. These are only a few examples from among many. For all these transgressions the white race will at last have to pay dearly.

The history of wars had in fact begun already with the first man. The serpent prevailed then and has ever since prevailed over Adam and Eve. Cain has ever again succeeded in killing his brother. Man has risen against man, clan against clan, tribe against tribe, nation against nation, empire against empire, and finally, in the twentieth century, all humanity wades through blood.

All this has already been so written, but man does not see nor hear nor understand and diligently continues to prepare his own destruction. Abyssus abyssum invocat!

In a long epistle, addressed to Henry II, king of France, Nostradamus, already 400 years ago, had warned all nations of world wars. He warned also of the great French Revolution, but it seems that only very few have been impressed by his words and have managed to escape misery and destruction. How many have turned to good account Nostradamus' predictions about the Second World War and have in time saved their money, property and life?

It is advisable for everybody to be informed about Nostradamus' prognostications of future events. If his gloomy predictions do come true, we will be prepared and will not suffer too great a shock and disappointment. If the predictions prove to be false, deceptive and illusory—so much the better!

*   *   *   *   *

The announcements by a seer of events in times to come can rouse our interest only if his previous predictions have been fulfilled. In this respect Nostradamus is known to be singularly unsurpassed. In his numerous prophecies all astrological elements of interpretation agree with direct indications of place and particular circumstances. It would be hard to deny that Nostradamus possessed a true, authentic gift of clairvoyance. Many prognostications are so exact in all particulars that it would be impossible to explain it as a matter of mere chance.

This is what urges us to assume that also the prophecies that have not been fulfilled have a likelihood of coming true, and it would be worthwhile to try to correctly solve them. But how to interpret these misty, incoherent verses? As soon as a prediction comes true, it is as if scales fall from our eyes: Yes, this is exactly as it had been predicted. Yet the interpretation of unfulfilled predictions remains as hard a task as before. In this respect great help can come from the comparison with the manner in which other of Nostradamus' prophecies have come true and what symbols, allegories and metaphors have been used. The elements of interpretation must be adjusted to the form under which the prophecy has been hidden. That is the only logical approach to this task. But perhaps the interpreter must be similarly inspired and zealous as was the prophet or the clairvoyant himself?

Well, in such a case our work can be successful only to the degree such inspiration is accessible to ourselves.

The interpretation of prognostications by Nostradamus will become easier if we will consider his personal political and religious convictions and his personal opinion about questions which interested the society in those days. As he was living in France, it is easy to understand why the plurality of his predictions pertain to France and the history of France. But there is no such country whose history could be considered and comprehended in isolation from other countries. Therefore even from these predictions it is possible to draw conclusions about events in other European countries. Besides, a great many other predictions refer directly to other nations, countries and rulers.

Nostradamus lived at a time when religious dissension in France began to rise and to grow deeper, finally leading to a civil war. These questions too play an important part in his predictions. It seems that Nostradamus had been a zealous, active Catholic. He was pitted against the Reformation and Protestantism, although he also had to face accusations that he secretly sympathized with Calvinists. In this respect polemics were caused by the 14th and 45th quatrains of the first century. The latter reads:

Founder of sects great grief to the accuser,
Beast in theater, the stage show prepared:
The inventor ennobled by the ancient fact,
The world confused and schismatic because of sects.

Protestants were enraged by this quatrain, because in the word "beast" ("beste") they discerned insult against the Calvinist scholar Theodore de Beze, who signed his name "Besze." Chavigny, the disciple of Nostradamus, comments on this quatrain: "He (i.e., Nostradamus) reproaches their ministers with ignorance and ridicules their congregations."

Nostradamus was a true French patriot and a convinced monarchist. Monarchy poses in his quatrains as a "lady" with descendants, because a king's son inherits the throne and crown by the right of succession. Nostradamus despised revolution and her daughter, the republic, and called them "nonnaria" and "pellix" (both words mean prostitute), "monstre" (monster) and other disgraceful names. Already three centuries before the events, he foretold social conflicts and revolution. Often he used the word "red" to designate revolutionaries, and "white" as a term for legitimists. Paris during the revolution he named the "red city."

Nostradamus' symbol for the empire is "l'aigle" (eagle). With this name he designates Napoleon and, according to the opinion of several commentators, also the future emperors of France. In several quatrains Nostradamus calls France or her ruler "le coq" (cock). The Gallic cock was chosen as symbol for himself and all France by King Louis Philippe, who reigned from 1830 to 1848. By way of inference, "cock" in Nostradamus' quatrains could be applied to this ruler or possibly other, future rulers of France from this royal family of Orleans. In other quatrains Nostradamus designates French rulers with the name "Ogmion" (a Gallic deity and orator). These could be future military and political French leaders or dictators or rulers belonging to a new royal dynasty, after the collapse of the French republican constitution.

The sun may mean monarchistic, the moon democratic government. On other occasions the sun may represent Christianity, in opposition to Islam, represented by the moon. "Fleur de lis" (lily) means the Bourbons, because lily is to be found in the coat-of-arms of the Bourbons. "Aemathion" (Greek sun god) means King Louis XIV, nicknamed the Sun King.

In Nostradamus' quatrains we find very many anagrams. I shall mention only a few: "noir" (black) means "roi" (king).

The circumstance of one letter missing does not disturb Nostradamus. "Ripas" means "Paris." "Nizaram" means "Mazarin" (French statesman).

As soon as a symbol used in one of Nostradamus' quatrains has been solved, it becomes much easier to solve all other quatrains, in which we come upon the same symbol. So, for instance, the name "la pille" (snatcher, i.e., robber) always refers to England, a country hated by Nostradamus.

3
SURVEY OF FULFILLED PREDICTIONS

Before we commence to construe the future, as prognosticated by Nostradamus, let us briefly linger over predictions that have already been fulfilled. It is known that the first edition of Nostradamus' prophecies was published in 1555, and the first predictions began to come true soon after, consequently, 400 years ago. Four centuries! How much has occurred during that time! And about all the most important historical events we find testimony in the works of Nostradamus.

It would be impossible to explain and analyze here, one by one, all the fulfilled prophecies. Such analysis would comprise at least two thick volumes, and we, of course, are more interested in the future. Therefore, I shall restrict this part to an enumeration of the fulfilled predictions, stopping to comment only on such as seem to be the most significant and characteristic. In many cases I have quoted also the only reliable source of the prediction, namely, the original text itself. All interpreters of Nostradamus who either have not studied his original texts or, having done so, operate only with translations, deceive themselves and their readers, and the readers have no chance to verify the author's assertions.

There is no lack of such of Nostradamus' predictions that can easily be assigned to several events, because they could be interpreted in several ways. Just as many could easily be applied to a certain event or a historical period, except for an included trifle which destroys our pretty solution and makes us assume the prediction must refer to the future.

For this reason my main purpose has been to provide the reader with material for independent interpretation and racking of the brain. My solutions, attached to quatrains, pertaining to the future, may be entirely wrong and should not be considered indubitable and correct interpretations. I hope that the reader will condone my mistakes, and I do not doubt that future events will disclose many such mistakes. Nevertheless, if the general trend of events will have been to some degree correctly indicated, my work, although incorrect, will have given to the reader a profitable incitement and possibly will have caused him to revise his opinion about prophecy in general and astrological or clairvoyant prognostication in particular. Within the text of this book and especially at the conclusion I have supplemented Nostradamus' prophecies with visions and predictions by other clairvoyants, assembling for the American reader material still very little known.

There follows a chronological enumeration of events, correctly foretold by Nostradamus:

War between France and Spain, abdication of Carlos V, king of Spain, and conclusion of peace, the journey to Spain of Philip II and his accession to the Spanish throne, the marriage of François II with Mary Stuart, the death of Henry II, king of France, in single combat (see commentary in the previous chapter on the life of Nostradamus), Montgomery's arrest, Admiral Coligny's acceptance of Protestantism, the conspiracy of Amboise (IV-62):

Un coronel machine ambition,
Se saisira de la plus grande armée,
Contre son Prince mal feinte invention:
Et descouvert sera sous la ramée.

(An ambitious colonel plots, will seize the greatest army against his Prince with faint invention and will be discovered under branches.) The word "machiner" means to make secret, malevolent preparations, from which verb is derived the substantive "machination." This quatrain tells about the conspiracy of Amboise, whose visible leader had been Renaudier, but the real instigator was Prince Condé. Conspiracy was discovered and the conspirators captured in a forest (i.e., under branches) and condemned to death.

The regency of Catherine de Médicis and her years of mourning (VI-63):

The lady left alone in the realm
By the unique one extinguished first on the bed of
　　honour:
Seven years she will weep in grief,
Then long life in the realm by good fortune.

Catherine de Médicis lived for almost thirty years after the death of her husband, King Henry II. To a great extent she influenced the country's destiny and several times became regent of France. For seven years (from July 10, 1559, to August 7, 1566) she wore mourning, having loved her husband dearly. Before the king's death her device had been the rainbow, but as a widow she changed it to another, which symbolized dew, falling on glowing ashes, with the verse "Ardorem extincti testandur vivere flamma" (the glow of ashes testifies that the flame is living).

The death of Antoine Bourbon, Henry IV's father (IV-88):

Le grand Anthoine du moindre fait sordide
De phythiriase à son dernier rongé.

These lines exactly describe Antoine's life, because he indeed had been "wasted by skin diseases to his end."

Disturbances in Lyons, Vienne and Mâcon (IX-70):

Sharp weapons hidden in the torches
In Lyons, the day of Sacrament,

Those of Vienne will all be hacked to pieces
Of the Latin cantons Mâcon does not lie.

This quatrain was commented on by Chavigny thus: "On June 13, 1560, on the day of the Holy Sacrament, in Lyons, during the usual procession, an imprudent heretic knocked the holy wafer out of the priest's hands. An uproar and riot began, during which Barthelemy l'Anaud was killed, an educated man, but still an apostate. . . . In 1562, on the last day of April, Protestants captured Lyons and a few days later the nearby towns of Vienne, Mâcon and Salon on the Saône."

Luther and the future of the Reformation (I-95):

Deuant moustier trouué enfant besson
D'heroic sang de moyne et vetutisque:
Son bruit par secte langue et puissance son
Qu'on dira fort esleué le vopisque.

(Before the monastery a twin child found of the ancient and heroic blood of a monk: His fame through sect and tongue and his power such that one will say the better twin has well been raised.) "Vetutique" is derived from Latin "vetustus." "Vopiscus" is the healthier and stronger of prematurely born twins. Luther was the only reformer who had a connection with a monastery, and his movement is still alive. The other, weaker twin was the movement of Anabaptists, which was born at the same time in Zwickau and Wittenberg.

The numerous victims of Calvinism, burned at the stake in Geneva (III-36 and X-92), the assassination of Prince Louis de Condé, the Huguenot wars, Admiral Coligny's secession to the Huguenot side (VI-75):

Le grand pillot par Roy sera mandé,
Laisser la classe pour plus haut lieu atteindre.
Sept ans aprés sera contrebandé,
Barbare armée viendra Venise craindre.

(The great Pilot will be commanded by the king to leave the fleet to fill a higher post. Seven years later he will be in rebellion. Barbarian army will come to frighten Venice.) *Classe* in this case is derived from the Latin *classis* and means "fleet." King Henry II in 1555 appointed Admiral Coligny (the great Pilot) for his merits to the post of a councilor of state. A few years later occurred Coligny's conversion to Protestantism. In 1562, when the war between Catholics and Huguenots began, Coligny sided with the Huguenots, who appointed him Lieutenant General. The last line of the quatrain refers to 1571, when the Turks seized Cyprus from the Venetians.

The attempt on Coligny's life (V-83):

Ceux qui auront entreprins subvertir,

Nompareil regne, puissant et invincible,

Feront par fraudes, nuicts trois advertir,

Quand le plus grand à table lira Bible.

(Those who will have undertaken to subvert, an unparalleled realm, powerful and invincible: tney will act through deceit, three nights to warn, when the greatest will read the Bible at a table.) The young King Charles IX had settled his dispute with Admiral Coligny, but Catherine de Médicis was alarmed by the admiral's influence on the king. Together with the Catholic "league" (although it had not yet been officially organized) she conspired to make away with Coligny. Louvier de Maurevert, a supporter of the duke of Guise, was engaged to kill Coligny, at the moment when he in the morning was leaving his apartment. Historians report the admiral had the custom every morning of sitting at the table and reading the Bible. According to the historian Joseph de Croze, Maurevert had in vain been waiting on the street in front of Coligny's windows for three days and nights. At last on Friday, August 22, 1572, Coligny left his apartment. Maurevert fired, but the bullet struck only Coligny's leg.

The massacre of St. Bartholomew (III-51):

Paris coniure vn grand meurtre commetre,

Bloys le fera sortir en plein effet:

Ceux d'Orleans voudront leur chef remetre,

Angiers, Troye, Langres leur feront grand forfait.

(Paris conspires to commit a great murder, Blois will cause it to be fully carried out: Those of Orleans will want to replace their chief, Angers, Troyes, Langres will commit a wicked deed against them.) In Paris a strong Catholic party prevailed at the time when Catherine de Médicis on August 23, 1572, managed to persuade the weak, enfeebled Charles IX to give his consent to a general massacre of the Huguenots. On the night of August 24, 1572, the night of St. Bartholomew, the slaughter began in Paris and spread to other French cities. The king's court was then at Blois. Orleans for a time had been a stronghold of the Huguenots.

The death of Admiral Coligny (III-30):

Celuy qu'en luitte et fer au fait bellique

Aura porté plus grand que lui le pris:

De nuict dans lict six lui feront le pique,

Nud sans harnois subit sera surpis.

(He who during struggle with steel in warlike deeds carried off the prize from one greater than he: By night in bed six will sting him, nude without armour he will be surprised suddenly.) In order to understand the first two lines, we have to remember Coligny's career as a Protestant. He was a popular army commander, fought together with Prince Condé against the party of Guises and finally settled his dispute with King Charles IX. This adjustment completely upset the hitherto existing political situation. Only a few months before, as a leader of the revolutionaries, he had laid siege to almost the whole of Paris and had burned down one of its suburbs, and now he arrived in the city as the king's ally. An unbelievable event! The king's mother, perceiving that the royal honor would suffer through the admiral's fame, managed to inspire the king with suspicion against Coligny, referring also to the possibility that the throne could be endangered by the king's brother-in-law, Henry of Bourbon, who was a Protestant and who later indeed did ascend the throne as Henry IV. The two first lines of the quatrain make reference to this complicated situation. During the bloody night of St. Bartholomew Coligny was assassinated in his bed. The murderers were the duke of Guise, Karel Danowitz (called Boem, because he was a Bohemian) and four Swiss mercenary soldiers. This fact is confirmed by history.

Henry III's abdication of the Polish throne, continuation of the civil war (IV-44):

Lous gros de Mende, de Roudes et Milhau
Cahours, Limoges, Castres malo sepmano
De nuech l'intrado, de Bourdeaux vn cailhau
Par Perigord au toc de la campano.

(Two large ones of Mende, of Rodez and Milhau, Cahors, Limoges, Castres bad week, by night the entry, from Bordeaux an insult, through Périgord at the peal of the bell.) This quatrain, written in Provençal, can be interpreted only by contemporaries, and Chavigny does it thus: "This quatrain is written in Gascon language, in which country our author has spent considerable time. The rich town of Castres was surprised by Protestants, and it experienced a bad week in August, 1574, when all its garrison of 334 men was massacred. The town was taken by a cunning trick. One of the townsmen set a house on fire and, while people were busy putting it out, others from the outside, in connivance with conspirators, who were inhabitants, found their way into town and captured it. Later, in the beginning of 1577, the king of Navarre captured Reole, a small town on the Garonne, a few miles from Bordeaux. The inhabitants of Bordeaux, seeing the authority of the Protestants gaining ground in so near a vicinity, arrested 300 of the most prominent Protestants of their city as hostages, to insure against their getting the upper hand. And in December,1579, at midnight, when people were assembled for the Christmas Eve service, Captain Merle in a surprising assault captured Périgord. A little later, in 1580, Lavardin, the commander of the Protestant force, captured Cahors.''

The destruction of the Spanish Armada, Henry III's conflict with Henri Guise and the assassination of the duke of Guise (III-55):

En l'an qu'un oeil en France regnera,

La Court sera en un bien fascheux trouble,

Le Grand de Bloys son amy tuera,

Le regne mis en mal et doubte double.

(In the year when one eye will reign in France, the court will be in a very unpleasant trouble. The great one of Blois will kill his friend, the realm placed in harm and double doubt.) The first two lines refer to the already mentioned Henry II, who in a single combat on June 29, 1559, lost his right eye and died on July 10. Henry II is the only ruler of France who has reigned as a one-eyed man, be it only for a few days. His death brought great trouble to the court. The supposition exists that the ruler did in fact die much earlier and that his death had been kept a secret in order to insure in the meantime the accession to the throne of François II, who was only 15 years old. It has to be remembered that at this period the throne was desired also by the Guises and the Bourbons. François died already in the following year. After his death his brother, Charles IX, ascended the throne, and after Charles IX's death, the third brother, Henry III. The quatrain's two last lines refer to the latter King Henry III, full of vice and low passions, an unsuccessful king. Alleging the defence of religion as their pretext, the Catholics founded the "Holy League" (1576-1577), which in reality was directed against the king. This event laid in balance the whole dynasty, the monarchy itself and the destiny of the whole of France. A new period of civil war began. The leader of the league was Henri Guise. The king, the last one of the house of Valois, wanting to destroy the opposition, declared himself to be the leader of the league, but was expelled from the capital city and wandered with his followers around the kingdom, all the time battling with his opponents. The angry Pope Sixtus V excommunicated him, together with his adversary Henry, king of Navarre. Finally the king, cunningly pretending to come to terms with the league and with Guise, appointed Guise to the post of the commander-in-chief of the army, summoned the parliament to the city of Blois and invited Henri Guise to come also. Guise did not suspect the trap and followed the invitation. He was put to death on the king's order. It happened in 1588. His brother, Cardinal Guise, met with the same fate. Henry III finally came to an arrangement also with Henry, the king of Navarre, and restored his authority in 1589. The insurrection nevertheless spread and soon after the king was stabbed to death by Jacques Clément, a monk and a fanatical partisan of the league. With Henry III the dynasty of Orleans came to an end, and the representative of the Bourbons, Henry of Navarre, became king and reigned as Henry IV.

To all these events Nostradamus dedicated several quatrains, for instance (Presages 40):

De maison sept par mort mortelle suite,
  Gresle, tempeste, pestilent mal, fureur . . .

(Of the house of seven mortal sequence in death, hail, tempest, pestilent evil, furor . . . .) Nostradamus reminds us that Henry II had seven children (four sons, three daughters). To these seven orphans, by Nostradamus called "the house of seven," have been dedicated several quatrains. On other occasions he calls them "those of Blois," because the royal pair had invited Nostradamus in 1556 to the castle of Blois to see the children and to cast their nativities (see the chapter on the life of Nostradamus). One of Henry II's sons died at an early age, but the rest, the last offsprings of the house of

Valois, succeeded one another on the throne. All died without descendants.

The decline of the house of Guise, Henry III's assassination by Jacques Clement, unexpected attack on Marseilles by Spaniards, Henry IV's life and disappointments (VI-60):

The Prince outside his Celtic land

Will be betrayed, deceived by the interpreter:

Rouen, Rochelle through those of Armorica

At the port of Blave deceived by monk and priest.

This is a list of betrayals, as experienced by Henry IV. In the course of his encounters with Savoy, the king, in person leading his army into battle, had carried the military actions forward into the territory of the duchy. He then appointed Biron as his commissariat officer to conduct negotiations with the adversary, but Biron turned out to be a traitor. Earlier Henry IV was deceived by Brittany (Armorica is the Latin name for Brittany), which had, contrary to the treaty, permitted to foreigners, allies of the league, the use of the harbor of Blavet. Finally, after the publication of the edict of Nantes (in 1598), the king had hoped that the wars of religion would cease, but lived to see the Catholic Rouen defy the treaty and for fully ten years refuse the ratification of the edict. Even La Rochelle, although it had ratified the edict, did not show willingness to comply with it.

The death of Giordano Bruno (IV-31):

La lune au plain de nuict sur le haut mont,

Le nouueau sophe d'un seul cerueau l'a veu:

Par ses disciples estre immortel semond

Yeux au mydi. En seins mains, corps au feu.

(The Moon in the full of night over the high mountain, the new sage with lone brain has seen it: By his disciples to be immortal invited, eyes to the south. Hands on the chest, body in fire.) Here we see Giordano Bruno, the great Italian philosopher, inquirer after and proclaimer of truth, persecuted by the Pope's power and finally burned at the stake, on the Piazza dei Fiori in Rome, on February 17, 1600. During his nocturnal astronomical observations this former monk ("the lone one") had arrived at the same revolutionary ideas about the movements of celestial bodies as the great contemporary astronomers Ticho Brahe, Copernicus, Kepler and Galileo. He imagined having found the scientific basis for these ideas and created a magnificent, lofty metaphysical teaching about the world and the universe which was in contradiction with the dogmas of the church. The disciples of Bruno wished him to return from his exile to his native Italy and to proclaim there his teaching, thus making himself immortal, but the Inquisition apprehended this disobedient searcher for truth, held him imprisoned for eight long years, then tore out the tongue from his throat and then burned him at the stake. Later on the same square a monument was built to him as one of the greatest thinkers of the Renaissance, who had to die a martyr's death.

The assassination of Henry IV (III-11):

The arms will fight in the sky a long time,
The tree in the middle of the city fallen:
Verbena clipped, steel facing the firebrand,
Then the monarch of Hadrie fallen.

"Verbena" means sacred bough. The shadow of a long war rose over Western Europe when the (genealogical) "tree" of the house of Bourbon, Henry IV ("Hadrie") was cut down in the very center of the inner city of Paris. In 1610 a fanatic thrust a dagger into his heart. His death caused a renewal of political complications.

The reign of Stuarts in England, conspiracy against Richelieu, the army of Gustavus Adolphus in Germany (V-19):

Le grand Royal d'or, d'airain augmente,
Rompu la pache par ieune ouverte guerre;

Peuple afflige par vn chef lamente,
De sang barbare sera couuerte terre.

(The great golden king, augmented by brass, the agreement broken, war opened by the young one. People afflicted because of a lamented chief, the land will be covered with barbarian blood.) Gustavus Adolphus was in Germany called "the golden king." After the peace treaty of Lubeck between Germany and Denmark in 1629, a truce became established also between Catholics and the German states, allied with the Protestants. The truce was broken by Gustavus Adolphus when he with the Swedish army in 1630 got ashore in Pomerania. "Brass" refers to Gustavus Adolphus' new, easy to maneuver, brass cannons, which were superior to the artillery of other countries. "Barbarians" are the Swedes and Finns, since Nostradamus, brought up in the center of Mediterranean culture, could not look in any other way upon nations living "near the North pole." The army of northerners treated their vanquished enemies and the peaceful populace with indulgence, contrary to the army of the German-Roman emperor, which consisted of mercenaries and often fell into arson and robberies. The Germans therefore gave to Gustavus II (Adolphus) the nickname of "the golden king" and they bewailed his death.

The death of Marshal Montmorency (IX-18):

Le lys Dauffois portera dans Nansy,
Iusques en Flandes Electeur de l'Empire,
Neufve obturée au grand Montmorency,
Hors lieux prouuez deliure à clere peine.

(The lily of the Dauphin will reach into Nancy, as far as Flanders the elector of the empire. New confinement for the great Montmorency, outside proven places delivered to celebrated punishment.) Since old times this quatrain has been acclaimed as a convincing proof of Nostradamus' clairvoyancy. This prophecy contains two names of historically known persons. The first of the house of the lily (the Bourbons), who as the successor to the throne was called by the title "Dauphin," was Louis XIII. This king in 1633 recaptured Nancy from the Huguenots. When the Spaniards in 1635 arrested the Elector of Trèves and took him to Brussels, the French army penetrated deep into Flanders, then part of Netherlands and belonging to the Spaniards. Finally, when Henry II, the duke of Montmorency, demanded the abdicaton of the king and the accession to the throne by the king's brother Gaston, duke of Orléans, he was arrested and confined in the newly built prison at Toulouse. On October 30, 1632, he was executed in the courtyard of the prison by a soldier, named Clerepeyne. This fact is confirmed by two contemporary historians, Chevalier de Jant (1637) and Etienne Jaubert (1656).

The election of João IV, king of Portugal (IV-97):
The year when Mercury, Mars, Venus in retrogression,
The line of the great Monarch will not fail:
Elected by the Portuguese people near Gaudole
One who in peace and reign will come to grow very old.

In 1640, when the Portuguese expelled their Spanish masters and elected as their king João IV, the descendant of the great Manuel (1495-1521), Mercury, Mars and Venus were in retrogression.

Peace of Westphalia, Oliver Cromwell's dictatorship in England (VIII-76):
Plus Macelin que Roy en Angleterre,
Lieu obscur nay par force aura l'empire:
Lasche sans foy sans loy seignera terre.
Son temps s'approche si prés que ie souspire.

(More butcher than king in England, born of obscure place, he by force will have the empire. Left without faith will without law bleed the country. His time approaches so near that I sigh.) The armour-bearer of Protestantism in England in the 17th century was Oliver Cromwell, who did not shun acts of violence. This bellicose usurper tried to exterminate

Catholicism in Ireland, thus laying the foundation for the later Irish hate of Englishmen. It is easy to comprehend the reasons for the depreciative assessment of Cromwell by the Catholic, peaceable Nostradamus.

The execution of Charles I, king of England (VIII-37):

The fortress near the Thames
Will fall when the king is locked up within.
Near the bridge will be seen in his shirt
One confronting death, then barred in the fort.

Charles I of the Stuarts, delivered up by Scots to Cromwell's adherents, was taken to the Windsor Castle, i.e., fortress near Thames, in January, 1649. To get to the public place of execution he had to cross a small bridge, erected for that purpose. He took off his cape and coat (consequently, was seen in his shirt) to unlace the Order of the Garter, which he gave to the present bishop. His dead body was buried in the same Windsor Castle.

The peace treaty of the Pyrenees, Louis XIV's campaign against Spain, war of the Camisards, the revocation of the Edict of Nantes and emigration of the Protestants (I-97):

That which sword and fire did not know how to accomplish,
The mild tongue in council will achieve:
Through repose, a dream, the king will have to meditate,
The enemy more in fire, military blood.

What sword and gunfire in the fight against Protestants could not accomplish, was gained by Fenelon's mild words in the "council of conscience," set up by Louis XIV. The ruler entertained a dream about some international treaty which would assure peace to citizens of both confessions, but the Protestants too were hoping for support from abroad. After the revocation of the Edict of Nantes new riots occurred and blood was shed again. These facts were foretold by Nostradamus in several quatrains, but he did not lay stress on the loss, suffered by France, when part of her most capable citizens were forced to go into exile.

The battle at Edinburgh, the conquest of Gibraltar by Englishmen, the Spanish War of Succession, the partition of Persia, the death of the last Barberini (quatrain VIII-49 tells that the "chief Barberini" will die on February 6 in the year when Saturn will be in Taurus, Jupiter in Aquarius, Mars in Sagittarius; the last representative of the Barberinis, an Italian house of nobility, died in 1738 on an unknown day, but the planetary constellation mentioned by Nostradamus took place, according to the data published by the Astronomical Bureau of Paris, in February, 1738), the plague in Marseilles (II-53):

La grande peste de cité maritime
Ne cessera que mort ne soit vengée
Du iuste sang par pris damné sans crime
De la grande dame par feincte n'outragée.

(The great plague of the maritime city will not cease until there be avenged the death of the just blood, condemned for a price without crime, lest the great lady remains wronged by pretense.) "The great lady" in Nostradamus' texts symbolizes the monarchy, "the sterile lady," on the contrary, the republic, which lacks a ruler with legitimate descendancy. During the last period of his reign Louis XIV had to see death mysteriously visit rapidly, one after another, his son, the Dauphin, his grandson, the duke of Bourgogne, his granddaughter and soon after that even the last of his grandsons. The suspicion arose that they all had been poisoned. The plague killed in Provence 85,000 persons and the epidemic ceased only in 1723, after the death of Regent Philippe. From 1715-1723 the reins of government had been in the hands of Regent Philippe of Orléans. Loose, licentious habits had penetrated the court of this regent, which circumstance prepared the ruin of the old regime and gave substance to new republican ideas. The 18th century was, par excellence, the century of brilliant and refined mundanism. The philosophers Montesquieu, Voltaire, Rousseau, Diderot and all encyclopedists set against the politics of the old regime ("ancien régime") their system of reason and of natural laws. Gradually the way was made smooth for the revolution of 1789 (III-15):

Coeur, vigueur, gloire le regne changera
De tous points contre aiant son aduersaire:
Lors France enfance par mort subiuguera
Le grand régent sera lors plus contraire.

(In heart, vigor and glory the realm will change, from all points having its adversary opposed: then France through death an infant will subjugate, and the great regent will then be yet more contrary.) This quatrain can refer only to the Regent Philippe, he being the only male regent in the history of France. After the famous and brilliant "age of glory" under the reign of Louis XIV, France experienced a rapid downfall under the regency of Philippe and during the infancy of Louis XV. The "sun king" Louis XIV was the last king of France to make a pilgrimage to Salon in order to do honor to the memory of Nostradamus. Louis XV did nothing of the kind and not without reason. The prophet had not loved him and had dedicated to him and to his reign only a few quatrains and sharply critical at that. Let me mention one (V-38):

He who will succeed the great monarch on his death
Will lead an illicit, wanton life:
Through nonchalance will give way to all,
So that in the end the Salic law will fail.

"The Salic law" regulates the right of succession to the throne. Louis XV lived the life of scandalous debauchery. In unconcern and indolence he ignored the intrigues of the encyclopedists and freemasons, enemies of the throne and of the Christian faith. In such a manner he himself paved the way for communism. At his death in 1774 the end of the dynasty was not far.

To the great French Revolution of 1789 Nostradamus has dedicated about 30 quatrains, in which he characterizes King Louis XVI as a benevolent, well-meaning ruler, but the people as already saturated with anti-Christian modes of thinking. This is especially emphasized also in the letter to Henry II, where he describes the revolutionary events up to 1792 as a fierce persecution of the Christian church. Undoubtedly the revolution of 1789 was not directed merely against the power of the king and against the aristocracy, but also against the Catholic church, the maintenance of which the impoverished population felt to be a heavy, detestable burden. The great acrimony against the priests, monks and Jesuits was upheld in freemason's lodges, which Catholics were forbidden to join. Freemasonry became the shelter for free thinkers and instigators of subversion. It is significant that almost three-fourths of the number of members of the National Assembly of 1789 were freemasons. The anti-Christian nature of the revolution can be clearly seen also from the fact that Christianity was abolished and the "cult of reason" substituted as the official "religion" of France. The revolution introduced also a new calendar and ceased to count years from the birth of Jesus, declaring that the Christian era had ended. The computation of time was begun on September 22, 1792, the first year of the new era beginning from that date. Nostradamus too registers this important fact in his epistle to Henry II, saying that the persecution of the Christian church will last to the year 1792, which will be marked as a "renewal of the era" (B.90). Nostradamus was not the first who with the help of astrological computations foretold extraordinary events between 1789 and 1793, but nobody had foretold these events as minutely as he did, analyzing also the psychological climate favorable to the revolution, the course of the revolution and finally, the situation which led to the establishment of the Consulate, then to the empire and ultimately to the restoration of the monarchy. A separate book would be needed for the quotation, interpretation and evaluation of these quatrains.

The tornado of the revolution, the character and fate of King Louis XVI (X-43):

Le trop bon temps, trop de bonté royale,
Faicts et deffaicts prompt, subit, negligence.
Leger croira faux d'espouse loyale.
Luy mis à mort par sa benevolence.

(The too good times, too much of royal goodness, made and unmade quickly, suddenly, neglectfully. Lightly he will believe falsely of his loyal wife; he will be put to death through his benevolence.)

The resolution of the National Assembly and the discord between the Bourbons (VIII-17):

Those well off will suddenly be removed,
Through the three brothers the world put in trouble.
The marine city seized by enemies,
Famine, fire, blood, plague and all evils doubled.

In one night, August 4, 1789, the National Assembly abolished the rights of the clergy and the aristocracy and seized their property. At the same time the three Bourbon brothers—the liberal count of Provence, the conservative count of Artois, and the wavering, indecisive King Louis XVI—with their discordant actions created confusion, which reverberated throughout the world. In reality all three brothers unwittingly helped communism to become still more deeply rooted. Englishmen, the ancient enemies of France, exploited the confusion in occupying Toulon. The evils were doubled by famine and a sanguinary civil war.

Louis XVI's flight to Varennes (IX-20):

De nuict viendra par la forest de Reines
Deux pars voltorte, Herne la pierre blanche,

Le moyne noir en gris dedans Varennes:

Esleu cap. cause tempeste, feu, sang tranche.

(By night will come through the forest of Reines, two couples by detour route Herne white stone, the black monk in gray in Varennes: elected Capet causes tempest, fire, blood through slicing.) This is a very famous prediction of Nostradamus and, although full of modified words and differently interpretable anagrams, still contains many remarkable elements that all were fulfilled when Louis XVI fled to Varennes. The quatrain mentions the name of Varennes in unaltered form. There exists no forest of Reines in France, but there is a forest of Beynes. The letter B has been substituted by the letter R. An error of transcription, a misprint or intentional alteration? Be it as it may, the fact remains that the king on June 22, 1791, after sundown at about half-past eight, did cross the forest of Beynes, at half an hour's distance from Varennes (in Argonnes). The word "voltorte" is combined from old French "volte" (way) and "tort" (roundabout). The chariot of the king indeed went to Montmedy by a roundabout way, because the fugitives lost their direction in the vicinity of St. Menehould. The word "Herne" could be interpreted in different ways, but mostly is considered to be an anagram of the word "Reine" (queen). Two couples took part in the flight: the king with the queen and Mme Tourzel with the Count Fersen. The word "noir" (black) should be taken as an anagram of the word "roi" (king). We can be reasonably sure of this, because the same word with the same meaning has been used in other quatrains. One missing letter does not bother Nostradamus. If "noir" means "king," this line clearly indicates the fact that the king arrived in Varennes attired in grey clothes like a monk. The word "cap." is an abbreviation of the word "Capet." As is well known, the kings of France did belong to the lineage of the Capets (the Bourbons being one of the several branches of the Capet family). At the time of the flight Louis XVI, formerly an absolute monarch, had become an "elected," constitutional ruler. The last line clearly indicates his manner of death: execution with a guillotine (decapitation).

The flight and apprehension of the king and the imposition of the Frigian beret becomes even more clearly visible in IX-34:

Le part soluz mary sera mitré,
Retour conflict passera sur le thuile,
Par cinq sens vn trahyr sera tiltré
Narbonne et Saulce par couteaux avons d'huile.

(The separately afflicted will be mitred, return conflict, shall pass over the tile. Of five hundred one traitor will be titled Narbonne and Sauce for knives we have oil.) Even this seemingly unintelligible quatrain has become famous, because for scholars of history it is easily deciphered. Louis XVI fled from Paris on June 20, 1791. He was apprehended in Varennes and was forced to return. A year later, on June 20, 1792, occurred the great Jacobin demonstration with an assault on the Tuilleries, and the king was "mitred" (mitre, the Frigian beret, is a peculiar headgear for bishops). The populace put the Frigian beret on the king's head at a moment, when he alone ("separately and afflicted") was staying in one of the drawing-rooms, separated from Marie Antoinette and the Dauphin, who both were in a different part of the palace. Extraordinarily notable here is the designation of the Tuilleries as the place of assault, because in the times of Nostradamus the kings did not reside in the Tuilleries. Catherine de Médicis did not initiate the construction of this palace until 1564, when the prophecies of Nostradamus already had been published. The palace was built on a place where a tile factory had been, from which fact the palace got its name (*thuille* means "tile"). So, after the king's return, an assault on the Tuilleries did indeed take place. A second assault followed 40 days later, on August 10.

The assailants were 500 men, federalists from Marseilles, under the leadership of Barbaroux, a Girondist. One of the king's traitors was Count Louis Narbonne-Lara, who had the post of the secretary of war under Louis XVI. With cunning duplicity he tried to oblige both the royalists and the people's party. History accuses him as a traitor to his king! As such he is named also by Nostradamus. As for "Saulce" (the archaic form of the word "Sauce"), such indeed was the name of a historical personage made famous by the revolution. Sauce was the man who in Varennes recognized the king, called the guards and caused him to be arrested. Sauce was a shopkeeper, the son and grandson of chandler-grocers. It would be advisable to remember that the word *avons*, "we have," could be considered as an anagram of the word *savon*, "soap." "Soap and oil" then refer to Sauce's trade. The only word remaining incomprehensible in this prophecy is *couteaux*, "knives," which when pronounced recalls the Latin *custos*, "guard." According to some commentators, this Latin word has been hidden and replaced by the other word.

The execution of King Louis XVI (VII-44):

Alors qu'un bour sera fort bon,
Portant en soy les marques de justice,
De son sang lors portant long nom
Par fuite injuste recevra son supplice.

(When a Bourbon will be quite good, bearing in himself the marks of justice, bearing then the longest name of his blood, through flight will unjustly receive his punishment.) *Bour* and *bon* is a play upon the word *Bourbon*. This quatrain can be applied only to Louis XVI and his death. His name is longest because no other monarch of France had up to that time been the sixteenth of the same name. One of the arguments of the indictment had been his attempt to escape.

The fall of the monarchy, the cult of the deity Reason and the abolition of religion and of religious service (VIII-80):

> Des innocents le sang de veufve et vierge,
> Tant de maux faicts par moyen se grand Rouge,
> Saints simulachres trempez en ardent cierge:
> De frayeur crainte ne verra nul que bouge.

(The blood of innocent widows and virgins, so many evils done by means of this great Red, holy images, dipped in burning wax, frightened by terror none will be seen to move.)

Death of Philippe d'Egalité, the duke of Orléans (III-66):

> Le grand Bailli d'Orléans mis à mort
> Sera par vn de sang vindicatif:
> De mort merite ne mourra, ne par sort,
> Des pieds et mains mal le faisait captif.

(The great bailiff of Orléans put to death will be by one of vindictive blood: of death deserved will not die, nor by chance, by his feet and hands evil had made him captive.) The duke of Orléans played a great role in the revolution. He went over to the side of the republicans, was elected a member of the Assembly and even voted for the death of Louis XVI, but later on order by Robespierre was decapitated himself.

The death of Marie Antoinette (IX-77):

> The realm taken, the king will conspire,
> The lady taken to death by the jury by lot . . .

The National Assembly, after taking over the authority of the state, indicted the king for conspiracy and treason. The queen also was arrested and condemned to death by the revolutionary tribunal. The sentence was pronounced by a jury which had been chosen by lot. The jury is an English institution created after the English revolution (in the middle of the 17th century), but introduced into France only in 1791.

The death of Robespierre (VIII-19);

> A soustenir la Grand Cappe troublée
> Pour l'eslaircir les rouges marcheront,
> De mort famille sera presque accablée,

Les rouges rouges le rouge assommeront.

(To uphold themselves the great Capets have trouble, to clear them up the reds will be marching. The family by death almost effaced, then the red red ones will knock down the red one.) When the Montagnards (the doubly reds) began to decapitate the Girondists (the red ones), even Robespierre had to fall.

The execution of Elisabeth, the sister of Louis XVI, the reign of the National Assembly, invention of the air balloon (V-57):

From Mont Gaulfier and Aventin will come one

Who through the hole will warn the army . . .

"Mont Gaulfier" refers to the brothers Montgaulfier, inventors of the air balloon. The newly invented balloon had a hole at the bottom into which flowed heated air to lift it up. This balloon was first used by the French in 1794 to observe army movements in the battle of Deflery (Belgium) during the war against the Austrians.

The liberation of the English colonies in North America and the foundation of the United States (VII-80):

L'Occident libre les îles Britanniques

Le reconnu passer le bas, puis haut

Ne content triste Rebel corss. Escotiques

Puis rebeller par plus et par nuit chaud.

(The Occident free of the British Isles, the recognized one to pass low, then high; the discontented, sad rebel of Scottish corsairs, then to rebel much more and by warm night.) Here we have a reference to the American Revolutionary War between 1773 and 1783. The third line clearly indicates the famous American hero John Jones of Scottish descent, who as a corsair endangered the west coast of England and earned distinction from American and French governments. The last line is incomprehensible and may refer to George Washington's encounter with the French on the rainy night of May 27, 1754, with the result that the Americans eventually captured from the French all territories along the Ohio and Mississippi River valleys. It is also possible that the night of April 18, 1775, has been meant, when the famous ride of Paul Revere took place, giving alarm for battle.

The Republic of America and her future importance (IV-96):

La soeur aisnée de l'isle Britannique,
Quinze ans devant le frere aura naissance,
Par son promis moyennant verifique,
Succedera au regne de Balance.

(The elder sister of the British Isle will be born fifteen years before her brother; because of her promise proving to be veritable, she will succeed to the realm of balance.) During the American fight for freedom against England, France stood on the side of the Americans, and this "brotherhood" is mentioned by Nostradamus, in a reference to the formation of both republics. The republic of the United States was born on July 4, 1776, with the Declaration of Independence, but Nostradamus speaks about October 17, 1777, when, after the victory at Saratoga, America and France became allies. Exactly 15 years later in 1792, France arrested Louis XVI and became a republic. The *Balance* is a sign of the zodiac, considered by astrologers as a locality of equipoise. The expression "realm of balance" indicates that the new republic of the United States will ensure balance and peace in the world, after England in the future will cease to be capable to fulfill this task.

Rebellion in Nantes, the conquest of Sardinia, the capture of Rome (V-30), the death of Pius VI (VIII-46):

The great hermit will die three leagues from the Rhône,
Two nearest kin will flee, oppressed by the bogey:
For Mars will make the throne most horrible,
Of Cock and of Eagle, of France's three brothers.

The great hermit, Pope Pius VI, died not far from the Rhône (1799, in Valence). For the word *bogey* Nostradamus is using *tarasc,* the legendary Provençal hobgoblin whose effigy is carried in the procession of St. Marthe's day. Fleeing the bogey, i.e. the revolution, only two of the Bourbon brothers managed to escape and reach safety, namely the count of Provence (afterward Louis XVIII) and the count of Arthois (afterward Charles X). The third brother, King Louis XVI, as everybody knows, was decapitated. Mars (the civil war and the war with foreign countries) made the throne of France the most dangerous throne not only during the reign of the Cock (the cock became the emblem of the French Republic and of Louis Philippe) and of the Eagle (the eagle was the emblem of Napoleon resp. the empire), but also during the reign of the three brothers of France (Louis XVI, Louis XVIII and Charles X).

The birth of Napoleon (I-60):

Vn Empereur naistra prés d'Italie
Qui à l'Empire sera vendu bien cher,
Diront avec quels gens il se ralie
Qu'on trouuera moins prince que boucher.

(An Emperor will be born near Italy, one who will cost his Empire quite high a price: they will say that, with such people as rally around him, he will be found less prince than butcher.) The birthplace of Napoleon was neither France nor Italy, but Corsica (an island near Italy). The wars begun by Napoleon made France bleed almost to death (did cost a high price). Later he was blamed for having covered all countries of Europe with corpses (of being more butcher than prince).

Napoleon's conflict with the church (VIII-57):

De soldat simple parviendra en empire,
De robe courte parviendra à la longue:
Vaillant aux armes en église où plus pyre,
Vexer les prêtes comme l'eau faict l'espongé.

(From a simple soldier he will attain to empire, from a short robe he will attain the long: valiant in arms, in church the very worst, to vex the priests as water does to the sponge.) From the rank of lieutenant Napoleon rose to the glory of emperor and exchanged his short robe of an officer for the long mantle of an emperor. In war he was brave and severe, but still more severe against the church and Pope Pius VII.

The deliverance of Toulon and the length of Napoleon's reign (VII-13):

De la cite' marine et tributaire,
La teste raze prendra la Satrapie:
Chassez sordide qui puis sera contraire,
Par quatorze ans tiendra la tyranie.

(From the marine and tributary city the shaven head will take the satrapy: to chase the sordid ones who later will be against him, for fourteen years he will hold the tyranny.) The shaven head is Napoleon, because up to his time all rulers of France had been wearing wigs. Soldiers used to nickname Napoleon *Petit Tondu*, "the Little Crop-hair." Napoleon captured Toulon (the marine city) and chased away the English, who had subdued Toulon under their control since the early days of the revolution. The English never forgave Napoleon this deed and became adversaries to all his projects and finally vanquished him on the battlefield. Napoleon's length of reign, from the day of overthrow of the Directory, November 9, 1799, to April 13, 1814, was 14 years and 5 months.

The coup d'état by Napoleon (IV-26):

Lou grand eyssame le leuera d'albelhos,
Que non sauran donte sigen venguddos;
De nuech l'embousq, lou gach dessous las treilhos
Cieutad trahido per cinq lengos non nudos.

(Great swarm of bees will arise, such that nobody will know whence they have come; by night the ambush, the jay under the vines, city delivered by five babblers not naked.) This quatrain is written in Provençal. It was Napoleon, who on his emperor's mantle replaced the royal lilies with bees as the symbols of his empire. Five babblers very strikingly characterizes the five members of the Directory. They used to attire themselves like jays with headgear, adorned with luxuriant feathers. Napoleon overthrew the Directory and became the autocratic ruler of France.

The apportionment of the conquered territories among Napoleon's brothers and sisters, the apprehension and assassination of the duke of Enghien, the proclamation of Empire, the arrest of Pius VII, capture of Siena, Savona and Ancona, Napoleon's divorce from Josephine and his wedding with Marie Louise (IV-54):

Du nom qui oncquez ne fut au Roy Gaulois,
Jamais ne fust un fouldre si craintif:
Tremblant l'Italie, l'Espagne et les Anglois,
De femme estrange grandement attentif.

(Of the name which no Gallic king ever had, never was there so fearful thunderbolt, trembling Italy, Spain and the English, but greatly attentive to a foreign woman.) Since the times of Nostradamus Napoleon was the first crowned monarch of France with a new name. Before Nostradamus there had been six Louises, two Henrys, two Charleses, and one François. The second and third lines of the quatrain too can be applied only to Napoleon and no other monarch of France. In 1809 Napoleon obtained a divorce from Josephine in order to be able to marry the Austrian Marie Louise toward whom he always behaved with great respect.

Napoleon's fame throughout the world (I-76):

D'un nom farouche tel proféré sera
Que les trois soeurs aura fato le nom:
Puis grand peuple par langue et faicts duira,
Plus que nul autre aura bruict et renom.

(With so wild a name he will be brought forth that the three sisters will have the name for destiny: then he will lead a great people by tongue and deed, more than any other he will have fame and renown.) Napoleon had a wild name, which already proclaims his own destiny. The name is derived from Greek *Ne Appolyon,* "the new destroyer." The three sisters are the three *moiras,* "Greek deities of destiny," who are spinning the thread of man's destiny. The Italians called them *parces.* Nobody else but Napoleon had so great a renown. On the Vendôme column in Paris we read the inscription: "Neapolio, Imperator Augustus."

The conflagration of Moscow (IV-82):

Amas s'approche venant d'Esclavonie,
L'Olestant vieux cité ruynera,
Fort desolée verra sa Romanie,
Puis grand flamme esteindre ne scaura.

(A throng approaches coming from Slavonia, the destroyer will ruin the old city. He will see his Romania quite desolated, then he will not know how to put out the great flame.) The name Napoleon, as mentioned before, means "the new destroyer." The last lines refer to the insurrectional movements that after Napoleon's disastrous campaign in Russia arose in all European countries subjected by Napoleon. *Sa Romanie* refers to "his Roman empire."

The abatement and decline of the empire (IV-75):

Prèst à combattre fera defection,
Chef adversaire obtiendra la victoire:
L'arrière-garde fera defension
Les defaillans morts au blanc territoire.

(Ready to fight they will be deserted, the chief adversary will obtain the victory: the rear guard will make defense, but the exhausted ones will die in the white territory.) During the war against Russia Napoleon's army was ready to fight, but the Russian armies were avoiding battles and retreated ever deeper into the interior of the country. Napoleon's army was defeated by the cold of winter. The rear guard under General Ney insured the safety of retreat, but the exhausted soldiers found death in the snowfields (in the white territory).

The return of Louis XVIII, Napoleon's escape from the island of Elba and the Hundred Days (X-24):

Le Captif prince aux Itales vaincu
Passera Gennes par mer jusqu'à Marseille,
Par grand effort des forains survaincu
Sauf coup de feu, barril liqueur d'abeille.

(The captive prince conquered in Italy, will pass Genoa by sea as far as Marseilles, through great effort will be overcome by foreigners, from gunshot saved, but the bees' liquor will flow by barrels.) Defeated, captured and interned on the island of Elba (the classical name of Elba is *Aethalia*), Napoleon did escape across the bay of Genoa to France, but his army was defeated by a new, strong foreign coalition. He himself was spared by the bullets of his enemies, but the blood of his adherents (the bees' liquor) was shed by barrels.

Appraisement of Napoleon's reign (V-60):

Par teste raze viendra bien mal eslire,
Plus que sa charge ne porter passera:
Si grand fureur et rage fera dire,
Qu'à feu et sang tout sexe tranchera.

(By the shaven head a very bad choice will have been made, overburdened will not pass the door: he will speak with such great fury and rage, that to fire and blood he will consign the entire sex.) France will make a bad choice, choosing the "little crophead," as the people were calling Napoleon. France will be overburdened by him. With his fury and bellicosity Napoleon will exterminate almost the whole masculine sex, sending all Frenchmen, old and young, to the battlefields.

Capitulation of Paris, second entry of Louis XVIII into Paris (II-44):

L'aigle posée entour des pavillons,
Par autres oyseaux d'entour sera chassée.
Quand bruit des cymbres, tubes et sonnaillons
Rendront le sens de la Dame insensée.

(The Eagle driven back around the tents, from there will be chased by other birds, when the noise of cymbals, trumpets and bells will restore the senses of the senseless lady.) After Napoleon's eagle had flown over the territories of the eagles of Austria, Prussia and Russia, he was chased away, and when the sound of foreign military orchestras was heard in Paris, France (the senseless lady, who had overthrown the monarchy, chosen the republican form of government and then had suffered the Napoleonic dictatorship) regained her senses and invited the return of the king. The term "lady" in Nostradamus' quatrains, in most cases, means the government or form of government.

Many other quatrains of Nostradamus could be applied to the Napoleonic period, but the mentioned ones will suffice. They speak a clearly understandable language. Neither after nor before Napoleon has there been in France another soldier who ascended the throne of an emperor, nor has there been another monarch whose mantle was covered with bees, who made all nations of Europe tremble and whose armies were lost in the snowfields of Russia. But let us reflect on the Frenchmen of the revolutionary period. How many of them were capable of discerning their nearest future in the quatrains of Nostradamus, which for us, looking back into the past, are so easily explainable? How many of them could divine the rapid advance of the empire? Could they imagine that bees would be the symbol of the coming empire? Hardly. The quatrains of Nostradamus must have seemed to them only incoherent gibberish, and only after Napoleon had chosen for himself the emblem of bees, a few rare readers of Nostradamus would have been called to direct their attention to the quatrains which mention bees. We have to be mindful of this fact when we try to interpret those quatrains that have not yet been fulfilled. Their real meaning too may become evident only after a very attentive inquiry and scrutiny. And the meaning of many quatrains will reveal itself only much later and gradually, simultaneously with the unfolding of historical events.

Let me quote further fulfilled predictions of Nostradamus at a more rapid pace:

The reign of Louis XVIII, the assassination of the duke de Berry (the son of Charles X), the murder of the last prince of Condé (I-39):

De nuict dans lict le supresme estranglé . . .

(By night the last one strangled in bed.) Louis Henri Joseph, duke of Bourbon, the last prince of Condé, was strangled by Madame de Feuchéres.

The protest of Louis Philippe of Orléans, the revolution of 1830 and the change of dynasties, the accession to the throne by Louis Philippe, the republican insurrections against him, the substitution of his personal power for parliamentary government, the repression of 1830-1837 (IX-89):

Sept ans sera Philipp. fortune prospere . . .

(For seven years Philip will be by fortune favored.)

His plebeian character (IV-64):

Le defaillant en habit bourgeois . . .

(The transgressor in bourgeois garb.)

The tricolor and the conquest of Africa, the campaign against Belgium, the riots in Paris, the 17-year reign of Louis Philippe, the death of Napoleon's son (the "king of Rome," duke of Reichstadt) (IV-7). This event is also described in VIII-32:

Gallic king, beware of your nephew
Who will do so much that your only son
Will be murdered, making a vow to Venus,
Accompanied at night by three and six.

Here Nostradamus addresses Napoleon I and warns him of his nephew Louis (afterward Napoleon III), who in his youth was a very active and enterprising adventurer and became the hope of the Bonapartists in 1831. At the same time Napoleon I's only son (Napoleon II) was a prisoner in Austria and died right after coming of age in 1832. The latest research has come up with the hypothesis that he was poisoned in the "interests of the Austrian state."

The marriage of Ferdinand Philippe, the duke of Orléans, the coronation of Queen Victoria (X-19), the government of the National Assembly in Paris, dictatorship of General Cavaignac, the proclamation of Napoleon III as emperor, the Crimean war, the attempt on the life of Napoleon III, the wars in Italy, the Garibaldi expedition, the acquisition of Nice (VII-19, where Nostradamus tells us that France would conquer the fort of Nice not by combat but by "shining metal"; as is well known, France indeed obtained this town from Italy by the agreement of 1860 as a fee for assistance rendered in Italy's efforts to throw off Austrian dominion), the peace treaty of Zurich, the battle of Sedan (I-92):

Morts et captifz le tiers d'vn million.

(Dead and captives one third of a million.) In the war with Germany France lost 303 thousand men in the battles of Sedan and Metz.

Napoleon III in captivity and exile (VI-82):

Par les deserts de lieu libre et farouche,
Viendra errer nepueu du grand Pontife:
Assommé à sept auecques lourde souche,
Par ceux qu'après occuperont le cyphe.

(Through the deserts of a free and wild place the nephew of the great pontiff will wander, felled in September with a heavy club by those who afterward will occupy the cipher.) Although the word *sept* means "seven," here it is an abbreviation of the word September. Napoleon III, the nephew of Napoleon I, lost his throne on September 4, 1870, when the Chamber of Deputies, as though with a stroke of club, decided to abolish the empire. A few years later, on February 25, 1875, the constitution of the new republic came into force. It was the third republic successively and therefore occupied the same "cipher" as the overthrown emperor, Napoleon III, who was forced to spend some time as prisoner in Germany and afterward emigrated to England.

Proclamation of the Third Republic, the inutility of the efforts by Thiers and MacMahon in favor of the count de Chambord, the rivalry of the Orleanists with their tricolor and the Legitimists with their white banner, the untimely death of Prince Louis Napoleon, the son of Napoleon III, in South Africa in combat with the Zulus, the social condition of Europe in the 19th century (X-28):

Second et tiers qui font prime musique
Sera par Roy en honneur sublimée
Par grace et maigre presque demi eticque
Rapport de Venus faux rendre deprimée.

(Second and third make prime music and are by the king sublimated in honor by his grace, and the thin almost emaciated; report by Venus falsely made depressed.) The first class, aristocracy, gradually lost its power and influence, whereas the second and third class, i.e. clergy and middleclass, became the leaders of society (makers of prime music). The kings began especially to support the commoners, because from this middleclass arose men who fashioned and developed new industries on a scale never before witnessed. The more prominent representatives of clergy and commonalty were by monarchs rewarded with decorations, titles and honors. Entirely different was the treatment of the "thin" industrial workers who were depressed into poverty and misery. Similar fate was experienced by the "people of Venus," i.e., the primitive nations in European colonies and the black slaves in tobacco and cotton plantations in the United States and elsewhere.

The Balkan war of 1912-13 (IX-35):

Et Ferdinand blond sera descorte,
Quitter la fleur, suivre le Macedon,

Au grand besoin defaillira sa route,

Et marchera contre le Myrmidon.

(And fair Ferdinand will in disagreement abandon the flower and follow the Macedonian; in great straits his course will fail and he will march against the Myrmidons.) The German Prince Ferdinand in 1908 became czar of Bulgaria. After the collapse of Turkish power in the Balkans war broke out because of Macedonia. Bulgaria was at war with Greece and Serbia. Myrmidons were an ancient Greek tribe. In this quatrain they symbolize Greece.

The First World War (II-100):

Dedans les isles si horrible tumulte,

Rien on n'orra qu'vne bellique brigue,

Tant grand sera de predateurs l'insulte

Qu'on se viendra ranger à la grand ligue.

(Within the isles so horrible an uproar that nothing will be heard except a party of war. So great will be the insult of plunderers that there will come to be a joining of the great league.) It seems that here is described the commotion in England after the German army had entered Belgium during World War I. Then the English were not only indignant about the open violation of Belgium's neutrality but also fearful about their own security, seeing the German army right across the English channel. When the attacks by German submarines (the insults of plunderers) increased, the United States of America "joined the great league" in the war against Germany.

Austria at war against Italy, the German attempt to capture Paris (IX-65):

Dedans le coing de Luna viendra rendre,

Où sera prins et mis en terre estrange.

Les fruits immurs seront à grand esclandre,

Grand vitupere, à l'un grande louange.

(In the coin of Luna will be rendered, where will be captured and put in a strange land. The unripe fruits will cause a great scandal, great blame, but to one a great praise.) After the occupation of Belgium, the German army in a wide front invaded France and was nearing Paris, which at one point was only four miles away. But the Germans were weakened and tired after the long marches and the unceasing battles. The French counter-offensive on September 5, 1914, under the leadership of General Joffre halted the Germans on the Marne River. The Germans had been so convinced of the imminent fall of Paris that Kaiser Wilhelm had in advance ordered the mintage of a silver medal to commemorate the capture of Paris (Luna, i.e., the Moon in the quatrain, symbolizes silver). The incident with this Parisian medal put the Kaiser to great shame, but ever so much greater were the honors received by his lucky adversary, Joffre.

The use of poison gas during the First World War (IV-46):

Bien defendu le faict par excellence,

Garde toy Tours de ta proche ruine:

Londres et Nantes par Reims fera defense

Ne passe outre au temps de la bruine.

(The fact well defended by excellence, guard thyself, Tours, from thine near ruin. London and Nantes will make defense through Reims. Do not pass further in the time of sprinkle.) Skirting Paris, the German front moved further south of Reims, for the possession of which town fierce battles were fought. The small town of Tours (on the Marne) is to be found south of Reims, and the Germans captured it in the first assault. The French recaptured it in a counter-offensive and then it stood right behind the frontline. After the first encounters this section froze into the so-called Position War. This prophecy is interesting because it warns the civilians from sprinkling, i.e., from poison gas, which was used in this sector.

The Position War of four years duration, death of Kaiser Franz Joseph, Lord Kitchener's shipwreck, the devastation of Reims (III-18):

En plusieurs lieux de Reims le ciel toucher . . .

(In several places in Reims the sky touched.)

Jerusalem occupied by the English, the Bolshevistic revolution in Russia, Lenin's return to Russia (VII-33):

Par fraude, regne forces expolier,
La classe obsesse, passages à l'espie,
Deux feincts amys se viendront rallier,
Esueiller hayne de long temps assoupie.

(Through guile, to despoil the forces of the realm, the fleet blockaded, passages for the spy. Two feigned friends will come to rally, to awaken hatred long dormant.) "Classe" from the Latin *Classis* is the fleet. England and France have been for centuries not only open adversaries, but also at times ostensible friends. A real friendship and cooperation was obstructed by the competition for supremacy on the European continent. Policy often has brought both countries together as companions in arms, but subsequently hatred has often flared up anew. So it has been in the past, and it may happen again in the future. But the Swedish commentator Gustafsson has found for this quatrain a new interesting interpretation. Although Nostradamus with the word "classe" often designates the fleet, Gustafsson on this occasion translates it literally and attributes it to the combat between classes. *Classe obsesse* literally means "obsessed class." The new interpretation is as follows: When on March 8, 1917, the first revolution took place in Russia, Lenin lived in exile in Switzerland. He petitioned the Allies to help him return to Russia, but England declined the request, because the revolution, which had occurred in Russia, was an annoying surprise. Lenin had better luck with the Germans, who hoped that a real communistic uprising would paralyze the Russian army. Kaiser Wilhelm permitted Lenin to cross Germany in a sealed-off railway car. Lenin's further course led him through Sweden and Finland. The two feigned friends are Lenin and

Trotsky, the latter having returned from America. Both friends are mentioned also in IV-95:

Le regne à deux laisse, bien peu tiendront,
Trois and sept mois passes feront la guerre,
Les deux Vestales contre rebelleront:
Victor puis nay en Armonique terre.

(The realm left to two, they will hold it very briefly, three years seven months will pass in making war. The two Vestals will rebel in opposition: Victor the later born in the land of Armenia.) Since Lenin with Trotsky attained to power in November, 1917, they did not continue the state of war with Germany for long, but concluded separate peace with Germany in March, 1918, exactly three years and seven months after the beginning of war. After the death of Lenin (January 21, 1924) Trotsky and Stalin became rivals. They are compared with Vestals, because they built a sepulchre, resembling an altar, for Lenin on the Red Square in Moscow. The competition was won by Stalin, the younger one (the later born). Stalin was born in Georgia, not in Armenia, but Armenia has been mentioned here the same way as in V-94, where Armenia did serve better as a rhyme than Georgia. It has to be noted that for the sake of a rhyme Nostradamus often transforms the last words of a line, sometimes even using grammatically incorrect endings. Besides, in this case, it should not be forgotten that in olden times Armenia indeed included parts of the present Georgia.

The collapse of Austria, England's victory, collapse of Germany, France regains her territory, including Alsace and Lorraine (IV-12);

Le camp plus grand de route mis en fuite,
Gueres plus outre ne sera pourchassé:
Ost recampé, et legion reduicte
Puis hors des Gaules du tout sera chassé.

(The greater army put to flight in disorder, scarcely further will it be pursued: army reassembled and the legion reduced, then it will be chased out from the Gauls completely.)

The conclusion of armistice (V-2):

Sept coniurez au banquet feront luire,
Contre les trois le fer hors de nauire,
L'un les deux classes au grand fera conduire,
Quand par le mail dernier au front lui tire.

(Seven conspirators at the banquet will cause to flash the iron against the three out of the ship. One will have the two fleets brought to the great one, when on the mall the latter shoots him in the forehead.) The conditions in postwar Germany were characterized by the wrestling between the adherents of the Republic of Weimar and the nationalists, who demanded revenge and exploited the general indignation about the severe terms of the peace treaty. Extremely painful for the Germans was the circumstance that they had to dismantle both fleets: the navy and the merchant fleet. Especially violent indignation was directed against the person of Dr. Mathias Erzberger, who had been the leader of the German delegation and the signer of the armistice on November 11, 1918. The word "seven" of the first line represents the United States and six European countries, the adversaries of Germany during the world war. The German delegation consisted of three men. In an act of revenge Erzberger, then a member of the German government, was shot to death on August 26, 1921, by German nationalists, as he took a stroll on the mall of Griesbach-Freudenstadt.

Irish insurrection in 1919, the "dagger stab" legend, invented by the German nationalists (V-5):

Sous ombre feincte d'oster de seruitude,
Peuple et cité usurpera lui-mesme,
Pire fera par fraux de jeune pute,
Liuré au champ lisant le faux proësme.

(Under the shadowy pretense of revoking servitude, he will himself usurp people and city. He will do worse because of the fraud of the young prostitute and will deliver to the field, reading the false poem.) Referring to the theory that Germany had lost the war and had fallen under the servitude of the Treaty of Versailles because of treachery by Jews, communists and socialists, Adolf Hitler stirred up the unemployed and needy classes, promising to free Germany of this bondage. Thus the leadership gradually passed into the hands of the National-socialists. The matter was made worse by the actions of the French Republic (the prostitute) and her attitude regarding the question of reparations. (As is well known, Nostradamus, being himself a Christian monarchist, always called the republican form of government by the name of "fallen woman.") As a result, Hitler with his false poem, *Mein Kampf*, delivered the German nation to the battlefields. Similar scepticism about the peace treaty of Versailles and its results is disclosed by Nostradamus in II-88:

Le circuit du grand faict ruineux
Le nom septiesme du cinquiesme sera:
D'vn tiers plus grand l'estrange belliqueux.
Mouton, Lutece, Aix ne garantira.

(The circuit of the great ruinous deed will be the seventh name of the fifth. Of a third greater the strange bellicosity, sheep, Paris, Aix will not guarantee.) The Allies delivered the final terms of the peace treaty to the Germans on the seventh day of the fifth month (May) in 1919. The French consider this as a day of triumph, the greatest of the whole war. The Second World War was the third and the greatest of all contests between Germany and France. Hitler, born in the constellation of "sheep," i.e. "ram" (Aries), on April 20, 1889, captured not only Lutecia (Paris) but also the small Aix in Nostradamus' native Provence.

Mussolini's low descent and his further career (VII-32):

Du mont Royal naistra l'vne casane,
Qui caue, et compte viendra tyranniser:
Dresser copie de la marche Millane,
Favene, Florence d'or, et gens espuiser.

(To the royal mountain from a cabin will be born one who boring and calculating will come to tyrannize. He will prepare a march from Milan and will drain Faenza and Florence of gold and men.) Although of low descent, Mussolini, after the organized "march to Rome," became the real ruler of Italy. The incipient Fascist headquarters was in Milan, and in Milan Mussolini in 1917 founded his newspaper *Popolo d'Italia.* Therefore, it could be said that "the march to Rome" was begun in Milan. With the towns of Faenza and Florence, Nostradamus makes reference to all of Italy, which was drained of gold and men by the dictator's many military expeditions. The aggression against Ethiopia in 1935 is not mentioned by Nostradamus, but in his epistle to Henri II he disapproves of Italy's harsh administration of Africa, saying "the Barbarian sect (the Islam) everywhere will be greatly afflicted and persecuted by the Latins."

National-socialism (III-76):

En Germanie naistront diuerses sectes,
S'approchent fort de l'heureux paganisme.
Le coeur captif et petites receptes,
Feront retour à payer le vray disme.

(In Germany will be born diverse sects, approaching very near happy paganism. The heart captive and receipts small; they will return to paying the true tithe.) To modern German paganism belongs also the movement propagated by General Erich von Ludendorf, which had in its program the return to the ancient Germanic cult. Later the movement of National Socialism, which was ill disposed toward the church, came into existence with manifold subsidiary organizations, for instance, "Kraft durch Freude," the aim of which was to promote athletic events and exalt physical strength and beauty. Postwar elections in West Germany have proved that the masses, which had previously supported Nazism, have returned to Catholicism and again are paying the "true" tithe, as foretold by Nostradamus.

Dictatorship in Germany: in II-87 Nostradamus asserts that the German republic will not be able to overcome difficulties and will be overturned by a German dictator who will come from abroad; as is well known, Adolf Hitler was an Austrian. About the Italian dictatorship Nostradamus foretells that it will by its own exertion rise on wings so high as if to compete with ancient Rome, and that both dictatorships (II-89) will befriend each other and will combine their forces. As one of the causes of war, VIII-100 mentions the immense armament in small and big nations (*le haut en bas par le bas au plus haut*) and that this excessive power will bring disaster to all nations. In another quatrain we read that the Pope will condemn communism and fascism (the new sects of philosophers) but with no avail, because war will break out, causing misery to all countries.

The people's front in France (politicians, although regarding communism as their enemy, will ally themselves with it, in order to partly retain power and influence, and they like chameleons will change their color, depending on the situation), inflation in France, abdication of Edward VIII in December 1936 (X-22 and X-39):

Pour ne vouloir consentir au divorce,
Qui puis aprés sera connu indigne,
Le Roi des Isles sera chassé par force,
Mis à son lieu qui de Roi n'aura signe.

(For not wishing to consent to divorce, which then afterward will be recognized as unworthy, the king of the Isles will be driven out by force, and in his place put one who will have no mark of a king.)

Premier fils vefve, malheureux mariage,
Sans nuls enfans deux Isles en discord,

Avant dixhuict incompetent aage,

De l'autre prés plus bas sera l'accord.

(First son, widow, unfortunate marriage, without any children two Isles in discord, before eighteen, incompetent age, for the other, younger one, will be in accord.) The first of these quatrains has been formerly attributed to Charles I, king of England. His successor, Oliver Cromwell, of course, had no marks of a king, but the first line of the quatrain remained unexplained. After Edward VIII's abdication this quatrain has become easily explainable. The English society did not consent to King Edward VIII's marriage with a divorcee and forced him to abdicate. His mother was a widow and he was her first, oldest son. The other son, afterward George VI, had not been educated as a successor to the throne and was not prepared for the rôle of a monarch. From January 20, 1936, the day George V died, to May 18, 1937, the day of George VI's coronation, were sixteen months, i.e., less than one and one half years (eighteen months).

Of the many quatrains dedicated to England, let me mention also III-70, where we are told that Great Britain, including England, will be quite powerful on the seas, but a new Ausonia's treaty of alliance will cause war with Great Britain (Ausonia is a poetical Latin name for Italy, and Ausonia's treaty of course indicates the axis of Rome-Berlin).

Several quatrains bear upon the events during the civil war in Spain. First of all III-35 should be mentioned, where the birth of a dictator is predicted:

De plus profond de l'Occident d'Europe,

De pauures gens vn ieune enfant naistra,

Qui par sa langue seduira grande troupe:

Son bruit au regne d'Orient plus croistra.

(From the very depths of the Occident of Europe a young child will be born of poor people, he who by his tongue will seduce a great troop: his fame will increase toward the realm of the Orient.) The corner of Europe most extended toward the Occident is the northwestern coast of Spain. Exactly there, in the city of Ferrol, Francisco Franco, Spain's present head of state, was born on December 4, 1892, of a Spanish naval sergeant's family. He began his revolution from the territory of Spanish Morocco. In his first storm troops were many Moroccans. He was especially renowned in Morocco and other Arab countries as a staunch friend of the Arabs. The starting point of the civil war is referred to in VIII-85:

Entre Bayonne et à sainct Iean de Lux

Sera posé de Mars la promottoire . . .

(Between Bayonne and Saint-Jean-de-Luz will be placed the promoter of Mars.) Mars is the god of war, and it is a well known fact that the first fratricidal encounters between Spaniards began in the Pyrenean border region. Thereby the first stage has been marked. The second stage is announced in III-19:

En Luques sang et laict viendra pleuuoir:

Vn peu devant changement de preteur,

Grand peste et guerre, faim et soif sera voyr

Loing, où mourra leur prince recteur.

(In Lugues blood and milk will come to rain shortly before a change of the praetor. Great plague and war, hunger and thirst will be visible far away, where their prince and rector will die.) After the clashes in the north, blood began to be spilt in the south of Spain (Lugues is to be found near Cordova). Civil war broke out, and King Alphonse XIII died in Italy in 1941 during the World War, far away from his country.

Nostradamus furthermore presages that the flame of truth will devour the lady (the Republic) who wanted to execute innocent people, that the army will revolt and that the center of the revolt will be Seville (VI-19), that during the sanguinary revolution many inhabitants of the Spanish coast of Biscay will seek refuge in Bayonne (VIII-86), that the armies will be active near the Pyrenees, that the whole

Spanish nation will take up arms and many women will seek refuge in France (IV-2), that many Frenchmen together with numerous foreigners will join the civil war and will lose their lives (III-83), that because of the great number of Frenchmen and foreigners killed in Spain the representatives of the involved nations will draw up an accord to avoid the extension of this war (this prophecy came true in 1937) (III-38), that in a short time even the clergy will side with the one or the other of the combatant parties, and that the whole country will be stricken by blood, corruption, famine, fire and war (VI-10), that after the loss of the Duero River (Valladolid and Burgos), Irun and Santander also will fall, etc.

Coup d'état in Austria, death of Pope Pius XI, breach of the Versailles Treaty, rearmament of Germany, sedition, loss of faith and upheaval in the French nation (Présages 122), discord between workers and employers, brutal enmity, general uncertainty in the western part of Europe, i.e., France (Présages 123), new elections with odious results, augmenting the political discord (Présages 120), apparent truce between Russia and Germany, multitudes of Jews returning to Palestine (in VIII-96 Nostradamus maintains that the Jews will settle again in Palestine, but the Arabs will persecute them and make their lives miserable), the short life of the League of Nations, the withdrawal of Italy and the collapse of the League—all are presaged by Nostradamus.

Several quatrains relate to Hitler and his reign in Germany (X-46):

Vie sort mort de l'or vilaine indigne,
Sera de Saxe non nouveau electeur:
De Brunsuic mandra d'amour signe,
Faux le rendant au peuple seducteur.

(In life, fate and death a villain, unworthy of gold, will not become a new elector of Saxony. From Brunswick he will demand a sign of love, but with falsehood the seducer will restore it to the people.) Why Nostradamus has chosen the electors of Saxony as objects of comparison is explicit from the nicknames which people had given these rulers: Frederick the Wise (1486–1525), John the Steadfast (1525–1532), John Frederick, the Magnanimous (1532–1547), Henry the Pious (1539–1541). What kind of a nickname has Hitler earned?

> The next son of the old one will attain
> So great a height as the realm of the strongest:
> Everyone will fear his fierce glory,
> But his children will be thrown out of the
>   realm.   (II-11)

In a few words here has been outlined Hitler's rise to the highest place in the state, his reign of terror and the wretched end of his followers. As the successor to the old one (Hindenburg) he became the chancellor of Germany and later dictator. On April 27, 1942, the world's press spread reports about a surprisingly appointed meeting of the Reichstag, in which Hitler, in addition to the powers of a Führer (Leader), chancellor and supreme commander, demanded for himself also the rights of the supreme judge. In the whole of modern history there is no other parallel case, no other instance or counterpart of a similar concentration of power in a single person.

> Eyes closed, opened to antique fantasies,
> The garb of monks will be put to naught:
> The great monarch will chastise their frenzy,
> Ravishing the temple treasures before.   (II-12)

> A swashbuckler with twisted tongue
> Will come to pillage the sanctuary of the gods:
> To the heretics he will open the gate,
> Engendering the military church.   (VIII-78)

Here Hitler's disposition against the church is outlined. The treasures of the church were ravished and something like a military church instituted, because Hitler's name had to be mentioned in every prayer. The expression "eyes closed" implies that eyes were closed toward Christianity, but opened to ancient pagan beliefs. As is well known, in Hitler's time the ancient Germanic cult of Wotan was favored in every way.

> He who will have charge of destroying
> Temples and sects, changed through fantasy,
> Will do more harm to rocks than to living people
> Because of the din in ears by his polished
> tongue.   (I-96)

Before the time of Hitler this quatrain had been attributed to the edict of Nantes, which was revoked in 1685 by Louis XIV, who prohibited the freedom of cult and renewed the persecution of Protestantism. This act hurt only a few convinced Protestants, because the majority converted to Catholicism, letting themselves be persuaded by Fenelon's soft words. We could apply this quatrain as well to Hitler and his time. It seems that Nostradamus wanted to impress on us that everybody has a certain task within God's plan, although for men this plan more often than not remains incomprehensible. Thus even Hitler and Stalin, as the scourges of God, have had the task (have been "charged") to destroy churches and sects which had aroused God's wrath. The shallow Christianity of the masses, an outward sham piety; empty, hypocritical, trivial theological phraseology; the proliferation of sects through willful defiance ("through fantasy") of God's law—these demanded God's intervention and ordeal; but dictators do more harm to rocks than to people, because true Christianity has not been and cannot be destroyed.

Not only Nostradamus, but also many German clairvoyants have long ago foretold the era of Hitlerism in Germany. One of them, known as the "Seer of the Black Forest," in the twenties of this century issued a cry of warning to humanity with visions about events in Russia, England, France, Switzerland, Italy, Austria, Germany and America. Subsequently they were collected and published in book form by K. Friedrich. He warned the faithful of the imminent persecutions and sorrows in Germany with such words:

I see in the streets of Berlin the blood of brothers spilt and from its cellars rise the pack of destruction. Women and children suffocate and die of hunger, because the great nation annihilates itself in evils. It does not have the power to separate holy earnestness from impurity and does not possess the courage to sunder honest intentions from malice. But one will deem himself superior and more ingenious than others, and in this folly they will slay one another. The flock will be without shepherds, and the parsons will be chased from the pulpits. They have sold themselves to the state and have blessed the banners of murderers. They preach half-heartedly and live in haughtiness. They hate their enemies, protect the rich and threaten the poor with hell. God will afflict them, and only a few will prevail, because they are artisans, not priests.

An old prophecy, printed 1901 in Cologne, tells about a battle of the nations in Westphalia:

The people will revolt and conjure up a great general uprising. Loyalty and faith will not be found anymore. In this time the articles of faith in churches and schools will be forcibly distorted, and new books and new precepts will be introduced. Religion will then be severely harassed and subjected with great cunning, in order to abolish it altogether. After the separate nations will have made war against one another for a long time, and after thrones will have been overthrown and kingdoms will have collapsed, a tremendous battle will be unleashed such as the world has never seen before.

Then it will not be the matter of country, language or faith. They will unite to kill and to fight for the supremacy over the whole world. On one side will be all Russia and the North, on the other side all the West and the South. They will meet in the middle of Germany, will burn and destroy cities and towns, and the inhabitants will have to flee over the Ruhr to the southern forests. This dreadful battle will be decided in the region of Lower Germany. There they will encamp armies such as the whole world has not seen ever before. At the birch-grove near Budberg will this terrible battle be engaged. Woe! woe! woe! my poor country!

Many interpreters insist that these and similar predictions, as much as they remind us of the recent war, contain elements which still are waiting for fulfillment. A thick volume could be filled with ancient predictions and visions in order to prove that Hitlerism and communism are God's chosen scourges for humanity. In the same year (1938) when Emile Ruir's book about the imminent war was published in France, Louis Emrich in Germany published predictions which were fulfilled in the subsequent years during the war. Hitler's party arrested him and put him in a concentration camp. Several years later he managed to escape from the camp and to seek refuge in Switzerland.

Adolf Hitler was very much interested in occultism, clairvoyance and astrology. The careers of clairvoyant Hanussen and other soothsayers during Hitler's time provide ample material for special investigations. Many astrologers quite correctly predicted for Hitler a great future and glorious victories. After assuming power in Germany, Hitler in 1935 appointed astrology as a "science of state" (*Reichsfachschaft*), surrounded himself with astrologers and with their help made calculations about favorable periods, when to start successful military actions (occupation of Austria, the solution of the Sudeten problem, etc.). When the world war broke out, Hitler engaged as his adviser Germany's best astrologer, K.E. Krafft, in order, with his assistance, to elaborate plans for military operations. K.E. Krafft in reality was a Swiss, born May 10, 1900, in Basel. He was a very gifted linguist, studied in Basel, Geneva, London and had also taken up painting and astrology. He published many books and was an expert on Nostradamus' writings. On the strength of his astrological calculations Krafft was convinced that Hitler's life would be endangered between November 7 and 10, 1939. He sent Hitler a warning letter. Indeed, on November 8 an attempt on Hitler's life took place in a beer cellar in Munich. Krafft's letter was dated November 2 and held Hitler's interest. After the attempt on his life Hitler did show this letter to Goebbels and other wire-pullers of the party. Himmler was not able to interpret such a correct prediction in any other way than as evidence of Krafft's participation in the conspiracy and ordered him to be arrested. Goebbels was more clever and obtained his release, bade him to come to Berlin and appointed him to the post of a translator in the German news agency. Goebbels was enchanted about the way Krafft interpreted some of Nostradamus' quatrains, applying them to Hitler's person. He gave Krafft permission to publish a photographic reproduction of the best edition of Nostradamus' quatrains in the original French version with scientific German commentaries. In the form of proclamations and pamphlets Goebbels then spread abroad Krafft's interpretation of Nostradamus' quatrain V-94 (see on p. 101 the full text and a correct translation). Krafft was convinced that Nostradamus' text contained a misprint and instead of "duc d'Armenie" we should read "duc d'Arminie." Armenia thus would become the land of Armin, i.e., Germany, because Armin had been a famous chieftain of the Herusc tribe, in Germany known as Hermann the Herusc. Nostradamus' quatrain then could be translated thus: "The truce being feigned, the great leader (duc) of Germany (Arminia) will incorporate into Great-Germany Brabant, Flanders, Ghent, Bruges and Boulogne and will assail Vienna and Cologne." With Cologne Nostradamus supposedly had meant the whole Rhine valley, including the shore belonging to France. Today we know that there is no misprint, that only the first lines record the conquests of Great-Germany, that the text really means Armenia, and that the last part of the quatrain should be applied to Stalin, because in ancient times Armenia indeed extended into the present Georgia, Stalin's birthplace. Besides, "Armenie" did serve better as a rhyme, and we know that for the sake of a rhyme Nostradamus was ready to make any sacrifices (a fact which should be remembered by all interpreters wherever they have to deal with the last word of a line). All this then was correctly perceived also by German professor H.H. Kritzinger, who sharply protested against Krafft's interpretation but was unable to convince him. We know that Stalin actually occupied Vienna, but "Cologne" seems to be that Cologne which is a suburb of East Berlin and which did exist already in Nostradamus' time.

In order to find out and to repel Krafft's plans, which in this case were identical with Hitler's own plans, the British government engaged the well-known Austrian astrologer and writer Ludwig von Wohl, who became a British citizen and changed his name to Louis de Wohl (he later became famous as an author of religious novels). De Wohl tried to discredit Krafft and, to a certain extent, succeeded. Moreover, Krafft himself already in the summer of 1941 had begun to warn Hitler and even to predict failures. Hitler grew angry and ordered Krafft's arrest. Krafft died on April 16, 1944, in the concentration camp, Buchenwald. Already in 1942, when the number of unfavorable predictions steadily increased, Hitler proclaimed astrology a useless science which had to be prohibited. By a decree of Himmler the diffusion of

Nostradamus' predictions also was suppressed in Great-Germany.

About ineffectual astrologers and about the way fascists, nazis and communists worship their idols, Mussolini, Hitler and Stalin, Nostradamus scoffs in III-26:

Des Roys et princes dresseront simulacres,

Augures, creuz esleués aruspices:

Corne, victime d'orée, et d'azur, d'acre,

Interpretés seront les extispices.

(They will make idols of kings and princes and will elevate soothsayers and empty prophets. Gilded sacrificial horn with azure   point, the soothsayers will be interpreted.) *Acre* in Provencal means "pointed end," *extispices* (from Latin *extispicus*) were Roman soothsayers who tried to read the future from the entrails of sacrificed animals. Rulers always have readily listened to "empty" prophets, who foretell success and a glorious future, but truthful prophets are arrested and starved in concentration camps.

Several of Nostradamus' quatrains tell about Hitler as a hater of Jews, for instance, IX-17:

The third premier does worse than Nero,

Will empty valiant spilt human blood.

He will rebuild the furnace,

Golden age dead, new king great scandal.

The events in the Third Reich prove that this quatrain in all details pertains to occurrences under Hitler's reign. The third premier is the leader of the Third Reich. The rebuilt furnaces are the crematories that were built in concentration camps for the cremation of Jews and other "inferior people." Even the scandalous collapse of the German Reich became reality. Hitler is here compared with Nero. Historians testify that Nero, like Hitler, was proficient at painting. The beginning of his reign was good, which proves that the first administrative edicts of a ruler have no decisive value. Nero was despotic and cruel. Whoever stood in his way was done away with by the tyrant's servants. As long as he could be sure of the military forces, he had no need to fear conspiracies. Only after his tyranny had grown past endurance, discontent and commotion broke out in the army. Nero fled to a farm and decided to commit suicide, but could not find the courage to carry out his decision. He put a dagger to his throat, but had to ask one of his freed slaves to make the thrust. The hatred of Jews during Nero's time was so enormous that in the cities of Syria and Egypt, where they lived in great numbers, they were atrociously murdered by the thousands. In Egypt alone 60,000 of them were slain. Nero sent Vespasian, one of the best Roman generals, to Palestine, where he with his army of 60,000 men conducted a real war of extermination. At the siege and capture of Jotapat, for instance, not less than 40,000 Jews lost their lives and only 1,200 were taken captive by the Romans. During Hitler's time an estimated several million Jews lost their lives; consequently, the "third premier" had been worse than Nero.

The young Nero in the three chimneys
Will cause live pages to be thrown to burn:
Happy those who will be far away from such practices,
Three of his blood will ambush him to death.   (IX-53)

Here again a parallel is drawn between Nero and Hitler, and here we find also the crematories of concentration camps mentioned. According to Nostradamus, Hitler has lost his life through a plot, laid by three persons of his own party. Prof. Sauerbruch, the famous German surgeon, testified on July 17, 1945: "I do not believe that Hitler had the courage to commit suicide. Probably he has been 'suicided'. All signs seem to argue in favor of the assumption that he was already dead on April 20, 1945, in the chancery of state."

While in Nostradamus' writings we can find only about 40 quatrains about the First World War, not less than 84 quatrains have been dedicated to the Second World War, reflecting the events of the war comparatively in more detail. To begin with, the conclusion of the German-Russian pact has to be mentioned (VII-18):

Les assiegez couloureront leurs paches,
Sept jours aprés feront cruelle issue:
Dans repoussez, feu, sang, sept mis à l'hache,
Dame captive qu'avoit la paix tissue.

(The besieged will let their pacts to flow, seven days later they will make a cruel sortie. Among the repulsed fire, blood, seven put to the ax. The lady, who had woven the peace, captive.) *Couler* (from Latin *colare*) means "to flow," "to let flow" or "to seep." It was on August 23, 1939, when Hitler, with the new German-Russian treaty, torpedoed all previous treaties signed by Germany, from the peace Treaty of Versailles to the recently (in 1938) signed Agreement of Munich. News about it on the next day came upon the world like a bomb shell. Seven days later (on September 1) the Germans marched into Poland, which was "put to the ax," the same as later were France, Russia, Holland, Belgium, Yugoslavia and Greece (countries in which military actions took place, whereas Denmark, Norway, Hungary and Rumania were taken without bloodshed). The "captive lady" is the pacific Third French Republic.

Other quatrains characterize the occupation of Norway, the conquest of Holland, the invasion of Belgium (II-50):

Quand ceux d'Hainaut de Gand et de Bruxelles
Verront à Langres le siège devant mis...

(When those of Hainaut, of Ghent and of Brussels will see the siege laid before Langres...)

The breach of the Maginot line, capitulation of the Belgian army, capture of Paris and collapse of France. Of interest is the prophecy about the tragedy of Dunkirk (II-61):

Courage, you of Thames, Gironde and La Rochelle,
O Troyan blood! Mars in the port of church-spire.

Behind the river the ladder put to the fort,
Points in fire, great murder on the breach.

First, the names should be explained: "Those of Thames" are the English. The Troyans are the inhabitants of the town Troyes in France, but in a broader sense the French have been meant. The port with a church-spire is Dunkirk, in Flemish Dunkerk. "Duin" means "dune" or "downs" and "kerk" means "church." Mars is the God of war and reference to him means military actions. At Dunkirk the English and the French fought shoulder to shoulder and in the spring of 1940 suffered heavy losses. Nostradamus encourages them not to despair, because a time will come when even Gironde and La Rochelle after heavy bloodshed will be purged of enemies. The prophet in his visions had seen the Allied invasion on the Atlantic coast, when "from behind the river the ladder will be put to the fort" and the Allies will effect a landing. In spite of great losses the invasion succeeded and in 1945 the Germans were finally expelled also from Gironde and La Rochelle.

Bordeaux, Rouen and La Rochelle joined
Will hold around the great ocean sea.
English, Bretons and Flemings allied;
Will be chased as far as Roanne.   (III-9)

(After the capture of Bordeaux, Rouen and La Rochelle the enemies will hold the whole Atlantic shore. English, Breton and Flemish armies will be chased as far as Roanne.) Roanne was occupied by Germans on June 19, 1940. Three days later the French signed the armistice and agreed to a demarcation line, which permitted the Germans to occupy the whole Atlantic coast. In quatrain III-8 we read that Germans and their more or less willing allies will reach the northern borders of Spain: "The Cimbri joined with their neighbours will come to ravage as far as Spain."

The bird of prey flying to the window,
Before the conflict preparation made with the French.

    One will take it for good, another for sinister ambiguity,
    The weak party will hold it as a good omen.   (I-34)
The German eagle will fly to the window and before the conflict will flatter the French. As is well known, Germans sought to ingratiate themselves with the French nation and broke up not only France but also the whole French nation into two parts, causing discord in it. A good deal of the French people gave credence to German promises; the rest, on the contrary, were of the opinion that these promises were too vague and unreliable. The Vichy government too was vacillating between both extreme positions.

    Dame à l'absence de son grand capitaine
    Sera priée d'amour du Vice-Roy.
    Feinte promesse et malheureuse estreine,
    Entre les mains du grand Prince Barroy.   (VII-9)
(The lady in the absence of her great captain will be wooed by the viceroy. Feigned promise and unfortunate mishaps in the hands of the great prince of Barre.) If "the prince of Barre" can be interpreted as the prince of Bavaria and applied to Hitler, whose movement began in Bavaria, then this quatrain characterizes extremely well the dangerous situation of France during the German occupation, when the country was divided into two zones and when the Vichy government had to serve the French people and at the same time oblige Hitler. "The lady" is a frequently used designation of the French Republic, and "the captain in absence" could not be anybody else than General de Gaulle who had fled to England. "The viceroy" who tries to woo the French people is Marshal Pétain.

    Norueigre, Dace, et l'Isle Britannique,
    Par les unis freres seront vexées:
    Le chef Romain issu de sang Gallique,
    Et les copies aux forests repoussées.   (VI-7)
(Norway, Dacia and the British Isle will be vexed by the united brothers. The Roman chief, sprung from Gallic blood,

and his forces hurled back into forests.) The united brothers (Hitler and Mussolini) in their military expeditions involved countries as far one from another as Norway, Rumania (Dacia) and Great Britain. The third line refers to Victor Emanuel, king of Italy, from the house of Savoy (of Gallic blood). Savoy has belonged to France since 1860. During World War II Italy's army experienced rebuffs at the border of France and in Greece.

Nouuelle et pluie subite impetueuse
Empeschera subit deux exercites.
Pierre ciel, feux faire la mer pierreuse,
La mort de sept terre et marin subites.   (II-18)

(New, sudden and impetuous rain will suddenly halt two armies. Celestial stone, fires make the sea stony, the death of seven suddenly by land and sea.) Here in a concentrated form is described the first period of World War II, when Hitler in rapid assaults halted the combined French-English army in France, made air attacks on England, forced the evacuation of Dunkirk and with sudden surprise thrusts occupied, one after another, seven countries which were mentioned, as we have seen, also in VII-18.

Par les Sueues et lieux circonuoisins,
Seront en guerre pour cause des nuées;
Camps marins locustes et cousins,
Du Leman fautes seront bien desnuées.   (V-85)

(Through the Suevi and neighboring places they will be at war over the clouds. Locusts and gnats across marine fields. The faults of Geneva will be laid quite bare.) Nostradamus here scoffs at the League of Nations. The Sueves or Swabians are a German tribe, ancestors of the Swiss; therefore here they may mean Germans as well as Swiss. *Leman* (from Latin *Lemannus*) is the lake of Geneva. "Locusts and gnats" make reference to German "blitz" air attacks on England directed by Goering in the summer of 1940.

In addition to the military operations in France during World War II and to the fate of the Vichy government, Nostradamus' centuries mention also the heroic fighting of the Greek army, the unexpected attack on Yugoslavia, the escape of the king of Greece, capture of Athens, Rudolf Hess's flight to England (IX-90):

Un Capitaine de la grand Germanie
Se viendra rendre par simulé secours.
Au Roy des Roys ayde de Pannonie,
Que sa revolte fera de sang grand cours.

(A captain of Great Germany will come to deliver simulated help. To the king of kings the aid of Pannonia, so that his revolt will cause great flow of blood.) On the night of May 11, 1941, Hitler's deputy Rudolf Hess flew to Scotland. His task was to seek separate peace with Great Britain so that Germany would have its hands free against Russia. After the victory over Russia the Germans would have vanquished England also. The plan was cunning, but the English were not deceived. At about the same time "the king of kings," Hitler, who then, according to his whim, enthroned and dethroned kings and presidents, requested Hungary's (Pannonia's) help to transport the German army to the Balkans. In protest and indignation about the plan, Hungary's prime minister, Count Paul Teleky, terminated his political career by committing suicide on April 3.

Breach of the German-Russian pact (V-4):
The large mastiff expelled from the city
Will be vexed by the strange alliance;
After having chased the stag to the fields
The wolf and the bear will defy each other.

The wolf and the bear (Germany and Russia), after having conjointly torn the stag (Poland) to pieces, will break the strange alliance and will themselves start a war one against the other. About the war on the Eastern front, however, the number of prophecies in the works of Nostradamus is very small. The German invasion of Russia is described in II-9:

Neuf ans le regne le maigre en paix tiendra,

Puis il cherra en soif si sanguinaire:

Pour luy grand peuple sans foy et loy mourra

Tué par vn beaucoup plus de bonnaire.

(For nine years the lean one will hold the realm in peace, then he will fall into so bloody a thirst that because of him a great people, without faith and law, will die, killed by one far more debonair.) Here we are told about the outbreak of war between Germany and Russia, about great devastations and also about Stalin's crushing internal policy. The lean one is, of course, Adolf Hitler, who was a vegetarian and never lost his ascetic, martial appearance. Even Germany herself can be considered as a lean country, because she started the war with the pretense of having too small an expanse to be able to ensure proper subsistence for all of her people. But with Russia, which had more than enough living space, Hitler did not quarrel. Since he seized power in Germany on January 28, 1933, almost nine years had passed until June 22, 1941, when he invaded the Soviet Union, "the people without faith and law." Previously attempts were made to apply this quatrain to the religious strife in England and to Oliver Cromwell, although he was a believing Christian. Now, doubtless, the contents far better correspond to the conflict between Hitler and Stalin. Joseph Stalin had also a more debonair exterior, and he, no doubt, had "killed" or crushed his people by agrarian collectivization and had totally exterminated the Russian peasantry, delivering four million so-called "kulaks" to death.

Nostradamus further mentions the alliance of the Russians, British and Americans, Japanese capture of Rangoon, persecution of Jews in Paris, the tragedy of Toulon, German retreat in Russia, the misfortunes of Hitler's Spanish and Italian auxiliary forces in the Crimean peninsula (III-68), the war in Africa, the American army in Tunis, disembarkation of the allies in Sicily and the perpetually increasing distress in Germany (VIII-81):

The new empire in desolation,
It will be changed by the northern pole.
From Sicily will come disturbance,
To trouble the enterprise to tributary Philip.

Here commentaries are scarcely needed. The new German empire during the last period of World War II experienced rebuff after rebuff, the first great disappointment coming from the side of the northern pole (Russia). New turmoil was caused by the allied disembarkation in Sicily, and the Germans even had to worry about losing influence with Philippe Pétain, head of the French government, who was paying daily tribute of 400 million French francs to the German occupation army.

To the events in Italy in 1943, the collapse of Mussolini's power and to King Victor Emanuel III and his role in the coup d'état, II-55 can be applied, where we are told that "the great one, who in the conflict was worth little, at the end will perform a marvelous deed, and the Adrians then will see what was lacking and will be proud during the banquet of daggers." When the allied forces were nearing Rome, the king of Italy, at the instigation of Count Grandi, abdicated and permitted the arrest of Mussolini. All Italians (Adrians) afterward were proud about having in the last minute veered round to the side of the allies.

Further events mentioned by Nostradamus: the abduction of Mussolini, sparing of Rome, the English in Rome, Finland's fight against Russia, the destructive power of modern air warfare (VI-34):

De feu volant la machination
Viendra troubler au grand chef assiegez,
Dedans sera telle sedition,
Qu'en desespoir seront les profligez.

(The device of flying fire will come to trouble the great besieged chief. Within there will be such sedition that the profligates will be in despair.) During the last battles sedition arose among the German leaders, leading to the unsuccessful attempt on Hitler's life on July 20, 1944. Discontent in the army increased and caused collapse of discipline.

Amphibian boats (I-29):

When the terrestrial and aquatic fish

Will be put upon the beach by a strong wave,

Its form strange, attractive and frightful,

By sea the enemies very soon at the walls.

Here we are shown an amphibian boat, which can be used on land and in water. These boats were of great importance during the invasion of Sicily and Normandy as well as in the crossing of the river Rhine. Here is new proof that in Nostradamus' centuries can be found distinctive descriptions of all weapons of modern warfare.

Anglo-American invasion of Normandy (IX-97):

De mer copies en trois part divisées,

A la seconde les vivres failliront,

Desesperez cherchans champs Helisées,

Premier en breche entrez victoire auront.

(From the sea the armies divided into three parts, the second ones will run out of supplies. In despair looking for the Elysian fields, the first ones will enter the breach and will obtain victory.) British, French and American army units (the first ones) were much better supplied than Germans (the second ones), whose supply was insufficient and encumbered, because all major industrial plants and warehouses had been destroyed by air attacks. The Germans retreated in the direction of Paris. The French army under General de Gaulle entered Paris on August 20, 1944, thereby attaining the first object of the invasion, namely, the liberation of the capital of France. The *Champs Elysees,* "Elysian Fields," is the largest boulevard at the center of Paris.

American navy in the estuary of Rhone and the allied disembarkation in southern France (II-59):

Classe Gauloyse par apuy de grand garde
Du grand Neptune, et ses tridents souldats
Rousgée Prouence pour sostenir grand bande:
Plus Mars Narbon. par iauelotz et dards.

(Gallic fleet, through the support of the great guard of great Neptune and his trident soldiers, will redden Provence to sustain a great band. Moreover Mars at Narbonne, because of javelins and darts.) Allied disembarkation on the Mediterranean coast of France took place soon after the invasion of Normandy. French army units, supported by Anglo-Americans, entered Provence. Sea-god Neptune with his trident, as always, symbolizes England and her navy, which during World War II was still dominant upon the seas. The invasion of Normandy as well as of Provence was supported mainly by English ships. The allies in the course of a few weeks liberated the whole southern coast of France and finally, on August 31, 1944, also Narbonne. Mars here symbolizes military actions.

In II-1 Nostradamus tells about "great incursions by the British Isles" with French participation and about "mighty invasions from port Selyn." *Selene* in Greek means "moon" or "crescent," and "moon" symbolizes Islam. As is well known, the "incursions" into occupied France were made by English soldiers conjointly with soldiers of Free France, and all invasions of Italy and southern France originated from North African (Selyn) ports.

The expulsion of Germans from France, the end of Vichy government and Marshal Pétain's personal tragedy are described in IV-61:

The old one mocked and deprived of his place
By the foreigner who suborned him.
The hands of his sons eaten before his face,
The brother in Chartres, Orléans, Rouen will betray.

The situation of old Marshal Pétain during the German occupation was extremely precarious. He had to comply with the demands of the enemy and at the same time had to perform his duty to his people. Nostradamus tells us that the enemy (the foreigner) has compelled him to act contrary to his duty (has suborned him). He had to witness the forces of his own regime used against their brothers in arms when the Allies reached Chartres, Orleans and Rouen. On August 20, 1944, the German government ordered his arrest and brought him to Germany. On this occasion he addressed a manifesto to France, seeking to justify his actions. After the marshal, on April 24, 1945, was able to return to France, the French authorities on their part arrested him on July 23 and on August 15 condemned him to death as a collaborator (traitor). The sentence was later changed to imprisonment for life.

Subsequent periods of the war, as mentioned in Nostradamus' prophecies, are the severe battles in the rear of Belgium and the battles near the Danube (II-24):

Bestes farouches de faim fléuues tranner:

Plus part du champ encontre Hister sera,

En caige de fer le grand fera treisner,

Quand rin enfant Germain obseruera.

(Beasts, ferocious from hunger, will swim across rivers, the greater part from the fields against the Hister. In an iron cage the great one will be dragged when the German child will observe nothing.) *Hister* is the Danube. It cannot be discerned if here the German army in panicky retreat has been meant or really only a stampede of cattle in the Hungarian fields, fleeing from the din of war. "The iron cage" is the steel-clad, armored car in which Hitler used to inspect the front. During the last days of war Hitler secretly left the front and returned for the last stand to Berlin.

The last engagements in northern Italy (VIII-72):

Oh, what an enormous defeat on the Perugian field,

And the conflict very near to Ravenna.
Holy passage when they will celebrate the feast,
Conqueror's horse to eat the oats of the vanquished.

The Germans suffered an enormous defeat in the spring of 1945 when armies of the allies were not far from Ravenna. Among other things, the allies took as booty great stocks of oats, which the Germans had stored here, but which they could not take with them because of the rapid retreat. In such a way Nostradamus' prediction was literally fulfilled.

The two armies will be unable to unite at the wall,
In that instant Milan and Ticino trembling:
Hunger, thirst, doubt to thrust them so strongly,
They will not have a single morsel of meat, bread or
victuals. (IV-90)

Both German armies, which in the spring of 1945 were fighting in Italy and Germany, were unable to unite, prevented by the Swiss borderline (wall). The allies pushed the German army units back against Milan and later against the Ticino River, near the border of Switzerland, where these units, cut off from all supply lines, suffered hunger.

Because of the favour that the city will show
To the great one who will soon lose the field of battle,
In the Po and Ticino position blood will be shed,
Fires, deaths, drowned and cut off. (II-26)
The newly chosen will lead the army,
Almost cut off up to the proximity of the bank,
Seeking help from the Milanese elite.
The duke deprived of his eyes to Milan in an iron
cage. (IX-95)

The fascists together with the German army tried to hold Milan and extended their front of resistance along the Po and Ticino Rivers, until the whole occupation army of northern Italy with more than a million men, being cut off and isolated, had to capitulate. As Nostradamus had correctly foreseen it, the great one (Mussolini) lost the field of battle. Because of him, Milan had greatly suffered from military actions. Later Mussolini's corpse was publicly exhibited in Milan.

A few more quatrains about the last days of the war:

> Through blood and famine a greater calamity,
> Seven times it approaches the marine shore:
> Monaco from hunger, place captured, captivity,
> The great one led on a hook in an iron cage. (III-10)

The coast of the Bay of Genoa had been seven times (i.e., many times) drawn into the vortex of events, but during the last war Monaco fancied itself safe from all calamities. At a time when France fought for the daily bread for its people, Monaco almost continuously spun the roulette. But Nostradamus is warning that Monaco, whose ruler boasts of being a descendant of the Corsair Carlo Grimaldi, will suffer hunger. In the beginning refugees from war-torn northern France streamed into Monaco, then came the Germans, and Monaco suffered hunger. The last line of the quatrain refers to the manner in which Mussolini, the dictator of Italy (the great one) met his end. Mussolini was captured near lake Como in the hamlet of Nesso. The customs officer, who had Mussolini detained, delivered him up to the freedom fighters, who brought him to a country house at some distance from the lake. There he had to stay until the arrival on April 28, 1945, of the execution platoon of the freedom fighters' Garibaldi division, consisting of about 15 men who were led by Moscatelli, a communist. With Mussolini was only Claretta Petrucci, who remained at his side until the end and bravely met death together with him. They both were killed in the courtyard of the country house and afterward were brought to Milan. There both corpses were hung up on wire hooks in an iron cage, with heads down and feet up in the air, and exhibited to the public on Piazza Loreta.

> Brisk love does not prolong the siege,
> The holy barbarian will have the garrisons:
> The northern Adrians will pledge themselves for the Gauls,
> Surrendered in fear of the army in Grisons. (X-38)

The brisk love for their country will bring the war to an end, the entrenchments of the enemy will be overpowered and the enemy will be expelled from his positions. "The holy barbarian" is an allusion to the "Holy Roman Empire" (das *Heilige Römische Reich*), the revival of which was sought by Hitler. These barbarians were occupying the garrisons of northern Italy for quite a while, but then "the northerners of the Adria" (the Yugoslavs), who were fighting on the side of the Gauls (the French), pushed the Germans against the Swiss border (the canton of Grisons). The Swiss border was very well guarded, and in fear of the Swiss army the Germans had to surrender.

> Translatera en la grand Germanie,
> Brabant et Flandres, Gand, Bruges et Bolongne:
> La trefue feinte, le grand Duc d'Armenie
> Assaillira Vienne et la Cologne.   (V-94)

(He will transfer into Great-Germany Brabant and Flanders, Ghent, Bruges and Boulogne. After a feigned truce the great Duke of Armenia will assail Vienna and Cologne.) Here we see predicted not only the German conquest of the west, but also the German-Russian treaty of 1939 and the Russian capture of Vienna and Cologne. The first line mentions even the name Hitler gave to his Third Reich: Great-Germany. The feigned truce is the treaty concluded between Germany and Russia on August 23, 1939, afterward broken by Hitler with the result that Stalin, the leader (Duke) of Armenia, captured Vienna and Berlin. *Cologne* is the French name for the German city of *Köln*, which formerly had been a Roman "colony," but the same name *Kölln* was given also to the oldest suburb of Berlin, now part of East Berlin (see page 86). The offensive aginst Vienna began in April, 1945, with more than 1,000 tanks. Vienna was captured within a few weeks, and thus came to be fulfilled not only Nostradamus' prophecy but also the warning by the "seer of the Black Forest":

Charming city of Vienna—hear me! A violent wind will arise and if thou wilt stay as thou art, thou wilt fall. Sin walks thy streets and a disgusting sensation clings to thine houses. Thy affliction thou hast turned into a detestable and unworthy complaint, and brethren quarrel in thine alleys. Thou wantst to be beautiful, but thou still oglest dirty paramours. A little more, and thou wilt cease to exist, and thy sons will starve as prisoners and thy daughters will be sold as slaves.

Through hunger the prey will make the wolf prisoner,
The aggressor then in extreme distress.
The heir having the last one before him,
The great one will not escape in the middle of the
    crowd.   (II-82)

Is Hitler dead or alive? The world's press for a long time did not know how to answer this question and considered several suppositions. Nostradamus 400 years ago has given a clear answer: "The great one will not escape in the middle of the crowd." Hitler met his end in 1945, during the decisive battle over Berlin. Toward the end of the war, when the distress rose to an unprecedented high, Hitler drafted into the army even the oldest (the heirs) and the youngest (the last ones), but to no avail. Those whom the aggressor (the wolf) had intended to make his prey, made him their own prisoner.

Aupres du Rhin des montaignes Noriques
Naistra vn grand de gents trop tard venu,
Qui defendra Savrome et Pannoniques,
Qu'on ne saura qu'il sera deuenu.   (III-58)

(Near the Rhine from the Noric Mountains will be born a great one of people come too late, one who will defend Sarmatia and the Pannonians, and it will not be known what will have become of him.) The Noric Mountains are Austrian Mountains, because in Roman time Austria was called "Noricum." Sauromia is "Sauromatia," resp. "Sarmatia," the land between Austria and the Black Sea. Pannonia is the Roman name for Hungary. Hitler was born in a small Austrian mountain town, Braunau, on the River Inn, which is a tributary of the Danube and originates, like the Rhine, in the Rhaetian Alps. Why the Austrians have been called a people come "too late," is not evident. Perhaps here is a reference to the fact that Austria was left with empty hands when the great powers divided colonies in Africa and in other continents among themselves. During World War II in 1944 and 1945, Hitler defended himself against the attacking Russian army in Sarmatia and Pannonia. Under what circumstances he lost his life has not been clearly ascertained to this day. More or less creditable witnesses agree that, on April 30, 1945, he committed suicide in Berlin in a steel chamber under the state chancellery, and his corpse and that of Eva Braun, his mistress, were afterward cremated in the garden. Testimonies differ about the manner of his death, since some witnesses insist that he took poison, but others disagree, saying that he shot himself. Nostradamus is on the side of the former version, as can be seen from quatrain II-47:

L'ennemi grand viel dueil meurt de poison,
Les souuerains par infinis subiuguez:
Pierres pluuoir, cachés soubs la toison,
Par mort articles en vain sont alleguéz.

(The enemy in the great old duel dies of poison, the sovereigns subjugated in infinite numbers. Stones raining, hidden under the fleece. Through death articles are cited in vain.) Never before in world history, except the epoch of Gengis Khan, had a single state conquered and occupied so many countries as Hitler's Germany had done during World War II. Never before had so many sovereigns been ousted or subjugated and made subordinate. All this the prophet had seen as part of the great, old duel between France and Germany. It is to be wished that with the fulfillment of this quatrain the duel had been terminated and World War II had been the last contest between both countries. At least, there are in the quatrains no direct references to any future enmity between the two nations. The last part of the quatrain tells about the pitiless air bombardments by the Russians and by the allies during the last months of the war on countries occupied by the Germans and consequently on people who were no enemies of the allies and who therefore looked upon the pilots as wolves in sheep's clothing. It would have been of no avail to cite the articles of the international law.

The great one of lightning falls in daytime,
Evil predicted by bearer of demands.
According to prediction he falls in night time.
Conflict at Reims, London, Etruscan plague.   (I-26)

Hitler, the worshipper of Donar, the German god of thunder, had hoped to win in a *blitzkrieg* "lightning war," but he opened the attack too early (in daytime). No predictions or warnings could dissuade him from his design to become world conqueror. But the predictions came true in a late hour (in night time), at the end of the gigantic contest. Reims became a fatal city for the Germans (and indirectly also for the Italians or Etruscans), because there on May 7, 1945, they had to sign the unconditional capitulation.

Le gros airain qui les heures ordonne,
Sur le trespas du Tyran cassera:
Pleurs, plaintes et cris, eaux, glace pain ne donne.
V.S.C. paix, l'arme passera.   (Présages, 3)

(The large clock which decrees the hours, upon the death of the tyrant will strike. Tears, laments and cries, waters, ice does not give bread. V.S.C. peace, the arms will be left.) The collection of predictions (Présages) was edited and published by Chavigny after the death of Nostradamus. They are not a part of the centuries. The cited quatrain tells about the great British statesman and writer, Sir Winston Churchill, as the final victor of World War II. The "large clock" is the "Big Ben," the big clock in the tower of the Parliament building in London. This largest clock of England, on the day of victory, May 8, 1945, at 12 o'clock, pronounced the death of the tyrant Adolf Hitler and the end of his power. V.S.C. (Winston Spencer Churchill) as a triumphant victor could leave arms and dedicate himself to the work of peace and construction. This prophecy, having been fulfilled, can be considered as being authentic.

Le regne humain d'Angelique geniture,
Fera son regne paix union tenir:
Captive guerre demy de sa closture,
Long temps la paix leur fera maintenir.   (X-42)

(The humane realm of Anglican descendancy will cause its realm to hold peace and union. War, half captive in its enclosure, for long will cause them to maintain peace.) The word *Angelique* has a double meaning: "Anglican," rsp. "English" and "angelic." This quatrain can be applied to the United States, which is a "realm of Anglican descendancy." America's wish to maintain world peace has always been great. During World War I, under the leadership of President Wilson, it hesitated to interfere until the very last months of the war, and during World War II, likewise, it entered the war only after an open challenge by Japan.

Twice high, twice lowered,
The East also the West will weaken;
Its adversary after several struggles,
Routed by sea, will fail in the exigency.   (VIII-59)

The Pacific Ocean was the scene of changeful battles between the East (Japan) and the West (America and Great Britain). The luck of both sides was subject to frequent changes, bringing victory as well as defeat, until finally the last big offensive by the West followed, which led to Japan's capitulation on August 14, 1945. Japan was chased from all positions which it had conquered in the South Seas and in the Pacific Ocean, as prophesied by Nostradamus 390 years before.

> The senseless ire of the furious combat
> Will cause steel to be flashed at the table by brothers:
> To part them death, wounds and, curiously,
> The fierce duel will come to harm France.   (II-34)

At the time when negotiations about the peace of the world were in progress in San Francisco, a fierce duel broke out in the Near East where the French had opened fire on Damascus, the capital of Syria. For a time the relations between England and France, which had been brotherly during the recent world war, became precarious and almost hostile. After a while the stormy waves were smooth again, but the prestige of France had suffered, and France had to give up Syria. The world press reported on June 30, 1945 :

> The peace disappoints us. We had yearned for its coming, but now we have no reason to rejoice, because guns have gone off again. In Algiers alone there are 10,000 casualties, and the beautiful Damascus, a biblical city, is in flames. Also a number of other densely populated cities were bombarded.

> Near, far from the eclipse of the two great luminaries,
> Which will occur between April and March:
> Oh, what a dearth! but two great benevolent ones
> By land and sea will bring relief to all parts.   (III-5)

The expression "near, far" means "in between" or "in the middle" of two figures or two distances. In the middle of the two periods, in which eclipses of the sun and of the moon will occur in March and April, a great dearth will arise, but two great benevolent ones (the United States and Canada) will bring relief to all countries suffering from dearth and famine. It is to be noted that there were in 1941 eclipses of the sun and of the moon in March, in 1942 eclipses of the sun and of the moon in March, in 1949 eclipses of the sun and of the moon in April and in 1950 eclipses of the sun and of the moon in April. "In between" or "in the middle" of these years are the years 1945 and 1946, when Americans and Canadians were bringing relief to suffering Europe with substantial shipments of food.

Au grand de Cheramon agora,
Seront croisez par rang tous attachez;
Le pertinax Oppi et Mandragora,
Raugon d'Octobre le tiers seront laschez.   (IX-62)

A direct translation of this quatrain is impossible and would remain incomprehensible because in it we find many borrowed foreign words, expressions and contractions. *Cheramon* (from Greek) is "a rolling chair on wheels." *Pertinax* is a Latin word and means "hard," "pertinacious" or "persistent." *Oppi* is a contraction from French *opinant* and means "speaker," "debater" or "advisor." *Mandragora* or mandrake is an ancient medicinal herb used also in magic. Its root has the appearance of a deformed human figure. *Raugon* (from Greek) means "slitter" or "mangler." A rendering of this quatrain would be as follows: "To the great one of the rolling chair the crusaders will be attached by rank. The persistent speaker and mandrake, the mangler will be abandoned on the third of October." In this quatrain the blame for the fate of all the great Nazis has been laid at President Roosevelt's door, who had to use a wheelchair, being struck in his youth by infantile paralysis. Because of Roosevelt all Nazis met their death, one after another, as if by rank. The first who met death was the pertinacious speaker Adolf Hitler, who was notorious with his vehement speeches, and who in another quatrain is called by Nostradamus, in comparison with Wilhelm II, "the greater barker." Mandrake is Joseph Goebbels, who was of a queer, ludicrous appearance, and who in cartoons was usually depicted as a monkey. He stood by Hitler's side until the last moment and committed suicide by poison or bullet. The next "by rank" was Herman Goering, who had organized air bombardments over England and, therefore, is called the "mangler." He took poison in jail after he was sentenced to death on October 1, 1946, in the Nuremberg trial. The remaining ten Nazi leaders who had to meet death were hanged on October 16, which was October 3 according to the calendar style of Nostradamus' time.

> When the animal, domesticated by man,
> After great pains and leaps will start to speak:
> The virginal lightning will be very harmful,
> Taken from earth and suspended in the air.   (III-44)

The two first lines of this quatrain are a genuine rebus: the first domesticated animal was the dog, but that part of the rifle that we call "the cock," is by the French called "the dog" *chien*. The first two lines consequently tell us about the invention of the rifle in 1631, during the reign of Louis XIII. Forty years later in 1671 the rifle was introduced into the French army. But Nostradamus says that much more harmful a weapon of destruction will be the virginal lightning which will be taken from the earth and suspended in the air. This prophecy was fulfilled with the invention of the atomic bomb. The most important raw material for the production of atomic bombs is uranium ore, which is taken from the earth, as foretold by Nostradamus. The first atomic bomb was first tested on July 17, 1945, in southern Arizona. The bomb was hung up in a huge steel tower and provided with a detonating fuse, which could be ignited from afar. When the explosion occurred, a gigantic lightning bathed the whole vicinity with a blinding, dazzling white light. Atmospheric pressure shattered windows at a distance of 200 miles. The lightning was followed by a thundering, continuous rumbling with rapid, hard atmospheric thrusts, which knocked people down at a distance of 6 miles. A few weeks later, on August

8, 1945, the *United Press* cabled from Guam: "The last, here monitored Japanese radio messages speak of heavy damage in Hiroshima, caused by a new bomb which had been attached to a parachute." According to a later report by a Japanese news agency, in the first atomic bomb attack on Hiroshima more than 60,000 people were killed and 100,000 injured. Many of the injured died from burns suffered during the following weeks and months. The explosion turned into wreckage all houses for 20 miles around.

> After the conflict by the eloquence of the wounded one
> For a short time a false rest is contrived:
> The deliverance of the great ones is not attained,
> The enemies are restored at the proper time.   (II-80)

After the war the allies had to reckon with the eloquence of Germany and Russia. Both had suffered deadly wounds during the war. The peace, which had set in after the capitulation, was only a false peace. Soon the cold war began. As for the war criminals, the Nuremberg trial did not permit their deliverance, but many of the displaced persons were restored to their old countries.

Stalin too has been mentioned in several of Nostradamus' quatrains and called "the tiger" or "the bloody one" (IV-56):

> After the victory of the fierce tongue
> The spirit tempered in tranquility and repose:
> Throughout the conflict the bloody victor makes harangues,
> Roasting the tongue and the flesh and the bones.

After victory Stalin's fierce tongue grew more moderate. Nostradamus suggests unmistakably that behind his harangues were hidden intentions, calculated to deceive the allies. The Americans and British wanted sincerely to cooperate with Russia. The seer warns them that the bloody Russian leader will cheat them with his hypocritical speeches and promises. This warning came true.

A great number will be condemned,
When the monarchs will be reconciled:
But one of them will become such a bad impediment
That, barely together, they will not be united.   (II-38)

After the war one of the allied rulers became a great impediment. It was the Russian dictator, whose policy caused the cold war to break out between Russia and the western powers, a war which is still continuing with potential hot spots at other localities all over the world.

From where they will think the famine to come,
From there will come the satiation:
The eye of the sea through canine greed
For one and the other will give oil and wheat.   (IV-15)

When America, the purveyor of oil and wheat for many countries, actively joined the world war, it was generally feared that famine would occur in several countries because of the cessation of food shipments. The reality was different: America, due to rich harvests and a surplus of food, did not cease to provide the world with victuals and to alleviate the situation in already famine-stricken countries. Already during the war America continued to accumulate and to store up food reserves in order to prevent a catastrophe which seemed to be inevitable for postwar Europe. Conferences took place in Washington, with the participation of the United States, Canada, Australia, Argentina and England, to make provisions for the storage of surplus wheat and for constructive world-embracing international cooperation after the war.

Par les deux testes, et trois bras separez,
La cité grande sera par eaux vexée.
Des grands d'entr'eux par exil esgarez;
Par teste Perse Bisance fort pressée.   (V-86)

(By two heads and three arms divided, the great city will be vexed by waters. Some great ones among them astray in exile. Byzantium hard pressed by the head of Persia.) Here reference is made to the occupation of Austria. One of the heads is the Russian occupation power, the other one is the allied western power with three occupation zones, "arms." The "great city" is Vienna, which in July, 1954, suffered from heavy inundation by the Danube. The "great ones" are the members of the Hapsburg family with Archduke Otto as the family head. The last line mentions Mosadegh, prime minister · of Persia, who at about the same time (August 29, 1953) lost his power after he, in 1951, had caused agitation and turmoil in the whole Mideast (Byzantium) with the nationalization of oil wells.

There will be peace, union and change.
Estates, offices, the low high and the high very low,
Undertaking of journey, the fruit at first torment,
War to cease, civil process, debates.   (IX-66)

Here with short strokes of the brush has been painted a picture of the period after World War II. There will be serious consequences of the war for many people. The revolutionary · changes in the social structure will humble many persons of formerly high positions, but many lowly situated persons will be appointed to high offices. Social innovations will cause changes not only in the defeated countries, but in the victorious states as well. New ideologies will improve the essential conditions of the working classes. The changes will initially require certain sacrifices, and the fruits at first will cause torment. The transition from war to peace will necessitate great worries and financial burdens, but the new circumstances will gradually adjust themselves and bring improvement. International traffic again will be set in motion, and foreign travel will be in full swing. After the war the courts of arbitration in all devastated countries will have to deal with many civil suits, actions for damages, indemnifications and reparations of losses. Negotiations (debates) will arise about restoration of equilibrium between different countries and peoples, in order to build peace on a more durable foundation.

To conclude the survey of fulfilled predictions of Nostradamus, two more quatrains have to be quoted about England and her rôle in the world. These quatrains comprise long periods of time, which come to an end in these days of ours. These prophecies have come true or continue to come true before our eyes.

Nostradamus has dedicated to the powerful England a considerable number of his previsions, having clearly perceived the role of this first-rate power in European history. He has foretold not only the paramount might of Great Britain, but also her disastrous future with first the decline and then the complete ruin of her as an empire and a sea power. When England will feel the approach of the last cataclysm, she will forcibly try to restore her military power, but will lose in the contest, because she will lack the principal element: time (*Les Iles seront à sang pour le tardif ramer*).

Nostradamus affirms that England will have supremacy on the seas for more than three hundred years (X-100):

Le grand empire sera par Angleterre,
Le pempotam des ans plus de trois cens:
Grandes copies passer par mer et terre,
Les Lusitains n'en seront pas contens.

(The great empire will be by England, all powerful for more than three hundred years. Great armies will pass by sea and land. The Lusitanians will not be satisfied thereby.) The word *pempotam,* according to Le Pelletier, is borrowed from Greek *pan* "all" and Latin *potens* "power." The word *pempotam* Nostradamus has used in some other quatrains as a symbol for England proper. England's supremacy on the seas began in Elizabeth's time, when Drake in 1588 destroyed Philip II's invincible Spanish Armada. Ever since and, consequently, for more than 300 years England's fleet has been a power to reckon with on all seas. The beginning of Great Britain and simultaneously of the British colonial empire should be dated from 1603, when the Stuart dynasty amalgamated into one country England, Scotland and Ireland. During the war against Holland (1665-1667) the English fleet did suffer defeat, but even since this war more than 300 years have already passed. As for the Lusitanians, "the Portuguese," their "golden era" of dominion over the seas lasted from 1380 to 1580. Since then England has gradually expelled them from all of their more important colonies. Portugal, formerly a great world power, became economically dependent on England, and after the Treaty of Methwen, concluded in 1703, England completely consolidated her preponderancy over Portugal. Portugal herself became something like a British colony. No wonder Nostradamus says: "the Lusitanians will not be satisfied thereby."

Of great significance is III-57:

Sept foys changer verrés gent Britannique
Taintz en sang en deux cent nonante an.
Franche non point par apui Germanique.
Aries doute son pole Bastarnan.

(Seven times will you see the British nation change, steeped in blood for two hundred ninety years. Freed, but not with Germanic help, Aries doubts his Bastarnian pole.) The unraveling of this greatly important quatrain is made more difficult not only because the word *Franche* can be translated as "freed," but because it can refer to the French as a nation. *Aries*, "ram," is a Latin word, used as a designation of a certain sign of the zodiac. According to astrological traditions, the Aries sign corresponds to the eastern and northeastern region of Europe, including Austria. "Bastarnians" were a Germanic tribe, living beyond the Vistula, east of the Carpathian Mountains, which region before World War II was part of southern Poland. Around the year 200, Bastarnians partly inhabited also Pannonia (present Hungary). The first two lines of the quatrain announce that the British nation will experience seven changes within 290 years. What changes? And from which initial moment should we start the count of 290 years? This last question can be easily answered, because the prophecy mentions "the British," not the English. King James I (of the Stuart line) was the first who gave himself the title "Britannic Majesty," instead of simply "king of England." But what changes had Nostradamus in view? Perhaps the instances when a ruling dynasty becomes extinct and a ruler ascends to the throne from a different line? Or perhaps we have to reckon with all changes of the regime, including revolutions? Modern investigators of Nostradamus' texts, long before World War II, have had a general consensus of opinion about the starting point of the count of 290 years, to whit, that the count must start from the first change of the regime after the reign of James I, i.e., from 1649, when Cromwell overthrew Charles I (of the Stuarts). Adding 290 to 1649 we get 1939. In such a way the year 1939 has become the termination point of the time period set by Nostradamus. Such investigators, as the Germans, Kritzinger and Loog, the Frenchmen, Rochetaillée and Piobb, and the Englishman, Rupert Taylor, have all been in agreement, that 1939 would bring a war marking the end of the British Empire. We know that Great Britain at the end of World War II lined up among the victors, but hasn't Nostradamus' prediction nevertheless been fulfilled, like the aforementioned X-100? Hasn't World War II initiated the liquidation of the British colonial empire? Because of this war, England has lost her place among the great powers of this planet. Her economic resources have been exhausted, colonies in Africa and Asia lost, her naval force and merchant fleet seriously damaged and diminished during the war, and her dominant role on the seas relinquished to the United States. As far as can be seen from other quatrains by Nostradamus, the British Isles are approaching some great catastrophe. It is possible that they, like the rest of southern and western Europe, will experience invasion and occupation by barbarians. To this question we will return later, when analyzing Nostradamus' quatrains which are dedicated to future events. First we have to add up all changes of regime in England since James I:

1. In 1603 James I (of the Stuarts) succeeded Elizabeth I (of the Tudors).

2. In 1649 Cromwell overthrew Charles I (Stuart) and condemned him to death (see VIII-37, on page 50). From 1649 to 1660 England was a republic with Cromwell as protector.

3. In 1660 Charles II (son of Charles I), exhorted by General Monk, returned upon the throne.

4. In 1689 James II (Stuart), who tried to restore the influence of Catholicism in England, was succeeded by William III (of Orange), formerly governor of Holland. Nevertheless, his wife, Mary II, the daughter of James II, was considered lawful continuator of the Stuart line.

5. After an economic crisis, becoming more severe during the reign of Anne Stuart, the Stuarts were succeeded by George I, the elector of Hanover (of the Brunswick-Hanover line).

6. In 1901 the Hanoverians were succeeded by Edward VII (of Saxe-Coburg line, now called Windsor line). When this line will cease to reign because of revolution or some other circumstance, the seventh and last change will have occurred.

If the word *Franche* has to be translated as "the French," the puzzle can be solved differently, and, may be found to refer to‧ instances when the English and the French during 290 years were both involved in wars, alternately as allies or as enemies:

1. 1671–1674. England and France in war against Holland.

2. 1686. Holland, Austria, Spain, Sweden and other countries (League of Augsburg) were united against France. They were joined later by England, which became involved in war with France from 1689 to 1697, when peace was concluded in Ruyswick.

3. 1704–1713. War of succession in Spain. England, Austria and Holland at war with France. Peace Treaty of Utrecht.

4. 1740–1748. War of succession in Austria. England and Austria at war with France and her ally Prussia (under Frederic II).

5. 1756–1763. England and Prussia at war with France, Sweden and Austria.

6. 1914–1918. World War I. England and France at war with Germany and her allies.

7. 1939–1945. World War II. England again allied with France.

The second part of the quatrain shows Austria in an uncomfortable situation during World War II. In order for both parts of the quatrain to have some connection, 290 years and perhaps the seven changes as well have to be concluded at the same time, possibly with the year 1939, i.e., with World War II. After the war Austria regained her independence, but not with Germanic help, Germany then being divided into two parts and having no political influence. The last line may possibly point toward the future, when the ill-fated Austria will come to know fear from her ancient, now communistic sister-country, Hungary (her Bastarnian pole). What relation this circumstance will have with England only the future will reveal. In connection with this quatrain the reader is referred to II-90, where we are told about a revolution or uprising in Hungary, which prediction came true in 1956, and about a war between twin nations (Austria and Hungary). With these last quatrains we have arrived at predictions which extend into both the past and the future.

And when we turn to the quatrains that have not come true yet, it becomes evident that already during the past few years we have been witnessing signs and trends which make many of the predicted events ominously more and more probable.

I refer here, in the first place, to the predictions of an Islamic renaissance. Western civilization has in ever greater degree become dependent on Arab oil. This dependency has, in fact, already robbed many Western countries of the capability to pursue a fully independent economic and foreign policy. Such a state of creeping servility makes us suddenly realize that interruption of the flow of oil could, almost instantly, paralyze the whole Western world and abolish its technical superiority. Already once before, in the 8th century, an Arab invasion has reached Poitiers in France, after having submerged the territories of 12 former empires, winning 400 battles, and conquering 13 kingdoms, including Spain. Could it not happen again? The recrudescence of a spirit of religious and military conquest has now become evident in Iran, Iraq and several other Islamic countries. It could finally lead to the realization of the undying Arab dream of a re-birth and restoration of a Pan-Islamic confederation.

As for the prediction that Europe, some time in the future, will also suffer a wave of invasion by Asiatics, it too has already happened before. In the 13th century Mongol armies reached Central Europe. The great Swedish explorer Sven Hedin, in a book of his, has acknowledged the possibility and likelyhood of a repeat performance.

Another center of interest in the unfulfilled quatrains is the prediction of turbulent times for the Catholic church: a shortlived exaltation in status and power, and a subsequent period of decline and tribulation. Many quatrains refer to future popes. One of these found its fulfillment quite recently:

Elected pope, the chosen one will be mocked,

Suddenly, forthwith moved prompt and timid.

Through too much goodness and kindness provoked to die,

Fear extinguished guiding the night of his death. (X-12) This quatrain can be applied to the death of pope John Paul I. There is ample evidence that this naive, simple and timid man, during his short pontificate, was often openly ridiculed, mocked and sneered at by several highly placed members of the Curia. It can now be disclosed that the leader of the opposition has been the very influential Vatican Secretary of state, late French cardinal, Villot, who without any restraint divulged his contempt for the newly elected pope. John Paul I felt insecure and intimidated. His goodness and tender heart hastened his death, and only on the night of his death his fear was extinguished.

4
AMBIGUOUS PREDICTIONS

After having selected from Nostradamus' centuries all quatrains that in the course of 400 years have been fulfilled, there remain a good number of quatrains about which it cannot be ascertained if they should be referred to a past event or if they should be considered as such that are still waiting for fulfillment. There are also quatrains which could be applied to more than one past event. Let me quote, as a case in point, some of these ambiguous predictions:

De brique en marbre seront les murs reduicts,
Sept et cinquante années pacifiques,
Joye aux humains, renoue l'aqueduict,
Santé, grands fruits, joye et temps mellifiques. (X-89)

(From brick to marble the walls will be converted, seven and fifty pacific years, joy to mankind, the aqueduct renewed, health, abundance of fruit, joy and sweet times.) Fifty-seven years of peace. Aqueduct, i.e., free traffic between countries and nations, health, joy and abundant food. When will it be? Nostradamus could not have meant the period after World War II, because then it would mean peace from 1945 to 2002. And do we have peace today? If we read quatrains dedicated to the future, a lasting peace during this period does not seem likely. Perhaps the period after World War III has been meant, or perhaps after the expected combat with the so-called "second Antichrist" and before the Mahometan invasion of Europe? More likely, it is the reign of Louis XIV in France, called by historians the "golden era" in France. From the peace treaty of the Pyrenees in 1658 until the death of the "Sun King" in 1715, exactly 57 years elapsed.

> When a king will be against his people,
> A native of Blois will subjugate the Ligurians,
> Mammel, Cordoba and the Dalmatians,
> Of the seven then shadow to the king handsels and
>   lemures. (X-44)

An abstruse quatrain. Attempts have been made to attribute it to King Henry III's fight with the Catholic league, which included not only French but also Spanish and Italian soldiers. But what connection had Memel with the Catholic league? Or does "Mammel" designate some other city? In southern Italy there is a town called Mammola, but Nostradamus does not usually symbolize a whole nation or country with small, obscure towns or villages. The quatrain possibly refers to the future: When in Blois (the ancient French royal residence) a king will reign, who has a conflict with his own people, an invasion of northern Italy (Liguria) will occur. Seven nations will be entangled in this war, among others, in addition to France and Italy, also Spain and Yugoslavia. Again we have to ask: Which nation is represented by the word "Mammel"? The last line is unintelligible. It seems that the king will be tormented by nightmares and ghosts (lemures).

> Le chef de Perse remplira grand ΟΛΧΑΔΕΣ
> Classe trireme contre gent Mahumetique
> De Parthe et Mede: et piller les Cyclades.
> Repos long temps au grand port Ionique. (III-64)

(The chief of Persia will fill great tugboats, the trireme fleet against the Mahometan people from Parthia and Media, and the Cyclades pillaged. Long rest at the great Ionian port.) It seems that here the famous Battle of Lepanto has been described, when Don Juan of Austria vanquished the Turkish fleet in 1571, which event initiated the decline of the Ottoman empire. The great Ionian port is Smyrna. Nevertheless, many commentators apply this quatrain to the future, when Persia is supposed to play again an important rôle in world history, will extend her frontiers to the west, will through the Black Sea send a big fleet to the Turkish and Greek waters and will pillage also the Cyclades (islands between Greece and Crete). After this event a long peace is supposed to reign in the great Ionian port.

En terre neufve bien auant Roy entré
Pendant sujets luy viendront faire accueil:
Sa perfidie aura tel rencontré
Qu'aux citadins lieu de feste et recueil.   (VIII-74)

(In the new land well before king entered, while subjects come to welcome him: his perfidy will have such an effect that for the citizens a replacing of feast and gathering.) "The new land" is a well-known designation used since times long past for America. Thus was America called in Nostradamus' lifetime and so it is called by the people in many countries even today. Therefore this prophecy has always been attributed to America and particularly to Canada, since the subjects of a king are involved. But lately G. Gustafsson has come forward with a peculiar interpretation. He detects in this quatrain the religious strife between Protestant Sweden and Catholic Poland. After Johan III's death on November 17, 1592, his son Sigismund, king of Poland, inherited Sweden's throne by succession. Sigismund, raised in the Catholic faith, supported the efforts of Malaspinas, the pope's Nuntius, to catholicize Poland, and he wished to introduce Catholicism in Sweden as well. Learning about these intentions of Sigismund against Protestantism, the Swedish church summoned a convocation in Upsala in March of 1593, where the Resolutions of 1571 were confirmed and the readiness to sacrifice their lives for the Protestant faith was proclaimed. Also it was agreed to demand that Sigismund accept all resolutions of the Upsala convocation before he could be crowned king of Sweden. Sigismund at first refused, but later, obeying the advice of his confessor, yielded, arrived in Sweden (his "new land") in the autumn of 1593 and tried to obtain full religious freedom for Catholics. The Swedes revolted and raised to the throne Sigismund's uncle, Charles IX. Such an interpretation of the quatrain is very interesting, but, in my opinion, not likely to be correct, as it cannot be expected that Nostradamus, himself a Catholic, would describe Sigismund's actions as perfidy.

To the exploits of Charles XII, king of Sweden, in Russia, Gustafsson applies quatrain VIII-92:

Loin hors du regne mis en hazard voyage,
Grand ost duyra pour soy l'occupera:
Le Roi tiendra les siens captif, ostage,
A son retour tout pays pillera.

(Far from his realm set on a hazardous journey he will lead a great army and will keep it for himself. The king will hold his followers captive and hostage. Upon his return he will plunder the entire country.) After his campaigns in Russia, Charles XII, with the remains of his army, took refuge in Turkey, submitting to captivity. In vain he sought to incite the Turks to take up arms against Russia. Having for many years remained in Turkey, he left his voluntary captivity in October, 1714, to return to Sweden. He reached the Baltic Sea at Stralsund, where he with his followers were besieged for a whole year. To Sweden he could return only in December, 1715, and immediately he began to equip a new, strong army in such a hasty and forcible way that he seemingly pillaged his own country. It is a highly interesting interpretation of a quatrain which up to now has never been applied to a past event and always has been considered as one which still is waiting for fulfillment. The usual interpretation of this quatrain is: One of the future kings (of France) will make military incursions with a great army into foreign countries, but will think more of great booty and spoils than of his peoples' welfare. Returning, he will plunder his own country.

Ronge long, sec faisant du bon valet,

A la parfin n'aura que son congie.

Poignant poyson et lettres au collet

Sera saisi eschappé en dangie.   (VIII-82)

(Gaunt, tall, dry, playing the good valet, in the end he will have only his leave. Keen poison, and letters in his collar, he will be seized escaped in danger.) It seems that here we have a portrait of the great French philosopher Jean Jacques Rousseau. After his erratic youth, which was rich with dramatic, intricate adventures, Rousseau began to seek and to exploit every opportunity for literary studies. For some time he was employed as an assistant in a store, later as butler in several families of nobility. One of the latter secured for him an opportunity to get schooling from an abbot. Rousseau was "given leave" by all his employers, began to write books and became famous, but his ideas, as Nostradamus asserts, were poisoned. They were later adopted and exploited by Robespierre, the evil spirit of the French Revolution. Attempts were made to apply this quatrain also to Louis Philippe, king of France, a man with a dry heart, who exploited revolution and various intrigues to seize the throne in 1830, after the abdication of Charles X. He became king after Prince Condé de Bourbon (the last of the Condé line) was found dead from mysterious causes at his estate. Louis Philippe used diverse crises (the international crisis of 1840, the affair of Mehemet Ali) in order to keep his throne. Nevertheless, he finally was expelled ("was given leave") in 1848. Only with difficulty he escaped the officers, who were given orders for his arrest, and fled abroad.

Du lac Leman les sermons facheront,

Des iours seront reduicts par des sepmaines,

Puis mois, puis an, puis tous defailliront,
Les magistrats damneront leur loys vaines.   (I-47)

(The sermons from the Lake of Geneva annoying, from days they will grow into weeks, then months, then years, then all will fail, the magistrates will damn their useless laws.) The quatrain shows us those who were accused by Nostradamus as the forerunners of the French Revolution: Voltaire and Rousseau. Both were living and writing on the shores of Lake Geneva, but their work helped to prepare a favorable climate for communism. The revolutionary era will last for days, weeks, months and even years, but finally it nevertheless will experience failure and end. The successors of the revolution, the Empire and the Restoration, by degrees changed all the "useless laws." This quatrain could be applied as well or even better to the League of Nations located in Geneva. The League of Nations from the start was lacking authority, since the most powerful country of the world, the United States of America, did not participate in it. When the totalitarian countries, Italy and Japan and later also Germany and the Soviet Union, began aggressive actions, the League of Nations was unable to settle the conflicts. Verbally it condemned the culprit nations but, lacking power, could not give life to the imposed sanctions. The activity of the League of Nations consisted only of empty resolutions and endless discussions or, as Nostradamus puts it, of annoying sermons which lasted for weeks, months and years. Finally, the representatives of the nations in Geneva themselves had to admit that their decisions could not be carried out.

La republique miserable infelice
Sera vastée du nouueau magistrat:
Leur grand amas de l'exil malefice
Fera Sueue rauir leur grand contract.   (I-61)

(The miserable, unhappy republic will be ruined by the new magistrate. Their great accumulation in wicked exile will cause the Suevi to tear up their great contract.) With the

word "Suevi" (Swabians) Nostradamus usually designates
Switzerland or the Swiss since the Suevi or Swabians were the
ancestors of the Swiss. Should this quatrain be attributed to
Calvin's republic in Geneva or to the republican France
before the reign of Napoleon? Or perhaps to the future, when
a bloody (perhaps communistic) republican government will
cause the French to flee to Switzerland in such a great
number that Switzerland will be forced to close her borders
(i.e., to break with her traditions and to refuse to give to the
refugees asylum in her territory)?

> At Port Selin the tyrant put to death,
> Liberty nevertheless not recovered.
> The new Mars because of vengeance and slaughter,
> The lady honored through force of terror.   (I-94)

Greek *Selene* is the "moon," and "moon" or "crescent" as
symbol of Islam can be found in the flag of Turkey and
other Islamic countries. Does this quatrain pronounce the
assassination of Sultan Abd-el-Aziz on June 4, 1876, and the
Turkish acts of violence in the Balkans? Mars symbolizes war.
Who is the "lady"? With this word Nostradamus usually
indicates the monarchistic form of government or, more
usually, the French monarchy. It is very possible that this
quatrain tells us about a future event. Bauder interprets it
thus: "Regardless of the assassination of a Turkish tyrant, the
Turks will not regain their freedom. The Turks, subdued by
the future King Henry of France, will try to take revenge and
will kindle a new world war, during which France will attain
its goal through reign of terror."

> Quand le plus grand emportera le pris
> De Nuremberg d'Auspurg, et ceux de Basle
> Par Agrippine chef Francqfort repris
> Trauerseront par Flamans iusques en Gale.   (III-53)

(When the greatest one will carry off the prize of Nuremberg,
of Augsburg and those of Basel through Agrippine the chief
Frankfort retaken, they will cross through Flanders right into

Gaul.) *Agrippine* is "Cologne," a colony, founded by the Romans and called "colony of Agrippine" (in Latin *Colonia Agrippina)* in honor of Nero's mother and Caesar Claudius' wife Agrippine. "Gaul" is "France" *(Gale*=Gaule). Does this quatrain proclaim the invasion of Belgium during World War I? Or during World War II, for that matter, since on both occasions the Germans attacked France through Belgium? But how then to interpret the other lines and especially the expression "those of Basel"? Perhaps not the Germans, but the Americans have been meant, because Americans began the occupation of Germany from the direction of Basel. Indeed, American tank detachments coming from the direction of Basel, occupied Augsburg and Nuremberg. And the American commander in chief, General Eisenhower, the chief of Cologne, later occupied also Frankfort. The expression "Frankfort retaken," in such a case, could be taken as a reference to the historical fact that in 1792 during the French Revolution Frankfort for a short while was taken by the French army. But such an interpretation is contradicted by the last line which unequivocally speaks of a movement in western direction. It seems that we have to look for a different solution. The word *Francqfort* could be considered as a combination of *franc* and *fort* and could have the meaning of "fort of the Franks." The name "fort of the Franks" is traditionally attributed to Alsace-Lorraine. The new rendering now reads: "When the greatest one will gain possession of Nuremberg, Augsburg and those of Basel, the military chief of Agrippine will retake the fort of the Franks, and they will cross through Flanders into Gaul." "Basel" could possibly symbolize all of Switzerland. Such an interpretation refers to military actions during a future war.

L'horrible guerre qu'on l'Occident s'appreste.

L'an ensuyant viendra la pestilence

Si fort horrible que jeune, vieux, ne beste,

Sang, feu, Mercure, Mars, Jupiter en France.   (IX-55)

(The horrible war which is being prepared in the west. The following year will come the pestilence, so very horrible that young, old, nor beast, blood, fire, Mercury, Mars, Jupiter in France.) Does this quatrain refer to World War I, and does the word *pestilence* indicate the epidemic of influenza which ravaged the whole world right after the war? Or perhaps we are told here about the future hostilities with the Mohammedans, when several countries and nations will ally themselves against these foreign intruders? The fighting takes place in France, which fact is indicated in the last line by the expression "Mercury, Mars, Jupiter in France." The planets here represent nations. According to Cornelius Agrippa in his book *De Occulta Philosophia*, which was published in 1531 and certainly had been read by Nostradamus, Mercury represents the English and the Germans (among other nations), and Jupiter, the Spaniards. All these nations, consequently, will be engaged in combat within the territory of France.

Saturne en Cancer, Iupiter avec Mars,
Dedans Fevrier Chaldondon saluterre;
Saúlt Castallon assailly de trois parts,
Prés de Verbiesque conflict mortelle guerre.   (VIII-48)

(Saturn in Cancer, Jupiter with Mars, in February Chaldondon saluterre. Sault Castallon assailed from three sides, near Verbiesque conflict mortal war.) This quatrain is replete with inexplicable words. Many commentators have tortured their brains, trying to find an exact rendering, and everyone of them has brought to light a different solution. The word *Chaldondon* may mean "don Chaldon," and *Chaldon* could mean "a Chaldean." Chaldea is Babel. Commentator Boswell asserts that "Don Chaldon" is President Wilson, who organized the League of Nations, the Babel of our times. Furthermore, on February 3, 1917, Wilson severed diplomatic relations with Germany, thus giving answer to the German declaration on total submarine warfare. *Saluterre* derives from Latin *salus*, "safe, secure," and *terra*, "land," which results in the following rendering: "In February don Chaldon will give security to the land" or, in other words, "to the world." *Sault* derives from Latin *saltus*, "fall," but *castallon* from *castellum*, "stronghold"; consequently: the stronghold falls. *Verbiesque* is a typical Nostradamic anagram. There exists no place bearing such a name. Boswell splits it into three parts: V is the Roman "five," *erbies*, if considered as a cryptogram and the last letter "s" transposed to the front, results in "Serbie" (Serbia). The remainder *que* is the French word for "what." Translation: The stronghold (Germany) has to fight on three fronts (eastern, southern and western). Five countries in 1914 were involved in the initial dispute about Serbia: France, Belgium, Russia, Germany and Austria. Consequently, this prediction refers to World War I. But how about the first line of the quatrain? Saturn indeed was lingering in the sign of Cancer from August 1914 until June 1917. A conjunction of Jupiter and Mars occurred on June 6, 1917, but no significant event can be ascertained for this day. Possibly such a solution of this riddle is wrong and the fulfillment of the prophecy still to be expected. The reader is invited to come forward with his own solution. Some suggestions follow: Saturn enters the sign of Cancer approximately every 30 years, lingering there for about 2 years, in our times from 1973 to 1976, from 2002 to 2004 and so on. A conjunction between Jupiter and Mars recurs in about every 27 months, but only seldom does it fall in the month of February. It may be of interest to note that in southern France, near Avignon, a town Sault indeed exists. Castallon cannot be found anywhere, but in the same region of Avignon is Cavaillon. Verbiesque does not exist, but in the same department of Vaucluze, where Sault and Cavaillon can be found, exists Venasque. Perhaps between 1973 and 1976 or 2002 and 2004 a mortal war will take place in southern France, when Sault and Cavaillon will experience assault from three sides and a mortal combat will occur near Venasque (near Carpentras). The word "Chaldean" can be understood also as a symbol for "an astrologer" or "a soothsayer," since the Chaldeans were the first who (over 5000 years ago) practiced astrology, and Abraham, a patriarch of the Chaldeans, was the first astrologer. The second line in such a case can be translated thus: "When both constellations will coincide in February, it will be a fortunate sign." Some interpreters refer this quatrain to the coming Arab invasion, namely, to the phase in which the attack on Spain will take place. In Spain, a town of Castellon can be found northeast of Valencia. According to this version, the second great Mohammedan invasion of the Iberian peninsula will occur in the year when, in February, the mentioned stellar phenomena will be seen. The invaders will consider this planetary configuration a favorable sign. With the word "Chaldeans," the first nation of astrologers in ancient Babel, Nostradamus supposedly has labeled the invaders. The mentioned configuration will occur also in February, 2036, then in February, 2094, but in the 22nd century none of the Jupiter-Mars conjunctions occur in February. Therefore we have to assume one of the previously mentioned dates. This quatrain clearly shows the hazard of interpreting Nostradamus' texts and the difficulty of earning laurels in such a pursuit.

Encore seront les saincts temples pollus,
Et expillez par Senat Tholosain,
Saturne deux troix cicles reuollus,
Dans Auril, May, gens de nouueau leuain.   (IX-72)

(Again will the holy temples be polluted and plundered by the senate of Toulouse. Saturn two three cycles completed, in April, May, people of new leaven.) The astronomical Saturn cycle comprises 29 years and 167 days. But what meaning does "two three" cycles have? Does it mean "two to three" cycles or, perhaps, "two and three," i.e., "five" cycles? A confusion, which can be eliminated only by the events themselves. The events seem to be as follows: The senate of Toulouse will be hostile to the church and will utilize the holy temples for profane purposes. Two to three times 29 years after the profanation of the sanctuaries, people there will be of a "different leaven," i.e., again they will pay due honor to the church and to religion. But this quatrain also allows a different solution. Profanation of churches has already occurred during the French Revolution in Toulouse and other French cities. If we reckon five Saturn cycles, i.e., 147 years and 105 days from January 1, 1789 (the year of the French Revolution), we come to April, 1936, when, through the French elections of April and May, there appeared on the political stage "people of different leaven"; namely, the so-called "people's front" was born, which was used by communists to obtain participation in the government of France. Beginning with April and May, 1936, strikes and demonstrations were organized in France and riots arose, about which we can read also in another text of Nostradamus (sixain 36): "Those who thus far had been without influence, will try to seize power." But from still other quatrains of Nostradamus we can also deduce that Saturn here perhaps represents eastern countries and nations, and in such a case this quatrain may be referred to the period of Mohammedan invasion. That Toulouse then may have a senate, dominated by Mohammedans, who will persecute Christians, can be seen also from quatrain VIII-39 and from IX-73. If instead of "cicles" we read "siecles," it is possible to interpret the quatrain as meaning that the reign of Islam will last for less than three centuries, after which time it will be expelled by a people "of new leaven." With this expression the Germans could be meant, since there are indications in other quatrains, all of which refer to this period, that the Germans will be the leading nation in the liberated Europe and in the newly built "rule of peace," and that they, as if with a new leaven, will restore with their ideas the intellectual life of the whole of Europe.

Out of Castel Franco will come the assembly,
The ambassador not agreeable will cause a schism:
Those of Ribiere will be in the wrangle
And will refuse entry to the great gulf.   (IX-16)

In this prediction we detect the names of two Spanish dictators: Francisco Franco and Primo de Rivera. It makes us assume that this quatrain should be referred to the Spanish Civil War of 1936-1940. Indeed, *De Castel Franco* could be translated as "the Castilian Franco," since Castile formerly was the name for all Spain. Furthermore, *Ceux de Ribiere*, "those of Ribiere," could be translated as "those of Rivera," i.e., the adherents of Primo de Rivera, among whom was also General Franco. But how to interpret the fourth line? What connection does it have with the Spanish Civil War? On the other hand, we find in Italy several towns with the name of Castelfranco. If we apply this prediction not to Spain, but to Italy, it can be interpreted as follows: In Italy peace negotiations will be held, but the delegates will be unable to agree, and a wrangle will arise over the Gulf of Genova. Nevertheless, the aggressor will not obtain Riviera, because "those of Riviera will refuse entry to the great gulf."

Vn an deuant le conflict Italique
Germain, Gaulois, Espaignols pour le fort.
Cherra l'escolle maison de republique,
Où, hors mis peu, seront suffoqués morts.   (II-39)

(One year before the Italian conflict Germans, Gauls, Spaniards for the fort. The republican schoolhouse will fall, where, except for a few, they will be choked dead.) Probably, here we have a description of the Spanish Civil War. General Franco on June 18, 1936, took up the banner of insurrection against the republic and with Moroccan soldiers from Spanish

Morocco landed on the Spanish coast. Regardless of foreign aid, almost three years passed before he could vanquish the republicans and on May 19, 1939, enter Madrid. The Spanish Civil War ended in the same year that World War II began. But Nostradamus has a different timetable. Italy declared war on France only a year later (June 10, 1940), when Germany already had defeated the French, and when on the French-Italian front no major warfare could be expected. This impels us to think that the prophecy, regardless of the mentioned circumstances, still pertains to some future events. Furthermore, the majority of the French people were not on the side of Franco, although the French government observed a policy of nonintervention and thus, prohibiting French volunteers to openly join Spanish republicans, in reality was favorable to General Franco. More likely, this quatrain tells about a new war with a German, French and Spanish alliance, a war which will eventually involve also Italy.

Ambassadeur de la Toscane langue
Avril et May Alpes et mer passer,
Celuy de veau exposera l'harangue,
Vie Gauloise ne venant effacer.   (VII-20)

(Ambassadors of the Tuscan language in April and May to pass the Alps and sea. He of the calf will deliver a harangue about not coming to wipe out Gallic life.) The Italian language in general is most purely spoken in Tuscany (region of Florence) and around Rome. The dispute about the Italian literary language continued for centuries and during this quarrel the written Italian has now come nearer to, now deviated from the one that is spoken in Florence. In any case, it is safe to assume that the first part of the quatrain deals with ambassadors from Italy. Even "he of the calf" can be considered as an Italian, because the word Italy means "calf" or "cow" and derives from ancient Greek *italos,* "cow." This name was given to the Greek refugees, who became cowherds. Should this prediction be referred to the future, or can we assume it to have been fulfilled already in 1940? Italy declared war on France on June 10, 1940, but the fascists had already, long before, announced in sharp speeches their claim to French border regions including Nice. It is well known that Italian agents were active in France already in the spring of 1940, but at that time Italy was not able to create any serious danger for France.

II-16 tells about "forces from London, Ghent, Brussels and Susa celebrating triumphal festivities after great slaughter." Susa (Sousse) is a port in Tunisia. This quatrain could be referred to the allied invasion of Italy, which began on July 10, 1943, with the occupation of Sicily. But it is equally possible that this is a prediction about the future battles with the Mohammedans.

Au Roy l'augur sur le chef la main mettre,
Viendra prier pour la paix Italique:
A la main gauche viendra changer le sceptre
Du Roy viendra Empereur pacifique.   (V-6)

(The augur, putting his hand upon the head of the king, will come to pray for the peace of Italy. He will move the sceptre to his left hand, from king he will become pacific Emperor.) Augur is the name for priests-diviners of ancient Rome. According to some recent commentators it here denotes Count Dino Grandi, who on July 24, 1943, presented to the Italian government a proposal to declare withdrawal of confidence from their leader, Mussolini. On the following day the king, on Grandi's suggestion, abdicated from the throne, permitting the government to arrest the dictator, and thus secured peace for Italy. However, from the context of the quatrain, it seems that by the augur Nostradamus has meant the pope. In such a case the quatrain refers to the future: The Roman augur, the good shepherd of the Christians, i.e., the pope, will at the end of World War III become a mediator for peace. The mighty and victorious ruler of France, Emperor Henry V, upon the entreaty of the pope, will relent and will conclude peace with Italy.

> Par gent estrange, et de Romains loingtaine
> Leur grand cité apres eaue fort troublée,
> Fille sans main, trop different domaine,
> Prins chief, ferreure n'auvoir esté riblée.   (II-54)

(Because of people foreign and distant from the Romans, their great city much troubled after water, daughter without hand, domain too different, chief taken, the ironwork not having been filed off.) A German interpreter comments on this quatrain as follows: Here with a few catch-words the fate of Rome during World War II has been characterized. The foreign people are the Germans and the people who are "distant from Romans" are the Britons with their auxiliaries from Africa, Australia, Asia and America. By water or flooding the invasion by the aforementioned people has been meant, and these events have brought great trouble into the eternal city. From a fascist dictatorship Italy turned into a state, tributary to the allies, dependent on the wishes of the victorious countries, without any authority of her own (without hand). Chief Mussolini, not "filed off" with the capture of Rome, tried to continue to fight, but failed and was finally taken prisoner. French commentator Privat in July, 1938, maintained that this quatrain indicates imminent events in Czechoslovakia. The people distant from Romans are supposedly the Prussians; the daughter without hand (republic without power) is Czechoslovakia, because its people are of different domain (Czechs, Slovaks, Ruthenians). The great city is Prague, which after foreign occupation will be greatly troubled, and its chief will be taken. If we refer this quatrain to Czechoslovakia, the last line seems to have been fulfilled with the communistic coup d'état of 1948, when President Benes, made prisoner by the communists, abdicated.

> La loy Moricque on verra defaillir:

Apres vne autre beaucoup plus seductiue,
Boristhenes premier viendra faillir:
Par dons et langue vne plus attractiue.   (III-95)

(The law of More will be seen to decline, after another much more seductive, Boristhenes first will fail, through gifts and tongue to one more attractive.) This quatrain can be translated in two different ways, because *loy Moricque* can be understood either as "law of More" or as "Moorish law." *Boristhenes* is the ancient name for the Dnieper River. Therefore, by the word Boristhenes all Russia could be meant or, in a narrower sense, the Ukraine. If we read "Moorish law," then by this expression, of course, the Mohammedan Koran is meant. "Dnieper will fail first" means that Islam in Southern Russia will be replaced by a new, more attractive system," i.e., by communism, which does not promise pleasures of paradise after death, but right here on the face of earth. The prophecy, consequently, has been fulfilled. Of course, the Moorish version permits also another interpretation. We can attribute it to the final period of the future Mohammedan occupation of Europe, when the morale of the occupants begins to fail and some new religion (perhaps Christianity in a revived form) gains adherents among the believers of Islam. By translating *loy Moricque* as "the law of More," the English author, Thomas More, may be meant. In 1516 he published in Latin the first communistic book *Utopia.* In this book he proclaims the transformation of private property into joint property. Thus Thomas More can be considered as the ancestor of the doctrine of communism. Nostradamus doubtless had read this book. By the "law of More," therefore, the present communism could be meant, since the word communism did not exist in Nostradamus' times. In such a case the translation of this quatrain looks quite different: Nostradamus predicts the fall of the communistic doctrine and its replacement by another one, and this movement will begin in the Ukraine (see p. 139). Interestingly enough, in another quatrain Nostradamus characterizes communism by an expression in Greek Παντα Χοῖνα Ψιλῶν, "Panta Choina Philon," which can be translated as "all is common between friends." This quatrain reads as follows:

In the places and times, when flesh giving way to fish,
The communal law will be made in opposition:
The old will hold strongly, then removed from the midst,
'Panta Choina Philon' put far behind. (IV-32)

This quatrain too predicts the decline of communism. However, the fact should be mentioned that quite recently a French commentator has tried to attribute this Greek sentence to the policy of the Vichy government of France. The old one, in this case, is Pétain, but the motto "all is common between friends" is the opinion of the French collaborators. Communism, possibly, is the subject also of III-67:

Vn nouuelle secte de philosophes,
Meprisant mort or honneurs et richesses:
Des monts Germains ne seront limitrophes,
A les ensuyure auront appuy et presses.

(A new sect of philosophers despising death, gold, honors and riches, will not be bordering upon the German mountains: to follow them they will have support and crowds.) Russia, which has no common frontier with Germany, became the first communistic state. If the expression "a new sect of philosophers" is attributed to communism, the prophecy has been fulfilled. But, as we will see later, in quatrain III-2 Nostradamus proclaims the birth or the revival of another doctrine, which will be similar or related to the ancient Neo-Platonism. In such a case even this quatrain could be referred to the period after the Mohammedan invasion, when the German people will have changed and will be, as contrasted with Hitler, led by spiritual giants, by philosophers who "despise death, gold, honors and riches." This new sect or religion will not confine itself to Germany alone, but will like a stream overflow many countries. It will have great support by a crowd of followers.

> Vers Aquilon grands efforts par homasse,
> Presque l'Europe et l'Univers vexer,
> Les deux eclyps mettra en telle chasse,
> Et aux Pannons vie et mort renforcer.   (VIII-15)

(Toward Aquilon great efforts by human masses, almost to vex Europe and all the world, they will put the two eclipses into utter rout and will reinforce life and death for the Pannonians.) Aquilon is the north or a northern country. Pannonians are the Hungarians. This quatrain could be referred to the great territorial gains by Russian imperialism after World War II and to the political unrest and tension, created by international communism in all the world. The two eclipses could be the two world wars (as in the letter to Henry II) rather than astronomical phenomena, because due to both world wars communism has become a peace-disturbing factor and a menace to the whole world. The last line of the quatrain could refer both to the bloody regime of Bela Kun in Hungary in 1919 and to the suppression of the revolt against the communists in 1956. But there is no lack of commentators who refer even this quatrain to the future Asiatic invasion of Europe, i.e., to the yellow peril. According to them, the decisive battle with the Asiatics will take place in 1999, when there will occur an eclipse of the moon on July 28 and an eclipse of the sun on August 11.

*   *   *   *   *

These few examples clearly show that we cannot rely upon quatrains which could be ambiguously interpreted, if we wish to get a clearer view about future events. We should take into account only quatrains that cannot be attributed to any events of the last 400 years. The dubious quatrains should be left "in reserve." Maybe their real meaning will be disclosed by the future itself. Fortunately, certain important points and clues, left by Nostradamus himself, are substantially helping us to deal with many of these uncertainties. First of all, many essential and significant "nostradamic" expressions or symbols recur in several quatrains. As soon as we have found an indubitable solution for one of them, it is tolerably safe to assume that the same symbol in other quatrains can be referred to the same person, place or period. Secondly, Nostradamus has written introductory prefaces in the form of letters for both of his books. To an attentive reader these prefaces supply hints and even explanations about how the prophecies are to be interpreted. Especially the epistle to Henry II abounds with such hints. The acquaintance with these letters is indispensable for anyone who wants to scrutinize and evaluate the quatrains of Nostradamus. Therefore, I tender here unabridged versions of both letters, without having changed the then reigning, complicated style with its very long, involved sentences, which makes the meaning, more often than not, intricate and obscure.

The letter to his son Caesar is dated March 1, 1555, when the son was only a few months of age. In it Nostradamus informs the reader that his predictions reach until the year 3797. The epistle to King Henry II is dated June 27, 1558, and contains predictions, divided into three groups, with a short account of future events up to the millennium. About when this millennium is supposed to begin and what is meant by the figure 3797, the French commentator E. Ruir has developed an interesting theory, which I will review at the end of this volume.

So that it will be easier for me to refer in my commentaries to certain points within the text of the letters and for the reader to find the corresponding place in the text,

I have divided the letters with numerals into separate segments. The epistle to his son Caesar is referred to as letter A and the epistle to King Henry II, as letter B.

(See reference from page 136.)

Or in Southern Russia on the whole. At present only about 50% of the 250 million inhabitants of the Soviet Union are Russians. About 20% (50 million) are Mohammedans. Because of their very high birth rate, their number in the year 2000, according to an estimate made by Soviet statisticians will be 100 million The increase of population in the Republic of Soviet Russia from 1970 until 1979 has been only 6%, whereas in the Soviet Mohammedan republics as follows: inTadzhikistan 31%, Uzbekistan 50%, Turkmenistan 28% and Kirgizia 20%. The renaissance of Islam could place Soviet Union in a more precarious situation than the perpetual threat from the direction of China.

5
A. EPISTLE TO CAESAR

Ad Caesarem Nostradamum Filium

1. Your late arrival, Caesar Nostradamus, my son, has caused me to spend a great deal of time in continual nightly watches, so that after the corporal extinction of your father you might be left a memorial, revealing in writing, to the common benefit of mankind, what the Divine Essence has made known to me through the revolutions of the stars.

2. And since it has pleased the immortal God that you should have come into the natural light of this earthly shore but recently, and your years cannot yet be said to be made complete, but even during long months, spent in effort, your feeble understanding would not be capable of conceiving that which I am compelled to designate after my death: seeing that it is impossible to leave you in writing that which would be obliterated by the injury of time.

3. Indeed, the hereditary gift of occult prediction will be buried together with my body.

4. It should also be considered that events, defined by man, are uncertain, but all is regulated and governed by the inestimable power of God, inspiring us not through drunken fury nor by lymphatic movement, but by astronomical evidence: *Soli numine diuino afflati praesagiunt, et spiritu prophetico particularia.*[1]

1. Only those divinely inspired can predict particular things in a prophetic spirit.

5. For a long time and often I have predicted, far in advance, that which later came to pass and in particular localities, acknowledging all to have been accomplished through divine power and inspiration, and other predicted happy and sinister events with increasing promptness have later come to pass in different climates of the world.

6. However, because of possible injury, not only for the present time, but also for most of the future, I wanted to keep silent and to refrain from putting them into writing, for kingdoms, sects and religions will make changes, so diametrically opposite to the present situation, that if I came to reveal what will happen in the future, the chiefs of the kingdoms, sects, religions and faiths would find it so little in accord with what they would like to hear, that they would condemn that which future centuries will know to have been seen and perceived.

7. It is also in consideration of the saying by the Saviour: *Nolite sanctum dare canibus nec mittatis margaritas ante porcos ne conculcent pedibus et conversi dirumpant vos,*[2] that I have restrained my tongue from the vulgar and my pen from paper.

8. Later, nevertheless wishing to express myself for the common advent, I decided to tell by abstruse and entangled sentences of the future causes, even the most urgent ones, which I have perceived. Whatever future mutations of mankind will occur, my writings will not scandalize fragile sentiments, since all has been written under a cloudy figure, above all things prophetic.

9. Inasmuch as: *Abscondisti haec a sapientibus, et prudentibus, id est potentibus et regibus, et enucleasti ea*

---

2. Matt. 7:6. Give not that which is holy to dogs, neither cast ye pearls before swine, lest they trample them under their feet, and turning upon you, they tear you.

exiguis et tenuibus,[3] and to the prophets, who by means of the immortal God and the good angels have received the spirit of prophecy, by which they see distant things and foresee future events, for nothing can be accomplished without Him whose power and goodness to his creatures is so great that as long as these dwell in them, much as they may be exposed to other influences, they work in them similarly to their good genius, and this prophetic heat and power approaches us[4] like the rays of the sun, which cast their influence on bodies both elementary and non-elementary.

10. As for ourselves, who are but human, we can discover nothing of the obscure secrets of God the Creator by our own natural notions of our genial inclinations, since *Quia non est nostrum noscere tempora nec momenta.*[5]

11. However, in the present time may appear and exist persons to whom God the Creator through fanciful impressions wishes to reveal some secrets of the future in accordance with judicial astrology, in the same manner that in the past a certain power and voluntary faculty came over them like a visibly burning flame.[6]

12. Thus quickened, they have learned to discern between divine and human inspirations, for the divine works, which are totally absolute, are accomplished by God; those which are medial, by the angels; the third kind, by the evil spirits. But, my son, I speak to you here a bit too obscurely.

13. As for hidden prophecies, which are received through the subtle spirit of fire, they sometimes agitate the understanding like the contemplation of the remotest of stars, but in remaining alert until we hear the pronouncements, we surprisingly can take them down in

3. Matt. 11:25. Thou hast hid these things from the wise and prudent (that is, from the potentates and rulers), and hast revealed them to the little and weak.
4. Author suddenly switches to first person.
5. Acts 1:7. It is not for us to know the times nor moments.
6. Acts 2:3. Holy Ghost.

writing and can pronounce them without fear, without taint of disrespectful loquacity. But why? Because all these things did proceed from the divine power of the great eternal God, from Whom all goodness flows.

14. Furthermore, my son, though I have inserted the word "prophet," I do not wish to assume a title, for the present time so highly sublime, for: *qui propheta dicitur hodie, olim vocabatur videns.*[7]

15. Strictly speaking, my son, a prophet is one who sees things remote from the natural knowledge of all creatures.

16. When this happens, the prophet by means of the perfect light of the prophecy sees manifestly appearing before him things both divine as well as human, which he cannot apprehend, inasmuch as the effects of future prediction are far extending.

17. For the incomprehensible secrets of God and the materialization of their effective virtues far surpass human knowledge, which has its immediate origin in the free will. They bring about the appearance of causes which of themselves could not acquire enough attention to be known neither by human augury nor by any other hidden knowledge or virtue comprised under the concavity of heaven, even for the present fact of all eternity, which in itself embraces all time.

18. But if by means of epyleptic, heraclian agitation we consider some indivisible part of eternity, the causes are made known by celestial movements.

19. I am saying this, my son, in order that you should well understand, that the knowledge of this matter cannot yet impress itself upon your feeble brain, and that the causes of very distant events are not within the knowledge of reasoning man, except those that are simply the creation of the

7. Who today is called prophet, was heretofore called seer.

intellectual soul out of current events and are not by any means too greatly hidden nor revealed at all.

20. But the perfect concept of causes cannot be acquired without divine inspiration, since all prophetic inspiration receives its prime motivating force from God the Creator, then from good fortune and from nature.

21. For this reason, to the extent to which these independent causes have manifested themselves independently or have failed to manifest themselves, the prediction occurs in part or has been predicted correctly,

22. because the intellectually created understanding cannot see hidden things unless aided by the voice coming from limbo by means of a tiny flame,[8] showing in what direction future events incline.

23. And furthermore, my son, I beg you that you will never want to employ your understanding on such dreams and vanities as dry up the body and put the soul in perdition, causing trouble to the weak senses. Especially I caution against the vanity of the more than execrable magic, condemned of yore by the Holy Scriptures and the divine canons. This authority, however, has excepted the deductions of judicial astrology, and it is by means of this and by divine inspiration and revelation, that we have after continual nightly watches and calculations drawn up our prophecies in written form.

24. And although this occult philosophy was not condemned, I by no means did want to hold forth their excessive assertions, contained in many volumes, which had been hidden for a great many centuries and which I had at my disposal. But dreading what use might be made of them, after reading them I consigned them to Vulcan.[9] And while he came to devour them, the flame, licking the air, brought

8. Acts 2:3. Holy Ghost.   9. Fire.

forth an unusual brightness, clearer than could be caused by a natural flame. Like the light of thunder lightning it suddenly illuminated the house, as if in sudden conflagration.

25. Thus, so that in the future you might not be mislead by them in an investigation of the total transformation of the Selene[10] or the sun, and of the incorruptible metals under the earth and of hidden waves, I have reduced them to ashes.

26. As for the Judgment which is approaching, as proven by means of the calculation of the heavens, I want to make clear to you this: in order to have knowledge of the future, one has to discard completely all arising fantastic imaginations and to limit the particularity of places through divine, supernatural inspiration, in harmonizing with astronomical figures the places and periods of time, which have an occult property by divine virtue, power and faculty, in whose presence all three times comprise but one eternity. The planetary revolutions, conditioning events of past, present and future: *quia omnia sunt nuda et aperta.*[11]

27. Thus, my son, notwithstanding your tender brain, you can easily understand that things which are to happen can be prophesied by the celestial and nocturnal luminaries which are natural, and by the spirit of prophecy.

28. Not that I would assume the name or quality of a prophet, but by revealed inspiration, like a mortal man, no less remote by his senses from heaven than attached with his feet to the earth, to say *possum non errare, falli, decipi,*[12] and I am the greatest sinner in this world, subject to all human afflictions.

29. But being overtaken sometimes for a week by stimulations, which have rendered my nocturnal studies pleasingly distinctive, I have by long calculations composed books of prophecies, of which each contains one hundred

10. Moon.   11. Heb. 4:13. All things are naked and open.
12. I cannot err, fail or be deceived.

astronomical quatrains of prophecies. I have sought to shape them a bit obscurely: they are perpetual vaticinations from now to the year 3797.

30. It is possible that some will frown seeing such a long extension, but nevertheless all these events will occur under the concavity of the moon and will be intelligently and universally apprehended throughout the earth.

31. And, my son, if you will live the natural span of human life, you will see from your climate, in the skies of your own nativity, that it is possible to foresee future events.

32. Although the eternal God alone knows the eternity of the light which proceeds from himself, I say frankly that all to whom He in his immense magnitude, immeasurable and incomprehensible as it is, has wished through long and melancholy inspiration to reveal the future, are capable by means of this divinely manifested occult influence to discern the two principal causes, which are to be apprehended by the understanding of one who, being inspired, prophesies.

33. One cause comes by infusion, clearing the supernatural light for the person who predicts by the doctrine of stars; the other prophesies by inspired revelation, which is a certain participation of the divine eternity, by means of which the prophet comes to judge what has been given him by his divine spirit, through God the Creator and his natural incitement.

34. He also knows that what he predicts is true and has an ethereal origin, being as efficacious and as exalted as the light of the tiny flame. [13]

35. Just in the same manner natural clarity and natural light renders philosophers no less sure of themselves that by means of the principles of the first cause they have penetrated to the innermost depths of the loftiest of doctrines. But on this point, my son, I fear to extend too

13. Acts 2:3. Holy Ghost.

deeply for the future capacity of your senses, and also because writing about it may cause great and incomparable loss.

36. Furthermore, I find that before the universal conflagration the world will suffer by so many deluges and by so high floods that there will remain scarcely any land not covered by water, and this will last for so long that everything will perish except enographies[14] and topographies.

37. Before and after these inundations, in many countries the rains will be so slight and from the sky will fall such a great abundance of fire and of burning stones, that nothing will remain unconsumed. And this will occur suddenly, before the final conflagration.

38. For although the planet Mars will finish its cycle, it is not certain that at the end of its last period it will resume it, since some planets will assemble in Aquarius for several years, others in Cancer for an even longer, more extended time.

39. At present, by means of the supreme power of eternal God, we are led by the Moon. When she will have completed her entire circuit, the Sun will come and then Saturn. For according to the signs in the heavens the reign of Saturn will have returned when, to sum up, the world will draw near an anaragonic revolution.

40. At present I can write that during one hundred seventy-seven years, three months and eleven days, by pestilence, long famine, wars and, most of all, by inundations, the world between this and the fixed date, before and after, will be for several times so diminished, with so few left on earth, that no one will be found willing to work the fields, which will remain free for as long a period as they have been tilled.

14. Word of unknown meaning.

41. According to the visible judgment of the stars, we are now in the seventh millenary which finishes all. When we will approach the eighth millenary and the reign of the eighth sphere which will appear on the firmament in latitudinary dimension, then the great eternal God will come to complete the revolution, the heavenly bodies as well as the upper movement will return to their motion which render the earth stable and firm, *non inclinabatur in saeculum saeculi*,[15] but not before His will will be accomplished and not otherwise, regardless of ambiguous opinions which by Mahometan dreams exceed all natural reason.

42. Thus sometimes God the Creator, through the ministry of his messengers of fire, in a missive flame, reveals before our exterior senses, even our eyes, the causes of future predictions and the signification of future events so that the one, to whom He has willed these to manifest themselves, can make presages.

43. For the presage which is made by the exterior light, infallibly entrains a partial conception of it by means of the exterior vision, which one has had, although in reality the part which seemingly has come into the understanding by the eyes, has been only the lesion of the imaginative sense.

44. The reason is very evident. All is predicted through divine afflatus, and by means of the angelic spirit with which the man prophesying is inspired, rendering anointed the vaticinations, illuminating him, after having excited his fantasy through diverse nocturnal apparitions. Afterwards, in daytime, he gains certitude about the prophecy, harmonizing the most holy future prediction with astronomical calculations, which rest on nothing more than the free will.

45. Listen now, my son, to what I find by my calculations, which are in accord with revealed inspiration: the sword of death is now approaching us by pestilence, war

15. Ps. 104:5. Not inclining for ever and ever.

more horrible than has been known in three lifetimes, and famine, which will fall upon the earth and return there often, according to the rotation of the stars and also to the words: *Visitabo in virga ferrea iniquitates eorum, et in verberibus percutiam eos.*[16]

46. For the mercy of the Lord shall not be extended at all for a time, my son, until most of my prophecies will have been accomplished and will by accomplishment have become resolved.

47. Then several times during the sinister tempests the Lord will say: *Conteram ergo et confringam, et non miserebor.*[17]

48. And thousands of other events will come to pass because of floods and continual rains, as I have set forth more fully in writing my other prophecies, which are drawn out in length, in *soluta oratione,*[18] defining the places, times and prefixed duration, so that men of later ages, knowing the events that have occurred infallibly, will see also the others, which we have noted, speaking more clearly. For although they are under a cloud, the meanings will be understood: *sed quando submovenda erit ignorantia,*[19] the case will be cleared up still more.

49. I make an end here, my son. Take now this gift of your father Michel Nostradamus, who hopes that you will be able to solve each prophecy of the quatrains included here.

I beseech the immortal God that he will be willing to endow you with long life in good and prosperous happiness.

From Salon this first of March, 1555.

16. Ps. 89:33. I will visit their iniquities with an iron rod and their transgressions with lashes.
17. I will trample them and break them and not show pity.
18. In prose.
19. Only when the time comes for the removal of ignorance.

6
B. EPISTLE TO HENRY II
KING OF FRANCE

To the most invincible,
most powerful and most Christian
Henry, King of France the Second:
Michel Nostradamus,
his very humble and very obedient servant and subject,
wishes victory and happiness.

1. After my face had been long beclouded, O most Christian and most victorious king, I have had this sovereign sight, in presenting myself before the immeasurable deity of your majesty. Since then I have remained perpetually dazzled, not ceasing to honor and venerate properly that day when I first presented myself before a majesty so singular and so humane.

2. I have searched for some occasion on which to manifest stout heart and frank courage, thereby obtaining more extensive recognition of your most serene majesty.

3. But I saw how obviously impossible it was for me to declare myself, despite my singular desire to pierce through my long-lasting obfuscation and obscurity, when suddenly it was enlightened and I was transported face to face with the sovereign eye of the first monarch of the universe.

4. I also had been long in doubt as to whom I would dedicate these last three centuries of my prophecies, making up the thousand.

5. After having meditated for a long time on such rash audacity I have ventured to address your majesty. I have not been intimidated like those, mentioned by that most grave author Plutarch in his Life of Lycurgus, who were so astounded at the expense of the offerings and gifts brought as sacrifices to the temples of the immortal gods of that age, that they, attributing too great an importance to such outlays and donations, did not dare to present themselves in the temples at all.

6. Notwithstanding that, but seeing your royal splendor to be accompanied by an incomparable humanity, I have paid my address, not as to those kings of Persia whom one was never permitted neither to stand before nor to approach. It is to a most prudent and most wise prince that I have dedicated my nocturnal and prophetic computations, composed rather out of a natural instinct, accompanied by poetic furor, than according to the rules of poetry.

7. Most of them have been composed and integrated with astronomical calculations corresponding to the years, months and weeks of the regions, countries and most of the towns and cities of all Europe, including Africa and part of Asia, according to the changes which are approaching most of these regions. They are composed in a natural manner.

8. Someone, who would do well to blow his nose, may reply that the rhythm is as easy as the perception of the import difficult. That, O most humane king, is because most of the prophetic quatrains announce events so harsh that it is impossible to render means for their interpretation.

9. Nevertheless, I wanted to leave a record in writing of the years, towns, cities and regions where most of the events will come to pass, even those of the year 1585 and of the year 1606, beginning with the present time, the fourteenth of March, 1557, and going far beyond to the events which will take place at the beginning of the seventh millenary,

profoundly computed, as far as my astronomical calculations and other knowledge could extend—when the adversaries of Jesus Christ and his church will begin to multiply greatly.

10. All has been composed and calculated in well-disposed, choice days and hours, and as accurately as I could.

11. And with *Minerva libera et non injuria*[1] I have made computations for almost as many future events as have come to pass during past ages, including the present and that which in the course of time will be experienced in all regions, everything exactly as it has been written, with nothing superfluous added, albeit some may say: *Quod de futuris non est determinata omnino veritas.*[2]

12. It is quite true, Sire, that with merely my natural instinct alone, which has been given me by my ancestors, I would not believe in these predictions, but this natural instinct has been adjusted, brought into accord and combined with my long computations. At the same time I freed my soul, spirit and mind of all care, solicitude and vexation, by repose and tranquility of the spirit.

13. All has been coordinated and predicted in part *tripode aeneo,*[3] although there are some who would attribute to me not only what is mine but also what is not mine at all.

14. The eternal God alone, who is the thorough searcher of human hearts, pious, just and merciful, is the true judge, and it is to him I pray to defend me from the calumny of evil men, from those who in their slanderous way would likewise want to inquire by what means all your most ancient progenitors, the kings of France, have cured the scrofula, and how those of other nations have cured the bite of snakes, yet

1. With free and unconstrained mind.
2. Concerning the future no truth can be with certainty determined.
3. With brazen tripod.

others have had a certain instinct for the art of divination, and there are other instances which would be too long to recite here.

15. Notwithstanding those whom the malignity of the evil spirit will not permit to comprehend, my writings, as time elapses after my earthly extinction, will be understood better than during my lifetime. However, should I have made any errors in my computation of periods, it by no means has been done with purpose. I beg that your more than imperial majesty will forgive me.

16. I protest before God and his saints that I do not propose to insert any writings in this present epistle that will be contrary to the true Catholic faith, whilst consulting the astronomical calculations to the best of my ability.

17. Subject to correction by the most sound judgment, the extent of time past since our first forebears is such, that the first man, Adam, came about one thousand two hundred forty-two years before Noah, not reckoning the time by such Gentile computations as were written by Varro,[4] but simply by the Holy Scriptures, as best my weak understanding in my astronomical calculations can interpret them.

18. About a thousand and eighty years after Noah and the universal flood came Abraham, who was an eminent astrologer and, according to some, invented the Chaldean alphabet.

19. About five hundred fifteen or sixteen years later came Moses, and between the time of David and that of Moses have been about five hundred seventy years.

20. After that, between the time of David and the time of our Savior and Redeemer, Jesus Christ, born of the unique Virgin, have been (according to some chronographers) a thousand three hundred fifty years.

4. Roman author of historical works (116–27 B.C.).

21. Some one may object that this computation is not reliable, because it differs from that of Eusebius.

22. And from the time of the human redemption to the detestable seduction by the Saracens has been about six hundred twenty-one years.

23. It can be easily added up what time has elapsed after that. If my computation is not good and valid for all nations, everything, however, has been calculated according to the celestial movements, in association with emotions handed down to me by my ancient forebears, and which emotion is infused into me at certain hours of loneliness.

24. But the injury of the times, O most serene king, requires that such secret events should not be bared except in enigmatic sentences having, however, only one sense and meaning.

25. No ambiguities or amphibological calculations have been inserted, but all rather kept under a cloudy obscurity, with a natural infusion approaching the saying of one of the thousand and two prophets who have existed since the creation of the world, in accordance with the calculation and Punic chronicle of Joel: *Effundam spiritum meum super omnem carnem et prophetabunt filii vestri et filiae vestrae.*[5]

26. But such prophecy proceeded from the mouth of the Holy Ghost who was the sovereign, eternal power; aided by this celestial power, some of this number have predicted great and marvelous events.

27. As for myself, I by no means claim such a title, God forbid! But I readily admit that all proceeds from God and render to him thanks, honor and immortal praise.

28. I have mixed therewith no divination coming *à fato,* but *à Deo, à natura,* for the most part combined with celestial movements.

---

5. Joel 2:28. I will pour out my spirit upon all flesh and your sons and your daughters shall prophesy. (Cf. also Acts 2:17.)

29. As if in a burning mirror, with clouded vision, I have seen great events, sad, prodigious and calamitous occurrences approaching the principal factors of the cult. First, the temples of God, secondly those who, sustained by earth, will be approached by such decadence, with a thousand other calamitous occurrences which in the course of time will be known to happen in the future.

30. For God will look upon the long sterility of the great dame, who thereupon will conceive two principal children; but she will be declining, and the female who will be adjoined to her by the temerity of the hour of death, will decline in the eighteenth, unable to live beyond the thirty-sixth, leaving three males and one female, and of these, two will not have had the same father, so great will be the difference between the three brothers, but then they will unite and cooperate so that three and four parts of Europe will tremble.

31. The youngest of them will sustain and augment the Christian monarchy: the elevated sects will suddenly be cast down, Arabs will retreat, kingdoms will be united and new laws promulgated.

32. Of the other children the first will occupy the furious, crowned lions with their paws resting upon intrepid arms.

33. The second one, accompanied, will penetrate so far into the Latins that a second trembling and furious march will be made to the mountain of Jupiter;[6] he will descend to mount the Pyrenees, but will not be transferred to the ancient monarchy. Thus the third inundation of human blood will occur, and Mars will not remain long in fasting.

34. And the daughter will be given for the preservation of the Christian church, throwing her lord into the pagan sect of the new infidels.

35. She will have two children, one faithful, the other infidel, by the confirmation of the Catholic church, and the

6. Mons Jovis—the Great St. Bernard in the Alps.

other who, to his great confusion and later repentance, will want to ruin her, will have three regions with extremely different boundaries, namely, the Roman, Germany and Spain, which will set up diverse sects by military force.

36. Abandoning the fiftieth and fifty-second degree of latitude, they will all render homage to religions distant from the regions of Europe and of the septentrion.

37. Those of the forty-eighth degree of latitude will be the first to tremble in vain timidity, afterward those who are farther to the west, south and east; such will be their power, that what has been brought about by concord and union will prove insuperable by warlike conquests.

38. In nature they will be equal, but very different in faith.

39. After this the sterile dame, of greater power than the second, will be received by two nations, by the first, made obstinate by those who have had power over all, by the second and by the third, which will extend its forces toward the circuit of the East of Europe where, in the Pannonia, they will be overthrown and overcome, and by marine ships will make their expansions to the Adriatic Trinacria, by Myrmidons and Germans, will succumb wholly, and the Barbarian sect by all the Latins greatly afflicted and driven out.

40. Then the great empire of the Antechrist[7] will begin in Attila and Xerxes[8] and will descend in great and countless numbers, until the coming of the Holy Ghost, proceeding from the forty-eighth degree, will make a transmigration, chasing out the abomination of the Antechrist, who will have made war upon the royal person named vicar of Jesus Christ, and against his church and reign *per tempus and in occasione*

7. Antechrist—the one appearing before (*ante*) Christ's second coming; sometimes called Antichrist, an adversary (*anti*) of Christ.
8. Attila—ruler of the Huns. Xerxes—Greek name of the Persian king Akshayarsha.

temporis (for a time and to the end of time).

41. And this will be preceded by a solar eclipse more dark and more gloomy than any since the creation of the world until the death and passion of Jesus Christ, and thence to this time, and it will be in the month of October that a great transformation will occur and such that one will think the gravity of the earth has lost its natural movement and has been plunged into the abyss of perpetual darkness.

42. These will be precedent to the springtime,

43. and will follow after extreme changes, permutations of realms, mighty earthquakes, with the increase of the new Babylon, miserable daughter, enlarged by the abomination of the first holocaust.

44. It will last for only seventy-three years and seven months.

45. Thereafter there will issue from the stock, which had remained barren for so long, one who proceeding from the fiftieth degree will renew the whole Christian church.

46. And great peace will be established, union and concord between some of the children of misguided ranks, who have been separated by diverse realms.

47. And such will be the peace that the instigator and promoter of military factions by the diversity of religions, will remain chained within the deepest pit, and the kingdom of the Furious One, who counterfeits the sage, will be united.

48. And the countries, towns, cities, realms and provinces which will have abandoned their previous ways to gain liberty, will in fact have enslaved themselves still more profoundly. Secretly they will have been deprived of their liberty, and the perfect religion lost.

49. They will begin to strike to the left in order to return to the right, and holiness, for a long time overcome, will be replaced in accordance with the earliest writings.

50. Thereafter the great Dog will send forth the biggest of mastiffs, who will destroy everything, even as what before

had been perpetrated. Temples will be set up again as in ancient times, and the priest will be restored to his original position, and he will begin his whoring and luxury and will commit a thousand transgressions.

51. And at the eve of another desolation, when she will be in her most high and sublime dignity, potentates and warlords will confront her, and take away her two swords, and leave her only the insignia, whose curvature attracts them. The people will make him go rightly and will not wish to submit themselves to those of the opposite extreme with the hand in acute position, touching the ground, and will want to goad on until there is born of a branch long sterile one who will deliver the entire people from this benevolent and voluntary slavery, putting himself under the protection of Mars, stripping Jupiter of all his honors and dignities, and will establish himself in the free city, which is situated in another tiny Mesopotamia.

52. And the chief and governor will be cast out from the middle and hung up, ignorant of the complot of the conspirators with the second Thrasibulus,[10] who for a long time will have directed all this.

53. Then the impurities and abominations with a great shame will be brought out and manifested in the shadows of the veiled light,

54. and will cease towards the end of the change in his reign.

55. And the chiefs of the church will be backward in the love of God, and several of them will apostatize from the true faith.

56. And of the three sects, that which is in the middle, will be thrown a bit into decadence because of its own partisans.

10. Thrasibulus, Athenian statesman and military leader, who returned from exile and overthrew the thirty tyrants of Athens. Died 389 B.C.

57. The first one throughout Europe and in most of Africa will be exterminated by the third one, making use of the poor in spirit who, led by madmen to libidinous luxury, will adulterate.

58. The supporting mob will rise up and chase out the adherents of the legislators. In the realms weakened by easterners it will seem that God the Creator has loosed Satan from the prisons of hell to give birth to the great Dog and Doham, who will make such a great abominable breach in the churches that neither the reds nor the whites without eyes nor hands will have judgment anymore, and their power will be taken from them.

59. Then will again commence a persecution of the churches such as never before.

60. And meantime such a plague will arise that of three parts of the world more than two will perish in such a measure that it will not be possible to ascertain the true owners of fields and houses, and weeds will be growing in the streets of cities higher than the knees.

61. And for the clergy there will be utter desolation, and the warlords will usurp what is returned from the City of the Sun, from Melita[11] and the isles of Stechades,[12] and the great chain of the port which takes its name from the marine ox will be opened.

62. And a new incursion will be made on the maritime shores, wishing to deliver the fallen Castulum from the first Mahometan recapture.

63. And their assaults will not be in vain at all, and the place which was once the abode of Abraham will be assaulted by persons who hold the Jovialists in veneration.

64. And this city of Achem will be surrounded and assailed on all sides by a most powerful force of warriors.

11. Malta.
12. Isles of Hyeres, near the French Mediterranean coast.

65. Their maritime forces will be weakened by the westerners.

66. And great desolation will fall upon this realm, and the greatest cities will be depopulated and those who enter within will fall under the vengeance of the wrath of God.

67. And the sepulchre, an object of such great veneration, for the duration of a long time will remain in the open, exposed to the universal sight of the heavens, the sun and the moon.

68. And the holy place will be converted into a stable for a herd small and large, and adapted for profane substances.

69. Oh, what a calamitous affliction will pregnant women bear at this time.

70. And hereupon the principal eastern chief will be afflicted, most of his people vanquished and put to death, overwhelmed and the rest scattered, and his children, offspring of many women, imprisoned. And then will be accomplished the prophecy of the Royal Prophet: *Ut audiret gemitus compenditorum, ut solveret filios interemptorum.*[13]

71. What great oppression then will fall upon the princes and governors of kingdoms even those which will be maritime and eastern, and their tongues will be intermingled with a great group: the tongue of the Latins and of the Arabs, through Punic interchange.

72. And all these eastern kings will be chased, overthrown and exterminated but not at all by means of the forces of the kings of Aquilon[14] and by the proximity of our age, by means of the three secretly united in the search for death and traps, laying ambushes for one another. And the renewal of the Triumvirate will last for seven years, in order that the renown of this sect should extend around the world,

13. Let him hear the groaning of the captives, that he might deliver the children of those doomed to die.

14. The North.

73. and the sacrifice of the holy and immaculate wafer will be sustained.

74. And then the lords of Aquilon, two in number, will be victorious over the easterners, and so great a noise and bellicose tumult will be made amongst them that all this east will tremble in terror of these Aquilonian brothers, yet not brothers.

75. And therefore, Sire, in this discourse I present these predictions almost with confusion, and also as to when they will approach and take place. The enumeration of time which follows conforms very little, if at all, with that which has been set forth previously, although it was determined by astronomy and other sources, including the Holy Scriptures, and thus could not err any wise. If I had wanted to add the enumeration of time to each quatrain, I could have done so. But it would not have been agreeable to all, least of all the interpretation of the quatrains. It was not to be done, Sire, until Your Majesty would grant me full power to do so, lest calumniators be given cause for being injurious to me.

76. However, counting the years from the creation of the world to the birth of Noah one thousand five hundred and six years have passed.

77. And from the birth of Noah to the full completion of the Ark, at the coming of the universal deluge, six hundred years have passed (let the years be solar or lunar or the decades mixed). I hold in like manner as the Sacred Scriptures, that they were solar years.

78. And at the end of these six hundred years Noah entered the Ark to be saved from the deluge, and this deluge was on the earth universal and lasted one year and two months.

79. And from the end of the deluge to the birth of Abraham the number of years elapsed was two-hundred and ninety five.

80. And from the birth of Abraham to the birth of Isaac

one hundred years passed.

81. And from Isaac to Jacob sixty years.

82. Between the time he entered into Egypt and his exit from it, one hundred thirty years passed.

83. And from the entry of Jacob into Egypt to the exodus from it, four hundred thirty years passed.

84. And from the exodus from Egypt to the building of the Temple by Solomon in the fourth year of his reign, four hundred eighty years passed.

85. And from the building of the Temple to Jesus Christ, according to the computations of the hierographs, four hundred ninety years passed.

86. And thus, by this computation of mine, collected from the holy writ, it comes to about four thousand hundred seventy-three years and eight months, more or less.

87. The time from Jesus Christ until now I let remain, because of the diversity of sects, and have computed and calculated the present prophecies, all according to the order of the chain which contains its revolution and all by astronomical doctrine, in conformity with my natural instinct.

88. After a while and comprising in it the time after Saturn turns to enter on the seventh of April until August 15, Jupiter on June 14 until October 7, Mars from April 17 until June 22, Venus from April 9 until May 22, Mercury from February 3 until February 24. And after, from June 1 to June 24, and from September 25 to October 16, Saturn in Capricorn, Jupiter in Aquarius, Mars in Scorpio, Venus in Pisces, Mercury for a month in Capricorn, Aquarius and Pisces, the Moon in Aquarius, the Dragon's Head in Libra: its tail in its sign, in opposition to the following conjunction of Jupiter with Mercury, Mars and Mercury being in an aspect of quadrature, and the Dragon's Head coinciding with a conjunction of the Sun and Jupiter.

89. The year will be peaceful, without an eclipse, but not everywhere, and it will be the commencement, comprising all that will continue to happen.

90. And beginning with this year the Christian church will be persecuted more fiercely than it ever was in Africa, and this will last up to the year one thousand seven hundred ninety-two, which they will believe to be the renewal of an epoch.[15]

91. After this the Roman people will begin to re-establish themselves and to chase away some obscure shadows, recovering a bit of their ancient clarity, not without great division and continual changes.

92. Venice thereafter will raise its wings very high in great force and power, not far short of the might of ancient Rome.

93. And at that time great sails of Byzantium, allied with the Ligustians and through Aquilonarian support and power will impede so greatly that the two Cretans will be unable to maintain their faith.

94. The arks built by the ancient warriors will join the waves of Neptune.

95. In the Adriatic great discord will arise, and that which will have been united will be separated. To a house will be reduced that which formerly was, and is, a great city, including the Pempotamia, Mesopotamia of Europe at forty-five and others of forty-one, forty-two and thirty-seven.

96. And at this time and in these countries the power of the adversaries of the church of Jesus Christ will be set against His church by the infernal power; this will be the second Antechrist, who will persecute that church and its true

15. Exactly in 1792 the Republican calendar replaced the Gregorian calendar in France. On the night of January 1, 1792, an unknown person placed the *Prophecies* of Nostradamus, open at this sentence, on a desk, in the middle of the Pantheon Square at Paris. The passing Parisians had an opportunity to read and to ponder on what would take place during the coming year.

vicar by means of the power of three temporal kings who in their ignorance will be seduced by tongues which will cut more sharply than any sword in the hands of a madman.

97. The said reign of the Antechrist will last only until the determination of him who was born near the age, and of the other one in the city of Plancus,[16] accompanied by the elected one of Modone Fulcy, through Ferrara, maintained by the Adriatic Ligurians, and the proximity of the great Trinacria.[17]

98. Then the mountain of Jupiter[18] will be passed.

99. The Gallic Ogmios[19] will be accompanied by so great a number that from afar the Empire of his great law will be shown,

100. and then and for some time thereafter the blood of the innocents will be shed profusely by the recently elevated guilty ones.

101. It will be then that, because of great floods, the memory of things contained in such instruments will suffer incalculable loss, even letters: it will happen forth from the Aquilonians, by the will of God, and in the meantime Satan will be bound.

102. And universal peace will be established among men, and the church of Jesus Christ will be delivered from all tribulations, although the Azostians would like to mix in the honey bile and their pertinent seduction.

103. And this will be near the seventh millenary, when the sanctuary of Jesus Christ will no longer be trodden down by the infidels who come from Aquilon.[20] The world will be approaching a great conflagration, although, according to my

16. Lyon, founded by Lucius Minutius Plancus in 43 B.C.
17. Sicily.
18. The Great St. Bernard.
19. Celtic deity.
20. The North.

computations in my prophecies, the course of time runs much further.

104. In the epistle that some years ago I dedicated to my son Caesar Nostradamus, I declared some points openly enough, without presage.

105. But here, O Sire, are included several great and marvelous events which those to come after will see.

106. And during this astrological computation, making it conform to the Holy Scriptures, the persecution of the ecclesiastical folk will have its origin in the power of the kings of Aquilon, united with the easterners. And this persecution will last for eleven years, somewhat less.

107. Then the principal king of Aquilon will fail, and when his years will be accomplished, his southern ally will upstart and for three more years will persecute the church people even more fiercely through apostatic seduction of one who will hold all the absolute power in the militant church, and the holy people of God, observers of his law and the whole order of religion will be fiercely persecuted and afflicted in such a measure that the blood of the true ecclesiastics will flow everywhere, and one of the horrible temporal kings will be highly praised by his adherents for having shed more of human blood of innocent ecclesiastics than anyone else could have spilled of wine: and this king will commit incredible crimes against the church. Human blood will flow in the public streets and temples, like water after an impetuous rain, coloring the nearby rivers red,

108. but by another naval battle the sea will be reddened, so that one king will report to another: *Bellis rubit navalibus aequor.*[21]

109. Then, in this same year, and in those following, there will ensue the most horrible pestilence, more stupendous by

---

21. Battles have caused the sea to blush.

the famine which will have preceded it, and such great tribulations as will never have occurred since the first foundation of the Christian church, and within all Latin regions, leaving traces in some countries of the Spanish.

110. At this time the third king of Aquilon, hearing the lament of the people of his principal title, will raise a mighty army and will pass through the straits of his predecessors and ancestors, will put almost everything back in its place,

111. and the great vicar of the hood will be placed again in his former state, but desolated and then abandoned by all,

112. and as a consequence *Sancta Sanctorum*[22] will have been destroyed by paganism, and the old and new testaments thrown out and burned.

113. After the Antechrist will come the infernal prince; again, for the last time, all the kingdoms of Christianity will tremble, and also the infidels, for the space of twenty-five years, and wars and battles will be more grievous, and towns, cities, castles and all other edifices will be burned, desolated, destroyed, with great effusion of vestal blood, violations of married women and widows, sucking children dashed and broken against the walls of towns, and so many evils committed by means of Satan, prince infernal, that nearly all the world will find itself undone and desolated.

114. And before these events some strange birds will cry in the air: "Hui, hui," and some time later will vanish.

115. And after this has endured for a long time, there will be almost renewed another reign of Saturn and golden age: Hearing the affliction of His people, God the Creator will command that Satan be cast into the abysmal depths of the bottomless pit, and bound there.

116. And then a universal peace will commence between God and men, and will remain bound for around a thousand

22. Holy of Holies.

years, and the ecclesiastical power will evolve into its greatest strength, and then again will be unbound.

117. All these figures represent a just conformation of the divine scriptures with visible celestial bodies, namely, Saturn, Jupiter and Mars and others conjoined, as can be seen more fully in some quatrains.

118. I would have calculated more profoundly and made them even more conform: but seeing, O most serene king, that some of the censure would raise difficulties, I therefore have withdrawn my pen in order to protect my nocturnal repose:

Multa etiam, O Rex omnium potentissime, praeclara et sane in brevi ventura, sed omnia in hac tua epistola innectere non possumus, nec volumus: sed ad intelligenda quedam facta, horrida fata, pauca libanda sunt, quamvis tanta sit in omnes tua amplitudo et humanitas homines, deosque pietas, ut solus amplissimo et Christianissimo Regis nomine, et ad quem summa totius religionis auctoritas deferatur dignus esse videare.[23]

119. But I only beseech you, O most clement king, by this singular and prudent humanity of yours, to understand rather the desire of my heart and the sovereign zeal I have had to obey your most serene Majesty, ever since my eyes approached your solar splendor so near that the grandeur of my labor could never have had attained or required it.

From Salon, this 27th of June 1558.

Faciebat Michael Nostradamus Salonae Petrae Provinciae.

23. O most powerful of all kings, much more I could have told about the astounding future events, so briefly indicated in this epistle, but I neither could nor would them explain clearly. Nevertheless, in order to make comprehensible certain facts that are horrible strokes of destiny, some of them had to be delineated. So great is your grandeur and humanity before men, and your piety before God, that you alone are worthy of the great title of the Most Christian King, and to whom the highest authority in all religion should be deferred.

7

QUATRAINS OF NOSTRADAMUS' CENTURIES RELATIVE TO THE FUTURE

First century

How many times will you be taken, solar city,
Changing the barbarian and vain laws:
Your evil approaches, you will be more tributary,
The great Adria will re-cover your veins.   (I-8)

The solar city is identified with Rome, because the sun of Christianity shines in Rome. The Christians are called the *solaires,* "children of the sun," as contrasted with the *lunaires,* "children of the moon," the Mohammedans, who have chosen the crescent moon as their distinctive sign.

The evil will not fail to come to the "eternal city," the proud Rome. Rome will often have to change its barbarian and vain laws and it will be captured by different nations. Nostradamus evidently has had before his mind's eye the endless Roman wars and military occupations of Rome. Hannibal before Rome, Alaric before Rome, incursions of the Vandals and the Huns, Rome under the rule of the Ostro-Goths, attacks by the Arabs and the Longobards, Charlemagne in Rome, capture by Louis II, Rome under Napoleon, and so on, until the time of occupation by the Allies.

But that is not the end of it. Again and again, Rome will get involved in international conflicts and, after the Germans and the Allies, in the course of time will be occupied by still other nations. In days to come the great

169

ruler of Adria will also bring Rome under his sway. The identity of this formidable and mighty ruler can be divined from some of the later quatrains.

The motion of sense, heart, feet and hands
Will be in accord. Naples, Leon, Sicily:
Swords, fires, waters, then the noble Romans
Plunged, killed, dead because of weak brain.   (I-11)

Here we are told about an insurrection in Italy and, apparently, in Spain, because Leon is a Spanish province. In Naples (southern Italy) and in Sicily, as well as in Spain, movements will grow which will be in accord among themselves. They will call forth uprisings, perhaps with separatist tendencies. The battle for Rome will end with the downfall and massacre of Roman nobility. The expression "weak brain" refers either to an irrational, vain person or to the silly policy of Roman leaders in general.

The next quatrain (I-12) also tells about uprisings in Verona (Italy). The revolution, consequently, will spread to other Italian cities (cf. V-28, VI-76 and other quatrains).

Par quarante ans l'Iris n'aparoistra,
Par quarante ans tous les iours sera veu:
La terre aride en siccité croistra,
Et grands deluges quand sera aperceu.   (I-17)

(For forty years the Iris will not appear, for forty years it will be seen everyday. The parched earth will wax more dry, and great floods, when again she will be in sight.) Iris, the daughter of Thaumas and the oceanid Electra, acts as an intermediary between heaven and earth. In Greek mythology she personifies the rainbow. She is a winged messenger of the gods and swiftly hurries from one end of the world to the other and penetrates even to the depths of the sea. Considering the symbolism attributed to the rainbow in the Bible (in the story of Noah and the deluge), this quatrain could be interpreted thus: Rainbow, the sign of peace, will not be seen for forty years, i.e., there will be war which will last for forty years. It will be followed by forty years of peace, during which period great migration (floods) of people will take place. E. Ruir does not concur in such an interpretation. His opinion is that the quatrain has to be understood literally. Rainbows are caused by solar rays, which by raindrops are split up into their prismatic colors. Consequently, for forty years there will be no rainfall. After this period of draught and famine (cf. I-67), rainbows again will appear. A forty-year-long period of abundant rainfall will follow, causing wide, destructive floods.

Par la discorde negligence Gauloyse
Sera passage a Mahommet ouuert.
De sang trempe la terre et mer Senoyse
Le port Phocen de voiles et nefs couuert.   (I-18)

(Because of the Gallic discord and negligence a passage will be opened to Mahomet. The land and sea Senoise soaked in blood. The Phocean port covered with sails and ships.) The Mohammedans will engage in the invasion of the French Mediterranean coast. The Senons are an ancient Gallic (French) tribe. The Phocean port is Marseilles, founded by Greeks from Phocaea. The invasion will be facilitated by French discord and negligence (cf. I-73).

Lors que serpens viendront circuir l'are,
Le sang Troien vexé par les Hespaignes
Par eux grans nombre en sera faicte tare,
Chef fuyct, caché aux mares dans les saignes.   (I-19)

(When the serpents will come to encircle the altar, the Trojan blood will be vexed by the Spaniards. Because of them a great number will be made to suffer, the chief flies, hidden in the boggy marshes.) The Spaniards will see themselves encircled by a serpent, like the ancient Trojans, when assailed by the Greeks. This quatrain is probably one of those which foretell the coming Mohammedan invasion. The serpent could be the invading army (cf. V-25). In such a case this quatrain is connected with III-20.

Perdu, trouué, caché de si long siecle
Sera pasteur demy dieu honoré,
Ains que la lune acheue son grand cycle
Par autres vents sera deshonoré.   (I-25)

(Lost, found, hidden for so long a century, the pastor will be honored as a demigod. Before the moon finishes its grand cycle, he will be dishonored by other winds.) It is difficult to ascertain to which group of predictions this quatrain should be added. It could possibly be one of those which tell about the founding of a new religion or, to be more exact, of the revival of Christian faith, after the end of the Mohammedan occupation period. Some commentators assume that the words "lost, found, hidden" refer to the discovery of something hitherto unknown or forgotten about the main purport of the doctrine of Jesus Christ, and that the second line of the quatrain about the pastor or shepherd of souls testifies that Christianity will witness the appearance of highly qualified spiritual leaders and preachers with all the marks of a true Christian disciple (Mark 16:17-18).

Other interpreters are of the opinion that the word "pastor" signifies the pope. There is no unanimity about the length of the grand cycle of the moon either. Le Pelletier considers that the lunar epoch ended in 1887, but others have cast up the year 1797, when the authority of the church and of the priests, especially in France, was undermined by the ideals of the revolution of 1789 and by the attacks of Voltaire, Diderot and other encyclopedists. The long century alluded to by Nostradamus could be the period between 1309 and 1449. In 1309, under Pope Clement V, the Papal See was transferred from Rome to Avignon in southern France. Here it remained until 1377. This interval is usually referred to as the "Babylonian exile of the popes," because this period almost corresponds in the number of years to the length of captivity of the nation of Israel, brought to Babylon by Nebuchadnezzar. During the great schisms of the

Roman church from 1378 to 1416 two popes reigned simultaneously, one in Rome, the other in Avignon. After the conciliation in Rome's favor, the pope's authority rose and soon again he was honored as a demigod. Nostradamus reminds us that the pope will experience similar stormy times in the future, when the same old adversaries of the good shepherd will dishonor his repute. Here it is well to remember the predictions about the future of the popes by Saint Malachia, archbishop of Ireland. They are retold in the last part of this book. The greatest enemy of the pope is supposed to be Antechrist. The temporal ruler Antechrist can be expected before the second coming of Christ ("ante" means "before"). Lactantius, famous patristic writer and apologist, in about the year 312 described Antechrist thus:

In days to come the nations will be oppressed by a great prince from the north. A great destruction will then overtake the world. But when the end will be approaching, God will send a great prophet who through manifold miracles will convert people to the cognition of truth. But then the evil spirit will beget another great prince who will go forth as the betrayer of mankind. Then will be tribulation, such as had not been seen since the beginning, and blood will flow in streams. This infamous one, who is Antechrist, will at end flee, will lose his strength and will be defeated during the fourth war. Thereupon all impiety will be effaced.

Under the oaktree of Guien struck from the sky,
Not far from there is the treasure hidden,
Which for long centuries had been gathered,
Found he will die, the eye put out by a spring.   (I-27)

This quatrain is generally supposed to refer to old Arabian or Hebrew books on the art of clairvoyance. The Arabian art has long been famous. Many books on the art were burnt up by Nostradamus, as he himself tells in his letter to Caesar (A.24).

He was also a contemporary of the great Arabian seer Bumahur, whose works even today can be found at the library of the University of Tunis. The one who will seek and find this hidden treasure will perish (the spring of the box-lid will leap into his eye?) E. Ruir is of the opinion that among the books could also be the unaltered original text of Nostradamus' predictions. We cannot be sure that the word "Guien" in the first line means "Guyenne," a province in the southwest of France.

In I-28 we read that Marseilles (the coast of Provence) will be threatened by a barbarian fleet, but after a long while Hesperian ships will arrive. The Hesperians could be Americans (cf. IV-50). Between Taurus and Libra mortal quarrel will arise. Taurus reigns over the Arabic nation, and IV-50 clearly indicates that Hesperia is reigned by Libra. But why will American squadrons arrive to save Europe only "after a long while," perhaps "only after many years"? There could be many and different reasons. Not only North America but also South America itself at that time could be under the threat of an invasion by Asiatics, in which case even Russia might turn against Europe and America. The Russian and Asiatic menace might compel America to think first of her own security before she could yield to the calls for help by European nations. But the day will come when the United States of America again will fulfill her mission of saving the world from tyranny.

Tant d'ans en Gaule les guerres dureront,
Oultre la course du Castulon monarque:
Victoire incerte trois grands couronneront
Aigle, Coq, Lune, Lyon, Soleil en marque.   (I-31)

(The wars in Gaul will last for many years beyond the course of the monarch of Castulo. Uncertain victory will crown three great ones, eagle, cock, moon, lion, sun marked.) A quatrain hard to unravel. War will rage in France for so many years that change of rulers will take place twice.

Will any of these kings be the future Henri V? Should these events be classed with those of the time of Mohammedan invasion? Can the course of the monarch of Castulo be identified with the military expedition of the orientals from Spain into France, across the Pyrenees, which campaign is clearly indicated in another quatrain? Castulo is the Roman name for the present Spanish town, Caslon. Sun in Leo could mean Italy, and the moon generally represents Islam. Consequently, as long as the oriental ruler will be in Italy, and as long as the attacks will occur also from the direction of Spain, France will be forced for many years to defend itself on both sides. During this time France will twice experience change of her sovereigns. The eagle has been the symbol of Napoleon and may mean a ruler of his lineage or may symbolize empire in general. The cock may mean a sovereign from the family of Orléans.

In I-32 we read that after the destruction of Paris the king of France will transfer his government to a small town, which therefore rapidly will grow big. That this town will be Avignon can be seen from VIII-38.

Auant qu'auienne le changement d'empire,
Il auiendra vn cas bien merueilleux:
Le champ mué, le pilier de porphyre
Mis, translaté sus le rocher noilleux.   (I-43)

(Before the change of empire occurs, a very marvelous event will take place: the field moved, the placed pillar of porphyry transferred onto the knotty rock.) Before the change of form of government (perhaps in England?) earth will be astir and a pillar (probably a notable monument) will be shifted.

Very near Aux, Lectore and Mirande
Great fire will fall from the sky for three nights.
A very stupenduous and marvelous event will occur:
Very soon after the earth will tremble.   (I-46)

All three mentioned towns are in the department of Gers in southern France. Some commentators refer this quatrain to military actions between France and England, because from other quatrains it can be assumed that both these presently allied countries again will be adversaries in a future war. Nevertheless, there is no reason to deny that this quatrain could as well predict some natural disaster (cf. V-98 and VIII-2).

> Vingt ans du regne de la lune passés,
> Sept mil ans autre tiendra sa monarchie:
> Quand le soleil prendra ses iours lassés
> Lors accomplit et mine ma prophetie.   (I-48)

(Twenty years of the reign of the moon passed, seven thousand years another will hold its monarchy. When the sun will take on its tired days, then is accomplished and finished my prophecy.) This is one of those quatrains which speaks about the planetary periods of reign, permitting different interpretations (cf. I-25, I-56, III-92, among others). Some astrologers take 36 years as the influential period of each planet. In the twentieth century the militant Mars supposedly has had influence on global destiny from the year 1909/10 until 1944/45. Lunar influence has accordingly begun in 1945/46 and will last until 1980/81. If we accept this reckoning, no military events of world-wide scale can be expected during this period. In this respect we have to bear in mind that the calendar year does not correspond with the astronomical year, which begins with the arrival of spring on March 21. From the first line of the quatrain we gather that 20 years after the end of moon's reign, consequently at about the year 2000, one of Nostradamus' prophecies will be accomplished. Which one? Perhaps X-72, because it tells us that in July, 1999, the great king of terror will come from the sky to bring back life to the great king of "Angolmois" (Angoulême?) Possibly Henry V has been meant, the future, powerful king of France, who will ascend the throne in July, 1999, if this interpretation is correct. But some astrologers calculate the periods of planetary reign differently and assign to the influence of each planet a full 1000 years. This seems to be indicated also by the second line. In his letter to Caesar, speaking about these cycles, Nostradamus says: "At present we are led by the moon" (A.39). In III-92 he says: "The world nearing the last period, Saturn will come back." In his epistle to King Henry II we read that from the creation of the world to Jesus Christ 4173 years and 8 months have passed (B. 86). Combining all these statements and assuming 1,000 years as the length of each planetary reign, it follows that Saturn had the first cycle and will again return during the eighth millenary. The moon has reigned from the year 827 to 1827, and the sun is reigning from the year 1827 to 2827. In his letter to Caesar, Nostradamus maintains that his predictions reach until the year 3797 (A.29). Consequently, 30 years are wanting to make up full 8000 years. Are these 30 years to be deducted from one of the previous planetary cycles? Such a thought is suggested by the circumstance that in this quatrain the word *passés* can be translated also as "omitted." If we accept this translation and if 20 years have to be deducted from the cycle of the moon, the borderline between the moon period and the sun period is not 1827, but 1807. At that time Napoleon's war had its greatest extension, but we don't know if this circumstance has somehow influenced Nostradamus to choose this particular year. The remaining 10 years, consequently, have to be deducted from the period of the sun or of that of Saturn. If the period of the moon has ended and the period of the sun has begun in the year 1807, we can assume that the period of the sun will end in 2807, and that the period of Saturn, or the future millennium, will comprise only the years from 2807 to 3797, "around (i.e., approximately) a thousand years," as can be read in the epistle (B.116) about the bound Satan. Has this tranquil period of a thousand years with universal peace between God and men any connection with the "millennium" mentioned in St. John's Apocalypse? Hard to tell. Nostradamus never says anything about Christ's second coming on earth and his reign in power of glory. However, in several places he mentions the "end time" or "the time of the end" or simply the "last period." And as we have seen, he speaks about the binding of Satan for 1000 years (Apoc. 20:2). Although he does not directly speak about "new heavens and new earth," he nevertheless predicts that the world, i.e., earth, is drawing near an "anaragonic revolution" (A.39). It is possible that the millennium of Nostradamus is not identical with the one promised in the Apocalypse, and that the long period of peace, mentioned by Nostradamus, coming after so many world wars, disasters and upheavals, including the Mohammedan invasion, reminded him of the promised "millennium." In any case, Nostradamus too has foretold for mankind a long period of peace after many severe afflictions and sorrows.

> Chef d'Aries, Iuppiter et Saturne,
> Dieu eternel, quelles mutations!
> Puis après long siècle son maling temps retourne,
> Gaule et Itale quelles emotions!   (I-51)

(The head of Aries, Jupiter and Saturn. Eternal God, what changes! Then, after a long time, his malignant time returns. Gaul and Italy, what disturbances!) The first line is an astrological reference to the location of Jupiter and Saturn in the sign of Aries. "The malignant time" could be a period when it is necessary to struggle against barbarian invaders. After a long age a similar time returns, when new fighting is taken up, in order to again expel them from Europe. The simultaneous dwelling of Jupiter and Saturn in the sign of Aries is a rare phenomenon. It occurred lately in 1939 and in this century will not be repeated.

> Les deux malins de Scorpion conioincts,
> Le Grand Seigneur meurtry dedans sa salle:
> Peste à l'Eglise par le nouueau Roy ioinct
> L'Europe basse et Septentrionale.   (I-52)

(The two malignant ones conjoined in Scorpio, the Grand Seignior murdered in his hall. Plague to the Church by the new king joined Europe low and northern.) The two malignant planets in astrology are Mars and Saturn. When they will be in conjunction in the sign of Scorpio, the Grand Seignior (the pope?) will be murdered. It will be hard times for the church, possibly identical with the period when the Mohammedans will conquer Italy. Then also a king will unite southern and northern Europe, i.e., southern and central Europe, because Scandinavia, which today is called northern Europe, was by Nostradamus considered as belonging to the Polar region. This king may perhaps be identical with the one mentioned in II-29, who, after invading France, "will strike everyone with his rod." Saturn returns to Scorpio after every 29 years and remains there for 2 years. The next such period will be 1983-1985, when in February 1984 he will also meet Mars.

You will see great change made soon and late,
Extreme horrors and vengeances.
Because as the Moon is conducted by its angel,
The heavens are approaching their inclination.   (I-56)

Here again the moon and its period of influence has been mentioned (cf. I-25, I-48, III-92). If we assign to each planet a 36-year-long period of influence, this quatrain can be referred to the year 1945, when after the "extreme horrors" of World War II great changes were made: in other words, peace was established. The kind, peaceful moon, conducted as if by a guardian angel, reigns over a period of 36 years, during which time mankind is permitted to live in relative peace. But how then to interpret the last line? E. Ruir has about this and similar quatrains an entirely different and peculiar judgment, which I will discuss in a special chapter.

The scourges passed, the world shrinks,
For a long time peace, populated lands,

One will travel safely by skies, land, sea and wave,

Then the wars stirred up anew. (I-63)

For a long time peace! This is a rather interesting quatrain, because it foretells travel by air. Therefore it can be applied only to the twentieth century or later centuries. Because of more rapid travel the world seems to have shrunk. If the 57 years mentioned in X-89 are not applied to the past but extended into the future, we can hope, as does H. Bauder, that after the scourges of two world wars Europe and the greater part of the world will enjoy peace for 57 long years, consequently, until 2002. By land, water and air safe traffic will be maintained and only in the year 2002 the world again will be thrown into the misery of war. It would be very nice if we could believe in such an interpretation.

He who then will bear the news,

After a short while will come to breathe freely.

Viviers, Tournon, Montferrant and Pradelles,

Hail and storms will make them sigh. (I-66)

Here the suspension of the censorship of the press is indicated. The freedom of speech and writing again will be restored. But what connection has this forecast with the second half of the quatrain where we are told that the mentioned French localities will be afflicted by (military?) disturbances and storms? Montferrant is a suburb of Clermond-Ferrand, the seat of French government under Philippe Pétain.

La grand famine que ie sens approcher,

Souuent tourner, puis estre vniuerselle,

Si grande et longue qu'on viendra arracher

Du bois racine, et l'enfant de mammelle. (I-67)

(The great famine that I sense approaching, often turning, then becoming universal, so great and long that one will come to pull out roots from woods and infants from breast.) This is one of the quatrains which promise a long period of drought and famine (cf. I-17 and III-4).

I-70 imparts the news that rain, famine and war in Persia continue and that what had begun in France is finished. What connection can Persia have with events in France? Perhaps we are told here that at the time when war will rage in Persia, a movement which had its beginning in France will end. Could it be communism, since its beginnings are to be sought in the French philosophy of "enlightenment" and in the subsequent French revolution?

I-71 unmistakably tells that the Mediterranean coast of France will be ravaged by an army consisting of Spaniards, Barbarians (Arabs?) and Italians. Will France then be in a state of war with Italy and Spain?

From I-72 we gather that a hostile army (coming from Spain?) will attack Bordeaux in southern France, also Narbonne and Toulouse.

France à cinq pars par neglect assaillie
Tunys, Argel esmeuz par Persiens:
Leon, Seuille, Barcelone faillie
N'aura la classe par les Venetiens.   (I-73)

(France because of negligence assailed on five sides, Tunis, Algiers stirred up by Persians. Leon, Seville, Barcelona having failed. There will be no fleet from the Venetians.) *Argel* is an anagram for "Alger" (Algiers). Those commentators who are of the opinion that the present peace will last for 57 years foretell the outbreak of World War III in 2002 (cf. I-63). In this war France, supposedly under the future King Henry V, will be victorious and will subjugate all Mediterranean countries. After these triumphs France, more powerful than ever, will feel secure and, in luxury softened, will become careless and negligent. She will overlook the secret armament of her rivals and will be assailed on five sides. This will be the beginning of World War IV. France will again have to fight in order to maintain her hold over the Mediterranean. Tunis and Algiers will be stirred up against France by a powerful nation, which then will govern over

Persia. Even Spain will be involved in hostilities and will in vain be waiting for help from the Venetian, i.e., Italian fleet. Leon, Seville and Barcelona will be captured. It is more likely that this quatrain can be ranked with those which deal with the invasion by Mohammedans or Asiatics. After the Asiatic army will have captured Tunis and Algiers and will have under its sway all of North Africa, the invasion army will cross over to the Pyrenean peninsula. The conquest of Spain is treated also in other quatrains. Later will begin the assault against France, which will succeed because of the negligence of the defenders. France will suffer aggression also from the side of Italy and Switzerland (cf. II-29).

Entre deux mers dressera promontoire
Que puis mourra par le mors du cheual:
Le sien Neptune pliera voyle noire,
Par Calpre et classe auprès de Rocheual.   (I-77)

(Between two seas will be erected a promontory which then will die by the bite of a horse. His Neptune will fold the black sail by Calpre and the fleet near Rocheval.) The subject of this prediction is unmistakably Gibraltar, which was called Calpe by the Romans. The Moors built there a stronghold and called it Gibraltar. The English captured it in July, 1704, and since that day this British fortress on Spanish soil is for the Spanish patriot like a thistle in his flesh. More than once (already in 1705 and again in 1727 and 1782/83) have the Spaniards tried to recapture it, but in vain. Weakened by the civil war, Spain even after World War II did not dare to regain it by military means. Nevertheless, it is more than likely that during a future period of British weakness Spain may again try to exploit the opportunity for the occupation of this important naval base. Judging from Nostradamus' quatrains, it seems that the British will hold Gibraltar until the great Mohammedan invasion of southern and western Europe. Cape Roche is not far from Gibraltar. The English have now in Gibraltar "unfolded their sails," i.e., "pitched their tents," but will have to fold them again when the Mohammedans will have occupied all neighboring territory. "The bite of a horse" points toward the fact that the outlines of the western part of the Mediterranean resemble the head of a horse. Gibraltar is placed exactly in the horse's mouth.

From the sixth bright celestial splendor
It will come to thunder so severely in Burgundy:
Then of a very hideous beast will be born a monster.
March, April, May, June great tearing and
    clipping. (I-80)

The sixth planet by rank, according to the common sequence, i.e., the distance from the sun, is Jupiter. Under his dominion and influence "it will come to thunder" in Burgundy from March until June. Conceivably, it signifies military actions and fierce fighting, which will continue for four months with great "tearing and clipping."

Quand les colomnes de bois grand tremblée
D'Auster conduicte couuerte de rubriche,
Tant vuidera dehors grand assemblée,
Trembler Vienne et le pais d'Austriche. (I-82)

(When the columns of wood greatly trembling, led by Auster, covered with red ochre, will greatly empty outside grand assembly, Vienna and the land of Austria will tremble.) Ill fate will afflict Austria. An invasion army, led by Auster (the south wind), will devastate and lay waste (empty) towns and cities.

La gent estrange diuisera butins,
Saturne en Mars son regard furieux:
Horrible strage aux Toscans et Latins,
Grecs, qui seront à frapper curieux. (I-83)

(The strange nation will divide spoils, Saturn in Mars, his aspect furious. Horrible defeat of the Tuscans and Latins, Greeks, who will desire to strike.) Warfare in southeastern Europe. A conjunction of Saturn and Mars recurs so often (once in less than 2 years) that from this circumstance a previous determination of the time period is not possible. Saturn may here also symbolically indicate an aggressive nation in a state of war (in Mars).

> When the great queen will see herself vanquished,
> She will act with an excess of masculine courage:
> On horseback will pass over river entirely naked,
> Pursued by the sword, and the faith will be subject to
> outrage.   (I-86)

This puzzle about a modern Penthesilea (queen of the Amazons) remains for the present veiled in darkness. According to the myth, a bellicose nation of women lived on the shores of the Black Sea. These Amazons did not suffer any men among themselves, but used men of neighboring nations for the preservation of their sex. They brought up only girls and burned out their right breast, so that it would not hinder the bending of the bow. During the Trojan War Penthesilea with her nation supposedly came to aid the Trojans. Nostradamus foretells that a powerful nation (of the east or west?) will fall to the ground. Her masculine queen will save her naked life, but nevertheless will then choose voluntary death, lest she might suffer humiliation by her adversaries.

> Enosigaios, fire from the center of the earth
> Will cause trembling around the new city:
> Two great rocks will make war for a long time,
> Then Arethusa will redden a new river.   (I-87)

Enosigaios is one of the Greek names for Neptune. The new city is Naples, the meaning of whose Greek name, *Neapolis,* is exactly "the new city." Arethusa, the daughter of Nereus and Doris, was a nymph. She was pursued by the river god Alpheios and escaped over the sea to Sicily, where she implored Diana's help. Diana turned her into a spring. Even today a famous spring near Syracuse is called Arethusa. According to a different version Arethusa is a submarine river which has its source in Greece and appears in Sicily on the surface of the earth. This prophecy can be interpreted in several ways. Firstly, literally: a new eruption of Vesuvius will take place, together with earthquakes in the region of Naples. Secondly, if Enosigaios as the ruler of the sea symbolizes a nation, it could be, for instance, England, which always has been considered to be the ruler of the sea. England will assail Naples and its vicinity, because two great nations (rocks), for instance, France and England, will compete for supremacy over the Mediterranean. The sea again will be reddened by blood. But still another solution is possible, to which fact J. Monterey, a French engineer and assiduous interpreter of Nostradamus, directs attention in his recent book. From his point of view, "the new city" is "Geneva," and the prophecy can be associated with quatrains VI-97, VIII-10, X-49 and the apocryphal XII-69. "Fire from the center of the earth" is a plutonium, hydrogen, cobalt or some other kind of atomic bomb. Trying to name the thing which we today are calling "the nuclear phenomenon," Nostradamus, being a hellenist, could not possibly have found a better designation than "the fire of Enosigaios." Several already quoted quatrains testify that he had clearly foreseen all possibilities of scientific progress and development and had, for instance, in III-44 foretold also the invention of the atomic bomb, calling it "the lightning, taken from the earth." Consequently, it is to be feared that Geneva and the shores of Lake Geneva will be destroyed by "the nuclear phenomenon." J. Monterey maintains that these events will occur when the United States will seek to measure its strength with Russia on the national rather than the ideological battlefield. The result will be a long, extended struggle between two powerful blocks, involving disasters in air and on the sea. It will not be inopportune to quote here the interesting XII-69:

EIOVAS near to go far, Lake of Geneva,

Very great preparations, return, confusion:
Far from the nephews, from fire great Supelman,
All of their following.

The word "EIOVAS" is easy to decipher: spelled backwards it becomes "Savoie" (Savoy). The whole southern shore of Lake Geneva belongs to France and is part of the department of Savoy. The word "Supelman" is a harder nut to crack. It could mean "sup Leman," and the sentence then can be rendered as "great fire above the Lake Geneva," or it could mean "Superman," i.e., the fire of Superman. In both cases, the actual meaning remains unaltered.

I-89 tells us that the enemy will invade France and will devastate the shores of the Loire and Seine, and the Spaniards will "open every vein" (will commit cruelties? where? in France?).

Second century

II-5 mentions a conjunction of Mars and Mercury in the sign of Pisces. Then a certain country is going to make war and with her fleet will appear near Latin land. This conjunction recurs every 13 to 17 years. The calculations of a Portuguese commentator place this prophecy together with those which foretell an Arab invasion, supposedly some time between the years 1994 and 1996. On the other hand, Gustafsson foresees this event in 2088 or in 2090, in both cases in the month of April.

> Temples sacrés prime façon Romaine
> Reieteront les goffes fondements
> Prenant leurs loys premieres et humaines,
> Chassant, non tout, des saincts les cultements.   (II-8)

(Temples consecrated in the original Roman manner will reject the intricate foundations, taking their first and humane laws, rejecting, not entirely, the cult of saints.) This is one of the quatrains which speak about a new reformation of Christian faith. We understand that entirely new views will prevail regarding dogmas and rituals. The adornments of churches and cathedrals which assert fabulous wealth will be rejected, together with all the intricate ceremonies and colorful processions, which are so remarkable in the Catholic church. In quatrain V-16 Nostradamus says that the "Sabean tear" will no longer be at its high price. Saba was once famous as the exporter of frankincense. "The intricate foundations" are the testimonies, declarations, decisions and regulations, passed in the councils of the church (in the fourth to sixth centuries). At that time there existed many sects and faiths, ideologically very similar to the new Christianity. For this reason the church drew up strictly circumscribed dogmas, wishing to provide Christianity with certain, delimited "foundations." These speculatory, intricate dogmas and "fundamental laws" and statutes have been adopted by the councils on many occasions by only a very small majority of votes, and only contingencies were often determining the direction, in which Christian thought was allowed to develop further on. Nostradamus foretells that these "intricate foundations" will be rejected and replaced by first and humane laws, which formerly had been part of the teaching of Jesus, and which are so clear that they exclude all theological speculations. It is also possible that some writings of primitive Christianity will be found, the greater part of which were destroyed during the period of the formation of dogmas. This seems to be indicated by I-25.

Before long all will be set in order,

We will expect a very left-sided century.

The state of the masked and solitary ones much changed.

Few will be found who want to be in their place. (II-10)

Incomprehensible quatrain. The word "left-sided" could be interpreted also as "sinister," and this is the only word in this forecast with a negative meaning, since all else "will be set in order." The "masked ones" could refer to secret diplomacy, the mascarade between nations, with which they try to deceive each other and to hide their real thoughts and intentions. The "solitary ones" can be referred to dictators, who with their autocratic (solitary) rule oppress people and promote wars.

Le corps sans ame plus n'estre en sacrifice

Iour de la mort mis en natiuité:

L'esprit diuin fera l'ame felice

Voiant le verbe en son eternité.   (II-13)

(The body without soul no longer to be sacrificed, day of death comes to be birthday: the divine spirit will make the soul happy, seeing the word in its eternity.) This is one of the few quatrains in which Nostradamus does not speak about external historical events, but does touch the problem of life and death. The belief in the existence of the soul after death has belonged to mankind at all times and in all cultural phases. Many nations have believed also in an invisible tie, which connects and binds the soul with the body and which is severed at death, as can be read in Ecclesiastes 12:6, where this bond is called the "silver cord." Nostradamus too believes in existence after death, as proved by the contents of this quatrain. Possibly even this quatrain can be classified together with those which tell about the ascendancy of a new Christian or Neo-Platonic teaching, which will have to take on the fight against atheism and materialism.

> At Tours, Gien, guarded eyes will be searching,
> Discovering from afar the great serene:
> She and her suite will enter the port,
> Combat, thrust, sovereign power.   (II-14)

From the shores of Loire the French will discover from afar the approaching of a great power with her allies. This quatrain may refer to the future war of France against England, since it is to be expected that the interests of these two great countries will again intersect each other. After combat on land and sea unconditional capitulation will follow.

> Vn peu deuant monarque trucidé
> Castor Pollux en nef, astre crinite.
> L'erain publique par terre et mer vuidé,
> Pise, Ast, Ferrare, Turin, terre interdicte.   (II-15)

(Shortly before the monarch is assassinated, Castor and Pollux in the ship, bearded star. The public funds emptied by land and sea, Pisa, Asti, Ferrara, Turin land under interdict.) Here we have to deal with a celestial phenomenon, namely, with a comet, which will appear in the sign of Castor and Pollux, i.e., Gemini, the Twins (cf. II-43, VI-6 and perhaps also II-46, II-96). This comet (bearded star) will appear before significant and possibly catastrophic events in Italy. Shortly after the appearance of the comet the Italian ruler will be assassinated, northern Italy will secede from the rest of Italy and will become a land under interdict. In former times the pope with such an "interdiction" used to punish or condemn rebellious provinces and cities. The mentioned comet could be the same which was discovered in 1682 by E. Halley and which was lately seen in 1910/11. Its orbit is traversed in about 76 years, and we can reckon with a new appearance in 1986. Perhaps the comet will then be with its tail over the big twin stars Castor and Pollux, which will be like a warning about the events that will come to pass in Italy. But Nostradamus has mentioned also another comet, the time of appearance of which is not known.

> The field of temple of the vestal virgin,
> Not far from Ethna and the Pyrenees mountains:
> The great one conducted is hidden in the trunk,
> North, rivers thrown and vines battered.   (II-17)

This quatrain for the time being remains without a solution and even without localization. The ancient Italians revered Vesta as a goddess of the hearth and fire. Her rotund temple was built in the Forum of ancient Rome, where the vestal priestesses maintained an everlasting fire. The prophecy therefore could be meant for Rome, but other temples, dedicated to Vesta, were in ancient times built also in many other regions of Italy, as well as in Spain and France. The same can be said about the temples of Diana, because Diana too could be called a "vestal virgin." The second line of the quatrain does not make the meaning any more clear, because Etna is in Sicily and very far from the Pyrenean mountains. Perhaps "Ethna" is an anagram for another place-name. Here we have to remember that near the Pyrenean mountains flows the Elne. The third line tells about something or somebody hiding or hidden. It could be a hidden or disguised army. The word "North," moreover, spelled by Nostradamus in English, could be regarded as a hint that it is an invasion army from the "North," i.e., from England. "The battered vines" indicate devastations as the result of military actions.

Newcomers, place built without defense,
Settled in a region then uninhabitable:
Meadows, houses, fields, towns to take at pleasure,
Famine, plague, war land long arable.   (II-19)

Here we are told about mass resettlement. This quatrain permits different solutions. The more obvious is the following: Due to warfare a land or a country has been devastated and the inhabitants expelled. After war a mass settlement takes place in these abandoned, uninhabited regions. The new homesteads are portioned out without consideration of the rights of the previous owners. Houses are to be built and all land has to be tilled again, because war has destroyed everything. Some commentators are of the opinion that this quatrain can be applied to events in Palestine, where the Arabs will be resettled after the expulsion of the Jews by armed invasion. Such an event is forecast in the next quatrain.

II-20 tells about Jews and Jewesses (*frères et soeurs*, i.e., "brothers and sisters") experiencing a new captivity. They are led to diverse places.

In II-25 Nostradamus laments about the retreat of the foreign auxiliaries from an important section of the front, whereby the whole region south of the Loire and Saone is lost.

The divine word will be struck from the sky,
Which cannot proceed any further:
The secret closed up with its revealer
So that they will march over and ahead.   (II-27)

Incomprehensible. Is persecution of religion the subject of this quatrain? Such persecution is not limited to certain periods and has taken place at all times. Whenever people can live in affluence and opulence, they forget the Giver of all gifts. The assault against religion is commenced again, mankind experiences wars and revolutions and, through these ordeals exhorted, temporarily turns back to religion, seeking in it deliverance and comfort. There have been efforts to classify this quatrain as one of those which foretell the discovery of ancient Christian writings or even gospels and the revival of primitive Christianity: the heavens will reveal a secret which had been "closed up."

> The penultimate of the surname of the Prophet
> Will take Diana for his day and rest:
> He will wander far because of a frantic head,
> And delivering a great people from subjection.   (II-28)

If "the Prophet" is understood to be Mohammed, the penultimate syllable of his name is "ham" or "ho" (from "Mahomet"). This ruler, whose name will begin with the letter H, will worship Diana. Diana is the goddess of hunting. Since we know from other of Nostradamus' forecasts that one of the greatest future kings of France will have the name of Henric (Henry), this quatrain is usually referred to him. In his campaigns he will wander over faraway lands of the Mediterranean, but he will be successful, and France will experience happy days under this king (he will be "delivering a great people from subjection").

> L'Oriental sortira de son siège,
> Passer les monts Apennins, voir la Gaule:
> Transpercera du ciel les eaux et neige,
> Et vn chascun frapera de sa gaule.   (II-29)

(The Easterner will leave his seat, to pass the Apennine mountains to see Gaul. He will transpierce the sky, the waters and the snow, and everyone will be struck with his rod.) Unmistakable reference to the invasion of Europe by Orientals. Through Italy the hostile armies will advance toward France.

> In two lodgings the fire will take hold by night,
> Several within suffocated and roasted.
> It will happen near two rivers for one:

Sun, Sagittarius and Capricorn all will be
   exhausted.   (II-35)

If this prophecy is interpreted literally, it can have been
already accomplished more than once, because many cities
are located at the convergence of two rivers. Fires occur
often and also on December 22 they can have broken out
repeatedly (on December 22 the Sun leaves the sign of
Sagittarius and enters Capricorn). This quatrain can be
justifiably included in this section, however, only because
many commentators refer it to the future quarrel between
England and France. Both countries will all of a sudden as it
were, overnight, namely on December 22, clash and after
hard fighting both will be exhausted. But how then are we to
understand the line about the two rivers?

Of that great number that one will send
To relieve those besieged in the fort,
Plague and famine will devour them all,
Except seventy who will be destroyed.   (II-37)

Which fort will be besieged? Has the whole of Europe been
meant? The biblical (prophetical) meaning of "seventy" is "a
great number," i.e., "many." A great army will be sent to
relieve the besieged fort, but the resistance of the enemy will
require many reinforcements. On both sides many will die
through epidemics and famine, and many will perish in
combat.

The great star will burn for seven days,
The cloud will cause two suns to appear:
The big mastiff will howl all night,
When the great pontiff will change territory.   (II-41)

In the skies will be seen a strange cosmical event, the
character of which cannot yet be ascertained. Perhaps it will
be the emergence of two moons or the partition of an immense
comet. Even the explosion of an atomic bomb has often been
described by eyewitnesses as "a second sun." These cosmic
events will introduce a new, hard period, the first and

main sign of which will be the departure of the pope from either the world or the city of Rome. Only the accomplishment itself of this prophecy will bring certitude. However, the "changing of territory" is more likely to be a parting from the world, because the third line tells about a mastiff who will howl all night, and it is a generally well-known fact that a dog howls when his master dies.

> During the appearance of the bearded star
> The three great princes will be made enemies:
> From the sky struck peace, earth quaking,
> Po, Tiber overflowing, serpent placed upon the
>   shore.   (II-43)

Again a quatrain about a comet, which could be either Halley's or some other, less-known comet. This celestial body will so nearly approach the earth that great changes will be called forth. At first there will be geological and meteorological changes, namely natural catastrophes and earthquakes, but gradually the radiation from the comet will evoke changes also in mankind's spiritual spheres of action. In several quatrains Nostradamus has stressed the appearance of this comet and its consequences. Years will go by before earth will be released from the influence of this foreign celestial body, and it will then emerge transformed and cleansed, as if wrought and forged anew in a celestial furnace.

> Après grand trouble humain, plus grand s'apreste
> Le grand mouteur les siecles renouuele.
> Pluie, sang, laict, famine, fer et peste
> Au ciel veu feu courant longue estincele.   (II-46)

(After great trouble for mankind, a greater one is prepared. The great Mover renews the ages. Rain, blood, milk, famine, iron and plague, in the heavens fire seen, a long, streaming spark.) According to the best interpreters, Nostradamus here rebukes the revolution of 1789 and forecasts another, a still greater one.

La grand copie que passera les monts.
Saturne en l'Arq tournant du poisson Mars:
Venins cachez soubs testes de Saulmons,
Leurs chief pendu à fil de polemars.   (II-48)

(The great army which will pass the mountains. Saturn in Sagittarius, Mars turning from the fish. Poison hidden under the heads of salmon, their war chief hung with cord.) The most important part of this quatrain is the astronomically confined date: Saturn in Sagittarius, but Mars at the same time turning from Pisces into Aries. Such a spectacle is rare, but due to both Saturn and Mars retrograde, it will occur on January 8, 1987, July 13, 1988, and November 1, 1988. The third line is puzzling. If "poison" referes to the planet Venus, and the location of Venus too is required to be in the sign of Pisces, it will occur next only on May 1, 2107. At this time an army will pass the mountains, probably the Pyrenees. If there were any indication which would let us assume that the subject of this quatrain is the future assault on France by the Arabs, it wuld provide us with an important timetable not only for this but for many other quatrains, which deal with the Mohammedan invasion of Europe.

The blood of the just will commit a fault at London,
Burnt through lightning of twenty-three the six:
The ancient lady will fall from her high place,
Several of the same sect will be killed.   (II-51)

This quatrain proclaims revolution in England and the downfall of the ancient monarchistic regime, as well as death for several members of the dynasty. The second line is incomprehensible: who or what are the 23 or the 6? If we count English rulers since the Tudors, the introducers of Protestantism in England, we come to the number 24, including the present ruler Elizabeth II. Of these 24 rulers 6 had the name of George. If we count only rulers of the masculine sex, we get only 17. Some investigators have tried to find in the second line the number 66 (20 x 3 + 6), but would that bring us any nearer to a clear and lucid solution?

In II-52 we are told about an earthquake with the mentioning of Corinth and Ephesus, as in III-2. If both quatrains tell about the same event, the earthquake must be happening in Asia. Possibly not a literal earthquake, but political upheavals have been meant. After that in the spring, "Corinth and Ephesus will swim in two seas." Corinth is in Greece, Ephesus in Turkey.

Le parc enclin grande calamité
Par l'Hesperie et Insubre fera:
Le feu en nef, peste et captiuité,
Mercure en l'Arq, Saturne fenera.   (II-65)

(The sloping park great calamity done through Hesperia and Insubria. Fire in the ship, plague and captivity, Mercury in Sagittarius, Saturn will cleave.) Hesperia is "the land to the West," as the Greek of ancient times called Italy, but the Romans, Spain. In our times, from the viewpoint of Europe, Hesperia could be America. Here, however, Italy seems to be meant, because Insubria also is mentioned. The Insubrians were once a powerful Gallic tribe, living in northern Italy. Italy will experience a great calamity when Mercury will be in Sagittarius (which happens every year) and when Saturn coming from Scorpio will cleave to Sagittarius, i.e., will be on the border between Scorpio and Sagittarius. Such a position recurs every 29 years, but not always can Mercury then be found also in Sagittarius. Next possible date: 1985.

De l'Aquilon les effors seront grands,
Sur l'Ocean sera la porte ouuerte,
Le regne en l'isle sera réintegrand:
Tremblera Londres par voile descouuerte.   (II-68)

(The efforts of Aquilon will be great, the gate on the ocean will be opened, the reign on the isle will be restored, London will tremble, discovered by sail.) Aquilon is "land of the North." Such a name Nostradamus could have given to

Ireland as well as to England or any other northern country. If England has been meant, the prophecy can refer to future revolution in England or to the attack on England by a foreign country. London is directly mentioned. One of the possible solutions: The gate on the ocean (by which England is guarded) will be opened, i.e., through this gate an incursion into England will take place. The empire will diminish to the size of the isle itself, and a devastating attack will follow on London which will be devoid of the support of its fleet.

Le dard du ciel fera son extendue
Mors en parlant: grande execution.
La pierre en l'arbre, la fiere gent rendue,
Bruit, humain monstre, purge expiation (II-70)

(The dart from the sky will make its extension, the dead will be speaking: great execution. The stone in the tree, the proud nation restored, noise, human monster, purge, expiation.) A quatrain hard to comprehend. A quite interesting solution is rendered by those interpreters who perceive in this text the forecast that the Jewish nation, together with great difficulties, will experience also great joy when the dream of finding the Ark of the Covenant will be fulfilled. "The stone in the tree" refers to tablets of stone on which the Ten Commandments were written, and which were kept in an ark made of acacia wood (Exod. 25:10, 25:16, and 40:20). This ark was later placed in the temple built by Solomon and is mentioned in the Bible for the last time in 2 Chron. 35:3, where it is said that the ark in the future is not to be carried on shoulders anymore. The disappearance of the ark is hidden in the obscurity of history. The ark is not mentioned among the war booty neither in Nebuchadnezzar's nor Titus' time, when the temple of Jerusalem was destroyed. The Jewish physician and philosopher, Mosus Maimonides (1135–1204), in a writing discusses the mysterious disappearance of the ark and says that Solomon, when building the temple, already knew that it would be destroyed because the prophets proclaimed times of affliction for Jerusalem (2 Chron. 34:24). He, therefore, had supposedly stored the ark in a subterranean room to be reached through long underground passages. Exactly where this secret place is has been the subject of many speculations. The valley south of the temple, used as a place for sacrifices and later as cemetery (Jer. 7:31–32), has been mentioned as one such possible location. Since Nostradamus too speaks about the dead, other cemeteries around Jerusalem could be suspected as locations where the ark had been hidden. Jewish legends tell that the ark will be found without the help of the hands of man when the Jewish nation for the last time will be assembled in Palestine. Nostradamus mentions a dart from the sky which could be lightning or the explosion of a bomb. But when will it happen, before or after the desperate battle with the Mohammedans?

At the lake Fucino to the shore of Benac,
Taken from lake Leman to the port of Orguion:
Born of three arms the predicted bellicose image.
Through three crowns to the great Endymion.   (II-73)

Lake Fucino or Celano was once located in the Abruzzi Mountains and has been drained in the last century. Lake Benac is the former name of Lake Garda. Lake Leman is the Lake of Geneva. Orguion remains, for the present, unsolved. Could an upper Italian river Oglio, tributary of the Po, be meant? "Port" could mean also the "mouth" of a river. "Endymion" is in Greek mythology the son of Jupiter and could have the meaning of "a king's son." This prophecy promises warfare with the probable seat in upper or central Italy. Three allied armies will combine against a powerful ruler, the son of a king. Evidently a great man, descendant of a royal family, will then rule over Italy, and three nations will join forces ("born of three arms") in order to overthrow him.

La voix ouye de l'insolit oyseau,
Sur le canon du respiral estage:

Si haut viendra du froment le boisseau,

Que l'homme d'homme sera Anthropophage.   (II-75)

(The voice of the strange bird heard on the pipe of the air vent floor. So high will the bushel of wheat rise, that man of man will become anthropofagite.) The cries of strange birds are mentioned also in B. 114. Here it clearly means air attacks of a future war. The air vent floor could be an air raid shelter. In wartime (perhaps during the period of Mohammedan invasion?) long disastrous famine will break out and lead even to cannibalism.

Le grand Neptune du profond de la mer

De gent Punique et sang Gauloys meslé:

Les Isles à sang, pour le tardif ramer,

Plus luy nuira que l'occult mal celé: (II-78)

(The great Neptune of the deep of the sea with Punic race and Gallic blood mixed. The isles bled, because of the tardy propping. More harm will it do him than the ill-concealed secret.) "Punic race" refers to the Carthaginians, that is, the north Africans. It seems here we have to deal with an assault on the British Isles with the participation also of French-Arab halfbreeds. The invasion will succeed because the English will have been tardy with the building of fortifications. The last line indicates some secret means of defense, perhaps the long since discussed tunnel beneath the sea between England and France. It is also possible that it refers to the ill-guarded secrets of the British Intelligence Service. The aggressors will succeed in what neither Napoleon nor Hitler could obtain, namely, disembarkation on England's shores, but the prophecy does not say anything about their success in conquering England and the occupation of the country. Even this prophecy may belong to those which deal with the Mohammedan invasion of Europe.

The beard frizzled and black through shrewdness

Will subjugate the cruel and proud people:

The great Chyren will remove from far away

All those captured by the banner of Seline.   (II-79)

Selene is the crescent as seen on the banners of most Islamic countries. Chyren is an anagram for "Henryc" and must be attributed to the future king of France, the great Henry V, who will wrest from Turkish (or Arab) grasp all the captives which they had taken and moved far away. As can be seen from other quatrains, Henry V will conquer all lands of the Mediterranean.

II-83 forecasts the destruction and pillage of the city of Lyons during warfare. Lyons is mentioned by name. At the same time there will be "sprinkling" through the Jura mountains and Suevia, i.e., Switzerland. The meaning is not clear. Perhaps it means air raids or poison gas. Quatrain VI-97 too tells about the burning of a great city on the 45th degree, but Lyons is almost on the 46th degree.

Entre Campaigne, Sienne, Flora, Tuscie
Six moys neufz iours ne plouura vne goutte.
L'estrange langue en terre Dalmatie
Courira sus: vastant la terre toute.   (II-84)

(Between Campania, Siena, Florence, Tuscany six months nine days without a drop of rain. The strange tongue in the Dalmatian land will spread rapidly, devastating the entire land.) At the time when foreign people will conquer Dalmatia, in Italy long drought will be reigning.

Par vie et mort changé regne d'Ongrie:
La loy sera plus aspre que seruice,
Leur grand cité d'vrlements plaincts et crie:
Castor et Pollux ennemis dans la lyce.   (II-90)

(Through life and death the realm of Hungary changed, the law will be more harsh than service. Their great city cries out with howls and laments, Castor and Pollux enemies in the arena.) The expression "life and death" can be found also in the already mentioned VIII-15 (p. 137), which too deals with events in Hungary. It may refer to the Hungarian insurrection of 1956 against communism which took place after two eclipses, i.e., after World War I and II. Castor and Pollux are the two brightest stars in the sign of Gemini (Twins), but here we don't seem to have to deal with an astronomical or astrological situation. Here it seems to indicate Austria, because Austria and Hungary (Austro-Hungary) for over 200 years (1699–1918) existed as a twin nation, although against the will of the Hungarians. These nations will become enemies. Does it really mean war between both countries? If so, what will be the reaction of America and other countries, committed to maintaining Austria's independence? If the West will give military assistance to Austria, Hungary will be aided by other people's republics with the Soviet Union at the head. Such a conflict could widen into World War III.

Bien près du Tymbre presse la Libytine,
Ung peu deuant grand inundation:
Le chef du nef prins, mis à la sentine,
Chasteau, palais en conflagration.   (II-93)

(Very near the Tiber presses Libytine shortly before great inundation. The chief of the ship taken, thrown into the bilge, castle, palace in conflagration.) Near the Tiber is Rome. Libytine is the goddess of death. The chief of the (apostle Peter's) ship is the Pope. The bilge is a part of a ship's underwater body, where smelly water collects. This word could be interpreted literally as well as figuratively. The castle could be Castle Sant Angelo in Rome, the palace—the Vatican palace. This quatrain should be classified with those which foretell the decadence of the Roman church. Is the "great inundation" the one which will take place at the time of the earth's transformation (I-17)? The Pope will be taken and (perhaps literally) thrown in a cabin of a ship and transported (to Arabia?).

The populous places will be uninhabitable,
Great division to obtain fields:

Realms delivered to prudent incapable ones,
Then for the great brothers dissension and
   death.   (II-95)

In a war of extermination the great populous cities will be
consumed by fire and laid in ruins and will become
uninhabitable. The people will be flocking to the country and
will try to obtain fields for the living. Perhaps distribution or
repartition (division) of landed property will take place. The
realms will be governed by prudent, incapable men, who will
bring their countries to ruin and distress and between
brothers there will be dissension and hate. The picture
described in the two last lines is a very familiar one. Too
many times dictators, vaingloriously fancying themselves
godlike, have thrown the world into war and disaster. Only
the things promised by the first two lines have not yet come
to pass in such a manner and to the degree as forecast by the
text.

II-96 tells about a burning torch, which will be seen in the
sky at night, near the end and beginning of the Rhône,
which begins in Switzerland and empties itself into the
Mediterranean, west of Marseilles. The prophecy therefore
indicates all the region between both points. The last line of
the quatrain states that Persia is invading Macedonia.

In II-97 Nostradamus warns the pope to beware of
approaching the city through which two rivers flow, lest he
and his (as refugees from Rome?) be met by death, when
the roses will flourish.

Third century

III-1 informs us that after combat and naval battle the great Neptune will have reached his highest position, the red adversary will become pale with fear, putting the great ocean in dread. Who is the great Neptune? Is it England or America? Rather the latter, because other quatrains proclaim the decline of England's power. Consequently, American and Asian squadrons will be engaged in an unprecedented naval battle. A similar battle has been mentioned in the Epistle to Henry II (B. 108). One of the interpreters proclaims that he, by some obscure means, has been able to calculate the day of the battle, namely, March 29, 1998.

> The divine word will give (mastery) to the substance,
> Including heaven, earth or the hidden, mystic facts.
> Body, soul, spirit having all power
> As much under its feet (i.e., on earth) as the heavenly
>   see. (III-2)

Again one of those quatrains which foretell the rise of a new religion or philosophy. It seems that it will be kindred to the philosophical movement which became fashionable in the third century and strived to combine religious fervor with philosophy, attempting to give philosophical expositions to Pagan myths and allegories as well as to the then prevalent superstititons and conceptions of Oriental origin. To attain this goal, use was made of Platonic philosophy, wherefore this movement became know as Neo-Platonism. According to the indications by Nostradamus (in this and similar quatrains) the new religion or branch of Christianity will be homogeneous with this ancient movement and will similarly exploit Oriental mythological concepts, teaching men how to look into their inner self and how to approach God through meditation and contemplation. Such tenets are in reality not new and have formed the original character of Indian and Persian religions since time immemorial. Within Christianity many famous mystics have kept them alive until this day and many religious thinkers have in these primeval sources of wisdom refreshed their dry and withered philosophical ideas.

Mars et Mercure et l'argent ioint ensemble
Vers le midy extreme siccité:
Au fond d'Asie on dira terre tremble,
Corinthe Ephese lors en perplexité.   (III-3)

(Mars and Mercury and silver joined together, toward the south extreme drought. In the depths of Asia one will say the earth trembles, Corinth, Ephesus then in perplexity.) The first line can be understood either 1) literally—Mars, Mercury and silver, i.e., the moon, are in conjunction, or 2) symbolically—Mars is the god of war and symbolizes war or military armament, Mercury is the god of eloquence, communication and commerce. They both will be joined by money or speculation. The word *midy* can be rendered either as "south" or as "half." The word *extreme* can refer either to *midy* or *siccité*, consequently, can be understood either as "extreme drought" or "extreme south." Therefore the second line could mean one of two things: "half of the world will have drought" or "drought in the extreme south" (Africa?). Earthquake in Asia can be an actual occurrence or, it can be viewed symbolically, for instance, as political convulsions, which will have such far-reaching consequences that even Corinth in Greece and Ephesus in Turkey will be pulled into the whirl of events. The naming of Corinth and Ephesus (as in II-52) is interesting. Both cities were allied against Athens during the Peloponnesian War. Lysander's general quarters were in Ephesus, but after the decisive naval battle and victory over Athens, Lysander removed to Athens, where soon the rule of the so-called "thirty tyrants" was established. Some commentators refer this quatrain to the invasion by Asiatics, when in Asian depths the earth will tremble as immense armies move toward the west. The foreign invaders will also conquer Turkey and Greece.

III-4 states that at the end of the rule by "the lunar people" coldness, drought and danger will break out up to the frontiers, even where the oracle has had its beginning. "The lunar people" are the Mohammedans, since the crescent emblem can be found in the flags of all Islamic countries.

Within the closed temple the lightning will enter,
The citizens within their fort burdened:
Horses, cattle, men, the wave will touch the wall,
Through famine, thirst, under the weakest armed. (III-6)

Even the churches will suffer from warfare. Cities will be transformed into forts, where citizens will have to defend themselves against aggressors. The wave of war will cause men and animals to suffer from famine and thirst, and even the weakest will be called to take up arms.

The fugitives, fire from the sky on the pikes,
Conflict near, the ravens frolicking.
From land they cry for aid and help from heaven,
When the combatants will be near the walls. (III-7)

The fugitives will be more harmed by air raids than by bayonets; thousands of them will be massacred, when they, expelled from their country, will seek shelter in foreign cities. The ravens, the modern airplanes, will fight against one another in the air. On earth the misery through the horrors of war will become so great that people who did not want to know or hear about God anymore, will again cry for help from heaven, when the enemies will carry the war into their cities, sparing nobody.

Par les contrées du grand fleuue Bethique
Loing d'Ibere, au royaume de Grenade,
Croix respoussées par gens Mahometiques
Vn de Cordube trahira la contrade.   (III-20)

(Through the regions of the great Baetic River, deep in Iberia to the kingdom of Grenada, crosses beaten back by the Mahometan peoples. One of Cordova will betray his country.) This quatrain can be solved very easily and distinctly. It gives an account of treachery and hard fighting in Spain during the Mohammedan invasion. The great River Guadalquivir (in Spain) was by the Romans called *Baetis*. The ancient tribe of Iberians has given the name of Iberia to the whole Pyrenean peninsula. Consequently, in Andalusia, where all the mentioned places can be found, the Arabs, aided also by treachery, will completely vanquish the Christians.

> In the Crustamin by the Adriatic sea
> There will appear a horrible fish
> With human face and its end aquatic,
> Which cannot be taken with a hook.   (III-21)

Crustamin or Crustumius, now called Conca, is a river in central Italy. Most probably, this is an image of the submarine, since Nostradamus in his visions has perceived all modern weapons that have been employed in both world wars and will be used in future wars: tanks, submarines, airplanes, hydroplanes, radio and atomic bombs.

> Six days the assault made before the city,
> Battle will be given strong and harsh.
> Three will surrender it and to them pardon,
> The rest to fire and to bloody mincing, cutting. (III-22)

In a future war the siege of a great city will last only for six days. If Paris has been meant, then, as can be seen from another quatrain, it will be within a short time so greatly devastated that no men will be able to live between the Seine and the Marne for a long period due to the radiation from atomic bombs.

In III-23 Nostradamus warns France to be on its guard against a ruse by Italy, which could cause France to fall into a Mohammedan trap. It seems that this quatrain is connected with III-87.

III-27 tells that after the Arabs will have conquered the west, great interest in everything Arabian will arise in France. French scientists and writers will make translations of Arabian books into French; consequently, a wide cultural exchange will take place.

> The two nephews brought up in diverse places,
> Naval battle, land, fathers fallen:
> They will come to be elevated so high in making war,
> To avenge the injury, enemies succumbed.   (III-29)

A German interpreter offers this commentary: France will again have kings. After the great Henry V two nephews, brought up in diverse places, will have so great a success in naval battles and air attacks against England that the enemy will have to capitulate unconditionally. Thus France in a merciless campaign will have subdued England and avenged the injury, namely, the levelling to the ground of Paris during a previous war.

> Aux champs de Mede, d'Arabe et d'Armenie
> Deux grands copies trois foys s'assembleront:
> Près du rivage d'Araxes la mesnie,
> Du grand Soliman en terre tomberont.   (III-31)

(On the fields of Media, of Arabia and of Armenia two great armies will assemble thrice. The host near the bank of Araxes, of the great Suleiman will fall to earth [or fall in the land].) Great armies will march on the fields of Media (Persia), Arabia and Armenia. Consequently, we are here told about the triumphal progress of Asiatic armies along the Araxes River. This river forms the borderline between Persia and the Caucasus, which is part of Russia. Araxes empties itself into the Caspian Sea, but begins in Turkey. The Turkish name of the river is *Aras*. The last line of the quatrain is abstruse. Perhaps the name of Suleiman has been given to the commander-in-chief of the Asiatic armies, who in this case could be identical with the one mentioned in V-54. But in the days of Nostradamus the ruler of Turkey was Sultan Suleiman, also called "the great Suleiman." Consequently, Nostradamus may have had the intention to indicate that the Asiatic armies along the Araxes River will invade the land of

Suleiman, that is to say, Turkey. In such a way the Arabian assault on the whole Mediterranean territory will have been initiated.

> Le grand sepulcre du peuple Aquitanique
> S'approchera auprès de la Toscane,
> Quand Mars sera près du coing Germanique
> Et au terroir de la gent Mantuane.   (III-32)

(The great tomb of the people of Aquitaine will approach near to Tuscany, when Mars will be at the corner of Germany and in the land of the Mantuan people.) Aquitaine, a region of ancient Gaul, corresponds approximately to the present valley of Garonne and its environment (the southwestern part of France). Hence, when the French army (or navy) will be nearing Tuscany or the Gulf of Genova, it will meet with a total defeat. This quatrain may have some connection with III-23 and III-87. At the same time military actions will take place also at the corner of Germany (Hungary or Austria?) and in the region of Mantua (northern Italy).

> The child will be born with two teeth in his mouth,
> Stones will fall in Tuscany like the rain:
> A few years after there will be neither wheat, nor barley,
> To satiate those who will be weak from hunger. (III-42)

The first line is a hard nut to crack. Some interpreters are of the opinion that the expression "child will be born with two teeth in his mouth" indicates a ruler with innate propensity for contention and bellicosity. During his reign Italy will be drawn into a severe war. In air attacks bombs will be showered on the beautiful land of Tuscany with its capital city of Florence. The land will become so devastated that for several years there will be no gathering of crops, grain will be scarce, and people will die from hunger. As can be seen also from other quatrains, in future wars such destructive weapons will be used that in regions overrun by war, fields and even trees will not be fruit bearing.

Gens d'alentour de Tarn, Loth et Garonne,
Gardez les monts Apennines passer:
Vostre tombeau près de Rome et d'Anconne,
Le noir poil crespe fera trophée dresse.   (III-43)

(People from around the Tarn, Lot and Garonne, beware of passing the Appenine mountains: your tomb near Rome and Ancona, the black frizzled beard will have a trophy set up.) The French will have to pass through hard battles in Italian territory (near Ancona and Rome). But there is no certainty about who will be the enemy. Will it be the Italians themselves? The last line suggests that it could be Arabs, Asiatics or Africans, consequently, that the battles will be fought with Mohammedans. But will it happen at the time of Mohammedan onslaught or at the end of the period of occupation, when Mohammedans again will be gradually thrown out of Europe?

Throughout all Asia great outlawry,
Even in Mysia, Lycia and Pamphilia.
Blood will be shed because of the absolution
Of a young king filled with felony.   (III-60)

In the original text the word *noir* "black" has been used as an anagram for *roi*, "king." This anagram recurs in many quatrains, and the interpretation is indubitably correct. Mysia, Lycia and Pamphilia are Roman names for three provinces of Asia Minor which today are part of Turkey. A young king will throw all Asia (or only Turkey?) into lawlessness. People will not be protected by law anymore and deeds of blood will remain unpunished.

III-61 is a quatrain with a very vague meaning because of the hard problem imposed by the French term *secte crucigère*. E. Ruir refers it to the Jewish nation because "they made Christ bear the cross." His rendering: The Jews, again resettled in Judea and Palestine, will prepare to combat Arab partisans, who will be arrayed in Mesopotamia. The Arabs will consider Palestine as their own land and will strive to expel Jews from it. The expression *armée crucigère* can be found also in IX-43, which deals with the same subject.

Near the Duero, because of the closed Cyrene sea,
He will pierce the great Pyrenees mountains.
With the hand shorter and his penetrating speech
He will lead his throng to Carcassonne.   (III-62)

H. Bauder, explaining that the hand is shorter when the fist is clenched, comments on this quatrain as follows: Henry V, king of France, will invade Spain over the Pyrenean mountains because the way over the Mediterranean sea will be closed, due to strong Italian naval forces. The ancient fort of Carcassonne, even today surrounded by medieval ramparts, will become one of the main encampments during this French-Spanish war. So far H. Bauder. Well, but what prevents us from assuming that an army (Spanish or Oriental) will be led in the opposite direction from Douro over the Pyrenean mountains toward Carcassonne?

From III-65 we learn that on the day after the sepulchre of the great Roman is found a Pontiff will be elected, but he will not be approved by the Senate and will be poisoned with the sacred chalice.

The great army, led by a young man
Will surrender itself into the hands of the enemies,
But the old man, born to the half pig,
Will cause Châlon and Mâcon to be friends.   (III-69)

The first two lines need no explanation. It seems that the French army has been meant, since the cities, named in the last line, are in France. After the lost battle an old man, offspring of a person with the traits of a pig, will again restore friendship among the quarreling Frenchmen. Nostradamus may even have hinted that France will have split into two parts, with civil war raging between them. The borderline will evidently run between Macon and Chalon on the Saone.

III-71 reports that the inhabitants of England, who for a long time had not undergone a siege, will now themselves experience what they had done to their enemies. Those on the outside will die from hunger, but the English also will suffer a greater famine than ever before.

III-82 relates that the Mediterranean coast around Nice will suffer from the attack by locusts (airplanes) and will be thoroughly devastated by sea and by land, the wind being propitious (perhaps naval squadrons are meant, hidden in clouds of artificial smoke).

The great city will be thoroughly desolated,
Of the inhabitants not a single one will remain there:
Walls, sex, temples and virgins violated,
Through sword, fire, plague and cannon people will
    die.   (III-84)

Many interpreters agree that the great city is Paris, which in the next world war will be demolished to such a degree that nobody will be able to continue to live there. The weapons of destruction will not leave even stone upon a stone. For a considerable time Paris will not exist, but years later Paris, called *Lutetia*, "the luminous city," by the Romans, will again be rebuilt, more beautiful and radiant than ever. Who will be the devastators of Paris is not revealed by the quatrain, but some commentators are of the opinion that it will be the ancient rivals of the French, namely, the English, and that this war will take place at the beginning of the 21st century.

III-85 makes known that a handsome youth will through deceit take a city near the river Robine (in the region of Narbonne-Perpignan). Evidently, here it is the matter of an insurrection or even revolution.

In III-87 Nostradamus warns the French navy not to approach Corsica or Sardinia or it will have to rue it, since no help from the cape (Italy?) will arrive, and the result will be blood and captivity (cf. III-23).

III-88 foretells that from Barcelona a very great army will be transported by sea, and all Marseilles will tremble with terror. The isles will be seized, and all help from the sea will be shut off.

Le monde proche du dernier periode,
Saturne encore tard sera de retour.
Translat empire deuers nation Brodde,
L'oeil arraché à Narbon par Autour.   (III-92)

(The world near the last period, Saturn will come back again late. Empire transferred toward the Brodde nation, the eye plucked out of Narbonne by the goshawk.) This is a very significant quatrain, since it mentions "the last period" and the Saturn cycle (cf. I-25, I-48, I-56). *Brodde* is a word which even the many French interpreters have not been able to solve. The author, as on so many other similar occasions looking for a rhyme, has deviated from the original spelling or ending of the intended word. Brodde could be an abbreviation of *brodequin,* "boot," or it could be Old French *brode,* "dark." In any case, when the world will be nearing the last period, i.e., the millennium, the empire and the guidance of the world (or at least, of Europe) will be transferred to the "dark" nation or to the "nation of boots." Germans often have been referred to as "the nation of boots" i.e., of soldiers. In other quatrains too it has been implied that during the millenium the Germans will have become the leading nation. The last line remains incomprehensible. Narbonne is a town in southern France. Is this line a drastic attempt to depict the envy of Frenchmen for the Germans? It remains for us only to ascertain the beginning of the millennium. Le Pelletier assigns to each planet a period of 354 years. One of the moon periods supposedly began in the year 1533, a sun period in 1887 and a Saturn period will again begin in 2241. But such a calculation does not correspond with other indications, given by Nostradamus. In his letter to Caesar he asserts that his prophecies reach to the year 3797.

Accordingly, the millennium should begin around 2797. It seems very likely that Nostradamus, whose chronology spans 8000 years, has ascribed about a 1000 year-long period of influence or regency to each of the seven (then known) luminaries. The cycle was begun by Saturn, who will again return at the very end, "late." H. Bauder has for this quatrain an interesting solution: The last period of the world will be enacted before the dawn of the millenium. Once more the earth will be plunged into misery by national hatreds and jealousies. Terroristic attacks with destructive weapons will reduce Paris and other centers to rubbish and ashes. The government will therefore be compelled to transfer its seat into the mountainous region of Embrun. The word *Brodde* indicates the "Brodontians," a tribe which lived in the Alps. The name of this tribe has been given also to the town Embrun, called *Ebrodanum* by the Romans. This town has had a historical role to play already more than once, because former kings of France used to visit it on pilgrimage. During the last (fifth) world war, shortly before the happy times of the millennium, the world will once more be laid in ruins, and the government of France will find security only in the Alps. Narbonne, where Nostradamus once was working as physician, will also be badly ravaged during this war. The eye will be plucked out of Narbonne by a goshawk, in other words, the town will be damaged by air raids.

In III-93 we are distinctly told that the chief of the whole empire on the way to desolated Paris, will make a stop in Avignon (cf. I-32). Since Nostradamus speaks of an empire, it is possible that the period is meant when (in the opinion of many French commentators) the king of France will unite in his person three crowns and will reign not only over France, but over Italy and Spain as well and will expand the borders of France to the Rhine and the city of Cologne (cf. VI-4).

Nouuelle loy terre neufue occuper
Vers la Syrie, Iudée et Palestine:

Le grand empire barbare corruer,

Auant que Phebés son siecle determine.   (III-97)

(New law to occupy new land toward Syria, Judea and Palestine. The great barbarian empire to decay, before the Phebes completes its cycle.) Again one of those quatrains which mentions planetary cycles. Unfortunately, the solution is rendered considerably more difficult by the word *Phebes*, since we cannot be sure of its masculine or feminine gender. Phoebe (the bright or shining one) is in Greek mythology a name given to Artemis as a moon goddess. Poetically this word can mean the moon itself. The masculine form of the same word Phoebus (in Greek *Phoibos*) is one of the names used for Apollo and poetically can mean the sun. Now, does this quatrain speak about the cycle of the sun or of the moon? It is very important to find out, because Nostradamus here very clearly forecasts the decay of the great barbarian (Mohammedan) empire before the end of the cycle of "Phebes." And how long is the cycle assigned to each luminary? Even that still remains a mystery. We know only that in his letter to Caesar (A. 39) Nostradamus speaks about a certain chronology, according to which the period of Nostradamus' own lifetime (the middle of the 16th century) was ruled or "led by the Moon." According to the theory of Le Pelletier, the cycle of the moon ended already in 1887 and the cycle of the Sun will end at about the year 2241. Such a chronology, however, seems to be in contradistinction with some other indications by Nostradamus (cf. I-25, I-48, I-56, III-92).

Two royal brothers will wage war so fiercely

That between them the war will be so mortal

That both will occupy the strong places:

Their great quarrel will be of realm and life.   (III-98)

The prevalent rendering of this quatrain is that after the happy reign of Henry V, when France will have become the most powerful country of Europe, supposedly in the 21st century, the quarrel of two royal brothers will arise. This fratricidal war will cause the division of all France into two hostile military camps.

Fourth century

The chief of the army amid pressing crowd
Will be wounded by an arrow shot in the thighs,
When Geneva in tears and distress
Will be betrayed by Lausanne and the Swiss.   (IV-9)

In Switzerland too discord will arise when France, after becoming powerful, will again lay claim to Geneva. After France by the successful campaigns of the great King Henry V will have gained supremacy in Europe, Geneva will again be joined to France. History repeats itself. A situation will accrue for the Genevese analogous to that of the times of Napoleon. It will come to military actions, during which the chief of the army will be wounded in the thighs. Lausanne and the rest of the Swiss will yield before the superior power of France and will renounce Geneva.

IV-16 tells about a free city (or a free country) which will become "servile to liberty and asylum of profligates and dreamers." Some interpreters have seen the United States indicated here.

The legion in the navy,
Calcine, Magnes will burn sulfur and pitch:
The long rest of the secure place,
Port Selyn, Hercle, fire will consume them.   (IV-23)

"Port Selyn" is "port of the moon," consequently, one of the Turkish or Arab seaports. In this case, it must be Constantinople (Stamboul), because in its vicinity we also find a village named Heraclion. The great Turkish port, which had enjoyed security and peace for a long time, will suddenly be overrun by war and will be consumed by fire when a mighty fleet will bring troops to the Greek and Turkish islands. Chalcis, i.e., Chalkis, the capital of the Greek island Euboa, will be burned in sulfur and pitch. Magnes cannot be found on any maps. Perhaps Maina in southern Greece (Morea) has been meant? The ancient Magnesia, now called Manisa, is near Smyrna (in Turkey). From another quatrain we learn that Russia or some other eastern country will begin military actions against Turkey and will destroy Constantinople. It is well known that Russia has always shown interest in possessing the Dardanelles.

Quy soubs terre saincte Dame, voix fainte,
Humaine flamme pour diuine voyr luire,
Fera des seuls de leur sang terre tainte
Et les saincts temples pour les impurs destruire.   (IV-24)

(Beneath the earth holy lady, faint voice, human flame seen to shine as divine. It will cause the earth to be stained with the blood of the lonely ones and to destroy the holy temples for the impure ones.) Hard to comprehend, this quatrain, like IV-43, V-77 and V-96, is often referred to the Catholic Church and its struggle with and bloody repression of the future new religion or Neo-Christian sect. In such a case "the holy lady" can signify the Roman Catholic Church, in whose eyes the adherents of the new religion are unclean and their message false. Seeing the flame of the new religion shining and burning as divine, the Catholic Church tries to quench and to extinguish it, if not with other means, then with bloodshed (cf. also VI-66).

Corps sublimes sans fin à l'oeil visibles
Obnubiler viendront par ses raisons:
Corps, front comprins, sens, chief et inuisibles,
Diminuant les sacrés oraisons.   (IV-25)

(Lofty bodies endlessly visible to the eye: through these reasons they will obscure body, forehead included, sense, head and invisibles, diminishing the sacred prayers.) The new optical inventions will bring forth instruments so sharp that they will make visible to the eye those celestial bodies, which previously remained invisible to the unaided eye. This is a significant prediction, because in Nostradamus' time telescopes did not yet exist. The telescope was invented in 1610. Notions and ideas which by simple-minded Christians were accepted as facts will through this new knowledge be seen in a new light, and many believers will become confused and their faith will be shaken (their prayers will be diminished). Scientific discoveries and inventions, telescopes, microscopes, moving pictures and television have reduced the attendance at religious services, although a better knowlege of the miraculous material world should rather have strengthened the belief in the Creator of all these wonders.

> Salon, Mansol, Tarascon de Sex. l'arc,
> Où est debout encore la piramide,
> Viendront liurer le prince Dannemarc
> Rachat honni au temple d'Artemide.   (IV-27)

(Salon, Mansol, Tarascon, the arch of Sex., where the pyramid is still standing: they will come to deliver the prince of Denmark, redemption reviled in the temple of Artemis.) A quatrain hard to solve. The first line contains names of localities in the vicinity of Nostradamus' domicile: in Salon he spent the last years of his life, and Tarascon is only 10 miles north of Arles. *De Sex.* is probably identical with *Aquae sextiae*, as the Romans called the present Aix, now a health resort. Instead of *Mansol* we have to read "Mausol" (cf. VIII-34, IX-85); it indicates a mausoleum in the same vicinity or in Valence (as in VIII-46), but even Valence or Rhone is not far from the mentioned localities. Temples of Artemis, i.e., Diana, and their ruins can be found also in southern France, but with Artemis Nostradamus perhaps meant Artemisia, the queen of Halicarnassus who ordered a great, superb monument to be built over the tomb of her late husband Mausol. This structure, the so-called Mausoleum, became one of the seven wonders of the world. So far, so good. But what has all this to do with the prince of Denmark? Will a prince or a king of Denmark come to visit southern France, and will he there be delivered, captured, reviled, or perhaps even put to death, since the reference to a mausoleum may be an indication of a burial? And how to explain the second line? It is true that some mausoleums have been built in the form of a pyramid, and such mausoleums, no doubt, can be found also in southern France. Nevertheless, some interpreters persist in the following solution: At the time when the Asiatic invasion will have reached the Nile delta (the arch where pyramids are still standing), a Danish prince or king will visit southern France and will there be apprehended or even put to death. Only the future events themselves will disclose the connection between the diverse elements of this quatrain.

> The great one led captive of foreign land,
> Chained in gold offered to King Chyren:
> He who in Ausonia, Milan will lose the war,
> And all his army put to fire and sword.   (IV-34)

Chyren is an anagram for "Henry V," the future king of France who will overrun Italy (Ausonia) with his armed forces and capture the king of Italy. King Henry then will be offered ransom, but he nevertheless will cause the captured king to be brought to a place of exile in a foreign land. Upper Italy will become the seat of war and Milan the central point of the decisive battles. The Italian army will suffer a crushing defeat and will be completely wiped out by fire and sword.

> The Rhodians will demand relief
> Through the neglect of its heirs abandoned.
> The Arab empire will reveal its course,
> The cause set right again by Hesperia.   (IV-39)

The island Rhodos, which Turkey had to cede to Italy in 1911, will be neglected by its owners and greatly harassed by the might of the ascending Arab empire and will finally be conquered by the Mohammedans. Later the western powers or America (Hesperia) will intervene in the struggle and retake Rhodos from the Arabs, restoring the previous balance of power in the Mediterranean.

> The fortresses of the besieged shut up,
> Through gunpowder sunk into the abyss:

The traitors will all be buried alive,

Never did such a pitiful schism happen to the sextons.(IV-40)

In the future no fortifications will be able to offer a reliable protection against air raids, because the perforating effect of the new bombs will be enhanced to such a degree that at the explosion everything will be pulled into the abyss and the defendants buried alive.

Female sex captive as hostage

Will come by night to deceive the guards:

The chief of the camp deceived by their language

Will abandon them to the people, it will be pitiful to
see. (IV-41)

In the modern war even women will be called to participate in the defense of the country. To escape captivity, feminine cunning will be employed to deceive the guards, causing great disgrace to the officers.

Libra verra regner les Hesperies,

De ciel, et terre tenir la monarchie:

D'Asie forces nul ne verra peries

Que sept ne tiennent par sang la hierarchie.   (IV-50)

(Libra will see the Hesperias govern, holding the monarchy of heaven and earth. No one will see the forces of Asia perished, as long the seven will hold the hierarchy in order.) The first two lines foretell that the United States of America (Hesperia) will hold the monarchy on land and in the air. America will finally liberate Europe, but the forces of Asia will not be defeated "as long as the seven hold the hierarchy." Who are these seven? There is no consensus of opinion about it. Some researchers of Nostradamus' texts tend to discern in these seven the last seven heirs to Peter's see, i.e., the last seven popes, but with as good a reason some Islamic hierarchy could have been meant. The first line mentions the sign of Libra. In medieval astrology planet Venus in Libra or Taurus was dominant over Persia, Bactria and other regions east of the Caspian Sea.

The year when Saturn and Mars will be equally combust,
The air very parched, long meteor.
Through secret fires a great place scorched from heat,
Little rain, hot wind, wars, incursions.   (IV-67)

Both Saturn and Mars in traditional astrology are considered to be dangerously malicious. Saturn is often called the "great infortune." He is the harbinger of the inexorable fate and symbolizes delay, hindrance, repression, poverty, disgrace and imprisonment. He is the counterpart to the great luminaries, the sun and the moon. Mars, being the god of war, promulgates military actions and strife. He is characterized by his propelling force, passion, destructiveness, bellicosity and rashness. When Mars and Saturn will combine their malignant power to influence the history of the world, great natural catastrophes will occur, with subsequent periods of drought and aridity, with wars and invasions. Astrologically, a planet is called combust if it is in conjunction with the sun. Consequently, here we have to deal with a conjunction of Saturn and Mars with the sun. Saturn meets Mars once in every two years, but occasions when they, being in conjunction, are joined also by the sun are extremely rare, yet, one such occasion will arrive in March, 1996.

Selin monarch Italy peaceful,
Realms united by the Christian king of the world:
Dying he will want to lie in Blois soil,
After having chased the pirates from the sea.   (IV-77)

Henry V, the coming great king of France, after successful campaigns against Italy and Turkey or other "moon countries," i.e., Islamic countries (Selene is "the moon"), will unite many realms. On his deathbed he will utter the wish to be buried in the soil of Blois, the ancient French royal residence. Less clear is the last line of the quatrain, since we don't know what has been meant by the word "pirates." Perhaps, Nostradamus meant the Islamic fleet, but he may also have meant the English, because he hates them and often calls them by contemptuous names. From other quatrains we know that France will again have a military conflict with England. Therefore several interpreters are of the opinion that Nostradamus has here foretold Henry V's vengeance upon the English for the devastation of Paris (cf. III-84).

L'an que Saturne en eau sera conioint
Avecques Sol le Roi fort et puissant
A Reims et Aix sera receu et oinct,
Aprés conquestes meurtrira innocent.   (IV-86)

(The year when Saturn will be conjoined in water with the Sun, the strong and powerful king will be received and anointed at Reims and Aix. After conquests the innocent will be murdered.) Here it is clearly announced that the great French king will be crowned at Reims and at Aix in the year when Saturn will be conjoined with the Sun "in water." Unfortunately, we are not told in which of the signs of water (Pisces, Cancer or Scorpio) the conjunction will occur. Therefore during this century it could happen either in 1983/85 (Scorpio) or 1994/96 (Pisces). It is interesting to note that Reims is the traditional coronation site for French kings but Aix (Aachen) for emperors. After the death of King Henry V the world will again be engulfed by anarchy.

The Gallic duke compelled to fight in a duel,
The ship Mellela, Monaco will not approach,
Wrongly accused, perpetual prison,
His son will strive to reign before his death.   (IV-91)

A French ruler will, against his own wishes, be compelled to enter into a campaign and will suffer great defeat in the Mediterranean sea. The French navy will have no success either at Mellela nor at the Ligurian coast (Monaco). Mellela cannot be found on any maps. Has the island Malta been meant or, perhaps, Melilla, a Moroccan seaport? The defeat will cost the leader of the army the throne and untruthful reports will cause his imprisonment for life. His son, entangled in the intrigue, will try to snatch the throne for himself, while his father will still be living.

> The head of the valiant captain, cut off,
> Will be thrown before his adversary:
> His body hung on the sail yard of the ship,
> Confused he will flee by oars against the wind.   (IV-92)

After the cut-off head of the admiral will be thrown at the feet of his adversary, his body will be hung on the mast of his ship, but the murderer, perceiving that his deed meets with opposition, will have to flee in a rowboat, possibly together with other conspirators.

> The valiant elder son of the king's daughter
> Will hurl back the Celts so far,
> That he will cast thunderbolts, so many in such an array,
> Near and far, then deep of the Hesperias.   (IV-99)

It seems that Hesperias (lands of the west) here means Spain and Portugal, which countries King Henry V will have brought under his sway. But France will later lose sovereignty over her southern neighbors. A young Spanish king, after a fierce but successful battle, will drive the Frenchmen gradually back, and finally will expel them far over the frontiers of Spain. From other quatrains we learn that Spain will again be led by kings and will experience a happy future.

> Du feu celeste au Royal edifice
> Quand la lumière de Mars defaillira,
> Sept mois grand guerre, mort gent de malefice
> Rouen, Eureux au Roy ne faillira.   (IV-100)

(From the celestial fire on the Royal edifice, when the light of Mars will go out, seven months great war, dead the people of malignity, Rouen, Evreux will not fail the king.) From this quatrain we understand that after seven months of war a foreign, malignant nation will be subdued. Does this quatrain tell of the period when Mohammedans again will be expelled from France? Rouen and Evreux are both in Normandy (northern France).

Fifth century

Before the coming of Celtic ruin,
In the temple two will parley.
Dagger and pike to the heart of one mounted on the steed.
They will bury the great one without making noise.   (V-1)

A new (the fourth?) world war will be preceded by the assassination of an officer of high military rank. It will happen during negotiations in a holy place. The great one will be buried silently, in order to avoid the creation of a great stir, but the assassination will be followed by a war which will lead to the collapse of France.

The sea will not be passed over safely by those of the Sun,
Those of Venus will hold all Africa,
Saturn will no longer occupy their realm,
And the Asiatic part will change.   (V-11)

"Those of the Sun" are the Christians. "The people of Venus" are Mohammedans, or in a more restricted, typical sense, the Arabs. The Africans and Asiatics will some day turn into action everything they have in two world wars learned from the Christians. Under the leadership of the Arabs and of other Islamic nations, Africans will drive out all Europeans from their continent and will even make the sea unsafe for Christians. Similarly to Africa, where the battle cry "Africa for Africans" will be heard, in the countries of the Far East "Asia for Asiatics" will resound.

Saturne et Mars en Leo Espagne captiue,
Par chef Lybique au conflict attrapé:
Proche de Malte, Heredde prinse uiue,
Et Romain sceptre sera par Coq frappé.   (V-14)

(Saturn and Mars in Leo, Spain captive, by the Libyan chief trapped in the conflict, near Malte Heredde taken alive, and the Roman sceptre will be struck down by the cock.) Saturn and Mars simultaneously in Leo can be found in about every 30 years. The next time will be between 1975 and 1978, then again in the first decade of the 21st century. According to the experience of astrologers, this position portends a great activity of diplomats and statesmen. These are always dangerous times, but the danger can be alleviated by the aspects of other planets. In such a case the danger will make itself conspicuous only by unrest and insurrection in isolated countries instead of open warfare. The only incomprehensible word in this quatrain is *Heredde*. Does it denote a person or a place? It cannot be found on maps. Le Pelletier considers it to be an anagram for Rhodes. Or is it Hiera, one of the Spanish Canary Islands? The quatrain undoubtedly pertains to the period of Mohammedan invasion, since the first line reports that Spain has been brought under Libyan dominion. The Mohammedans, as the rulers of all North Africa, then will have extended their sphere of influence over Spain. At that time, Malta and Hiera also will change hands, and Italy will be conquered by Frenchmen, because "Cock" represents either the French republic or a ruler of the family of Orléans. Gustafsson's calculations have resulted in the determination of a certain date: year 2096.

> En navigant captif prins grand pontife
> Grand après faillir les clercs tumultuez:
> Second asleu absent son bien debiffe.
> Son favory bastard à mort tué.   (V-15)

(The great pontiff taken captive while navigating, the great one thereafter to fail clergy in tumult, second one elected absent, his estate declines, his favorite bastard slain to death.) The pope will be captured on the sea (by the Arabs?). After release he will return to Rome and will remove many clergymen from their posts. His surrogate successor (anti-pope), who had been elected during his absence, will flee, but his favorite will be put to death.

> The realm and law raised under Venus.
> Saturn will have dominion over Jupiter.

The law and realm raised by the Sun,

Through those of Saturn will suffer the worst.   (V-24)

Arabs are a people under the protection of Venus. They will get the upper hand over the Christians (those of the Sun). Then Jupiter, the planet of benevolence, will have less influence than Saturn, one of the malefic planets. Nostradamus here evidently wants to make apparent that there will be a certain period when Christianity, under the influence of Saturn, will be supplanted by a different conception of life (Islam or even paganism).

Le prince Arabe, Mars, Sol, Venus, Lyon,

Regne d'Eglise par mer succombera:

Deuers la Perse bien près d'vn million,

Bisance, Egypte ver. serp. inuadera.   (V-25)

(The Arab prince, Mars, Sun, Venus, Lion, the rule of the church will succomb by sea. Toward Persia very nearly a million men, ver. serp. will invade Byzantium, Egypt.) *Ver. serp.* could be an abbreviation of *vera serpens* "true serpent" or *serpent de verre* "serpent of glass." The quatrain otherwise is easily understandable. An Arab ruler (cf. III-31, perhaps also V-54), coming from the direction of Persia, will invade Asia Minor (Byzantium) and Egypt. The invasion army has been likened to a serpent coiling round the Meditteranean. The invasion will happen when Mars, the sun and Venus simultaneously will be joined in the sign of Leo (Lion). The sun is in Leo every year between July 23 and August 23, but occasions when both other planets are joining the sun, moreover both at the same time, are much more rare, but still far too frequent to give us a chance to calculate the point of time with any precision. Only Gustafsson has no doubts: it will happen in 2081, although similar configurations occur also earlier, for instance in August, 1987.

La gent esclave par vn heur Martial

Viendra en haut degré tant eslevée,

Changeront Prince, naistra vn Provincial,
Passer la mer copie aux monts levée.   (V-26)

(The Slavic people through luck in war will become elevated to a very high degree. They will change their Prince, one born a provincial, an army will pass over the sea, on mountains lifted.) This prophecy has found many different solutions, with reference to past events, which would make it already accomplished. The third line about the overthrown ruler could be applied to Czar Nicholas, who was dethroned in 1917 and on July 16, 1918, executed, and to the new Russian ruler Stalin, who was born a provincial and in another of Nostradamus' quatrains has been called the ruler of Armenia, i.e., Georgia. But at that time no army was passing over the sea, either toward the mountains or from them. The quatrain does not specify the army as Russian; therefore, some commentators have applied it to the English and French when they, during the Crimean War (1854–1856), crossed the Black Sea and disembarked on the mountainous Crimean peninsula. But then no changes of rulers occurred. There remains only the possibility that this quatrain refers to a future event, perhaps to the combined French and Russian assault on Sweden and Norway, prophesied by the Norwegian clairvoyant, Anton Johanson. His visions are related in the last part of this book.

Par feu et armes non loing de la marnegro
Viendra de Perse occuper Trebisonde,
Trembler Pharos, Methelin, Sol alegro,
De sang Arabe d'Adrio couuert onde.   (V-27)

(Through fire and arms not far from the Black Sea he will come from Persia to occupy Trebizond. Pharos, Mytilene to tremble, Sol alegro, the Adriatic Sea covered with Arab blood.) From Persia a powerful army will come and conquer Trebizond, a Turkish seaport on the Black Sea. The military expedition will extend farther over the Dardanelles to the

Aegean Sea and the Turkish and Greek islands. Mytilene, capital city of the Greek island Lesbos will fall, and so will Pharos, an Egyptian island near Alexandria, where once the famous lighthouse of Alexandria was built, one of the seven wonders of the world. The struggle between Persians, Turks, Greeks and Arabs will expand also into the Adriatic Sea. The general meaning of the quatrain is clear enough. Only the meaning of the expression *sol alegro* remains to be solved. Here again Nostradamus has changed the ending of a word to obtain an artificially created rhyme. Literally translated, the Latin word *sol* means "the sun," and the Italian word *allegro* means "joyful." In astrological geography the sun rules over Italy, and the expression "joyful sun" could mean that Italy will be able to repel the first Arab assaults coming from the direction of the Balkans and to inflict bloody losses to the Arabs on the Adriatic Sea. But we must not forget that *sol alegro* could represent the name or names of still other localities. One such possibility is *Sola + Leros*. In such a case the letter g would have been inserted only for the sake of a rhyme. Sola is a town on the beautiful island of Cyprus, and Leros is one of the Greek islands near the Turkish coast.

In V-28 we are told that three conspirators will plot against the life of "the great one of Genova." VI-76 reports on a similar matter. It seems that here we have to deal with a revolutionary period in Italy.

... La gent Lombarde fera si grand effroy

A ceux de l'Aigle comprins sous la Balance.   (V-42)

(The Lombard people will cause very great terror to those of the Eagle, included under the Balance.) These two lines are here quoted to show another instance of "the eagle" being mentioned. Lombardy is in northern Italy, but "the eagle" is the symbol of an empire. For this reason many commentators apply this and similar quatrains to Great Britain, but we should not disregard the possibility that it could be a reference to a future French emperor or even a member of the Bonaparte family. Significantly, VIII-9 mentions not only "the eagle," but also "the cock," which is a symbol of the French republic or of the family of Orléans.

La grande ruine des sacrez ne s'esloigne,
Prouence, Naples, Sicille, Seez et Ponce:
En Germanie, au Rhin et la Cologne,
Vexez à mort par tous ceux de Magonce.   (V-43)

(The great ruin of the holy ones is not far off, Provence, Naples, Sicily, Seez and Ponce. In Germany, at the Rhine and Cologne, vexed to death by all those of Magonce.) Here are included very wide regions: Provence (southern France), Naples (southern Italy) and Sicily, the valley of Rhine with Cologne (Germany). But where are Seez, Ponce and Magonce located? With Seez perhaps the town Sées (in northern France) or the river Sesia, a tributary of Po (in northern Italy) have been meant. Ponce could be either Pons (in western France) or the island Ponza in the Tyrrhenian Sea. Magonce could be the town Mayence on the Rhine. This quatrain reports that in a wide region, including all Italy, France and part of Germany west of the Rhine, persecutions of the holy ones (the clergy) are taking place. It seems the Rhine is forming something like a line of defense, since no persecution occurs east of it. One more possibility should be mentioned: Magonce could be the famous Carthaginian General Mago (or Magon), brother of Hannibal. Considering the fact that in several of Nostradamus' quatrains the Punians (Carthaginians) represent Africans, i.e., Mohammedans, and their attacks from the direction of Africa, such a rendering classifies this quatrain with those which deal with the Mohammedan invasion. In such a case this quatrain relates that during the occupation a great persecution of Christian clergy will take place and that the Germans will successfully defend themselves along the Rhine against the enemy's attacks from the direction of France.

The great empire will soon be desolated

And transferred to near the Ardennes forest.

The two bastards by the oldest one beheaded,

And Bronzebeard the hawk-nose will reign.   (V-45)

France, having become an empire under the reign of, and due to the successful campaigns of Henry V, will be in short time desolated during the next, i.e., the Fourth World War. After the (second) destruction of Paris the government will be transferred to the Ardennes forest. Two bastards will contend for the throne. The oldest one will be removed by decapitation, and a bronzebeard with hawk-nose will seize the reigns of government.

V-46 tells about quarrels and schisms among cardinals, arising on account of a pope (or anti-pope?) from the region of Sabine.

The great Arab will march far forward,

He will be betrayed by the Byzantines:

Ancient Rhodes will come to meet him,

And greater harm through other Pannonians.   (V-47)

First rendering: Since the great Arab will be betrayed by the Byzantines, i.e., the Turks, it denotes the fact that the Turks will be on the side of the Greeks and will conjointly with them defend Europe against the Asiatic assaults. In some way the island of Rhodes will play a fatal role. In Nostradamus' lifetime the invincible Turkish ruler Suleiman II in 1522 captured the fortress of the knights of Rhodes. They retreated to the island of Malta and during several centuries fought against the Turks from that bastion. A similar event will occur in the future and it is possible that instead of Rhodes we here have to deal with Malta. After the defeat of Turkey and Greece, the wave of invasion will move northward, and still greater harm will be done in Hungary or Austria (the other Pannonia).

Second rendering: This quatrain refers not to the initial days of invasion but to the period when the Arabs will again be thrown out of Europe, namely, during the reign of Henry

V, king of France. When the combined forces of Europe under the leadership of King Henry V and with the possible support by American troops will push the Arabs back, an insurrection against the Arab rule will occur in Turkey and will spread to the island Rhodes, with the following crushing defeat of the Arabs in Austria or Hungary.

Not from Spain but from ancient France
Will one be elected for the trembling boat,
To the enemy will be given assurance,
Who will cause a cruel plague in his realm.   (V-49)

A correct interpretation of this quatrain depends on the meaning of the expression "trembling boat." There are two possibilities: 1) "The boat" indicates the "bark of St. Peter," i.e., the papacy. In such a case these lines predict that one of the future popes will be a Frenchman. 2) "The boat" stands for "the ship of state." In this connection, it should be remembered that the Spanish line of the Bourbons also has legitimate claims on the French throne. At a time, when the French "ship of state" will be trembling and in danger of being upset, a decision about the succession to the throne will have to be made. It will accrue to a Frenchman of ancient lineage. This possibly is a reference to the future great king of France, Henry V.

The year that the brothers of the lily come of age,
One of them will hold the great Romania:
The mountains will tremble, Latin passage opened,
Pasha to march against the fort of Armenia.   (V-50)

The brothers of the lily are the princes of France, since the lily is the symbol of French monarchy. One of the princes will inherit the throne of France, the other will obtain "the great Romania," i.e., the Roman state. In Nostradamus' time Rome was within the papal territory. Therefore, the other prince perhaps will either become pope, or will conquer all Italy. The latter possibility is indicated in the third line by the expression "Latin passage opened." The fourth line tells about events in Turkey, since "pasha" is the title of Turkish noblemen. Will the ruler of Turkey try to seize Armenia from Russia?

> La gent de Dace, d'Angleterre, Polonne,
> Et de Boësme feront nouvelle ligue,
> Pour passer outre d'Hercules la colonne,
> Barcins, Tyrrans dresser cruelle brigue.   (V-51)

(The people of Dacia, England, Poland and of Bohemia will make a new league. To pass beyond the pillars of Hercules, the Barcinians and Tyrrhenians will prepare a cruel plot). Dacia is the Roman name for Rumania. The pillars of Hercules is the ancient name for Gibraltar. Barcelona was founded by Hamilcar Barca; hence its ancient name, Barcino. The Barcinians represent the whole of Spain; similarly, the Tyrrhenians represent the whole of Italy, since the sea, which laves the western coast of Italy, is the Tyrrhenian Sea, and the Greeks gave the name of Tyrrhenians to the Etruscans, the inhabitants of this coastal region. The quatrain predicts an alliance between Spain and Italy, and their intention to take Gibraltar away from England. The allies of England will be Poland, Czechoslovakia and Rumania. The quatrain does not mention any outbreak of open warfare, but such a possibility is not excluded.

> La loy du Sol et Venus contendus,
> Appropriant l'esprit de Prophetie,
> Ne l'un ne l'autre ne seront entendus,
> Par Sol tiendra la loy du grand Messie.   (V-53)

(The law of the Sun and of Venus in contention, appropriating the spirit of prophecy; neither the one or the other will be given a hearing, the law of the great Messiah will hold through the Sun.) The sun symbolizes Italy, i.e., the church of Rome and, in a wider sense, Christianity. Venus symbolizes the Near East, especially the Arabs and, in a wider sense, Islam. Christianity and Islam will be in contention, but it is not clear if the strife will be among themselves or against a third party. In the latter case the quatrain could be classified with those which relate about a new religion or a new sect arising during the period of Mohammedan expansion and gaining adherents not only among Christians, but also among Mohammedans. In either case, the last line shows that the Christians will keep the law of the great Messiah (Christ). Gustafsson deduces from this quatrain that the new religion will gain adherents not only among Christian Protestants, but also among Mohammedans, but that the Protestants will carry over into this new or reorganized faith the message of "the great Messiah," the gospel of Jesus Christ, changing only some dogmas and rituals (cf. II-8).

Du pont Euxine et la grand Tartarie
Un Roy sera qui viendra voir la Gaule.
Transpercera Alane et l'Armenie,
Et dedans Bisance lairra sanglante gaule.   (V-54)

(From the Black Sea and great Tartary there will be a king who will come to see Gaul; he will pierce through Alania and Armenia and within Byzantium will leave his bloody rod.) The Black Sea was called "Pontus Euxinus" by the Romans. Alans were an ancient Germanic people who lived in northern Caucasus and today are called Ossetins. This quatrain again tells about an invasion by the yellow race. One of the Asiatic rulers will arrive in France (Gaul), after having crossed the northern Caucasus and Armenia. Although the masses of Asiatic nations, which will take part in the invasion, will partly come also from the present Soviet Union, they will not invade Europe from the direction of northern Russia nor even Ukraine (north of the Black Sea), but will cross the Caucasus and conquer Asia Minor (Byzantium) first. Turkey will not willingly submit to the invaders and bloody battles will be fought on its territory. Should Russia then be an ally of Asia, then it follows from this quatrain, that a war between Russia and Turkey will form the prelude to a gigantic contest.

In the country of Arabia felix
There will be born one powerful in the law of Mahomet:
To vex Spain, to conquer Granada,
And more by sea against the Ligurian people.   (V-55)

Arabia is about thrice the size of France and by its climate belongs to the torrid zone. The greater part of it consists of deserts or bare, rocky plains. Only a few regions have an enduring vegetation. To these favored areas belongs Yemen, called of yore "Arabia felix" (the happy Arabia). From this Yemen a powerful Mahometan king will arise, march against Spain and capture Granada. History repeats itself. In 710 the Arabs conquered Western Africa, the domain of the West-Goths. At about the same time Arab military leaders Mohammed and Kuteiba had extended their sway over Turkestan up to Kashgar and over India up to Multan. It was therefore quite natural that they conceived the idea to expand also in a western direction, to attack the West-Goths and even to cross over to Spain. Not far from Cadiz, in the fields of Jeres-de-la-Frontera, was the decisive battle fought. It lasted for seven days, from July 19 to 26, 711. Both sides fought with equal endurance and equal luck, but on the eighth day Rodrigo, king of Spain, was not to be found on the battlefield. Nobody ever has found out what had happened to him or in what way he had perished. The Spaniards surrendered and the prosperous Andalusian provinces of Granada and Murcia were soon occupied. Thousands of the inhabitants were converted to Islam. In Malaga, Granada and other cities the Jews supported the Arabian army, welcoming the Arabs as their deliverers from misery and persecution. In a short time the Arabs subdued all Spain. We gather from this Nostradamus prediction, that simultaneously with the subjugation of Spain the Mohammedan invasion will be directed also against the Ligurian coast of Italy.

V-58 is not easy to solve. It tells about forests and inaccessible mountains from the aqueduct of Utica to

Gardone. In the second part of the quatrain a chief of Nimes is mentioned, who will be very terrible and will be pounded by a fist in the middle of the bridge. Because Nostradamus sometimes uses the French word *pont* (bridge) for the Greek word *pontos* (sea), the pounding perhaps will happen not on a bridge but "in the middle of the sea." Nimes is a town in southern France, in the department of Gard. Here also a famous Roman aqueduct can be found. Therefore, instead of "Gardone," we probably have to read "Gard," but there are no inaccessible mountains anywhere near the place. The town Nimes is mentioned also in the next quatrain. Could both quatrains have some connection?

V-59. The English chief will have too long a stay at Nimes; toward Spain Redbeard will come to the rescue (or he will be rescued?). Many will die by war which will begin on the day when a bearded star (most probably, a meteor) will fall in Artois (northern France, not far from the Belgian frontier).

V-61. The child (but not by birth, consequently, the stepson) of the great one will subjugate the high Appennine mountains, i.e., Italy, will cause all to tremble, and fire will burn from the mountains to Mont Cenis (in the French Alps, near the Italian frontier).

> Under the ancient vestal edifices,
> Not far from the ruined aqueduct,
> Of Sun and Moon are the glittering metals,
> Burning lamp of Trajan, with gold engraved.   (V-66)

In Nimes a great temple was built by the Romans in honor of Diana, the goddess of hunting. As can be seen from the inscriptions on the temple, it was dedicated also to Vesta, the goddess of the hearth. Not far from Nimes is also a great Roman water-conduit, the aqueduct of Gard. Under the ruins of the vestal temple, in days to come, a great treasure will be found, consisting of gold and silver (sun and moon). According to astrological and alchemical correspondences, the planets stand in some analogical relation to all classes of substances, among others, also to metals. Gold corresponds to the sun, and silver to the moon. Among the ancient treasures also a golden, "burning" lamp of Trajan will be found.

The regions subject to the Balance
Will trouble the mountains with great war.
Captives of both sexes detained and all Byzantium,
So that at dawn they will cry from land to land.   (V-70)

In general, Italy and parts of Austria are considered to be subject to the sign of Balance. These countries will be drawn into a terrible war, which will extend as far as Turkey (Byzantium). The inhabitants of these countries, of both sexes, will become captives. It is not clear when this will happen. Perhaps, it refers to Henry V, king of France, and his campaigns which, as is known from other quatrains, will extend not only into Italy, but into the entire eastern Mediterranean, including Turkey.

Persecutée sera de Dieu l'Eglise
Et les saincts Temples seront expoliez,
L'enfant la mère mettra nud en chemise:
Seront Arabes aux Pollons ralliez.   (V-73)

(The church of God will be persecuted and the holy temples will be plundered. The child will put its mother naked in her chemise. Arabs will be allied with the Poles.) A significant quatrain, in which it is clearly stated that during the time of the Arab invasion Poland will inflict a treacherous deed upon her "mother Europe" by allying herself with the Arabs. This act of Poland, in a situation critical for all Europe, is explained by Gustafsson in the following manner: After World War II Poland, in negotiations with the unrelenting Russians, was not able to regain the eastern part of her country, which Germany, already before the war, had allotted to Russia in the famous Hitler-Stalin deal. After the war, Russia did not give up either the Baltic States, which were included in the Hitler-Stalin deal, nor the appropriated

Polish territory. To compensate the Poles, Poland was given regions in the west, up to the rivers Oder and Neisse, which formerly did belong to Germany. In a future war, according to Gustafsson, communism will be defeated by the western nations, and Germany will regain her provinces, lost to Poland. As a consequence, Poland, a first-rate power by the number of her inhabitants, will be squeezed into so narrow a corner that it will be small wonder if the Polish nation will exploit the opportunity and, with Arab help, will try to wrest again from Germany the disputed provinces. Nevertheless, from a European standpoint, this act will constitute treason, but by a lucky circumstance, the Polish endeavor will not succeed, since the northern nations will give assistance to Germany, as can be seen from IX-94. Such an explanation, by Gustafsson, of the causes of the activities of Poland does not have a high degree of credibility, since it is not conceivable that after the collapse of communism Poland will not be reintegrated into her demographical boundaries. Or, will special circumstances indeed prohibit such a natural solution? Only the future will reveal it to us. In any case, whatever the causes or reasons, Poland will betray her mother Europe.

De sang Troyen naistra coeur Germanique
Qui deuiendra en si haute puissance:
Hors chassera gent estrange Arabique,
Tournant l'Eglise en pristine preeminence.　(V-74)

(Of Trojan blood will be born a Germanic heart, which will rise to very great power and will drive out the foreign Arabic people, returning the church to its pristine pre-eminence.) This quatrain permits several interpretations. First, the literal: German's defensive war against the Arabs has been compared with the ten-year-long war of the ancient Trojans against the Greeks (1197-1187 B.C.). Second version: Trojan blood is equivalent with Roman blood because, according to a legend, Romans are the descendants of Trojan refugees

Aeneas and his companions, who after the destruction of Troy settled in the region of Latium. Consequently, the Arabs will be expelled by someone who will have Roman blood and a Germanic heart. "Germanic heart" is equivalent with brave heart, because the ancient Germans were known to be fearless fighters. This Italian hero will again elevate the Catholic church to its pristine pre-eminence. Since several following quatrains refer to a pope, many interpreters discern a pope even in the person of this Italian hero.

> He will rise high over the estate more to the right,
> He will remain seated on the square stone,
> Toward the south facing to his left,
> The crooked staff in his hand, mouth sealed.   (V-75)

Incomprehensible. Only "the crooked staff" helps to attain to a solution, since we obviously have to deal here with the crozier of a bishop or a pope. A pope is also the subject of quatrains V-76 to V-79. This circumstance has suggested the search for a pope also in the previous quatrain (V-74). If all these quatrains have in view the same person, it is the only instance in all of Nostradamus' predictions where in connected quatrains an identical subject has been treated. In such a case we here have before us a pope to whom the seer has attributed an extraordinary importance. If we look at a map of Europe, to the right of Rome lies the East. The pope will rise high toward it (will be high-minded and magnanimous?). East of Rome is situated Greece, which since the 10th century deserted the Roman church and became alienated from the West. The Greek (Orthodox) church, her patriarchs and the whole Greek nation regarded the Roman popes with suspicion and irritation. Christianity was separated into two segments and could not be considered a uniform community anymore. However, the pope will remain seated on the cornerstone, which serves as foundation for the Church of Jesus Christ. Toward the south his look will be cast at the Mohammedans. To his left lies the West, whither he, with his crozier in hand, will wander, as can be seen from the following quatrain. He will not speak, but his actions will speak for him.

In a free place will he pitch his tent
And will not want to lodge in cities:
Aix, Carpen, island Volce, mount Cavaillon,
Throughout all these places will he abolish his trace.
(V-76)

The seer reports that the pope will emigrate to southern France, but will not reside in big cities and palaces. Aix is north of Marseilles, Carpentras (Carpen) is in the department Vaucluse. The Volces or Volques are an ancient Celtic tribe which lived in the region of Narbonne. The whole department Vaucluse (with the old papal residence Avignon and the fountain of Vaucluse, immortalized by Petrarca) got its name from the Volces. Cavaillon is a town on the river Durance, south of Avignon.

All the degrees of ecclesiastical honor
Will be changed to that of "dial quirinal":
The priest of Quirinus to one of Mars,
Then a king of France will make him one of Vulcan.
(V-77)

The Quirinal is one of the seven hills of Rome, and the Palace Quirinal is the seat of the Italian government. Consequently, "quirinal" here means "Roman." All dissident churches will be reformed according to the Roman rite. The pope is here seen as a warrior (man of Mars), as a Roman citizen and as a Roman priest. Then, through the protection by a king of France, he will become invulnerable. In this quatrain it is also possible to discern the prediction that the church of the pope will ruthlessly persecute a new anti-catholic sect or teaching, the rise of which has been predicted in other quatrains.

La sacrée pompe viendra baisser les aisles,
Par le venuë du grand legislateur:
Humble haussera, vexera les rebelles,

Naistra sur terre aucun aemulateur.   (V-79)

(The sacred pomp will lower its wings through the coming of the great legislator: he will raise the humble, he will vex the rebels, his like will not appear on this earth.) "The wings" are a symbol of power and freedom. This quatrain permits several interpretations: 1) A remarkable pope will suppress the outward "pomp" (the sacred ceremonies and processions) of the Catholic church. 2) This prediction does not refer to the Catholic church at all, but instead, to the coming of a new religion or sect, which will be founded by an extraordinary man, who will combine in his person eminent spirituality with external secular power. Since it is said that his like will not again appear on this earth, it may be even deduced that this prophecy announces the fulfillment of the biblical promise about the second coming of Christ.

Logmion grande Bisance approchera,

Chassée sera la barbarique ligue:

Des deux loix l'une l'estinique laschera,

Barbare et franche en perpetuelle brigue.   (V-80)

(Ogmion will approach great Byzantium, the barbaric league will be driven out. Of the two laws the heathen one will give way. Barbarian and Frank in perpetual strife.) "L'estinique" is derived from Latin "ethnicus." Ogmion or Ogmios is an eloquent Gallic deity. With this name Nostradamus symbolizes a French leader or king, under whose leadership the barbarians will be driven out of the Balkans or of Asia Minor (the ancient Byzantine territory). The battles there will be long and incessant.

Au grand marche qu'on dict des mensongers

Du tout torrent, et champ Athenien,

Seront surprins par les cheuaux legers,

Par Albanois, Mars, Leo, Sat. un versien.   (V-91)

(At the great market that they call liars' market, of the entire torrent and field of Athens, they will be surprised by the light horses and by Albanians, Mars, Leo, Saturn in

Aquarius.) From the second line it is evident that here the subject matter is an invasion of Greece, perhaps invasion by Asiatics, because heretofore all attacks on Europe from the East have taken place with the help of cavalry. But Nostradamus calls the attackers Albanians. Does he indicate thereby the place or direction from which the attack will come? Albania lies northwest of Greece, but we should not forget the well known fact that the ancient Albania was south of the Caucasus. The passage of Saturn over the sign of Aquárius takes place once in less than 30 years and requires approximately three years. In that period Mars also transits over the sign of Leo for a couple of times. The next such period will be between 1991 and 1993. Gustafsson's calculations have again provided him with an exact date: 1st of September, 2083.

> Soubs le terroir du rond globe lunaire,
> Lors que sera dominateur Mercure:
> L'isle d'Ecosse fera vn luminaire,
> Qui les Anglois mettra a deconfiture.   (V-93)

(Under the land of the round lunar globe, when Mercury will be dominating, the isle of Scotland will produce a luminary, who will put the English into confusion.) This quatrain permits several interpretations, depending on how the references to the moon and Mercury are understood (cf.III-3). According to astrological sources, lands of the moon could be Belgium and Northern France, and Mercury dominates over India and Egypt. But we should not disregard such authorities as Cornelius Agrippa, a contemporary of Nostradamus. In 1531 he published his "De occulta philosophia." This book, which most certainly was read also by Nostradamus, contains a chapter on astrological geography. Agrippa maintains that the moon reigns over such countries as Bithinia and Phrygia (both in Asia Minor) and partly over North Africa, but that Mercury reigns over, among other countries, Armenia, Assyria, Babylonia,

Mesopotamia and Egypt. If we accept the latter interpretation, this forecast could pertain to the period when the mentioned countries begin economically and militarily to arm themselves, prior to the attack on Europe, or perhaps to the period when the invasion of Europe has already begun. On the other hand, if Mercury, the ancient Greek god of commerce, navigation and communications, is understood as the symbol of trade, then this prophecy has no relevance to the Middle East, since England, together with Belgium and Northern France, has always been and still is a center of trade and navigation.

> The rose upon the middle of the great world,
> For new events public shedding of blood.
> To speak the truth, one will have a closed mouth,
> Then, at the time of need, the awaited one will come
> late.   (V-96)

For Catholic Christianity, the very center of the great world is Rome. Therefore, this prediction may refer to the pope. In the prophecy of St. Malachia (cf. the last chapter of this book) the 108th pope carries the descriptive name "flos florum," i.e., flower of flowers. If the flower of flowers is the rose (and not the lily), then this prediction refers to Pope Paul VI, who was elected in 1963. During his reign, new, tremendous events with great bloodshed will take place. It will not be permitted to preach the truth until, at long last, the eagerly expected rescuer will arrive. Gustafsson sees in this quatrain another indication of the bloody persecutions, instigated by the Catholic church, of the "Neo-Christians" (a new Christian sect).

> At the forty-eighth climacteric degree,
> At the end of Cancer so great a dryness:
> Fish in the sea, river, lake boiled hectic,
> Bearn, Bigorre in distress through fire from the
> sky.   (V-98)

Paris is situated in 48° 50′ 14″ north latitude. The sun travels through the sign of Cancer between June 21st and

July 21st. This event, consequently, will take place around the 20th of July. Dryness can be understood 1) literally, as drought and aridity, and 2) as military actions on land, on water and in the air, whereby the fury of man has been raised to fever point. In such a case the last line of the quatrain also can be explained by warlike activities, namely by air raids, which will cause great distress in southern France, the regions of Bearn and Bigorre. E. Ruir, on the contrary, takes this prediction in a literal sense and refers it, together with I-46 and VIII-2, to the period of terrestrial translation.

Le Boute feu par son feu attrapé,
Du feu du ciel à Calcas et Cominge:
Foix, Aux, Mazere, haut vieillard eschappé,
Par ceux de Hasse des Saxons et Turinge.   (V-100)

(The incendiary trapped by his fire, of fire from the sky at Calcas and Cominge, Foix, Aux, Mazères, the high old man escaped through those of Hesse, the Saxons and Thuringia.) This tells of retaliation against an incendiary. And again fire from the sky has been specified. All mentioned places are situated in the southwestern part of France, between the Pyrenees and the so-called southern canal. These localities have never experienced air raids before, and therefore this prediction can pertain only to the future. Only Cominge cannot be found on the map. Near the border of Belgium is the town of Comines, but more likely the ancient district of Comminges has been meant, which is east of Bigorre, in the same region where all the rest of the mentioned places are located.

Sixth century

Around the Pyrenees mountains a great throng
Of foreign people to aid the new king:
By the Garonne, near the great temple of Mas,
A Roman chief will fear him in the water. (VI-1)

In the department Garonne can be found Le-Mas d'Agénais, a small town. In its environs are the ruins of a Gallic temple, which was dedicated to the sun. The new king could be either the king of France or the king of Spain. One of possible solutions: Near the mentioned temple ruins a great battle will take place between the French under one of their future kings and an Italian army. The battle will end with the defeat of the Italians and the flight of their leader over the sea. The French in their fight against Italy will be aided by diverse foreign auxiliary troops.

En l'an cinq cens octante plus et moins,
On attendra le siecle bien estrange,
Et l'an sept cens et neuf cieux seront tesmoings
Que pour de l'or en bled non sans peine il
    change. (VI-2)

(In the year five hundred eighty, more or less, one will attend a very strange century: in the year seven hundred and nine the heavens witness thereof, that for gold in Bled the change will not be without difficulties.) Bled is a desert region of Africa. This is a very significant quatrain, which has caused great speculation and brain-racking, all the more because in some later editions of the centuries, published after 1568, the third and fourth lines have been altered, namely, to read: "in the year seven hundred and three the heavens witness thereof, that several kingdoms, one to five, will make a change." How to interpret these dates? At first, naturally, it would seem that the years 1580 and 1703 or 1709 rsp. have been intended. But such a solution does not give us any satisfaction, because the year 1580 was not historically significant, except that France then was in the midst of a civil war and that five years earlier (in 1577) the so-called "holy league" had come into existence. Nor have the years 1703 or 1709 been of importance. Therefore we have to look for a different solution. E. Ruir in one of his books, which was published in 1947, operates with numerical manipulations, which would cause us to sneer, if his previous interpretations of Nostradamus' quatrains had not been so miraculously realized. He considers both figures as indications of the beginning and the end of the Arabic or Asiatic invasion and occupation of Western Europe. Nostradamus wrote his last predictions between the years 1550 and 1555. If we take the last mentioned year and add 580 to it, then as the latest date for the conquest of Europe by Arabs or Asiatics we get the year 2135 (1555 + 580 = 2135). If the other of the mentioned figures indicates the year when Europe again will be freed from the barbarians, we similarly, assuming the 1568 version of the centuries as authentic, get the year 2264 (1555 + 709 = 2264) as the latest date for the liberation of Europe. This is not the only occasion when E. Ruir refuses to accept the literal meaning of numerals, mentioned by Nostradamus. For instance, in the sentence about the events of 1585 in the epistle to Henri the Second (B.9) he very ingenuously reads the date in reverse as 5851 and counts 5851 years from the creation of the world, according to Nostradamus' own chronology, contained in the same epistle. According to E. Ruir, Nostradamus in his epistle has some dates spelled out by letters, but others expressed by numbers, thereby sagaciously indicating that not all of his numerals have to be understood in the literal sense.

The river that tries the new Celtic heir
Will be in great discord with the empire:
The young prince through the ecclesiastical people
Will remove the sceptre of the crown of concord.　(VI-3)
One of the French successors to the crown will get into the

wrong groove with the empire. He will overestimate his strength and perhaps will even be defeated in a battle. The last two lines are abstruse. Will the conflict be provoked by the clergy, or will the clergy, on the contrary, help the prince to gain the throne?

> Le celtique fleuve changera de rivage,
> Plus ne tiendra la cité d'Agripine,
> Tout transmué hormis le vieil langage,
> Saturne, Leo, Mars, Cancer en rapine.   (VI-4)

(The Celtic river will change its shore, no longer will it include the city of Agrippina; all changed except the old language, Saturn, Leo, Mars, Cancer in rapine.) If we take the Seine for the Celtic river—and it most certainly deserves such a designation—then "the city of Agrippina" is Paris, and the whole prediction tells us about the German occupation of France during the Second World War, since Saturn in Leo is in Hitler's nativity and Mars in Cancer can be found in the astrological theme of the Third Republic (of 1870). So far, so good. Nevertheless, it is an entirely wrong solution, since Paris, formerly called also "Lutetia," has never been called "the city of Agrippina," and it has never had any connection whatsoever with Agrippina, the mother of Nero. However, a Roman military camp near the Rhine was once called "Colonia Agrippina" (Agrippina's colony), in honor of Nero's mother. In the course of time the name was abbreviated to "Colonia," which name the French changed into "Cologne" and the Germans into "Köln." "The city of Agrippina" is Cologne on the Rhine, which also can be called a Celtic river, since the ancient Celts, before they moved into France, were dwelling on both shores of the Rhine, from Belgium to Switzerland and even further on. They were a bellicose tribe, which made many marauding raids into several neighboring countries. Hence, the Rhine will be changing its shores. Will it change its course? More probably, there will be a change of the owners of its shores. The proud Cologne will no longer be on a "German river." Only the old language will still be heard in Cologne, but the city itself will no longer belong to Germany. Nostradamus specifies also the time with planetary positions: "Saturn in Leo and Mars in Cancer." The expression "in rapine" is used in an astrological sense and indicates that the planets will be in constellations where their influence will be weakened. Such an astrological situation will occur in the first decade of the 21st century and will be repeated once every 29 years.

So great a famine through pestiferous wave,
Through long rain along the arctic pole:
Samarobryn one hundred leagues from the hemisphere,
They will live without law exempt from politics.   (VI-5)

A very interesting quatrain, which seems to indicate events quite impossible at the time of Nostradamus. Of course, it is feasible to decipher this quatrain in an entirely simple fashion: continuous warfare (rain of projectiles or missiles) in arctic regions (for instance, in Norway, Finland and Siberia) will cause a terrible famine and epidemics in the countries concerned. Even in France, especially in Amiens, which in Roman times was called Samarobriva, the war will create lawless, anarchical and disorderly conditions. But "one hundred leagues from the hemisphere" can mean only one direction, namely, upwards, into space. One hundred leagues of Nostradamus' time are about 270 miles of present measurement. It seems that here we have to deal with an artificial satellite, projected into space. Perhaps the word "Samarobryn" has a different meaning? E. Leoni suggests: a space-station astronaut named Sam R. O'Brien. And does not the first line indicate bacteriological warfare? Of what kind will be these mysterious activities in the arctic regions?

VI-6 reports the appearance of a comet towards the north, not far from the constellation of Cancer. It will be a sign that the great one of Rome will die.

L'union feinte sera peu de durée,
Des uns changez reformez la pluspart:
Dans les vaisseaux sera gent endurée,
Lors aura Rome un nouveau liepart.   (VI-20)

(The feigned union will be of short duration, some changed, most reformed. In the ships people will be suffering, then Rome will have a new leopard.) Here a new Italian dictator has been foretold. He will appear after a "feigned union" has been dissolved. The line about "ships" may mean not only seagoing vessels and disasters on the sea, but also "ecclesiastical ships," consequently, the churches and, in the context, persecutions of the churches, in connection with the preceding revolution.

Quand ceux du pole arctiq vnis ensemble,
Et en Orient grand effrayeur et crainte:
Esleu nouueau, soustenu le grand tremble,
Rodes, Bisance de sang barbare teincte.   (VI-21)

(When those of the arctic pole are united together, in the East great terror and fear. The newly elected, upheld the great one trembling, Rhodes, Byzantium stained with barbarian blood). It seems that here we are told about the liberation of Europe from the constraint of occupation by the Easterners. The northern countries have been unmistakably mentioned as assisting in the war of liberation. When Nostradamus mentions the countries of Aquilon (the lands of the northern wind) we cannot be always sure that he means countries of Northern Europe, because from the context we often find that he has meant regions and lands that lie towards the north from his own domicile. As he lived in southern France, even such a country as Austria could have been a northern country in his conception. But when Nostradamus speaks of "those of the arctic pole," there can be no misconception about "those" being real Northerners. The "newly elected" seems to be a European leader and probably identical with the "king of Europe" of X-86.

Dedans la terre du grand Temple Celique,
Nepveu à Londres par paix fainct meurtry,
La barque alors deviendra scismatique,
Liberté faincte sera au corn et cry.   (VI-22)

(Within the land of the great celestial temple, nephew murdered at London through feigned peace: the bark will then become schismatic, feigned liberty will be with horn and voice proclaimed.) Here a new schism is forecast in the Roman church, since "bark" undoubtedly is "the bark of Peter." Simultaneously a kind of governmental crisis or change of government will occur in London, in connection with "a feigned peace," which could mean "demonstrations by so-called pacifists" or similar events.

VI-25 belongs to those texts which tell about a schism in the Catholic church. The seat of the pope will be seized by a "red black one," consequently, by a priest who is a communist.

Quatre ans le siege quelque peu bien tiendra,
Vn surviendra libidineux de vie:
Rauenne et Pyse, Veronne soustiendront,
Pour esleuer la croix de Pape enuie.   (VI-26)

(Four years the see will be held with some little good, one libidinous in life will succeed to it. Ravenna, Pisa and Verona will give support, longing to elevate the papal cross.) If this quatrain is connected with the previous one, the "red" pope will hold power for four years.

Within the isles of five rivers to one,
Through the crescent of the great Chyren Selin:
Through the drizzles in the air the fury of one,
Six escaped, hidden bundles of flax.   (VI-27)

This quatrain can be understood only in connection with other predictions. The former French province "L'Ile de France" (the island of France) was situated between five rivers: Seine, Marne, Ourq, Aisne and Oise. Ourq empties itself into Marne, but Aisne into Oise. Marne and Oise being tributaries of the Seine, Seine is thus comprised of five rivers. "Chyren" is an anagram of the name "Henry.""Selene" is the crescent, such as can be found in the flag of Turkey. Both names are here for the first time combined into one expression (cf.II-79). Here we are told that in France King Henri will reign, called "Henri of the Crescent" because of his victories over the Turks. In the interior of France a rebellion will take place, but six conspirators will escape the wrath of the ruler, having been hiding in bundles of flax (cf. also IV-77).

> The great Celt will enter Rome,
> Leading a crowd of the exiled and banished:
> The great Pastor will put to death every man
> Who was united in the Alps for the cock.   (VI-28)

A future king of France, "the great Celt," who may be identical with the repeatedly mentioned king Henry V of France, will enter Rome after a victorious battle against Italian forces. The pope will spiritually "put to death," i.e. ex-communicate all who as allies of France (the cock) were fighting in the Alps against Italy.

> The child of the realm through the capture of his father
> Will be plundered to deliver him:
> Near the azure lake Trasimen captive,
> The hostage troop becoming far too drunk.   (VI-39)

The lake Trasimen (lake of Perugia) was destined in the Roman and Italian history to become over and over again the locality for military actions. Lately, during the Second World War, sanguinary battles were enacted there between the Germans and the Allies. In times to come hostile armies will meet there again. An Italian prince will be taken captive because his soldiers will be given to drinking.

> Grand de Magonce pour grande soif esteindre,
> Sera priué de sa grande dignité:
> Ceux de Cologne si fort le viendront plaindre,
> Que la grand groppe au Rhin sera ietté.   (VI-40)

(To quench the great thirst the great one of Magonce will be deprived of his great dignity. Those of Cologne will complain so loudly that the great rump will be thrown into the Rhine.) "Magonce" could be 1) the city of Mainz (Mayence) and in such a case this is a forecast about a German dictator who will be deprived of his power, or 2) the Carthaginian name Magon (cf. V-43).

> Le second chef du regne d'Annemarc
> Par ceux de Frize et l'isle Britanique
> Fera despendre plus de cent mille marc,
> Vain exploicter voyage en Italique.   (VI-41)

(The second chief of the realm of Annemarc through those of Frisia and of the British Isles will spend more than one hundred thousand marks, exploiting in vain the voyage to Italy.) It seems that here, as in IV-27, we have to deal with a king (or the second chief) of Denmark, who in his military expedition (voyage in vain) has been joined even by people of Great Britain and of Frisia (i.e. Germany and Holland). Could this "second chief of the realm of Denmark" be identical with the "third Northern king," mentioned in the epistle to Henri the Second (B.110)? If so, then this "voyage to Italy" is the expedition mentioned in the epistle: "At this time the third king of Aquilon, hearing the lament of the people of his principal title, will raise a mighty army and will pass through the straits of his predecessors and ancestors..."

> To Ogmion will be left the realm
> Of the great Selin, who will in fact do more:
> Throughout Italy will he extend his banner,
> Ruled will be by prudent counter-act.   (VI-42)

Nostradamus has repeatedly referred to the future French national hero, king Henri V, and to his successful campaigns against Turkey and Italy. Not only with his soldier-like efficiency but also with his prudence he will lead his country to predominance in Europe. In this quatrain Nostradamus refers to Henri's successor, naming him Ogmion. Ogmion (or

Ogmios) was the Celtic Hercules. Ogmion is mentioned also in V-80 and VIII-44.

Long temps sera sans estre habitée
Ou Signe et Marne autour vient arroser.
De la Tamise et martiaux tentée,
Deceus les gardes en cuidant repousser. (VI-43)

(For a long time will she remain uninhabited, where the Seine and the Marne are laving around. Tried by the Thames and warriors, the guards deceived in trying to repulse.) Again, as in III-84, we hear about the total destruction of the French capital city Paris. Those of the Thames are the English, who with their auxiliaries will level Paris to the ground, and for a long time nobody will be able to live in the region between the Seine and the Marne.

The very learned governor of the realm,
Not wishing to consent to the royal deed:
The fleet at Melilla through contrary wind
Will give him back to his most disloyal one. (VI-45)

In the days of sailing vessels ships often had to wait for a propitious wind, before they could set sail and leave the port. Nostradamus is using this allegory to report on a learned governor, who from prudential considerations will not consent to a decree of his king, but who will be delivered to his traitor, the navy having taken the king's side.

The too false and seductive sanctity,
Accompanied by an eloquent tongue:
The old city, and Parma too hasty,
Florence and Siena will be rendered more desert. (VI-48)

Hypocrisy, supported by eloquence, will take up the attitude of sanctity and thus deceive the people. The old city, eternal Rome, will in alliance with Parma and in a precipitate manner wage war against Florence and Siena and will devastate these cities of art. Florence (in Latin "Florentia," i.e. the flowering one) was an inhabited town already around the year 1000 before Christ. Sulla destroyed Florence in 82

B.C. The Christian faith was brought to Florence mainly by Syrian merchants. Florence later became the center and focus of the movement of the Renaissance (the rebirth of antiquity), which sought to resuscitate antiquity (classicism) in poetry and oratory, art and science. Florence and Siena suffered comparatively little damage during the Second World War, but will be greatly affected by a future war which will break out among the Italians themselves.

VI-49 relates that assailants (perhaps Asiatics) will subjugate the confines of the Danube, pillaging cities and persecuting Christians.

Au poinct du iour au second chant du coq,
Ceux de Tunes, de Fez, et de Bugie,
Par les Arabes, captif le Roy Maroq,
L'an mil six cents et sept de Liturgie.   (VI-54)

(At daybreak, at the second crowing of the cock, those of Tunis, of Fez and of Bougie, by the Arabs the king of Morocco captured, the year thousand six hundred and seven of the Liturgy.) Tunis is a country in North Africa, Bougie is a fortified seaport in Algiers, and Fez is a city in Morocco. In the Mediterranean regions the cock's second crowing occurs at about three o'clock in the morning. The king of Morocco will then become a captive of the Arabs, evidently during an attack by the Arabs. This is a very significant quatrain, since here a certain date has been mentioned, a number, which has to be added to the "year of liturgy." G. Gustafsson attaches great importance to a correct calculation of this date and is of the opinion that still other dates of Nostradamus are to be considered as belonging to this "liturgical" time-table, for instance, in VIII-71, where it is predicted that in 1607 astrologers, whose number has become "very great," will be banished and persecuted. In 1607 by our chronology the number of astrologers was very small and they were by no means persecuted. Therefore, Gustafsson thinks that the persecution of astrologers will take place before the coming attack by barbarians, and that the inquisition (sacrées glomes, or the holy assemblies) of that time will persucute everybody who will cite Nostradamus' prophecies and predict the coming Arab invasion. Gustafsson considers I-49, where the year 1700 is mentioned, as similarly belonging to the "liturgical" chronology. In that year the Easterners will carry off many people and will subjugate countries even near the corner of the northern wind. Furthermore in III-77 is mentioned the year 1727, when there will be "conflict, death, loss and great shame to the cross." But what initial point has this "liturgical" chronology of Nostradamus? The Christian church has no uniform liturgy, and we cannot determine any particular year as the origin or inception of any national liturgy, for instance, of the French liturgy. Auxentius, who was the bishop of Milan from 355 until 374, developed an extensive liturgy. Adding 1607 to 374 we get the year 1981. The apostolic credo in France obtained its present form at about the year 500. If we choose this year as the initial point for the "liturgical" chronology, we get year 2107 as the year of the barbarian assault. Another possibility: in the *Confessions* (IX, sect. 7), St. Augustine says, "Then [in 386] it was first instituted that ... Hymns and Psalms should be sung ..."

> The Lady in fury through rage of adultery,
> Will adjure her Prince not to tell:
> But soon will the blame be known,
> So that seventeen will be put to martyrdom.   (VI-59)

In a land, ruled by a queen, her consort will be forced to reveal the names of those who accuse the queen of adultery. Seventeen will suffer the death penalty for it.

> Trop tard tous deux les fleurs seront perdues
> Contre la loy serpent ne voudra faire:
> Des ligueurs forces par gallots confondues,
> Sauone, Albingue par monech grand martyre.   (VI-62)

(Too late both the flowers will be lost, against the law the serpent will not want to act. The forces of the leaguers confounded by the Gallots, Savona, Albenga through Monech great martyrdom.) The gallots are the French, but what is "Monech"? It is either "the monarchy" or "Monaco," since Monaco's Latin name is "Portus Herculi Monoecis."

No peace agreed upon will be kept,
All subscribers will act with deceit:
In peace and truce, land and sea in protest,
By Barcelona fleet seized with ingenuity.   (VI-64)

All peace treaties, although they with many provisions regulate all particulars and details and have been solemnly ratified by the governments of numerous countries and proclaimed before the whole world, will nevertheless, as time goes on, be broken and ridiculed as merely scraps of paper. Wars and even world wars will be waged again, as clearly foretold by Nostradamus.

VI-66 tells that at the foundation of the new sect, when in April earth will quake, the bones of a great Roman will be found. Has this quatrain any connection with III-65? Is this new sect the revived primitive Christianity, which has been mentioned in other quatrains?

La dechassée au regne tournera,
Ses ennemis trouuez des coniurez,
Plus que iamais son temps triomphera,
Trois et septante à mort trop asseurez.   (VI-74)

(The chased out will return to the realm, her enemies found to be conspirators. More than ever her time will triumph. Three and seventy, to death very sure.) This is a famous, often quoted quatrain, because here the end of the French Republic seems to be foretold, as in the epistle to Henri the Second, where its duration is fixed at 73 years and 7 months (B.44). This quatrain has been interpreted in manifold ways. As usual in the prophecies of Nostradamus, a government or form of government has been represented by a feminine personage. Here perhaps the "goddess of reason" has been meant, which was worshipped by Frenchmen during the Great Revolution. The chased-out republic returned on September 4, 1870, and with 73 years and 7 months added, she should have ended in April 1944. But it happened otherwise. The Third French Republic ceased to exist in the summer of 1940, when Hitler's army occupied half of France and when marshal Pétain established his "collaborationist" government in the other half. The liberation followed in the end of summer 1944, and the men of resistance, the "conspirators" of the quatrain (if we translate the second line to read "her enemies will be found by the conspirators") began hunting the "collaborants." The Republic, which had been "chased out" for several times, returned again as the legal form of government. The constitution of the Fourth Republic was approved by a plebiscite on October 13, 1945, and came into force on December 24, 1946. If we add 73 years to 1944, 1945 or 1946, the end of this republic should come only in 2017, 2018 or 2019 resp. Again, it happened otherwise. The Fourth Republic ended on December 21, 1958, when the Fifth Republic (of De Gaulle) came into force. Consequently, either the interpretation with reference to the French Republic is wrong or the realization of the forecast is still a matter of the future.

VI-76 gives an account of an attempt on the life of an Italian dictator, who will be stabbed in a church.

VI-80 seems to be a continuation of VI-54, because it tells that the Arabian government from Fez will reach Europe, and first and foremost, of course, Spain (cf.III-20).

Pleurs, crys et plaints, hurlement effrayeurs.
Coeur inhumain, cruel Roy, et transi.
Leman les Isles des Gennes les maieurs
Sang espancher, profaim à nul mercy.   (VI-81)

(Tears, cries and laments, howls, terror. Heart inhuman, cruel king and chilly. Lake of Geneva, the Isles, Genoa the greater, blood to flow, famine, mercy to none.) A message of doom, with reference to Switzerland (lake of Geneva), England (the Isles?) and Italy (Genova).

> La grande cité de Tharse par Gaulois
> Sera destruite, captifs tous à Turban,
> Secours par mer du grand Portugalois,
> Premier d'este' le iour du sacre Vrban. (VI-85)

(The great city of Tharse by the Gauls will be destroyed, all captives of the Turban. Help by sea from the great one of Portugal, first day of summer, St. Urban's day.) A very interesting quatrain, but with numerous possibilities of interpretation. First, where is the city of Tharse? There exists no city of that name. Perhaps it is Constantinople, which previously was called "Bosphorus of Thrace"? In such a case, instead of "Tharse" we have to read "Thrace." In Nostradamus' text such transpositions are frequent. Consequently, the French will capture Constantinople and will destroy it. Indications of such an event can be found also in other quatrains, from which can be inferred that this city will first be captured and pillaged by the Russians, but later by the future great Henri V, king of France. All "of the Turban" will be taken captive. The Portuguese will be allied with the French and with their navy will support France in the war against the Turks. On May 25, St. Urban's day, which by some ancient people was considered to be the first day of summer (instead of June 22, as today), Constantinople will fall into the hands of the French. Such is one reading of the quatrain. There have been efforts to read the third line differently, as saying that Americans will take part in the struggle against the Arabs and will disembark on the shores of Portugal on May 25, St. Urban's day. But it is very well possible that the foretold events don't refer to Constantinople at all. Tharse could be the same as the Spanish river Tajo, called "Tarraeonensis" by the Romans. Tajo flows through Castile and reaches the Atlantic ocean near Lisbon, the capital of Portugal. "The great city of

Tharse" then is Lisbon, and the quatrain in its entirety deals only with the battle for the sake of Portugal. Lisbon will be destroyed by allied French forces in defending the city or in an unsuccessful effort to recapture it. All will be captured by the wearers of the "Turban," who will receive reinforcements through the great Portuguese port on the first day of summer, i.e. on St. Urban's day.

> The great Prelate one day after his dream,
> Interpreted opposite to its meaning:
> From Gascony a monk will come unexpectedly,
> One who will cause the great prelate of Sens to be
>   elected. (VI-86)

The great prelate, the pope, will interpret his dream opposite to its meaning. As is well known, many dreams have to be interpreted in a reversed sense. As yet, no occupant of the Holy See has come from Sens. Only once the archbishop of Sens was proposed for the seat of St. Peter. It happened in 1534, in Nostradamus' time. Then it was cardinal Duprat, the counsellor of King François I. Heeding the king's command, he withdrew his candidacy. But Nostradamus could not have meant him, since this prophecy was published in 1555, consequently, 21 years later. One of the future popes will become, first, the archbishop of Sens, and a monk from Gascony will help him to attain to the high position.

> Un regne grand demeurera desolé:
> Auprès de l'Hebro se feront assemblées,
> Monts Pyrennées le rendront consolé,
> Lors que dans May seront terres tremblées. (VI-88)

(A great realm will be left desolated, near the Ebro an assembly will be formed. The Pyrenees mountains will console him, when in May lands will be trembling). Here evidently Spain has been meant. Spain is in a sense an isolated country, since by the Pyrenees mountains it appears to be protected against attacks. The trembling in May could be either warfare or a real earthquake. In IX-83 Nostradamus also reports on an earthquake in the month of May.

> The stinking abominable disgrace,
> After the deed he will be congratulated:
> The great excused for not being favorable,
> Except for peace, Neptune will not be incited.   (VI-90)

This quatrain has been quoted here only as an example of so many other, no less incomprehensible and ambiguous quatrains. H. Bauder comments it as follows: "Pétain, the former chief of France, will be by many of his subjects abominably disgraced, because he had bowed down before Hitler, yielding to the necessity of that period. But after the war the old Pétain will be understood and forgiven. France has been promised happy times after the war, and "Neptune," the ruler of the sea, i.e. England, will strive to keep peace between France and herself and will take care not to incite France." The French original text, however, is so obscure that the last line could even be translated thus: "That Neptune will not be incited for peace."

VI-96, like III-84, reports on the destruction of the "great city" (Paris?)

> Cinq et quarante degrez ciel bruslera,
> Feu approcher de la grand cité neuve,
> Instant grand flamme esparse sautera,
> Quand on voudra des Normands faire preuve.   (VI-97)

(At forty-five degrees the sky will burn, fire will approach the great new city. In an instant a great scattered flame will leap up, when one will want to demand proof of the Normans.) Has Lyons been meant, as in II-83? But Lyons is on the 46th degree. If the foretold events will take place during the French-Italian war, we have to look for a city in northern Italy. It could be identical with "the city of the Insubrian region" (Lombardy), mentioned in VII-15, which will be besieged for seven years. The greatest city of Lombardy is Milan, situated between the 45th and the 46th degree. The same can be said of Venice. Only Turin is on the 45th degree.

The "great new city" can indeed be an entirely new, not yet existing city, because all afore-mentioned cities have existed already in Nostradamus' time and cannot be considered "new" cities. And who are the Normans? Some interpreters suspect that the English could have been meant, and that the city will be burned at the moment when one of the belligerents will ask for England's intervention. The French interpreter J. Monterey, however, is of the opinion that the "new city" is Geneva, although it lies on the 46th degree.

Between the sixth and seventh centuries, with a separate title "Legis cautio (var.: cantio) contra ineptos criticos," Nostradamus has inserted a warning against inept critics. This warning will be valid also in the future. The warning has been written in Latin:

Qui(d) legent hosce versus, mature (var.: nature) censunto,
Profanum vulgus et inscium ne attrectato:
Omnesque Astrologi, Blenni, Barbari procul sunto,
Qui aliter facit, is rite sacer esto.   (VI-100)

(Let those who read these verses consider it profoundly, let the profane and ignorant herd keep away, and far away all astrologers, idiots and barbarians. May he who does otherwise be subject to the sacred rite). The profane and ignorant herd should not obtain knowledge of these prophecies, because they would misapprehend them and only confuse the people. Nostradamus had many unpleasant experiences with such profane persons. Some ignorant peasants had called him a wizard and devil-worshipper. He had replied: "Go away, you miserable wretches, you will not be able to put your foot on my throat, not while I'm alive nor after my death." His remark came true literally, since the earthly remains of the seer were entombed in the Minorite church, inside a wall, to the left of the main portal. Nobody will ever be able to tread on the tomb of Nostradamus.

In the 1605 edition of Nostradamus' centuries the afore-mentioned quatrain has been replaced by a different one, and Nostradamus' warning was printed after it, without any numbering. We cannot be absolutely sure that even this duplicate VI-100 has been written by Nostradamus. The text is as follows:

Fille de l'Aure, asyle du mal sain,
Où jusqu'au ciel se void l'amphiteatre.
Prodige veu, ton mal est fort prochain,
Sera captive, et deux fois plus de quatre.   (VI-100)

(Daughter of the Aure, asylum of the unhealthy, where the amphitheater is seen on the horizon. When prodigy seen, your evil is very near. You will be captive, and two times more than four). In Le Pelletier's opinion, the daughter of Aure is the city of Orange, and the prophecy has already seen fulfillment. Other commentators disagree and say that here, as in X-65, the decadence of Rome has been foretold. Rome has supposedly been the asylum of the unhealthy, since anti-popes and other renegades have ruled there for long periods of time. In Rome also an amphitheater (Colosseum) can be found. The coming persecution of Christians during the Arab invasion can for good reasons be considered as a merited ordeal for all perfidies, the initiators of which, more often than not, have called themselves servants of God. And the coming prodigy, which will be seen, is supposedly the comet, whose appearance has been proclaimed by Nostradamus also in many other quatrains.

Seventh century

After the naval victory of France
The Barcinians, Saillimons, the Phokians,
Robber of gold, anvil enclosed in the ball,
Those of Ptolon will be content with the fraud.   (VII-3)

Instead of the names of cities, towns and regions, Nostradamus often uses the names of the original founders, inhabitants or native tribes. For the comprehension of these terms, some historical knowledge is indispensable. "Barcinians" are the inhabitants of Barcelona, because in the days of Arabian rule in Spain Barcelona was still called Barcino, which name is derived from the name of the city's founder, Hamilcar Barca. "Saillimons" are the Salians, the former inhabitants of Provence in southern France. "Phokians" are the inhabitants of Marseilles, because Marseilles was founded by the Phokians, i.e. the Phoenicians. Consequently, Spaniards from Barcelona, Frenchmen from Provence in southern France and the inhabitants of Marseilles will take part in the great naval battle. After the surprisingly swift naval victory of France the aforesaid populace, exuberant with joy, will put away the weaponry (forged on anvils). With that even the marines of Ptolon, i.e. Toulon, the great French naval base, will be content, although they will have anticipated a much longer war and their own participation in it, as may be concluded from the remark about "the fraud."

Le Duc de Langres assiegé dedans Dole,
Accompagné d'Autun et Lyonnois:
Geneue, Ausbourg, ioinct ceux de Mirandole,
Passer les monts contre les Anconnois.   (VII-4)

(The duke of Langres, besieged in Dole, accompanied by Autun and those of Lyons. Geneva, Augsburg, allied with those of Mirandola, will pass over the mountains against those of Ancona.) Dole is a town in the Jura mountains. The siege of Dole is mentioned also in V-82 (not quoted in this book). Langres is a plateau in the Haut-Marne (Upper Marne). Autun is a town in Bourgogne (Burgundy). Mirandola is a town in the province of Modena (northern Italy). Ancona is a town in Italy, on the Adriatic Sea. The quatrain deals with military actions, which Gustafsson places at the time when Europeans will again drive the Arabs or Asiatics out of Europe.

Naples, Palerme, et toute la Sicille
Par main Barbare sera inhabitée,
Corsique, Salerne et de Sardeigne l'Isle.
Faim, peste, guerre, fin de maux intentée.   (VII-6)

(Naples, Palermo and all Sicily through barbarian hand will be uninhabited, Corsica, Salerno and the Isle of Sardinia. Famine, plague, war, end of evils remote.) Here no comments are needed; the quatrain refers to the times of the Mohammedan invasion of Europe, when their attacks are directed against the great Mediterranean islands Sicily, Sardinia and Corsica and against the southern half of the Italian peninsula.

Flora, flee, flee the approaching Roman,
At Fiesole will battle be given:
Blood shed, the greatest ones taken captive,
Neither temple nor sex will be spared.   (VII-8)

"Flora" or Florentia, i.e. Florence, the city on both shores of the Arno, will be drawn into a terrible conflict with Rome. Not far from Florence, on the mountain summit near Fiesole, on the ancient battlefield, the decisive encounter between Florence and Rome will take place. Fiesole (Faesulae) is older than Florence, since the Faesulians laid the foundation of Florence in about 200 B.C., but this city was destroyed by Sulla in 82 B.C. The Roman colony Florentia was formed in about the year 59 B.C., to safeguard the crossing over the river Arno. Near Fiesole the Gauls had already, 2000 years ago, fought against the Romans and had vanquished them in 225 B.C. In 1010 A.D. the Florentians ravaged Fiesole, the town which had once founded Florence. Florence, the capital city of Toscana, battling the Hohenstaufen emperors, extended its power to a predominant position in Central Italy. Under the rule of the Medici family Florence passed through its true and essential "florescence." As already seen from the previously quoted quatrains, Florence will be drawn into a severe engagement with Rome and Parma, and will suffer great devastation. Florence has already weathered many storms, and in times to come will again act an important part in the history of Italy.

Entrée profonde par la grand Reine faite
Rendra le lieu puissant inaccessible:
L'armée des trois Lyons sera defaite
Faisant dedans cas hideux et terrible.   (VII-16)

(The deep entry made by the great queen will render the place powerful and inaccessible. The army of the three lions will be defeated, causing within a hideous and terrible event.) G. Gustafsson refers this quatrain to the events around Gibraltar. The great queen is Queen Victoria of Great Britain, who at the end of her reign in about 1900 ordered the fortifications of Gibraltar to be modernized and made into an impregnable stronghold, the most powerful in the world. "Three lions" can be found in the arms of England. Properly speaking, they are leopards. Nostradamus mistook them for lions, but it can be easily explained and excused, because leopards in arms are always depicted as having lion's manes, which real leopards never have. Even in heraldic atlases the arms of England are entered under "arms with lions." Neither the Spanish nor Italian arms have more than two lions, therefore, here only the English, i.e. British, army could be meant. As already stated, this army will be defeated. Gustafsson is of the opinion that it will happen at the time when the Mohammedans will occupy the Pyrenean peninsula.

Before that, according to Gustafsson, all efforts by Spain to recapture Gibraltar will be unsuccessful.

Par pestilente inimitié Volsicque,
Dissimulée chassera le tyran:
Au point de Sorgues se fera la traffique
De mettre à mort luy et son adherant. (VII-21)

(By the pestilential Volscian enmity, dissimulated will drive out the tyrant. On the bridge of Sorgues will be made the bargain to put to death him and his adherent.) The Volscians or Volsci are an ancient tribe that lived in Italy. But more likely the Volces must have been meant (see pp. 239,269). Sorgues is a small town in Provence (southern France), in the department of Vaucluse, near the Rone, about 2 miles north of Avignon. Hence, in Sorgues will take place a conspiracy against an (Italian?) tyrant. The word "dissimulated" seems to infer "underground" activities.

Dieu le ciel, tout le divin verbe, à l'onde,
Porté par rouges sept razes a Bizance:
Contre les oingt trois cnes de Trebisconde,
Deux loix mettront, et hourreur puis credence. (VII-35)

(God, heaven all the divine word in the waves, carried by reds seven shaven heads to Bysantium. Against the anointed three hundred from Trebizond will set two laws, and horror, then credence.) G. Gustafsson classifies this quatrain with those which relate to the new Christian sect. His commentary: "When the Catholic chrch under the pressure of the barbarian occupation will lose influence, and when the new faith will more and more spread over Europe, a general confusion will set in among those who are holding on to the traditional Christianity. Then the "red ones," i.e. the socialist parties or governments, will send a delegation of theologians (the word "shaven heads" refers to the tonsures of priests) to Byzantium (or to Turkey as the modern representative of Byzantium). There they will arrive in Trebizond (on the coast of the Black Sea), where the priests ("the anointed") of the new faith will assemble for a council. Here the delegates of European Christianity will acquaint themselves with a newly found, early gospel or another genuine document, containing the complete doctrine of Jesus. They will examine the submitted writings with distrust and fear but finally they will be convincing."

Eighth century

Condom et Aux et autour de Mirande,
Ie voy du ciel feu qui les enuironne,
Sol, Mars conioint au Lyon, puis Marmande,
Foudre, grand gresle, mur tombe dans Garonne.   (VIII-2)
(Condom and Aux and around Mirande, I see fire from the
sky encompassing them. Sun and Mars conjoined in Leo, then
at Marmande lightning, great hail, wall falls into the Garonne.)
All the mentioned places are near the river Garonne and the
city of Bordeaux (cf.I-46). The wall in the river may be a
dam or power station. Lightning and fire from the sky could
mean warfare, atomic bombs or a cosmic catastrophe. E. Ruir
refers this quatrain to the period of the transformation of the
globe. The sun and Mars pass through Leo once a year, but
passage seldom coincides with conjunction. Gustafsson's
date: August 22, 2113.

VIII-9 tells us that the eagle and the cock at Savona
(Italian Riviera) will be united, the sea, Levant, Hungary,
army at Naples, Palermo . . . An incomprehensible quatrain,
since it encompasses too many localities, which
geographically are quite remote from one another.

A great stench will come out of Lausanne,
Such that one will not know the source of the fact.
They will throw out all the remote people,
Fire seen in the sky, foreign people defeated.   (VIII-10)
S w i t z e r l a n d heretofore has given shelter to many
foreigners, but will some day earn great ingratitude for her
hospitality. The secret political agitation will remain hidden
for a long time, but then will suddenly come to light.
Switzerland instantly will react and begin an inexorable
action of purge and expulsion. But what about the fire in the
sky? Could not a connection be seen here still with I-87,
XI-44 and especially with X-49, which explicitly mentions

poisoned waters, reeking of sulfur?

> The crossed brother through unbridled love
> Will cause Bellerophon to die through Proitos.
> Fleet like hawks, the woman gone mad,
> The potion drunk, both thereupon to perish.   (VIII-13)

The purport of the quatrain can be discerned only with the help of a Greek myth, told by Homer in his "Iliad": Bellerophon was the son of Glaukos, king of Corinth. Accused of murder, he fled to Proitos, king of Argos, who received his kinsman hospitably and obtained his release. But Queen Anteia conceived a deep affection for Bellerophon and, as Bellerophon did not reciprocate her love, she slandered him, telling her husband that he had tried to seduce her. Proitos sent Bellerophon to his father-in-law, Iobates, king of Lycia, with a coded message, which contained the commission to kill Bellerophon. Referring to Proitos and Bellerophon, Nostradamus reports on a similar incident in Italy. This time it will be the king's brother, who is caught in forbidden love towards the queen. The desperately loving ("mad") woman will flee in a ship (to Italy or from Italy?) and will kill herself, having drunk a poisonous potion. Both lovers will be united in death. Nostradamus does not say where it will happen, but the quatrain contains an indication of Italy. Namely, the French word "milan" means "hawk," but it also may mean the Italian city, Milan. However, the third line of the quatrain cannot be translated as "fleet to Milan," because Milan is not a seaport.

> Au lieu que Hieron fait sa nef fabriquer,
> Si grand deluge sera et si subite,
> Qu'on n'aura lieu ne terre s'attaquer.
> L'onde monter Fesulan Olympique.   (VIII-16)

(At the place where Hieron had his ship built, there will be a flood so great and so sudden that one will have no place nor land to take hold of. The waves will mount Olympian

Fesulan.) A correct interpretation is stymied by the incomprehensible word "Hieron" and further complicated by the circumstance that in some texts, instead of "Hieron," "Hesion" appeared. In the last case, Jason could be meant, who led the Argonauts in their voyage from Iolcos (on the bay of Volo, Greece). But Fesulan could be only Fiesole (Fesulae) in Italy, and what kind of a flood could influence not only Greece but Italy as well? In the case of so immense a flood Nostradamus would not have mentioned two such insignificant localities in Greece and Italy. G. Gustafsson has a different solution. Being as preoccupied with the Arab or Asiatic invasion as he is, he thinks that the term "flood" refers to the flood of Asiatic invaders. The waves of attack will roll over Egypt, then along the Mediterranean coast westwards to Fesan (the present Libya). Instead of "Hieron" Gustafsson reads "Heron," who was a Greek thinker and inventor and lived in Alexandria (Egypt). In the second century B.C. Heron was the first to invent the steam engine and use steam as a motor power.

> Within Toulouse, not far from Beluzer,
> Digging a deep pit, palace of spectacle,
> Treasure found will vex everyone,
> And in two places quite near the Basacle.   (VIII-30)

This quatrain can be comprehended only with the help of an ancient Toulousian legend, which tells that the Volces (an ancient Gallic tribe which lived in the region of Toulouse) together with other Gauls, marauding in Greece, had pillaged the Delphian oracle, for which transgression they were inflicted with diseases. The local Toulousian oracle ordered them to throw all booty into the lake. Since there are no lakes in the vicinity of Toulouse, scientists are of the opinion that instead of a lake an excavated pit must have been meant. The legend is supported by historical facts. The Gauls (or Galls) in 390 B.C. attacked Rome, in 279 B.C., Greece. They even crossed over to the Asian coast and settled there in a province which thereupon was called Galatia. But the inhabitants of Toulouse are convinced that their own Volces (the Tectosages) did return home, laden with gold and other treasures. Nostradamus now tells us that these treasures will be found after a deep pit will be excavated not far from "Beluzer," which probably means Beauzelle, a suburb of Toulouse. The pit will be dug at a place chosen for the construction of a theatre, or at a place where formerly a theatre had stood. The treasure will be found at two places, not far from the famous mills of Basacle, a locality well known to every inhabitant of Toulouse.

> After the victory of the lion over the lion,
> Upon the Jura mountain hecatomb,
> Slaughter and dusky ones seventh million,
> Lyons, Ulm at Mansol death and tomb.   (VIII-34)

A terrible war will rage in southern France and in the Jura mountains. This calamity will happen after France will have fought a victorious war against a rival power. Who is the lion that has defeated another lion, has been disclosed in other quatrains, but confusion is caused by the last line: instead of Mansol, we have to read ''Mausol'' (mausoleum, cf. IV-27, IX-85), but what, in this context, could be the meaning of Ulm (a city in Germany)? Or should we read ''ulmus'' (Latin for ''elm'')?

> Within the entry of the Garonne and Bayse
> And the forest not far from Damazan,
> "Mar saues" frozen, then hail and cold,
> In the Dordonnais frost through error of "mesan."
>   (VIII-35)

The correct rendering of this quatrain is made difficult by several incomprehensible expressions: 1) "Mar saues" could be translated as "discoveries of the sea" (from Old French "save," to discover), but may mean something entirely different; 2) "mesan" (a word evidently changed by Nostradamus to rhyme with "Damazan") could be the inverted Latin "mensa" (month), or the town Mezin, not far from all the other localities mentioned in this quatrain. One thing is certain: the quatrain refers to the southwestern part of France, which will be affected by a cold wave. This region of the Gascogne being famous for its wines, the "mar saues" could be vineyards. The region of Dordogne too will suffer from frost caused by an "error of the month," i.e. frost in a wrong month.

> The king of Blois to reign in Avignon,
> Once again the people flock together,
> In the Rhone by walls will cause to bathe,
> Up to five the last one near Nolle.   (VIII-38)

Blois has been a favourite residence of several kings of France. One of the future kings of France will transfer the seat of government to Avignon. Avignon has been the papal see from 1348 to 1377 and remained under papal jurisdiction until 1791. The French republic will again flock around the king's throne. They will finally get weary of the endless disputes of the political parties and will try to eliminate internal wrestling by conferring power on a king. The third line could mean that the king will build a palace there, which will be bathed by the Rhone. But how to interpret the last line? Will the king spend in Avignon the first five years of his reign? And what is Nolle? No such place can be found on maps. A hypothesis has been offered, that the word Nolle or Nole is an anagram for "Leon" and may refer to a pope. The last pope with the name of "Leon" was Leo XIII. According to the prophecy of St. Malachia, the present pope will be succeeded by only four more popes. If one of the last ones will be Leo XIV (always assuming that such interpretation of "Nolle" is correct), what connection will he have with the king, residing in Avignon? Or will the prophecy be realized in Leo XIV's time? Or will Avignon again become the seat of the popes as well? (cf. VIII-52).

VIII-44 makes known that the natural offspring of Ogmion (or Ogmios) will turn aside from the road from seven to nine, and that Navarre will have to destroy the fort of Pau (cf. VI-42). Pau has been the capital of Navarre, and Henri IV was born in the fort of Pau.

> The pestilence around Capadille,
> Another famine approaches Sagunto:
> The knight, bastard of the good old one,
> Will cause the great one of Tunis to be decapitated.
> (VIII-50)

Capadille (a name which sounds Spanish) cannot be found on any maps. Northwest of Barcelona, however, lies Capellades. Regardless of whether we read "Capellades" or "Castille" (Castile), a place in Spain has been meant, because Sagunto too is in Spain. The mentioned Capellades or Castile (central part of Spain) will become the central point of hostilities during the war between Spain and the Mohammedans. An epidemic will break out and Sagunto also will suffer from famine, caused by the war. The ruler of Tunis will come to a bad end: a knight, born out of wedlock, will decapitate him. Not quite clear is the expression "the good old one" (bon sénile). It could mean the good character of the old one or his "good age." To be of a "good age" means to be at least 60 to 70 years old.

> The Byzantine making an oblation,
> After having taken Corduva to himself again:
> His road, long rest, vines lopped,
> On sea passing prey by Colongna taken.   (VIII-51)

"Byzantines" are the inhabitants of Constantinople, because this city was called "Byzantium" by the Romans. Consequently, the Turks, i.e. the Mohammedans, will rule again over Spain. After the conquest of Corduva (Cordoba) they will impose great tribute of war on the Spaniards, and they will enjoy Spanish wine. The name "Colongna" remains incomprehensible. Does it stand for "Corogna" (Spanish

"Coruna"), a city on the northwestern coast of Spain? Or, perhaps, for the "columns of Hercules," i.e. the Strait of Gibraltar?

> The king of Blois to reign in Avignon,
> From Amboise and Seme will come along the Indre,
> Claw at Poitiers, holy wings to ruin
> Before Boni.   (VIII-52)

The word "Seme" is incomprehensible. Could the river Seine be meant? Or Saumur? The fourth line is unfinished. In some apocryphal editions of the centuries, instead of "Boni," "Bonieux" is printed. Nostradamus once more confirms that one of the future kings of France will reign in Avignon. After Poitiers will be taken in his "claw," to wit, will be vanquished or subdued, the enemy will be routed, and the war will end before Bonnieux (a small town in the Vaucluse).

VIII-58 relates to events in England, where something like a civil war will take place. The country will be split, and the Anglican church will approach the "Gallic air," i.e. Catholicism.

> Le vieux frustré du principal espoir
> Il parviendra au chef de son Empire:
> Vingt mois tiendra le regne à grand pouvoir
> Tiran, cruel en delaissant un pire.   (VIII-65)

(The old one, disappointed in his principal hope, will attain to the head of his empire. Twenty months he will hold the realm with great power, tyrant, cruel in giving way to one worse.) This prophecy was very often quoted after the First World War. The commentators were convinced that it refers to George Clemenceau, the "old tiger," as he was called. It was expected that he would take on the role of a tyrant. And afterwards, when during the Second World War the 84 year-old marshal Pétain became head of the Vichy government, he was identified with the "old one" of Nostradamus. But Pétain's reign lasted 28 months, from July 1, 1940, until November 11, 1942, when the Germans seized all power in

France. Furthermore, Pétain was no dictator, and he could not be called a tyrant. Terror in France began only after November, 1942. President De Gaulle as well cannot be meant, since he ruled over France much longer than 20 months, and he too was no tyrant. Consequently, the forecast about the old dictator is still awaiting realization.

Auprès du ieune le vieux ange baisser,
Et le viendra surmonter à la fin:
Dix ans esgaux au plus vieux rabaisser,
De trois deux l'un huictiesme seraphin.   (VIII-69)

(Beside the young one the old angel will fall, and he will come to rise above him in the end: ten years equal in most, the old one to fall again, of three two one the eighth seraphin.) Here we have a contest between the old and the new. Are certain personages meant? Hardly, because the contest is between angels, consequently, between spiritual currents. G. Gustafsson, who very much favors the foretold "new faith," sees even in this quatrain a prophecy about the contest between Protestantism ("the old angel") and the new line of faith, which will finally prevail by fusion with Protestantism. The "third one," mentioned in the last line, could be Catholicism, which still will retain a certain position of power, although weakened during the Arab occupation. Gustafsson foresees that the new form of Christianity will gain many adherents also among the Islamites. But who or what is the "eighth seraphin"? Is it the eighth millennium?

VIII-70 makes known that an ugly, wicked tyrant will arrive in Mesopotamia, and that the whole land will be full with black-faced people. What is here meant by "Mesopotamia"? Mesopotamia is a land between waters, consequently, something like a peninsula (as contrasted with "Panpotamia," which would mean an island). E. Ruir is of the opinion that this quatrain relates to the period of Arab reign in Italy.

L'Antechrist trois bien-tost annichilez,

Vingt et sept ans sang durera sa guerre:
Les heretiques morts, captifs, exilez,
Sang, corps humain, eau rougie, gresler terre.   (VIII-77)

(The Antechrist three very soon annihilated, seven and twenty years of blood will his war last. The heretics dead, captives, exiled, blood, human body, water reddened, hail on land). In his epistle to Henri the Second, Nostradamus mentions several Antechrists, during whose reign the Christian church will be persecuted. This quatrain speaks about the "third" Antechrist. It is important to distinguish among these Antechrists, and therefore it is advisable to make a careful analysis of the epistle. It will be of great help in deciphering Nostradamus' quatrains. In counting the Antechrists, E. Ruir has counted eight of them, including fascism and communism, the seventh being Mohammedan victory over Europe and the eighth the invasion by Asiatics. However, it should be kept in mind that Antechrists, which are represented by certain political systems, may reappear at different periods of history.

The greatest sail out of the port of Zara
Near Byzantium will carry out its enterprise:
Loss to the enemy and the friend will not be caused,
The third upon both will inflict great plunder and
capture.   (VIII-83)

Zara is in Yugoslavia and now is called Zadara. From there, i.e. from the Adriatic Sea, a great naval squadron will set out to the waters of Constantinople. But no encounter will take place between this fleet and the Turks, because a third one will interfere, will inflict great loss upon both rivals and will be the only one which gains advantage from this quarrel. Who is the third one—Russia? and who is the adversary of the Turks—Greece? Or England? In another quatrain Nostradamus warns the English to abstain from alliances with the Russians, lest it later bring them great disgrace. No eternal friendship between England and Russia is possible.

In order not to fall into the hands of his uncle,
Who slaughtered his children in order to reign:
Speaking to the people, putting his foot on Peloncle,
Dead and dragged between barded horses.   (VIII-89)

An heir to the throne will be put to death, but in which country will it happen? The solution must be sought in the incomprehensible word "Peloncle." The word being at the end of a line, it is clear that Nostradamus has changed the ending of the word in order to get a rhyme. As is well known, he has done it more often as not. A possible solution: Pelorum, the ancient name for Cap Faro, the northeastern point of Sicily. If this solution is correct, the foretold event will take place in Italy.

VIII-97 tells us that the all-powerful England will witness three new, beautiful children (three new countries) to be born near the shores of Var (on the Bay of Genoa, near the French-Italian frontier). The English nation itself will have lost its faculty to reign and will never regain its former power and glory. If Var is an abbreviation, the river Vardar in Macedonia (southern Yugoslavia and northern Greece) may have been meant.

Des gens d'Eglise sang sera espanché
Comme de l'eau en si grand abondance,
Et d'un long temps ne sera restranché
Vae, Vae au clerc, ruine et doléance. (VIII-98)

(The blood of the church people will be poured out like water in such great abundance and for a long time will not be stopped. Woe, woe, for the clergy ruin and wailing.) Antechrist will try to exterminate the clergy, and for a long time all pious people will be outlawed and their murderers will not be brought to justice. Whether it would happen in just one or several countries, is not revealed by Nostradamus, but we know from his other predictions that the pope will have to flee from Rome.

Through the power of the three temporal kings,

The Holy See will be put in another place:
Where the corporal substance of the spirit
Will be restored and received as the true see.   (VIII-99)

This prediction confirms the previous one. A new exile is forecast for the pope, where the eucharist (the holy communion) will be presented and received as in the proper place (Rome).

Ninth century

From the top of the Aventin hill a voice is heard,
Be gone, be gone all of you on both sides:
The anger will be appeased by the blood of the red ones,
From Rimini Prato, Columna expelled.   (IX-2)

Not only in Rome, from the Aventin hill, will the warning voice
"Be gone, be gone" be heard, but in all Italy, from Rimini to
Prato; i.e. from the Adriatic Sea in the east to Prato in Tuscany
in the west, the believers will hear the warning. The red ones
will put an end to the clergy, and the pope, called here
"Columna" (the pillar of the St. Peter's church in Rome) will
be expelled from his see in Rome.

The great cow, at Ravenna great trouble,
Led by fifteen shut up at Fornase:
At Rome there will be born two double-headed
   monsters,
Blood, fire, flood, the greatest ones in space.   (IX-3)

"The great cow" is Italy. The first Greek colonists in Italy
were cowherds. As mentioned previously, the name "Italy"
comes from an ancient, obsolete Greek word, which means
"cow." The chief of these cowherds was Italos, king of the
Siculians, father of Siculus and Roma. In Italy, at Ravenna, a
rebellion will be staged under the leadership of fifteen
ringleaders (former prisoners?). Fornase is a town near
Venice. This word being at the end of the line, it is possible
that Nostradamus has changed the ending of the word for the
sake of a rhyme and, in reality, another place-name with
a similar first syllable may have been meant, for instance, Forli.
At that time in Rome two double-headed monsters will
appear and be up to mischief. It is hard to discover the
meaning of this allegory. The Roman god Janus was
double-headed. His temple was opened or closed, in
accordance with Rome being in a state of war or of peace.
Possibly, Nostradamus has wanted to infer that during the

time of these two "monsters," in Rome will reign now war, now peace.

> Who will open the monument found
> And will not close it promptly,
> Evil will come to him, and unable to prove
> If it had better be a Breton or Norman king.   (IX-7)

What kind of a monument will it be: a document or a tomb? The main point of this quatrain is that it will not be known if the future king of France will be a descendant of the Valois line or the Bourbon line. Bretagne was incorporated with France under François I of the house of Valois, and Louis XVII bore also the title of the duke of Normandy.

> The child of a monk and nun exposed to death,
> To die through a she-bear, and carried off by a glazier,
> The army will be camped by Foix and Pamiers,
> Against Toulouse Carcassone will send fore-runners.   (IX-10)

An illegitimate, exposed child would have suffered death by a she-bear, if it had not been rescued by a glazier. In France woods with bears can be found only in the most southern part of the country, at the foot of the Pyrenees. This foundling will later become captain or commander of a body of soldiers and will erect a camp by Foix and Pamiers and from Carcassone will send forerunners against Toulouse. The first line of this quatrain still requires a more particular commentary. During the Middle Ages a common popular belief existed that the Antechrist will be born as an offspring of a monk and a nun. When Luther, who belonged to the Augustine order, in 1525 married the nun Catherine Bora, his antagonists did not fail to exploit this belief, trying to augment the popular prejudice. Nostradamus lived in Luther's time, and we cannot know if he wanted us to comprehend the first line of this quatrain literally. Anyway, he has wanted to underscore that the "child of a monk and a nun" will not be a peace-loving, pious man, but a murderous, destructive spirit, who will take active part in the civil war in southern France.

> So much silver of Diana and Mercury,
> The images will be found in the lake:
> The potter looking for new clay,
> He and his own will be steeped in gold.   (IX-12)

A poor potter, looking for fresh clay, will by a lucky chance find silver images of Diana, the goddess of hunting, and of Mercury, the god of commerce, in a lake. The find will make him and his family rich.

> The younger son playing outdoors under the arbor,
> The top of the roof in the middle on his head,
> The father king in the temple of Saint-Salonne
> Sacrificing will consecrate festive smoke.   (IX-23)

The crown prince will meet with a fatal accident. We are in uncertainty only about where to seek Salonne. It could be Salon in Provence, where Nostradamus was laid to rest, or Salonnes in Lorraine, or Salone between Rome and Tivoli. The most likely place, however, is the cathedral of Blois, before 1730 called the church of Saint-Solenne. This interpretation is the most credible because the subjects of this prophecy are a king and a prince. Blois has been a famous residence of the kings of France and, in case of the restoration of monarchy, may again become one.

> Passing the bridges to come near the rosebushes,
> Arrived late, yet sooner than he will believe,
> The new Spaniards will come to Béziers,
> So that this chase the enterprise will break.   (IX-25)

In the first line two words have been in the original designedly changed, in order to render the riddle more difficult. Instead of "the bridges" we have to read "Saint-Pons" ("pont" means "bridge"), and instead of "rosebushes" we have to read "Rosis." Both localities are situated near Béziers. "The new Spaniards" is an allusion to the incursions, made by the West-Goths (Visigoths) from

Spain three times (in the fifth to seventh centuries) against France. At that time Béziers was captured, but in the future, when a similar raid into southern France will be undertaken by the Spaniards, the enterprise will not succeed (it will be "broken").

> Allied fleet, port of Marseilles,
> In the port of Venice to march to the Pannonias:
> To leave from the gulf and bay of Illyria,
> Destruction to Sicily, cannon shots for the
>   Ligurians.   (IX-28)

Naval battles in the Mediterranean. It's hard to discern if the allied fleet will sail to or from Marseilles. Let us assume that it will first arrive in Marseilles, then proceed further to Venice. From Venice the army will march to the Pannonias (Austria or Hungary). After leaving the Adriatic, the troops will devastate Sicily and will bombard the Ligurian coast. Possibly, it will be a different detachment from the one that had marched off to the Pannonias.

> Hercules Roi de Rome et d'Annemarc,
> De Gaule trois le Guion surnommé,
> Trembler l'Italie et l'une de sainct Marc,
> Premier sur tous Monarque renommé.   (IX-33)

(Hercules king of Rome and of Annemarc, from Gaul three surnamed leaders. Italy and the one of St. Mark to tremble. First monarch renowned above all.) Here we are told about three leaders. Hercules symbolizes a king of France. The two others are the king of Rome and the king of Denmark (d'Annemarc). Apostle St. Mark is the patron of Venice. According to a legend, his bones are buried in the church, which has been built on the square of St. Mark in Venice. All Italy will tremble in warfare when these three leaders will lead the attack (against the positions of the Mohammedan occupation army in Italy?).

> Bridge and mills in December carried off,
> To so high a place will rise the Garonne.

Walls, edifices, Toulouse pulled down,
So that none will know his place, likewise
   Matronne.   (IX-37)

The Garonne will overflow and demolish the whole region of Toulouse. At the same time the "Matronne" will do the same. "Matronne" is the river Marne, called "Matrona" in Latin. E. Ruir is of the opinon that the catastrophe will occur during the translation of the terrestrial globe.

The great Chyren will seize Avignon,
From Rome letters in honey, full of bitterness:
Letter, embassy to leave from Chanignon,
Carpentras taken by a black duke with a red
   feather.   (IX-41)

The future King Henry, in Nostradamus' quatrains often called "Chyren" (anagram of "Henryc"), will seize Avignon. The pope in Rome will deplore this procedure with bittersweet words in a letter to King Henry. A special ambassador will leave from Chanignon with the king's reply. Since no such place as Chanignon can be found on any map, and since it is the last word of a line, we can be sure that here again Nostradamus has had some difficulty in finding a suitable rhyme for "Avignon." Let us assume that it will be Cavaillon, a town near Avignon. At the same time a military leader (wearing a hat adorned with black and red tufts of feathers, or whose escutcheon includes a similarly colored heraldic crest) will capture Carpentras, a nearby city. If king Henry the Fifth's coming is foretold for July, 1999 (as H. Bauder interprets X-72), these events will occur only after the year 2000.

From Barcelona, from Genoa and Venice,
From Sicily pestilence Monaco joined:
They will take their aim against Barbarian fleet,
Barbarian driven back as far as Tunis.   (IX-42)

The Spaniards and Italian coastal towns, which had much suffered in previously mentioned wars against the

Mohammedan onslaught, will join forces to put the barbarian fleet to flight and to drive it back as far as Tunis.

> On the point of landing the crusader army
> Will be ambushed by the Ishmaelites,
> From all sides struck by the pirate ship,
> Rapidly attacked by ten elite galleys.   (IX-43)

E. Ruir is convinced that this quatrain predicts Arab victory over the Jews in Palestine, and that the Jews will be speedily and easily overcome on land and on sea, because on the side of the Arabs will be fighting soldiers from all Islamic countries of Africa and the Middle East. But the expression "crusader army" makes us think that the Christians rather than the Jews will be the ones ambushed by Arabs (Ishmaelites). Ishmael, son of Abraham and Hagar, was the ancestor of the Arabs. Consequently, this quatrain could be interpreted also thus: an attack by Arabs will surprise the fleet of the Christians and will destroy it. Of course, both interpretations can be fused into one. It is more than possible that the Pan-Arabian movement will be directed also against the Christians. The Arabs look upon Palestine as their country, and that the Arabs will for some time occupy and desecrate the Christian holy places in Palestine, has been foretold by Nostradamus also in his epistle to Henry the Second.

> Migrez, migrez de Geneue trestous,
> Saturne d'or en fer se changera,
> Le contre *Raypoz* exterminera tous,
> Avant l'aduant le ciel signes fera.   (IX-44)

(Leave, leave Geneva every one of you, Saturn will be converted from gold to iron, Raypoz will exterminate all who oppose him. Before the coming the sky will show signs.) Geneva and the lake of Geneva are often mentioned in the centuries. The reasons can be easily explained. The times of Nostradamus were times of religious wars. Geneva was a land of freedom and occasionally a land of terror, since Calvin was as furious and cruel as the inquisition. For Nostradamus

Geneva was also the cradle of Jean Jacques Rousseau and of humanitarism. The teachings of Rousseau to some degree already foreshadow the fourteen points of Wilson and the League of Nations. We can read about it in quatrain IV-59: "The fort polished, and an old dreamer to the Genevans from Nira will show the tracks." It can be seen that the prophet of Salon did not set a high value on the League of Nations and deemed it to be a feeble, vain crowd of chatterers, who lull the nations into a false, foolish sense of security. Alas, history has confirmed it. The hopes of the old dreamers have not been realized. Such a sincere, generous humanitarian has been Briand, who some interpreters see mentioned by Nostradamus as "Nira" (phonetical anagram of "Briand"). One or two letters wanting or in excess was a permissible variation in Nostradamus' times (for instance, Nostradamus often uses "noir" as an anagram of "roi"). Nostradamus was especially interested in Geneva as the seat of the League of Nations. New buildings, new palaces, all the new spirit influenced him to such a degree that he possibly named Geneva itself "the new city" (cf. I-87). Geneva in times to come will be visited by a cataclysm. There is no doubt about it, because too many indications point toward such a conclusion. In the second line of this quatrain astrological symbolism has been employed. Nostradamus' astrology is often occult, symbolic, esoteric, and his symbols do not always reflect astronomical chronology. In this respect many commentators have often been led astray by literal interpretations. The expression "le contre *Raypoz*" presents difficulty. For Foubrine *"Raypoz"* is "rapace." (bird of prey), and the whole expression is rendered as "adversary of the rapacious ones." To Colin de Larmor this expression means "contre Paris" (against Paris). Gustafsson has gone so far as to compare the Swiss with the Rajputs, the courageous warriors of northern India, who in the days of the Grand-Moguls, in 1526, created a separate Indian state. In

Saturn Gustafsson sees a symbol of the Asiatic invaders, who will not be able to persuade the Swiss to take part in a victorious expedition against France and Germany. According to Gustafsson, the Swiss will resist, and Switzerland will become another victim of the Mohammedan thirst for conquest. J. Monterey's solution of *raypoz* is *zopyra*. In fact, such a rendering supplies us not only with an absolutely perfect anagram, but also with a key to the meaning of the whole quatrain. Zopyra was the man who, pretending to be a fugitive, delivered Babylon into the power of the Persian king, Darius. Our epoch is rich with such fugitives—let me mention only the Russian general Vlasov and the German general Von Paulus. Here, evidently, we have to deal with a pseudo refugee, a counterfeit turncoat, who in reality will be spying for the enemy.

IX-49 predicts, that Ghent and Brussels will march against Antwerp; i.e. Belgium will experience a revolution. The Flemings will clash with the Walloons, splitting the country and the people into two inimical parts. At the same time, a revolt will occur in England; revolutionaries will seize power and put the king to death.

Conflit Barbare en la Cornette noire,
Sang espandu, trembler la Dalmatie,
Grand Ismaël mettra son promontoire,
Ranes trembler, secours Lusitanie.   (IX-60)

(Conflict barbarian in the black headdress, blood shed, Dalmatia to tremble. Great Ishmael will set up his promontory, frogs to tremble, aid for Lusitania.) Arab invasion of the Balkans. The shores of the Adriatic have to suffer. For the present, the real meaning of the word "frogs" remains incomprehensible. The reference to Portugal (Lusitania) may mean that after Arabs will have taken Rome and Venice, the western powers, for instance, France and England, will assemble their forces for a contrary action and will concentrate their armies in Portugal (cf. I-28 and IV-50).

It is significant that Portugal will play a positive rôle in this contest in later years, "after a long while" (I-28), as the bridgehead for the United States of America on the European continent.

> The plunder made upon the marine coast,
> In *cita nova* and relatives brought away:
> Several of Malta through the deed of Messina
> Will be closely confined, poorly rewarded.   (IX-61)

This time "the new city" (cita nova) is spelled out in Italian. Therefore, we can assume that Naples has been meant, since the name of this city in Greek "nea polis" means "new city." In other quatrains too a "new city" is often mentioned in French. Then, as we have seen, there is some reason to doubt that Naples has been meant, one of other possibilities being, for instance, Geneva, which became "a new city" after it had been chosen as the seat of the League of Nations. Ever and ever again Naples will become a bone of contention, partly among the Italians themselves, partly being coveted by foreign nations. Also those of Malta (the English?) will hurry to render the harassed city assistance, but will be poorly rewarded for it.

IX-63 mentions the destruction of Narbonne and Foix in southern France.

> On the mountain of Bailly and La Bresles
> The proud ones of Grenoble will be hidden.
> Beyond Lyons, Vienne on them so great a hail,
> Like locust on land, not a third will remain.   (IX-69)

In southeastern France such fierce battles will occur that people will be crushed like swarms of locusts and only less than a third of the fighters will remain alive.

> At the holy places animals seen with hair,
> With him who will not dare the day.
> At Carcassonne propitious for disgrace,
> He will be set for more ample stay.   (IX-71)

Carcassonne is one of the few medieval towns which have

been preserved up to this day with all enclosing walls, towers and ditches intact. This medieval fortress will become for a long time the retreat for a man to whom nothing is sacred and who should have been rejected instead of being welcomed. In Carcassonne will reign irreligiousness, and in churches animals will be kept.

Dans Foix entrez Roy cerulée Turban,
Et regnera moins évolu Saturne,
Roy Turban blanc et Bisance coeur ban
Sol, Mars, Mercure ensemble prés la hurne.   (IX-73)

(Into Foix will enter Blue Turban King and will reign less than an evolution of Saturn. The White Turban King Byzantium heart banished, sun Mars, Mercury together near the urn.) Here the Mohammedan invasion of Europe is announced. A Blue Turban King or Emir will capture Foix. Could this mean only a temporary Arab expedition from Spain over the Pyrenees into France and a brief attack on Foix, before the concentrated invasion of France? Saturn's revolutionary period is approximately twenty-nine years. Will this Arab emir reign in Foix for less than twenty-nine years? Or perhaps Foix symbolizes the whole of France, and the Mohammedan reign in France will be less than twenty-nine years? All these questions will be answered only by the future events themselves. A White Turban King or Emir will reign in Byzantium. The word "ban" could mean also "banner," and the third line could be rendered thus: "The White Turban King will plant his banner in the heart of Byzantium, i.e. in Turkey." Does the last line indicate the length of his reign? In such a case, it will not last longer than nine years, because the sun, Mars and Mercury meet in the sign of Aquarius once in approximately nine years. In the original instead of "Aquarius" we read "the urn." The urn is an attribute of the Aquarius (Aquarius, the Water Bearer, pours water from an urn). However, the last line could be also an astronomical indication of the time period of the invasion. If a conjunction of all three luminaries has been meant, then it must be stated that such an occasion occurs comparatively seldom. The expression "near the urn" could also mean that the conjunction can occur not only in the end of January or in February, but even in the first days of March, because the stars, which constitute "the urn," extend far into the sign of Pisces. Gustafsson's date: March 15, 2105.

> In the city of Fertsod homicide,
> Deeds, harsh deeds for sacrificing plough-oxen.
> Return again to the honors of Artemis,
> And to Vulcan dead bodies to sepulchre.   (IX-74)

For the time being, the word "Fertsod" remains unsolved. Perhaps Rome has been meant, since it is known as the city of Jupiter Feretrius, in honor of whom all cloaks belonging to the enemy's generals, who had perished in combat, were collected and brought to Rome. Artemis, the goddess of hunting, is known also as Diana. Her honors again will be restored, and the dead will be dedicated to Vulcan, the god of Fire. This is a prediction of a return to the pagan customs in at least a section of Europe.

> From Ambraxis and the country of Thrace
> People by the sea, evil and help to the Gauls:
> Perpetual trace in the Provence,
> With vestiges of their custom and laws.   (IX-75)

Ambraxis, now called Arta, is a city in western Greece. From this city and from Thrace (northwestern Greece) people by the sea will bring assistance to France. But the Greeks will also become a nuisance, because they will not want to return to their country. They will intermarry with the inhabitants of their host country, and their habits and customs will gain firm footing in France. History repeats itself. Formerly, Phoenicians settled in Marseilles and became residents of that region; in the future it will be Greeks, who will settle in the Provence, not to be ousted.

> With the rapacious and bloodthirsty king,

Issued from the pallet of the inhuman Nero:
Between two rivers, on the left wing of the army,
He will be murdered by a young tenant (or
    baldy?). (IX-76)

An unworthy king will become a dreadful scourge for his country (France?). During a military action this bloodthirsty king will be murdered by a young farmer. The word "tenant" can be understood also as "baldy."

IX-78 makes known that an ugly Greek lady, who has had countless suitors, will emigrate to Spain, where she will be taken captive and will die a miserable death. This quatrain would not be worthy of citation, if we had not known of Nostradamus' habit of symbolizing governments and forms of government by feminine personages. Now, the history of ancient Greece permits us to compare dictatorship with an ugly Greek lady. Consequently, if such an interpretation is correct, the dictatorship of general Franco may come to as bad an end as the red republic (Captive prise mourir mort miserable).

The chief of the fleet through fraud and stratagem
Will make the timid ones come out of their galleys.
Come out, murdered, the chief, renouncer of chrism,
Then, through ambush, they will pay him his
    wages. (IX-79)

An admiral will use a stratagem to make the timid ones to disembark, and he will put them to death. The chief of the fleet, who had become untrue to his king, "the anointed one," and had corrupted his soldiers, to induce them to this betrayal, will be repaid in kind.

The duke will want to exterminate his followers,
Will send the strongest ones to strange places.
Through tyranny will ruin Pisa and Lucca,
Then the barbarians will make vintage without
    wine. (IX-80)

An Italian leader will through tyranny ruin Pisa and Lucca,

two famous cities of Central Italy. Pisa is known all the world over through its "leaning tower," the construction of which was begun in 1174 and completed in 1350. The famous pioneer of science Galileo used the tower's incline to make experiments with gravitation. Pisa, in rivalry with Genova and Venice, rose during the 11th century to be one of the chief commercial cities of the Mediterranean, owing its predominance mainly to the circumstance that it took the lead in the fight against the infidels. Lucca was once a great Roman city. The ruins of an amphitheatre give evidence of the city's former magnitude. After the collapse of the Roman empire Lucca was yielding obedience successively to the Ost-Goths, Langobards and Franks, then became a dukedom and, finally, after the death of the margravine Mathilde, a republic. In 1805 Napoleon I gave Lucca to his sister Elisa Baciocchi as a principality, but in 1847 Lucca became part of Toscana. In times to come, the cities Pisa and Lucca will again play a great rôle, but ill fortune will befall them because of the tyranny of their ruler.

> To pass Guienne, Languedoc and the Rhône,
> From Agen holding Marmande and La Réole.
> To open through faith the wall, Marseilles will hold its
> throne,
> Conflict near Saint-Paul de Mausole.   (IX-85)

The places mentioned in the second line are situated in the Gironde and in the department Lot-et-Garonne. Adding the regions of the first line, we have all of beautiful southern France. Over the years, many battles will be fought for the sake of it.

> In the cleared forest of Touphon
> By the hermitage will be erected a temple.
> The duke of Etampes through the ruse he invented
> Will teach a lesson to the prelate of
> Monthléry.   (IX-87)

Here commentaries are superfluous. Monthléry is in the

department Seine-et-Oise.

> Foibles galeres seront unies ensemble,
> Ennemis faux le plus fort en rempart:
> Foibles assaillies Vratislaue tremble,
> Lubecq et Mysne tiendront barbare part.   (IX-94)

(Weak galleys will be joined together, false enemies the strongest on the rampart. Weak ones assailed, Bratislava trembles, Lubeck and Meissen will take the barbarian side.) A very interesting quatrain. As barbarians have been mentioned, it pertains to the period of Arabian invasion of Europe. Possibly, this prediction is connected with V-73. Although Bratislava (called Pressburg in Nostradamus' time) is a city in Czechoslovakia, it is not impossible that Nostradamus meant Vrotslav (Polish name for Breslau). The Poles siding with the Arabs, the "weak galleys" must belong to the fleet of the countries of Northern Europe, which have joined their forces to combat the Polish fleet in the Baltic. The Poles will be vanquished; consequently, to the Northern countries will belong the decisive role during this period of the invasion. Even Bratislava (or Breslau?) will tremble. In Gustafsson's opinion, the last line should be read thus: "Lubeck and Meissen (i.e. the Germans) will hold the barbarian line," will repel the enemies in southeastern Saxony, where Meissen is situated, and will pursue them even into Czechoslovakia. If this interpretation is correct, Germany will be the only Central European country which the Arabs will not be able to conquer.

Tenth century

At midnight the leader of the army
Will save himself, suddenly vanished:
Seven years later, his reputation unblemished,
On his return will never say yes.   (X-4)

In France, in a future war, the commander-in-chief of the
army, deeming the campaign lost, will save himself by flight.
For seven years he will keep in hiding in a foreign country,
before venturing to return to France. He will never admit the
flight, in order not to damage his reputation.

Gardon, Nemaus so high over the banks,
That Deucalion will be believed reborn.
Into the colossus the greater part will flee,
In Vesta's tomb fire to appear extinguished.   (X-6)

Gardon is a tributary of Garda. Garda, in its turn, empties
itself into the Rhône. Nemaus is a brook near Nîmes. It seems
that with "Nemaus" Nostradamus may have meant the city
of Nîmes itself, its Latin name being "Nemausus." The first
line, consequently, means: "The river Gardon will flood the
city of Nîmes." The mentioned localities are near Salon,
where Nostradamus lived and was buried. Deucalion and
Pyrrha were, in Greek mythology, the couple which escaped
"the great flood" or deluge. The word Deucalion, therefore,
stands here for "deluge." The colossus or colosseum is the
famous Roman amphitheatre in Nîmes, where many people,
the flood being imminent, will take refuge. Vesta is the
goddess of the hearth, and the last line can be interpreted as:
fire will be extinguished in all fire-places. But Vesta, being a
goddess of fire, reigns also over the fire that dwells in the
bowels of the earth. Therefore, simultaneously with the
catastrophe, caused by water, another catastrophe may
occur, caused by fire, which will gush forth from the earth.

In the Figueras of Castillon on a misty day
A sovereign prince will be born of an infamous woman.

Surname of "Breeches," made posthumous,
Never was there a king so very bad in his
   province.   (X-9)

Castillon is the present Catalonia. Figueras is a town near the French border. There the birth of a very eminent Spanish prince will become a great misfortune for the whole of Catalonia (or perhaps for the whole of Spain). The prince will be born of an infamous, vile woman. The third line can be understood in two different ways: 1) the prince, because of his slovenly dress, will earn the surname "Breeches" and will have been born after the death of his father, 2) a man with a surname "Breeches" will make him be born after the death of his father, i.e. will murder his father. Spain will never have had so bad a ruler.

Stained with murder, enormous adulteries,
Great enemy of the entire human race,
One who will be worse than his grandfathers, uncles or
   fathers,
In iron, fire, waters, bloody and inhuman.   (X-10)

This is a continuation of the previous quatrain. All mentioned crimes can be attributed either to the Spanish ruler alone or they may characterize the whole generation of his time. Murders and adulteries will be daily occurrences, worse than ever. A blood-thirsty, inhuman race will annihilate itself with sword and fire. Taking into account the fact that the next quatrain also reports about the same inhuman ruler, the suspicion is aroused that he could be one of the Antechrists, mentioned by Nostradamus in his epistles.

Below Junquera, at the dangerous passage,
The posthumous one will have his band cross,
To pass the Pyrenees mountains without his baggage,
From Perpignan the duke will hasten to Tende.   (X-11)

"The posthumous one" is the same Spanish ruler who was mentioned in the two previous quatrains. He is called "posthumous" because he will be born after his father's death. According to one source, Junquera is the name of a valley near Pampeluna, at the foot of the Pyrenees mountains. More probably it is another Junquera, situated approximately twelve miles north of Figueras, which was mentioned in X-9. Here the Spanish king will cross the Pyrenees mountains without his baggage. The fourth line, dealing with the adversary of the Spanish ruler, can be translated in different ways. Tende is a town in Piemont, near the French-Italian border. Nearby is also the Pass of Tende. The "duke," the foe of the Spanish king, will either hasten from Tende to meet his enemy, or he will flee from Perpignan to Tende, in other words, from France to Italy.

> Elected pope, the chosen one will be mocked,
> Suddenly, forthwith moved prompt and timid.
> Through too much goodness and kindness provoked to
> die,
> Fear extinguished guiding the night of his
> death. (X-12) (see also page 118)

A newly elected pope will be mocked and sneered at. He will feel insecure and timid. His goodness and tender heart will hasten his death and only in the night of his death his fear will be extinguished.

> Beneath the food of ruminating animals,
> Led by them to the fodder market town,
> Soldiers hidden, their arms making noise,
> Tried not far from the city of Antibes. (X-13)

Soldiers, hidden in haycarts, will imagine themselves safe, will be betrayed by the noise of their arms and will be attacked not far from Antibes, on the French Riviera.

> Father duke old in years and tormented by thirst,
> On his last day his son denying him the ewer.
> Into the well plunged alive he will come up dead,
> Senate at the rope death long and light. (X-15)

An old duke will meet with death, being thrown into the well by his son. The senate will sentence his son to be hanged.

The remonstrances made to the ungrateful people,
Thereupon the army will seize Antibes.
In the region of Monaco will be placed the complaints,
And at Fréjus the one will take the shore from the
    other.   (X-23)

Again there will be struggles for the sake of Antibes, Monaco and Fréjus, the beautiful cities of the French Riviera. In Nostradamus' time the seaport Fréjus was still a very important commercial town and naval stronghold.

Through the Nebro to open the passage of Bisanne,
Very far away will the Tajo make a demonstration.
In Pelligouxe will the outrage be committed
By the great lady seated in the orchestra
    (senate?)   (X-25)

A quatrain hard to solve, because all place names have been changed, except the Tajo river in Spain and Portugal. In Spain also a river, named Ebro, can be found, but since it is indicated that Tajo is "very far away," we have to look for "Nebro" somewhere outside the territory of Spain or Portugal. A possible solution: the Nebrodi mountains in Sicily. Through these mountains a "passage" will be opened. Perhaps a (French?) fleet will pass the mountains towards the port Brindisi(?) in Italy. We know from other quatrains that in days to come France will undertake several campaigns against Italy and that finally Italy will be brought under the dominion of France. Very far away, in another country, the river Tajo, which flows through Spain and Portugal (consequently, the inhabitants of both countries) will make a demonstration. In the original we read in Spanish: "fara muestra," an expression with the meaning "to make known one's intention or will." At the same time, a French queen (?) will commit a crime in Périguex. What the crime consists in is not disclosed by Nostradamus and will be revealed only by future events.

Le sainct Empire viendra en Germanie,

Ismaëlites trouueront lieux ouuerts,

Asnes voudront aussi la Carmanie,

Les soustenants de terre tous couuerts.   (X-31)

(The Holy Empire will come into Germany. The Ishmaelites will find open places. The asses will want also Carmania, the supporters all covered by earth.) It is hard to understand the meaning of this quatrain. The Holy Empire once was synonymous with the German Reich. Probably, Germany again will become the dominating power in another Holy Empire. The prophecy mentions also Ishmaelites. Ishmael, son of Abraham and Hagar, was the ancestor of the Arabs. Carmania is the Roman name for a province of Persia. By the word "Ishmaelites" Gustafsson understands only those Arabs who have joined the new Christian sect, which will rise in Europe during the Arab occupation. The last two lines he interprets in the following way: this new teaching, which will have found many "open places" and will have spread especially in Germany, will find Persia "closed."

The great empire should belong to everyone,

One will obtain it over the others,

But his realm and existence will be of short duration,

Two years will he be able to maintain himself in the
    ships.   (X-32)

It seems that the great empire will have to be partitioned. Everyone of the victorious states will want to have the lion's share, but the one which will get the greater portion will be able to keep it, however, only for two years. The contention between the rivals will be decided at the conference table, after a long squabble with all modern pressure methods. The allies will be united only seemingly, not in reality.

The cruel faction in the long robe

Will hide thereunder the sharp daggers.

To seize Florence, the duke and the vicinity,

Its discovery by immature ones and idlers.   (X-33)

The rebels will hide their weapons under their long robes, to seize power in Florence and the surrounding country. The conspiracy will be betrayed by adolescents and idle sycophants.

> The Gaul who will take possession of the empire
>   through war,
> Will be betrayed by his minor brother-in-law.
> He will be drawn by a fierce, prancing horse,
> The brother will be hated for the deed for a long
>   time.   (X-34)

The Frenchman, who will obtain the sway over the empire through war, will be betrayed by his younger brother-in-law. The king will fall from and will be dragged by a wild, untrained horse. His brother-in-law will be blamed for this accident for a long time.

X-40 has for the subject a heir to the British throne. After his father's death his ascendance to the throne will be due, but revolution will take place, and from the son "the realm will be demanded."

> The shadow of the realm of Navarre untrue,
> It will make the scion's life unlawful.
> The vow promised in Cambrai uncertain,
> King Orléans will give a lawful wall.   (X-45)

The scion of the king of Navarra will turn out to be a wrong claimant to the throne, and his power of a sovereign unlawful. A court of arbitration in Cambrai will have to settle the question of the disputed succession to the throne, but the decision arrived at will not contain the desired positive realities. Protection for the lawful king will come from Orléans.

> Garden of the world near the new city,
> In the path of the hollow mountains,
> Will be seized and plunged into the Tub,
> Forced to drink waters poisoned by sulfur.   (X-49)

This is one of the quatrains which are quoted by J. Monterey when he tries to illustrate the meaning of I-87 and

IX-44. The garden of the world is the League of Nations, which made a new city of Geneva. This city will be destroyed in a nuclear explosion. Obviously, even Lausanne will suffer (VIII-10). The explosion will poison also the water of Lake Geneva, since the phenomenon will occur not only on land or air, but also in the water. For contemporaries of Nostradamus and also for later generations these quatrains must have seemed insignificant and even ridiculous with the "odor of sulphur" and "poisoned water," but today these predictions have assumed a sinister and horrible character.

> The three whores will fight each other from afar,
> The greatest least will remain listening.
> The great Selin will no longer be her patron,
> He will be called fire, shield, white route.   (X-53)

The words "pellix" and "nonaria" ("whore") in Nostradamus' texts mean "revolution." Selin, as we know from other quatrains, is the "conqueror of the Crescent," i.e. of the Turks or Arabs, namely, the great Henry V, king of France. The French army will be proud of the successes of the king, and even after his death he will be called fire that gives light, shield that protects, white path that leads to victory.

> The royal prelate his waning too prolonged,
> A great flow of blood will come out of his mouth.
> The angelic realm by his reign proclaimed,
> For a long time dead alive in Tunis as a stump.   (X-56)

The royal prelate is the pope, who during his reign will have proclaimed "angelic realm." His decline of life will be miserable and for a long time he will hover between life and death in Tunis. "As a stump" and "dead alive" indicate that he either will be paralyzed, or that he, who in his time has had proclaimed so many angelic messages, now will be forced to keep silence. It is strange that he will waste away not in the Vatican City, but on African soil, in Tunis, across the Meditteranean from Italy. From this fact many interpreters conclude that he will have been imprisoned by Arabs.

> Within Lyons twenty-five of one mind,
> Five citizens Germans, Bressans, Latins,
> Under a noble one they will lead a long train,
> And discovered by barks of mastiffs.   (X-59)

A group of conspirators in Lyons, consisting of twenty-five persons, including five Germans or at least five foreigners, namely, Germans, Bressans and Italians, will make long preparations for an attempt, but will be discovered by a dog's bark. The last line could be understood also allegorically: the warning will come by vigilant and alert guards. Bressan is a region in Savoy, which in Nostradamus' time did not yet belong to France.

> Ie pleure Nisse, Mannego, Pize, Gennes,
> Sauonne, Sienne, Capuĕ, Modene, Malte:
> Le dessus sang et glaiue par estrennes,
> Feu, trembler terre, eau, malheureuse nolte.   (X-60)

(I weep for Nice, Monaco, Pisa, Genoa, Savona, Siena, Capua, Modena, Malta: for the above blood and sword for a New Year's gift. Fire, the earth to tremble, water, unfortunate unwillingness.) "Nolte" is derived from Latin "nolutas" (unwillingness) or "nolo" (I do not want). Here are depicted fierce battles on sea and land. When will they take place? Probably, during the Arab or Asiatic invasion of Europe.

> Betta, Vienna, Emorre, Sacarbance
> Will want to deliver Pannonia to the Barbarians,
> Enormous violence through pike and fire,
> The conspirators discovered by a matron.   (X-61)

Betta could be Pettau in northern Slovenia. It now belongs to Yugoslavia and is called Ptuj. Emorre could be Emona, a town in Bulgaria. Sacarbance is Scarabance (from Latin "Scarbantia"). It is situated south of the Austrian capital Vienna, inside the territory of the present Hungary. The Austrians call it Odenburg, but the Hungarians, Sopron.

Pannonia is either Austria or Hungary. Since the quatrain mentions Vienna (in Austria) and Sopron (in Hungary), it is not clear against which of the countries will be directed the conspiracy of delivery to the barbarians (some powerful neighbor country). But as all the mentioned cities, except Vienna, lie in countries under the dominion of communism, it can be assumed that the conspiracy, if it is expected in the near future, will be directed against Austria, but will fail, because it will be discovered by an elderly woman.

Près de Sorbin pour assaillir Ongrie,
L'heraut de Brudes les viendra aduertir:
Chef Bisantin, Sallon de Sclavonie,
A loy d'Arabes les viendra conuertir.   (X-62)

(Near Sorbin, to assail Hungary, the herald of Brudes will come to warn them. Byzantine chief, Salona of Slavonia, will come to convert them to the law of the Arabs.) By Sorbin, apparently, Serbia has been meant. Salona (in Latin "Salonae") was in Roman times a great seaport of Dalmatia. Brudes can nowhere be found, but it is very likely Brindisi (in Latin "Brundisium"). In V-99 Nostradamus has already used the word "Brundis" to designate Brindisi, but in his quatrains the same geographical name can be found under many forms and with different spellings. Since during the Arab attack the Balkans will be conquered simultaneously with Italy, the Mohammedans, very likely, will transfer their headquarters to Brindisi, from where the Byzantine chief will easily cross to Split, in the vicinity of which port lies the ancient Salona. The military front will advance through Serbia towards Hungary.

O vaste Rome ta ruine s'approche,
Non de tes murs, de ton sang et substance: --
L'Aspre par lettres fera si horrible coche,
Fer pointu mis à tous jusques au manche.   (X-65)

(O vast Rome, thy ruin approaches, not of thy walls, but of thy blood and substance. The harsh one by letters will make so horrible a notch, pointed steel driven in up to the hilt.) It seems that here is meant not the total ruin of all of Rome with its monuments, which will happen only during the transformation of the terrestrial globe, but instead, the decadence of the Catholic church. In Rome anti-popes will appear and will make agreements with the Arabs. This quatrain is connected with VI-100.

> L'an mil neuf cens nonante neuf sept mois,
> Du ciel viendra un grand Roy d'effrayeur,
> Ressusciter le grand Roy d'Angolmois,
> Avant après Mars regner par bon heur.   (X-72)

(In nineteen hundred ninety nine and seven months, from the sky will come a great king of terror to bring back to life the great king of Angolmois, before and after Mars to reign by good luck.) This is a very often quoted quatrain, because it contains a distinct numeral, indicating a certain year. "Angolmois," correctly "Angoumois," was an ancient feudal land, later called by the name of its capital Angoulême. Before 1714, when it was incorporated into the French "crown lands," it was esteemed as an independent, separate branch of the reigning house of Bourbons. Many interpreters are of the opinion that in July, 1999, the arrival of the greatest king of France, Henry the Fifth, can be expected. He will reign in his country with good luck before and after the next (i.e. the third) world war. With his bellicose, soldier-like character, he will recall François I, the first ruler from the house of Valois-Angoulême. François I reigned in Nostradamus' lifetime for thirty-three years, from 1515 until 1547. François I through his victory over the Swiss at Marignano on September 13 and 14, 1515, conquered the dukedom of Milan and concluded with Pope Leo X a concordat, advantageous to France. François I was also the first who had on open field vanquished the Swiss, up to that time considered to be invincible. His two first wars against Emperor Carlos V from 1521 until 1526 and from 1526 until 1529 definitely determined the loss of Milan and the resulting Spanish predominance in Italy. The third war against Carlos V lasted from 1536 until 1538 and the fourth from 1542 until 1544. François I enlarged the territory of France towards the north and aspired to the German emperor's crown. On his accession to the throne François I was only 21 years old. He was, from the French point of view, an ideal king, a gallant and elegant courtier and a splendid, brave knight. He was very nationalistic and did not squander away the property of the citizen and of the peasant, as his predecessors had done, in gifts to lords, courtiers, knights, ladies and scholars. Even up to this day he has remained for many Frenchmen the image of an ideal sovereign. In childhood he liked to play shuttlecock, practiced archery, used to set traps and to lay snares as well as to hunt deer and stags. In more advanced years he liked to break in horses, to break a lance with his companions or to clear ditches and turnpikes on horseback. The future king of France, Henry V, too will be a hunter like François I, as already proclaimed by Nostradamus in II-28. If the fifty-seven years, mentioned in X-89 (quoted in the chapter "Ambiguous Predictions"), can be referred to the period from 1945 until 2002, then during the third year of Henry V's reign the world will experience the commencement of a terrible war, the Third World War, from which France will come off victorious, emerging as a first-rate military power. G. Gustafsson does not share this opinion and believes that the end of the French republic can be expected only in 2017 (cf. VI-74). He therefore is convinced that Nostradamus with this quatrain announces only a monarchistic attempt to seize power in France (with war before and after this event) and that the proud, emphatic words are being used in an ironical sense. According to Gustafsson, the attempt, made by the Bourbons, will meet with as little success as the one made in 1836 by Louis Antoine de Bourbon, the duke of Angoulême.

France in 1950 repealed the law, which had been effective for sixty-four years and did prohibit the residence in France of members of families, claimants to the throne of France. Of these families the house of Bourbons has been extinct since 1883. Only the Bonaparts and the house of Orléans still exist, the last one being one of the many lesser branches of the Bourbons. The symbols of these two families appear in Nostradamus' quatrains as "the eagle" and "the cock." The eagle is a symbol of the Roman empire and in prophecy can serve as a substitute for "the empire" in general. This symbol in 1804 was revived by Napoleon I and since then has become a symbol of the French empire. The cock is a symbol of the house of Orléans. When in the revolution of July, 1830, Louis Philippe, a member of this family, replaced the Bourbons on the throne of France, the cock became a symbol of the whole French nation and even to this day is very popular in France. Nostradamus has not let us know to which of these two families the king will belong, who will ascend the throne of France after the demise of the republic. The symbols of both families are mentioned in quatrains which tell about the period of invasions of southern and western Europe from Asia and Africa. Therefore, it can be assumed that members of both families will play a significant rôle in the future history of France. Still another, quite interesting rendering of this quatrain should be mentioned: the word "Angolmois" can be taken as an anagram for "Mongolois." The great king of the Mongols, of course, has been Genghis Khan, and this personage is aptly described by the expression "king of terror." If such a rendering is correct, the year 1999 will see the appearance of the great Asiatic ruler, the future conqueror of Europe. E. Ruir, on the contrary, is of the opinion that 1999 will already bring an end to the Asiatic dominion and that, before and after 1999, Mars (the war) will be reigning with good luck, i.e. will be favorable to the Christian armies. As many interpretations exist as interpreters. It remains for us only to underscore the fact that this is one of the very few quatrains in which Nostradamus has included a certain, indisputable date. If the meaning of many other quatrains seems to be clear and there remains only uncertainty about the period of time, then in this case we are given a distinct date, but we still are left in the dark about the real meaning of this prophecy.

> The present time with the past
> Will be judged by the great Jovialist.
> The world late will be to him tiring
> And disloyal through the clergy, learned in
>   law. (X-73)

The great Jovialist (adherent of Jupiter) will judge all of humanity. Does this refer to the future king of France, Henry V, whose campaigns during the Third World War will victoriously cover the territory of all Europe?

> Au reuolu du grand nombre septiesme
> Apparoistra au temps ieux d'Hecatombe:
> Non esloigné du grand âge milliesme,
> Que les entrez sortiront de leur tombe.   (X-74)

(At the completion of the great seventh number it will appear at that time the games of hecatomb, not far from the great millennial age, when the buried will go out from their tombs.) This is a significant quatrain with apocalyptic contents. It has some connection with I-48 and III-92. The great seventh number is the year 7000 according to the Jewish chronology. The forefathers of Nostradamus were of Jewish descent and they calculated time according to the Jewish calendar. Nostradamus too took as the basis for his calculations the seven 1000-year periods. The so-called "millennium" will comprise the following, i.e. the eighth 1000-year period. According to the Jewish calendar, Jesus was born in the year 3761. In order to find the year in which, according to our own chronology, the mentioned games of hecatomb will take place, we have to deduct 3761 from

7000. The result is 3239 A.D. Then the world will not be far from the millennium and will experience great events. Hecatomb means slaughter. It is probably identical with the one, mentioned in B.113, which will occur before the end of the seventh one-thousand-year period and will continue for a long time. But we should not forget the letter to César, where it is said that Nostradamus' prophecies extend to the year 3797. Accordingly, the millennium should begin already around the year 2800. Of course, we cannot be sure that "the millennium" of Nostradamus is identical with the one promised in the 20th chapter of the Apocalypse, although in Nostradamus' epistle we read farther on (B.115) also about the binding of Satan, like in the Book of Revelation. The binding of Satan was mentioned also in B.101. Be that as it may, from B.113 can be inferred that before "the millennium" of Nostradamus a long war will rage. From the 20th chapter of the Book of Revelation can be seen that during the millennium the wise and just law of Christ will be reigning, and the witnesses of God's word and all martyrs of the Antechristian period, together with Christ himself, will rule for a thousand years, and it will be the first resurrection. Even as in the days between Easter and the Ascension Jesus made himself visible, so also these righteous ones and the martyrs will make evident their presence on this earth. After the 1000 years, according to the inconceivable will of God, Satan will be released for a short while. This short interval will be used by the evil spirit to goad and provoke Gog and Magog against God. But the Almighty God will destroy Gog and Magog, and this judgment will mean good fortune for Israel and all other people and nations. Who are Gog and Magog? The answer is found in the 38th and 39th chapter of prophet Ezekiel. "Son of man, set thy face against Gog in the land of Magog, the prince of Rosh, Meshech and Tubal, and prophesy of him." Gog is prince in the land of Magog. Magog (cf. Genesis 10:2) was the son of

Japhet and became the ancestor of many northeastern nations, for instance, of the Scythians and Russians, among which Ezekiel includes Rosh (Russia), Meshech (Moscow) and Tubal (Tobolsk). After the crushing of Gog will come the day of judgment or doomsday, and it will be the second resurrection, when also the rest of the dead will assemble before the white throne and will be judged according to their deeds, all of which have been registered. Excluded will be the faithful of the first resurrection, who already will have ruled the world, together with Christ, for 1000 years. That in the opinion of St. John "to rise and to step forth from the tombs" and "the earth will give up (or restore) its dead" and similar expressions are not to be understood literally, can be seen from the Book of Revelation, chapter 6, verse 9-11, where the subject is "the souls of the slain." Although in Leviticus 17:11 Moses speaks of the soul as equal to the blood, it is a primitive conception, connected with the ritual of blood-sacrifices. Jesus, to the contrary, makes his opinion about this question very clear, saying (Matth. 10:28): "Do not fear those who will kill the body, but cannot kill the soul." With these words he affirms that the soul is distinct from the body and cannot be killed or annihilated simultaneously with the body. In Luke 20:35-38, conversing with the Sadducees, he expounds a spiritual conception of the resurrection. In what way Nostradamus has apprehended the resurrection, cannot be seen either from this or any other of his quatrains.

Tant attendu ne reuiendra iamais,
Dedans l'Europe, en Asie apparoistra:
Vn de la ligue yssu du grand Hermes,
Et sur tous Roys des Orients croistra.   (X-75)

(The long-awaited will never return in Europe, in Asia will appear one of the league issued from the great Hermes, and he will grow over all the kings of the East.) A quatrain permitting diverse interpretations. First of all, who is "the long awaited one"? Upon first reading it would seem that Nostradamus indeed has mentioned Jesus Christ, because for His return Christians have been waiting for countless generations. But after we have penetrated deeper into the meaning of the quatrain, we must admit that somebody else or something else has been meant. Europe or, for that matter, the whole world anxiously awaits peace. But peace, even if it comes, will not be reigning for long, regardless of the United Nations, the existence of which organization itself will not be of long duration. Over and over again discord will arise between the many nations of the small European continent, and all the beautiful words about democracy and lasting peace will turn out to be vain desires and beautiful hopes, which will be abruptly shattered by the furies of war. The intermittent periods of peace will not be long ones. And, according to Bauder, in the year 2002 (X-89) at the latest but possibly much earler, another world war will break out. And wars will recur for many centuries, up till the millennium. And Europe will cease to rule over the world. Asia will be the new ruling continent, and "one of the league, issued from the great Hermes" will grow over all the kings of the East. Will it be China, Japan or Indonesia? Which one of these states has arisen from the "league of Hermes"? Hermes, or the Roman Mercury, was the god of communication, trade and commerce. The greatest commercial nation in the world, up to now, has been England. England has concluded agreements and alliances with many countries, among others, an alliance with Japan in 1902, which country on December 7, 1941, declared war against her former allies. Japan was defeated, but the weight of a total defeat cannot last forever. Japan, the land of the rising sun, may again become the leader of the yellow race. Or will it be China, the land of the red dragon? Be that as it may, this quatrain permits still another, quite different rendering. The expected one may not be a political leader at all, but a spiritual teacher instead. As a matter of fact, such a teacher is today expected by all initiated in esoteric doctrines. According to ancient traditions, the world may soon expect the commencement of a new epoch. Such epochs supercede each other, in round numbers, every 2160 years, in which time the astronomical vernal equinox has advanced full 30 degrees. The epoch of Christianity was ruled by the zodiacal sign Pisces (Fish). Now we are expecting the commencement of the epoch of Aquarius. According to this doctrine, the change of epochs or eras is always conjoint with the appearance in the world of a new, great spiritual teacher, called either Messiah or having other similar names, according to the hopes of the nation expecting him. This deliverer of the world, although appearing at great intervals, may even have the same spiritual identity. He comes to proclaim or to again present to human minds, in a new form, the same old, immortal and eternal truths. When these esoteric epochs alternate, the whole world is always ravaged by immense political, social and even geological convulsions and upheavals. The spiritual aspect of this problem of change and transformation Nostradamus has supposedly presented in this quatrain. Accordingly, those who expect that the annointed one (the one issued from the league of the great Hermes) will appear in Europe, are mistaken. He again will appear in Asia. With the word "Hermes" has been meant not the divine messenger of Greek mythology, but Hermes Trismegist (the thrice great Hermes), the Greeks' name for Toth, the Egyptian god of Wisdom. Toth may be a historical personage. According to Egyptian legends, he supposedly lived about 18,000 years before Christ, was a great teacher and lawgiver and had written many books, establishing with them the basis for all existing sciences. Jamblich, a Neoplatonic philosopher (in the 4th century) claims that the number of these books has reached a thousand or more. In the Middle Ages many books with theosophical subject matter, supposedly written by Hermes Trismegist, were circulating in Greek, Latin and

Arabic languages. They had a great rôle to play in both Christian and Arabic medieval mysticism. Nostradamus now asserts that the new, great prophet and lawgiver and possibly even a founder of a new religious movement will appear in Asia, probably, in the Near East. It remains for us only to hope that he indeed "will grow over all the kings of the East," and that his spiritual influence and authority over the masses will surmount the influence of the materialistic and political leaders of the East, and that the expression: "Ex oriente lux!" will again regain validity.

> In the great realm of the great one reigning,
> Through force of arms the great gates of brass
> Will be opened, the king and duke joining,
> Port demolished, ship on the ground, day
>   serene.   (X-80)

After the great monarch will be crowned, his armies will capture the most powerful strongholds. Combining in his person both king and commander of the army, he will demolish ports and give a new foundation to the ship of Peter (the church). Those will be bright and happy days.

> A treasure placed in a temple by Hesperian citizens,
> Therein withdrawn to a secret place.
> The hungry bands to open the temple,
> Retaken, ravished, horrible prey in the midst.   (X-81)

In a Spanish (or American?) town a treasure will be hidden in a secret place within a temple. A hungry gang will force open the doors of the sanctuary, but they will be taken by surprise and apprehended. In the midst of the booty a horrible discovery will be made.

> Comme vn gryphon viendra le Roy d'Europe
> Accompagné de ceux d'Aquilon,
> De rouges et blancs conduira grand troupe,
> Et iront contre le Roy de Babylon.   (X-86)

(Like a griffin will come the king of Europe, accompanied by those of Aquilon. He will lead a great troop of reds and whites, and they will go against the king of Babylon.) Who will be this king of Europe, who together with his allies will fight against the Orientals (the king of Babylon) and will again liberate Europe from their dominance? Most likely, no other than Henry V. From the epistle to Henry the Second can be seen that the war against the Orientals will be enacted in two episodes. B.72 says that "these Eastern kings will be chased, overthrown and exterminated but not at all by means of the forces of the kings of Aquilon." And further on, in B.74, we read that "the lords of Aquilon, two in number" will make all the East tremble in terror. It proves that the Europeans will not put down their arms before the Mohammedans have been expelled not only from Europe, but also from the eastern part of their previously powerful dominion. It is possible that after the first period of the war the Europeans will be in discord about whether to carry the war into the countries properly Islamic. After an agreement on this question, the war, under the leadership of Germany and other northern countries, will be extended to the east and will acquire the character of a crusade, about which we can read also in VI-21 and III-97.

> The new barque will take trips,
> There and nearby they will transfer the empire.
> Beaucaire, Arles will retain the hostages,
> Near two columns porphyry found.   (X-93)

The new pope who represents the barque of Peter, i.e. the Catholic church, will undertake pilgrimages similar to those of Jesus' disciples, who as the proclaimers of the kingdom of God had no permanent domicile. Likewise the pope, when expelled from Rome, will undertake pilgrimages and will be received by Beaucaire and Arles. In the latter town two immense columns of marble can be found, remains of a great ancient theatre. Near these ruins the head of the church will take up his domicile.

To Spain will come a very powerful king,

By land and sea subjugating the south.
This evil, lowering again the crescent,
Will clip the wings of those of Friday.   (X-95)

Spain too will meet with better times under a powerful king. The old ideals of days long past will revive. Spain will regain the lost provinces and will be reminded of the days of Ferdinand and Isabella, when Moors were expelled for the first time. The attack will be directed against the south, i.e. toward Morocco. "Those of Friday" are the Mohammedans, whose sabbath is Friday.

Religion du nom de mers vaincra
Contre la secte fils d'Adaluncatif,
Secte obstinée deplorée craindra
Des deux blessez par Aleph et Aleph.   (X-96)

(The religion of the name of the seas will win against the sect of the son of Adaluncatif. The stubborn, deplorable sect will be afraid of the two wounded by Aleph and Aleph.) Which is the religion of "the name of the seas"? The word "sea" in Latin is "mare," phonetically very close to the word "Maria." Nostradamus often propounds similar logogriphs. As is well known, the Catholic church worships the Virgin Mary in preference to the Son, who is the central figure in Protestantism. A riddle, much harder to solve, is the word "Adaluncatif." Let us assume that it is a word in Arabic, since most Arabic cognomens begin with the letter A. The name of the letter A in Hebrew is "aleph," in Greek "alpha," but in Arabic "aliph." Consequently, the word sought for begins with the letter A. Supposing that the word is Allah (name of God in Arabic), the rendering of the quatrain could be as follows: The Christian religion, disseminated across all the seas over the whole world, will win out against the adherents of Islam. The stubborn Mohammedans, worshippers of Allah, will fear reprisals for having wounded two Christian leaders. Evidently, this quatrain refers to the period when the struggle between Christians and

Mohammedans will be resumed and the adherents of Islam will again be expelled from Europe. In days past, the Turks had occupied southeastern Europe, including Hungary, and were threatening Vienna, but in the southern and western part they were laying waste all Mediterranean shores and islands, carrying away into slavery thousands of Christians every year. The Iberian peninsula (Spain and Portugal) too was under the sway of the Mohammedans. In days to come history will repeat itself. Arabs will bring devastation to the countries of southern Europe and will penetrate into the interior of the continent. Great atrocities and depredations will take place. Towards the end of this period Mohammedans again will be gradually driven back, out of Europe. The European army and fleet will rally in Portugal or Spain. During fierce battles two Christian leaders will be wounded, before a complete victory over the barbarians will be achieved. The strongholds and seaports of the ancient Arabic pirates, Algiers, Tripolis, Tunis and the island Djerba will again be attacked. A new crusade will ensue, with the participation of France. Such is one of the possible interpretations of this quatrain, obtained with the aid of forecasts, taken from other quatrains. Nevertheless, some interpreters have a different understanding of the two last lines. They say that in having quoted the name of the letter A in Hebrew and not in Arabic, Nostradamus has wanted to indicate that the last part of the quatrain refers to Jews, even if the word "Aleph" has to be rendered as "Allah." The Mohammedans intend to drive the Jews out of Palestine and are preparing for a combined attack. Nostradamus was a Christian and the Jews seemed to him just a stubborn, deplorable sect, which persevered in maintaining antiquated religious ideas and consequently, as a nation, would meet with catastrophe. The "two wounded by Allah" are two vindictive nations, hostile to Israel, namely, the Syrians and the Egyptians, which both have vowed never to conclude peace with Israel. Sooner or later, the western bastions in Palestine will be victims of Arab nationalism, at the latest, when Europe will be inundated by masses of Asiatics. But even after the liberation of Europe, battles in Palestine will continue (or will be resumed), about which fact we find further information in the epistle to Henry the Second (B.67-68).

8
THREE VIEWS OF THE FUTURE

To translate the incongruous quatrains of Nostradamus and to solve all riddles propounded therein is, indeed, a very hard task. Many quatrains permit different solutions with, more often than not, even diametrically opposed meanings. Harder still it is to arrange the unraveled quatrains into a correct sequence of the approaching events.

The first step toward that purpose is—to classify into separate groups all quatrains that seem to have for subject matter the same identical event. Next, we have to try to arrange chronologically the quatrains of each separate group. In such a way separate fragments of the future unfold before our eyes. The most important of these fragments are: 1) the Mohammedans will invade Europe, 2) the Asians will invade Europe, 3) the Arabs will succeed in expelling the Jews from Palestine, 4) monarchy will be restored in France, 5) France will temporarily become the dominant power in Europe, 6) England will lose her status of a first-rate power and will never regain it, 7) the Catholic church, after a short consolidation, will again become decadent, and the power of the pope will come to an end, 8) a new sect or religion will arise, 9) a cosmic catastrophe, called "translation of the terrestrial globe" by Nostradamus, will occur. Besides these main prospects many minor ones are revealed, for instance, revolution in and partition of Italy, revolution in England, a new crusade against the Mohammedans, and other events.

Many commentators on Nostradamus' texts, after careful evaluation of these separate prospects, have tried to combine them into one comprehensive view of the future. In order to show how different can be the results, I will in a condensed form relate three such views, offered by commentators of three different nations—1. H. Bauder, a German, 2. G. Gustafsson, a Swede, and 3. E. Ruir, a Frenchman.[1]

* * * * *

H. Bauder founds the chronology of all his commentaries on the fifty-seven years of peace, promised in X-89 (cf. the chapter on ambiguous predictions). He refers them to the period from 1945 until 2002. His concept of the future is as follows:

All reports on impending disasters and wars, promised by Nostradamus, will be realized only in the 21st century. Only small wars of local nature are possible before the year 2002, for instance, a war between Russia and Turkey for the sake of the Dardanelles, with possible involvement of Greece.

King Henry the Fifth will ascend the throne of France in July, 1999 (X-72). It is confirmed also by I-48, since the reign of the moon will come to an end in 1980/81, and about twenty years later Nostradamus' prophecy about Henry V will be realized.

The Third World War will begin in 2002. France will have to fight against England, Spain and Italy. The English will devastate Paris, but the French will later wreak their revenge upon them. France will first conquer Spain, then Italy, and finally will gain dominance over all countries of the Mediterranean, including Turkey. During the reign of Henry V France will obtain control also over Geneva, which now belongs to Switzerland.

1. The most useful and complete investigation in English, so far, has been E. Leoni's contribution. Unfortunately, his commentaries, although well elucidating the historical background, depend too much on Le Pelletier and, consequently, are not quite abreast of our times.

After Henry V's reign dissension and discord will again arise in France. One after another the neighboring countries will escape from French domination. Spain will become an independent monarchy. A complete collapse of France will follow during the Fourth World War, which calamity is reported in I-73.

After a revolution, communists will come to power in Italy. The pope will be forced to leave Italy and will move to southern France, where he will reside in a new exile.

The next century will experience also an invasion of Europe by Mohammedans. In course of the expansion, they will first capture Palestine and then extend their sphere of influence along the Mediterranean coast and over the Mediterranean islands toward Spain, where they will reign for a long time. They will capture also Italian coastal towns in Liguria and will reign over France for less than twenty-nine years (IX-73). After their period of dominance, a new crusade will be organized by the Europeans.

Neo-Platonism will revive, gain influence and play a rôle, similar to that of a religion.

Asiatics will be roused to move westward. They will conquer the Middle East, Turkey, Greece and islands up to the Adriatic. Japan will become the dominant representant of the yellow race. Since every action is followed by a reaction, Japan will repay America in kind for the fatal atomic bomb of the Second World War.

The last world war will take place shortly before the millennium. Paris will then be devastated again. Great events are to be expected in 3239 A.D., when the world will be nearing the millennium (X-74).

At some time before 3797 A.D. the terrestrial globe will come under the influence of a new comet. The comet will approach the earth so greatly that it will bring about great convulsions and geological changes on our globe, and only after the lapse of many years the earth will regain equilibrium and emerge from the ordeal purified and rejuvenated.

The more significant passages of Nostradamus' epistles are interpreted by H. Bauder as follows:

B.43: Although in some quatrains Babylon means Paris, the "new Babylon," mentioned here, is New York, as a pseudonym valid for the whole of America. This Babylon is mentioned also in the Book of Revelation, chapters 17 and 18. Ten great countries will ally themselves against this modern Babylon and in a single hour will reduce the greatest city of the world to rubbish and ashes.

The golden calf is adored and worshipped in America. The attraction and economical power of America will grow fast. The attention of all nations, of all merchants and politicians will be directed towards America. Such are the predictions of Nostradamus. In his lifetime (1503-1566) America was in its first phase of development. Columbus had discovered it in 1493, and only in 1614 Dutchmen laid the foundation of New Amsterdam, the present New York. Nobody could foresee then that this small Dutch colony would speedily rise and grow to become the greatest city of the world. But even over New York, which now feels secure, will come a terrible ordeal: destruction of the city. Nostradamus refers to the biblical images of the Book of Revelation. All St. John's visions of the Babylon will be accomplished. Oriental legends tell that Babylon, in the Old Testament called Babel, "the gate of god," has been made into a marvel and wonder of the world on account of its buildings, which were constructed by the order of queen Semiramis. According to ancient reports, Babylon had a perimeter of sixty miles. Through the center of the city run Euphrates, the largest river of the Middle East. On the shores of the river two royal palaces were built, but in the center of the city a tower was set up, in honor of god Bel. The most famous marvels of the city, however, were the hanging gardens, that is, great masses of stone walls with immense terraces, which were covered with soil and laid out into gardens. The Babylonian rulers and courtiers lived in luxury, which circumstance advanced the growth of the trades and professions and all lines of business in the city. Weaver's trade in fine linen and wool, embroidery, dyer's art and manufacture of carpets, perfumes and other articles flourished already in the early days of Babylon. Babylon engaged also in a lively trade with neighboring countries. Already from the first days of Babylon's history, its citizens appear as an unwarlike, flabby, effeminate nation, which loves magnificence, luxury and life of pleasure. Already in the time of Jesus Babylon was decaying and desolate. Today the only remnants are heaps of rubbish and ruins.

Exactly so will end the great modern Babylon. New York is situated on several islands and on the mainland, on the shores of the Hudson, which with several branches empties itself into the Atlantic, forming many bays and inlets. Manhattan constitutes the heart of the city, in the southern part of which today the main business quarter can be found, with Wall Street as the principal seat of world finance. Gigantic houses of business and numerous skyscrapers, the most remarkable buildings of the world, are in this section of the city. The inhabitants form a babylonic mixture and jumble of all nations and all languages of the world. Furthermore, New York is the greatest Jewish city of the world with over two million Jews. New York takes also the leading position in America and in the world as the central point of industry, commerce and banking. This great Babylon will come to a bad end as a deserved punishment for having chosen idol Mammon as her god. Ten countries of the earth will agree to hate her, and shall make her desolate and naked, and shall eat her flesh, and burn her with fire (Rev. 17:16). Nobody will render aid to her and the kings of the earth shall lament for her when they shall see the smoke of her burning, standing afar off for the fear of her torment, saying: "Alas, alas that great city Babylon, that mighty city! for in one hour is thy judgment come" (Rev. 18:9-10). The power of atomic bombs will make the skyscrapers collapse like houses of cards and cover the neighboring houses with concrete, glass and steel, burying thousands of people under the rubble. Then the prophecy of St. John will have been accomplished.

Nostradamus in his letter to his son Cesar, written in March, 1555, refers to the periods of punishment which will repeatedly befall humanity. Always, when men for a long time have fared well and have lived in abundance and prosperity, they become arrogant and insolent, renounce God and rely only on their own "reason." God's wrath does not fail to visit them, and man's reason alone is incapable of saving him from war, famine and disease. Under the symbols of water and flood, the seer warns of periods of war, when hardly any region will remain unaffected. During the future world wars such a great abundance of fire and of burning stones (incendiary bombs and explosive bombs) will fall from the sky, that nothing will remain unconsumed (A.36-37). No one will be found to work the fields, because their owners will be dead or carried off to slavery and captivity (A.40).

In his epistle to king Henry the Second Nostradamus leads us in spirit to the empire of the Antechrist. After the "Myrmidons," that is, the Germans, who in Greek legends were considered invincible, will be subdued, and the barbarian sect by all the Latins greatly afflicted and driven out (B.39), the great empire of the Antechrist will begin.

B.40: Attila, the king of the Huns, with Xerxes will descend in great and countless numbers from the steppes of China and Russia. As Xerxes, the king of Persia, in days past, about 480 years before Christ, organized a military expedition from the whole of Asia, assembling an enormous army from all nations of the powerful Persian empire, including the Scythians from southern Russia; so the descendants of these rulers and of their subjects will undertake an expedition against the Christian Europe.

A transmigration will result, proceeding from the 48th degree north latitude. In this degree are also situated southern Russia, Romania, Czechoslovakia, Hungary, Austria, Germany and France.

The abomination of the Antechrist, who will have made war upon the royal person who is the great vicar of Jesus Christ, upon the pope and his church and his "temporal and time-restricted" reign, will be chased out, but this will be preceded by a period more dark and more gloomy than any since the creation of the world to this time. Extreme changes will follow, permutations of realms, mighty convulsions of a political and social nature. To determine the hour in which, according to the divine will, the purification and dissolution is bound to take place, men have to look for the promised, partly supernatural, signs in the skies.

Antechrist should not be comprehended as an individual person, but thereunder are included, for instance, also the bearers and representatives of the temporal religion, who have built up their personal power without regard for the one and truthful faith in and through the Son of God. Antechrist is not only *Ante*christ (who comes before the coming of Christ), but also *Anti*christ (who fights against Christ and the salvation of man). The wordly, human reason drives man to fight against Christ. But behind each such contention stands Lucifer himself as a personification of the Antichrist. He is the one who dares to raise his head through the permissiveness of man, since in his battle against the will of God he makes use of almost the whole humanity, bringing it to meet God's wrath and its own perdition. All slaves of human reason are in reality servants of Lucifer and accessories to the prodigious collapse, which now must come for the whole humanity. Prophecy proclaims that this Antechrist will raise his head and reach the zenith of his power shortly *before* the day of judgment begins.

B.59-61: The City of the Sun is Rome, Stechades are the

isles of Hyeres, and the great chain of port, which takes the name of the marine ox, is Bosphorus or Bosporus. Bosporus is the straight which connects the Black Sea with the Marmara Sea. The name "Bosporus" means "cow's ford" or "cattle ford," since, according to a Greek legend, it was here, where Io, turned into a cow, swam across the strait.

Inachos, the ancient ruler and king of the Pelasgi, had a daughter of dazzling beauty, named Io. When she once tended her father's cattle on the meadow of Lerna, Zeus, the ruler of Olympus, cast his eye on the maiden and was inspired to passionate love for her. He walked up to her in the shape of man and began to tempt her with flattering words, but the maiden flew from him in haste and would have escaped, had not the god in pursuit misused his power and wrapped the whole land in dense gloom. The fugitive saw herself surrounded by a dark vapor and arrested her steps, afraid of running into a rock or of falling into a river. Thus the unfortunate Io fell into the hands of the god. The goddess Hera had long since been aware of the faithlessness of her husband, Zeus, but was not able to tame her wrath and jealousy and, with her distrust always awake, watched each step of Zeus upon the earth. Zeus had foreseen the arrival of his spouse and, to save his beloved Io from her revenge, turned the lovely daughter of Inachos into a pleasant, snow-white cow.

The Marmara Sea and Bosporus, together with the narrow, important Dardanelles strait form the line of communication between the Black Sea and the Mediterranean Sea. For centuries Russia has tried to establish there her power and to extort free passage through the straits. After the First World War the allies tried to find a solution, instituting there a militarily neutralized zone. The treaty of Sévres left the administration of the zone to Turkey, with the stipulation that Turkey had to give free passage to all ships. But the treaty of Sèvres was the first one in the gigantic postwar structure of treaties which fell to the ground, because the

Turks, with consent of the allies, have long since refortified the straits. The Dardanelles have ever been a bone of contention. Xerxes and Alexander with their armies have crossed there from one continent to the other. The fall of the Turks has been prophetically proclaimed long ago, especially in Russia of the czars, where the "testament of Peter the Great" has been repeatedly unearthed, with the expectation that the Greek cross is about to shine again on the dome of the Agia Sophia in Constantinople. According to Nostradamus, the Dardanelles strait will be opened, and the great wish of the Russians will thus at last be realized.

For the "beginning of the seventh millenary" Nostradamus predicts the coming of extraordinary events, "when the adversaries of Jesus Christ and his church will begin to multiply greatly." Nostradamus takes as the basis for his calculations of dates the Hebrew calendar. The beginning of the seventh millenary, the year 6001, is the year 2239 according to our chronology. Then and during the following years a wave of impiety will be engrossing the world. Temples for ancient heathenish rites will again be set up, and the clergy will begin to indulge in luxury and whoring and will commit a thousand abominations (B.50). Nostradamus, evidently, refers to the religion of the Phoenicians and other Syrian peoples, who worshipped Ishtar or Astarte, the immoral and unchaste cult of which goddess is frequently mentioned in the Old Testament.

B.51: Beside Paris, at that time there will be in France another free city, which will be situated, like the French capital, between two rivers ("Mesopotamia"). Lyons is situated between two rivers, the Rhône and the Saône.

B.52-54: "The second Thrasibulus," as stated here by Nostradamus, will be a young officer with great aptitude for military strategy. He will liberate his native city Lyons from tyrant's rule (like the first Thrasibulus, who did the same for Athens in 410 B.C.). Together with refugees, friends of democracy, he will carry Lyons by surprise, will cast out the tyrant from the middle and send him to the gallows.

B.58: Satan's reign. Dog and Doham are Gog and Magog.

B.62: New wars. Even Spain and Arab countries will be seized with fever of war. As in the eighth century, when Arab power, with the assistance of a mighty Berber tribe, was extended into Europe, the Mohammedans will again extend their empire to Spain. But the Islamic reign in Spain will not be of long duration, because an alliance of the Christian nations will dislodge the invaders and push them out of Europe.

B.63-70: The profanation of the Holy Sepulchre. Achem is Shehem or Sichem, the ancient capital of Israel (today called Nablus).

B.71-74: Victory over the Orientals. Instead of Phoenicians we have to read: Tunisians.

A.41: In the eighth millenary of the Jewish chronology, i.e. between the years 3239 and 4238 of the Christian calendar, a new cosmic system will be created. In his letter to his son César, Nostradamus specifies the year 3797 as the date to which his predictions extend. We therefore are justified in assuming that at that time the changes will take place, which the seer has predicted in reference to the reorganization of the celestial constellations.

*　*　*　*　*

The view of the future, as presented by G. Gustafsson, is much more thoroughly considered and calculated and provides many isolated details. Its chronology is based on the supposition that the 73 years of VI-74 refer to the lifespan of the French "fourth republic" from 1944 to 2017, and that in about 2018 France will become a monarchy.[2] His other

2. The "fourth republic" came to an end already on December 21, 1958, when the constitution of the "fifth (DeGaulle's) republic" came into force. Adding 73 years, we get the year 2031. De Gaulle's death in 1970 did not result in a termination of the "Fifth Republic."

conjecture is that the initial point of the "liturgical" chronology (cf.VI-54) is the year 500 and that the dates, mentioned in VI-2, also are calculated "liturgically."

Gustafsson does not believe that the word "Chiren" or "Chyren," which can be found in some quatrains, should be translated as "Henry." Therefore, in forming his view of the future, he ignores these quatrains. His interest is concentrated on the future invasion of Europe by Arabs and Asiatics and on the particular stages of the invasion. He pays special attention to the appearance of a new religion and in his book dedicates many pages to it. He is convinced that it will be a revival of the original, primordial Christianity as it existed before 543, when the council of Constantinople rejected the teaching of Origen and of other patristic writers on apocatastasis (the return of man into the state of innocence, which teaching in modern times has been propagated by the German theologian Fr. Schleiermacher) and on pre-existence of the soul (or reincarnation, a doctrine lately accepted, for instance, by the English theologian Leslie Weatherhead). G. Gustafsson is also convinced that Jesus was a vegetarian (Romans 14:2) and was teaching compassion for all living created beings, and that these tenets will be confirmed by the discovery of old authentic manuscripts.

The view of the future, as conjectured by Gustafsson, is as follows:

The next great event, predicted by Nostradamus, will be the long awaited and dreaded conflict between Europe's western and eastern countries. This war is not called a world war by Nostradamus, as have been the previous great wars, which he in VIII-15 and in the epistle to Henry the Second calls "the two eclipses" because of their range and fatality. In Nostradamus' eyes the future conflict between East and West is merely an uprising against Antechrist, resulting in his banishment from the Russian satellites of Eastern Europe. The first Antechrist, consequently, is the modern East

European communism, hostile to religion in all forms and trying to abolish religion together with the capitalistic social order. The struggle with the first Antechrist will take place on different levels and arenas, being conducted so relentlessly that it will call forth armed conflicts in different corners of the earth and finally will convert itself into a contest on the important European front. The emancipation movement in Eastern Europe may acquire also a religious or even Catholic trait, since B.40 mentions the "Holy Ghost" as the antagonist of communism. The movement will first arise in Austria, through which runs the 48th degree of latitude, and which is identical with the "Northern country of 48th degree," mentioned in B.37. It is entirely possible that the war will break out because of Austria. I venture to surmise that archduke Otto may be identical with the prince, opposed by communists in connection with the religious movement on the 48th degree. Therefore, the prediction is that the Habsburgs will return to Austria, with probable reconstitution of monarchy in that country, which event would be in line with Catholic (papal) interests. If this would happen, the communistic governments of the neighboring countries would not tolerate it, especially Hungary would interfere, to prevent the occurrence of a fait accompli. The Hungarians would demand the expulsion of the Habsburg family as pretenders to the throne. This war between Austria and Hungary may expand into the Third World War. According to the aforesaid B.40, this great conflict will end with the complete defeat of the communists. The victory of the Christian anticommunists will ensure a general long-wished-for peace and concord (B.46) among "some" children, including the French republic. By "the misguided and separated children" have been meant the adherents of the ideas of Marx, Lenin and Stalin. Consequently, the communistic party will retain its power over the Russian people, but the so-called satellite countries, including East

Germany, will have changed their political and social regimes. Peace will last almost till the end of the century. All this is conceived by Nostradamus as a victory for the Christian, especially the Catholic, church. Catholicism will then experience its last great increase in power.

The seer does not say exactly when this war will break out. We have to try to conjecture the approximate date from his indirect disclosures. First, we see (B.45) that simultaneously with the great movement of peace "will issue one who will renew the whole Christian church." From B.44 can be seen that this renovator of the church will come after the end of a seventy-three year and seven-month long period. If we could establish the initial point of this period, we could easily fix also the date for the end of the Third World War. Assuming the Bolshevistic revolution of November, 1917, to be the initial point, we arrive at June, 1991, as the beginning of a long period of peace.[3] But X-72 reveals that Mars, the god of war, will reign before 1999. Consequently, the initial point has to be sought differently. In a Benedictine monastery (Maria Lesach on the Rhine) a prophecy was found in the 17th century about three wars, the last of which will begin a half-generation span after the previous war and will be of a much shorter duration. How long is a half-generation? How many years have to be added to 1945, in order to arrive at the beginning of the third war? During the First World War, a prediction was circulating, originating from an old monastery, that in a future war "the ruler with the cross" will be victorious, and that the "people of the Pleiades" will attack the "bearded people" from the rear. "The ruler with the cross" could be the one who is mentioned in B.40, and "the bearded people" could be the Russians, the attack from the rear coming from the direction of Asia, either by the

3. Gustafsson neglects to consider the possibility that the 73 years and 7 months, mentioned in the epistle, may be identical with the 73 years of VI-74, on which the whole chronology of his prospect of the future is based.

Americans (people of the starred banner), the Japanese or the Chinese. The old Chinese novel, *Chin-Ping-Mei*, includes a passage about the future magicians of China, who, while praying, will gaze toward a certain constellation of stars. Therefore, the prophecy may have meant the Chinese. In such a case, the defeat of Soviet Russia is quite possible and even likely. If the predicted conflict between Hungary and Austria breaks out and the Russians intervene, their Asian frontiers would remain unprotected. An insurrectionary movement may start there or the Chinese Peoples Republic may attack, since Russia now owns lands (Outer Mongolia, part of Sinkiang and western Tibet) which in previous times were part of the ancient Chinese empire. A clash between the new, despotic China and the Russian people, who belong to the white race, is sooner or later inevitable anyway.

Should the Third World War break out and should it end with the defeat of communism, extensive political revolutions with renewed, vivid interest for religion can be expected in countries neighboring Russia. As predicted by Nostradamus in B.49, the activities of the church will not be restricted any more. That will be the "transmigration" (B.40) which, regardless of oppression by communism, will have grown and will help to destroy its oppressors, reaching the culmination point after the war. Another result of the revolution will be the fact that many Protestants will join the Catholic church, because the Catholics will have shown far greater activity in the struggle against the rule of Antechrist. In B.45 is mentioned someone "who proceeding from the fiftieth degree will renew the whole Christian church." This degree west of the iron curtain traverses the Catholic countries France, Belgium and southern Germany. The renewal of the church will take place immediately after the Third World War, but already now the Roman church is experiencing something very much like a renewal or reformation. The movement, mentioned in this prophecy, will lead the church on a path which will become reactionary and violent against dissidents. In B.50 the seer says that the priests will again become perverted and corrupt. Such things cannot happen unless the church collaborates with a secular dictatorship which can last only as long as its rule is based on methods of terror. Further on, in B.51, we read that the church will be deprived of both her "swords." It means that the church will have acted jointly with *two* dictatorships, but will lose her connection with them. The political influence of the priests will wane, and they will retain only their "insignia." Of these dictatorships one is certainly Italy, but the other will perhaps rise on monarchistic foundations in Austria. Or, if fascism in Spain will then still exist, it could as well be Spain, which country always has been more Catholic than the pope himself.

The "feigned union," mentioned in VI-20, is the French-Russian alliance, as confirmed by B.46. It will come into existence after the next war (war of liberation against the first Antechrist). This alliance will be terminated after the new Roman "leopard," i.e. fascist dictatorship, will have come to power. Consequently, the Catholic church will lean upon two fascist dictatorships, Spain and Italy, in their joint struggle against communists and Protestants. Both dictatorships will be allied politically and militarily, looking upon the Mediterranean Sea as "mare nostrum." These dictatorships will be involved in a war against England (V-51) and her allies. The war between both political constellations will result in a victory by England and her allies, because B.51 confirms that Catholicism will be deprived of both "swords"; i.e. both Catholic fascistic dictatorships will collapse. Nevertheless, the very next sentence admits that the Catholic church even after that event will continue to attract people with methods of her own "until that there is born of a branch long sterile" one who will deliver the people from "this benevolent and voluntary slavery," i.e. the authority of the church. However, the similarity between what has been said about the origin of this man in B.51 and the one mentioned in B.45 proves that both statements refer to the same man, and that he will be rather a renovator or reformator than an enemy of the church.

About the further fate of Spain nothing has been said, but from B.51 we can infer that armed insurrection will take place in Italy. In the North Italian region which with its rivers reminds one of ancient Mesopotamia, namely, in the valley of the Po, will be created a new state, free from Rome and the church. This state will become the central point for the power of communism, the second Antechrist. The leader of the revolution will be a modern counterpart to Thrasibulus of ancient Greece (B.52), consequently, an emigrant, head of a movement of resistance, who will return to his native land, stir up revolution and, throwing fascists out of power, will put communists in charge, at least in a great part of Italy. All these dramatic events have been described in VII-21. The "dissimulant" will be the same Italian Thrasibulus, who as a political refugee will have emigrated to southern France and from there will direct the underground movement against the neo-fascist dictatorship in his native land. The time is astronomically fixed in II-15, where we are told of the slaying of an Italian ruler, presumably the neo-fascist leader. In such a way communists will come to power in northern Italy. The fascistic regime in Italy will have resulted as a consequence of the victory of Catholicism over the first Antechrist, Eastern European communism. The second Antechrist is mentioned in B.95, where we are told that in the "Adriatic," i.e. in Italy, which had been united, discord and separation will arise. Thereby it has been underlined that the task of the unification of Italy, which was completed in 1861, will be annulled, after the communists will have come to power in a section of Italy. Initially it will happen in the "Mesopotamia of Europe" on the 45th degree, namely, in the

Po valley. There communism even now has many adherents among the industrial workers. Later, revolution will expand to the 41st degree (Naples and Bari) and the 42nd degree with the capital city Rome. Finally, the 47th degree is mentioned, which crosses the strategically important Brenner Pass. Contrary to the 1568 edition of Nostradamus' works, which mentions the 47th degree, in the 1600 edition the 37th degree is substituted, which crosses southern Sicily. In either case, the Italian frontier is involved, which fact shows that all of Italy will come under the "infernal" power of the second Antechrist, as Nostradamus in B.96 characterizes communism in Italy, which will be fiercely hostile to the church. With harsh words he further on condemns communistic propaganda, with which the leaders will try to justify their actions. An end to the power of the second Antechrist will be marked out by the death of two important persons (B.97). One of them will be a Frenchman, adversary to the ultra-red regime, but the other will be in alliance with the church and free Sicily. On this occasion too, it will be impossible to overthrow communism without military intervention, since the epistle is continued with the statement that a great French army under the leadership of "Gallic Ogmios" will cross the Alps (the mountain of Jupiter) and invade Italy.

According to Le Pelletier, the "Gallic Ogmios" is a counterpart to the ancient demigod Heracles, who is mentioned in IX-33 as the future great king, battling Mohammedans. Ogmios actually was the Gallic god of oratory and corresponded to Hermes of the Greeks and Mercury of the Romans. Having used the name of a god as the designation of the French commander-in-chief, Nostradamus will not have indicated a lesser rank than the rank of a king. Therefore, at the time of the collapse of the communistic northern Italy, France will be a monarchy and the event referred to cannot take place before the year 2017 when, according to my calculations, the republican constitution of France will be abolished. A description of the second Antechrist is the main purport of the epistle's second prophecy; it could therefore be considered as a supplement to the first prophecy, where the second Antechrist is indicated only indirectly (B.51) as the adversary of the neo-fascist regime of Italy. In continuation, Nostradamus comments on the reasons for people's renunciation of the Christian faith and on the situation of the three most important religions (B.56-57). Catholicism, before its ruin, will have to some extent supplanted Protestantism in Europe, but Islam will have spread in the major part of Africa, where the churches of Christian missions will fail.

But the greatest danger yet to the European civilization, according to Nostradamus, will come from the manifold colored people. They will form a world of their own, and this world, like an infernal boiler, will explode. Nostradamus foresees Mohammedan and Asiatic invasion of Europe. The great Swedish naturalist and explorer Sven Hedin in a book, published in 1939, says that the migration of Asian people towards the west recurs regularly after a certain number of centuries like the attacks of locust swarms. "Therefore," he says, "no wonder that Nostradamus has foreseen the outbreak of a racial war between Asia and Europe in the year 1982, since a similar event can be presaged even without having to ask the stars for a solution of the riddle of the future." Sven Hedin has supposedly found the year 1982 indicated in a German commentary on Nostradamus' quatrain III-3. Here the words *"Mars et Mercure et l'argent ioint ensemble"* may not at all mean a celestial phenomenon, of which the temporal date can be calculated, but, quite contrary, a military, industrial and financial armament of Asia in preparation for the invasion of Europe. The population of Asia is rapidly growing, and the expansive pressure of the many millions of Asians from the direction of the east will be felt sooner or later. Then the Mongolian masses will unite and consolidate and, obeying the command of a new Gengis Khan, will begin a military expedition towards the west. At that time the Europeans and the Americans will have lost all their colonies, concessions and bases in Asia and finally also in the Middle East, which fact is confirmed by Nostradamus in B.58, where he says that "the realms will be weakened by Easterners."

Besides the prophecy incorporated into the epistle, Nostradamus has dedicated 227 quatrains to this future epoch of Europe, when it will suffer an incursion by the Asiatics. From what the seer has given us to understand, we perceive belligerent masses from Central Asia attacking the more civilized and modernized Arab peoples so swiftly that they will not be aware of the danger until too late. After the old Arab hatred against the Christians will be kindled anew, Arabs will join the Asians and, by reason of having a higher culture and religion, they will become the dominating power in the gigantic military enterprise. Therefore, taking into account words and expressions used by the quatrains, the barbarian invasion of Europe may be characterized also as a Mohammedan onslaught.

It would seem that Europe should be capable of repelling such an attack. But perhaps a long period of peace will precede and Europe will have disarmed herself? Or, perhaps, Europe will be exhausted because of internal wars? It should be remembered that Europe then will have lost all sources of raw materials in Africa and Asia, and will not be able to arm itself and to prepare for war. It would suffice to prevent the importation of oil from the Middle East, and the whole European industry would be paralyzed. Perhaps England at that time will experience the catastrophe foretold in V-93, and will not be able with its navy to protect the Mediterranean Sea. Perhaps even the United States at that moment will be itself in a state of war in the Pacific, against Japan, China and other East Asian countries, and will not be able to give aid to Europe. Nostradamus does not say that Russia will oppose the attacking Asians. In all probability, Russia will have already previously lost all her possessions in Asia and will be reduced to a power of the second or third rank. Nor is there in Nostradamus' prophecies anywhere an indication that the Russians will become allied with the Asians and Africans. Yet it has been clearly stated that exactly such will be the case with the Poles, moreover at a moment most critical for the future of Europe.

Assuming the year 500 as the initial point of the liturgical chronology (VI-54) and relying on the astronomical indications which are given in other quatrains, it is possible to construe the progress of the whole barbarian invasion. As in the days past the Huns, Turks and Tatars, so now again the strange invaders will come from Central Asia and, as disclosed by V-54, also from the great Tartary (Turkestan). The further stages of the assault are related in III-31, V-54, V-27.

In V-25 we read that the wave of Arabic people will flow into the Balkan peninsula and into Egypt at about the same time, namely, when "Mars, sun, Venus in Leo." Such a configuration occurs quite often, for instance, already on August 21, 1987, but such a a solution does not agree with V-91, according to which the Asians, coming from the direction of the conquered Balkans, will overwhelm Greece from the north in the year 2083. Accordingly, the invasion of the Balkans (across the Bosporus and the Dardanelles), of Greek islands and of Egypt must take place only a few years earlier, namely, in 2081, and the attack on Greece, coming from the north, will follow in 2083.

In the Balkans the further progress of the Arabs will be stopped due to the heroic resistance of the Greeks and also because of the remarkable fact that the Turks will have consolidated their interests with those of Europe (V-47). According to the prophecy, a complete occupation of the

Balkan peninsula will follow only after the conquest of all North Africa, Spain and part of Italy. The conquest of Morocco is mentioned in VI-54. The attack on Spain will take place in 2094 (VIII-48), and two years later, in 2096, Spain will be subdued (V-14). Italy and the Italian islands in the Mediterranean will have seen attacks already much earlier, in 2088 or 2090 (II-5), but the great offensive on Italy will follow only after the Pyrenean peninsula will be conquered. The stages of the attack are described in V-55, X-60 and VII-6. From III-32 we can infer that the French will assist the Italians in their war of resistance, but the French navy will suffer a catastrophic defeat near the coast of Tuscany. Simultaneously with the battles for the possession of Italy, the Mohammedan invasion of the Balkans will have proceeded so far that the peninsula will be taken, including perhaps also Hungary and Austria. The occupation of Hungary is indicated in X-62, and the ill fate of Austria is described in I-82. Either before or after the occupation of Hungary and Austria, the Mohammedans will be engaged in a decisive battle for northern Italy, since the prophecy mentions a siege of the ancient city Mantua (III-32). Italy will be completely conquered only in 2103 (II-65). A year later, on November 22, 2104, when Mars and Saturn will be in conjunction in Scorpio, an event in Italy will resound in the whole world (I-52), namely, the assassination of the pope. The prophecy does not mention the conquest of Czechoslovakia, but it may take place simultaneously with the occupation of Austria. Even Switzerland will become a victim of aggression, as shown by IX-44.

France will be assailed from several directions, but an astronomical date exists only for the onset from across the Pyrenees (II-48). The stages of the invasion of France have been mentioned in I-73, I-18, II-29, II-25. Fighting along the Garonne river is described in VIII-2. The invaders will be engaged in battles inside French territory for several years (I-31), for so long a time that during the war two kings will be crowned. Only after the resistance of the French and their allies will be broken, power will be arrogated by one of the Oriental rulers of occupied Italy. In II-29 we can read about an Arab leader who, coming from Italy, will enter France and will become its ruler (I-31 and I-52). The conquest of all France is foretold in I-51. Jupiter and Saturn will be in Aries on May 10, 2118. It will not be a conjunction of both planets; however, such an exact phenomenon has not been specified by the prophecy.

The texts don't mention the conquest of Belgium and Holland, but they will hardly been able to escape a similar fate, the latter at least as far as the western shores of the river Rhine. As for Germany, it can be seen from V-43 that the region west of the Rhine has been occupied by a foreign power. In Germany the will to offer resistance will gain momentum, and a new "Siegfried line" will be the result, which will help to keep the enemy in check and to protect Germany from invasion. The enemy's efforts to break the line of defense will peter out, and the attention of the assailants will turn in a different direction, namely, toward the British Isles. It seems that the invasion of Great Britain will succeed (II-78).

Consequently, only Germany and Scandinavia will remain unconquered. At the time when the Mohammedans will try to cross the Rhine, in order to occupy Germany, Germany will be attacked from the rear by Poland (V-73). The northern countries will give assistance to Germany, as can be seen from IX-94, where it is related that "the weak galleys," probably coming from the north, will save Europe, giving at this juncture a decisive turn to the events.

From VI-2 we can see that France, and possibly all Europe as well, will again be free in about the year 2264.

Consequently, the stages of the Mohammedan invasion of Europe are as follows:

Invasion of the Balkans, 2081.
Attack on Greece, 2083.
Skirmishes in Italy, 2088.
Attack on Spain, 2094.
Spain conquered, 2096.
Italy conquered, 2103.
Assassination of the pope, 2104.
Battle near Foix, 2105.
Big offensive against France, 2107.
Battles near the Garonne, 2113.
France conquered, 2118.
All western Europe occupied, about 2135.
France (possibly Europe) liberated, about 2264.

Of course, during the 150 years of occupation, a mingling of languages and races will take place, including a rich, mutual cultural exchange, which fact is registered also in Nostradamus' epistle and quatrains. Considering the relatively small extent of Europe, races so different as the Europeans, Asians and Africans will not be able to co-exist without conflicts. Especially the multiple religious differences will cause strife and contention. Nostradamus reports on long, bloody persecutions of Christianity. This period of persecutions by the Mohammedans is called by him "the third Antechrist" (the first was Russian communism, the second—Italian communism). Persecutions are described in detail in B.58-61 and in a long section of the epistle, beginning with B.106. The expression "third Antechrist" cannot be found in the epistle; it is in VIII-77. According to B.58 this third persecution of the Christians will begin when the previous enemies of the church (fascists and communists) will be powerless, and it will take place during the last decade of the occupation, since B.62 already tells about "incursions on maritime shores," possibly by Americans, with the intention to deliver Spain from the "first Mahometan recapture." Spain's occupation is here called "recapture," because the initial capture took place in the 8th century. Since the inhabitants of that part of Europe, which will be occupied by the Mohammedans, are predominantly Catholics, the representatives of the Roman church will be the principle targets of the cruel persecution by the "third Antechrist." In a similar manner, they in their time themselves have persecuted so many sects and societies of their antagonists. The Roman Catholic Church will be ruined. The great, proud theological edifice will collapse, and "the old and new testaments will be thrown out and burned" (B.112). The pope himself, "the great vicar of the hood," will be "abandoned by all."

At that time the German nation will greatly differ from the one which yielded ready obedience to the garrulous sabre rattler, Kaiser Wilhelm, or to the "biggest of mastiffs," Adolph Hitler. Nostradamus assures us that it will be the Germans who will help to restore Christianity to its true, pristine essence, disclosing its deeper purport, which has been hidden from the first. But II-27 promises that "the secret will be revealed." Fortified by this new faith, humanity will be able to proceed on its historical course. This new Christian faith will be the one that will be dominant during the "millennium."

After the Germans together with the Northerners will have defeated the Mohammedans on the Rhine, the task of liberation will extend westward and southward. If, as was possibly indicated in II-78, Great Britain will have been conquered by French-African half-breeds, she will free herself by insurrection and, probably, by invasion of American and free European forces. Later the English will take part in battles against the foreign invaders in France. After a war of seven months duration (IV-100) the foreign people will be vanquished. The participation of Spaniards in military actions in France proves that the Iberian peninsula will be swept clean earlier. This fact is registered in B.62, where the expression "incursion on maritime shores" means that liberation has come from the sea, perhaps from England or America.

After that, German and French armies will deliver one country after another. From V-12 it can be seen that Switzerland, with German help, will regain sovereignty. The same will happen to Austria. After the liberation of France, resistance will grow in northern Italy (V-42). French and Italian commanders, representatives of the families Bonaparte and Orléans (eagle and cock) will join forces (VIII-9). From Savona (Italian Riviera) and from still another direction the armies will move towards the interior of Italy, in order to crush the Mohammedan power and to push the hated invaders into the sea (VII-4 and III-43).

After Italy in such a manner will be liberated, hostilities will begin in the Balkans or Byzantium (V-80). Warfare in the Balkans will be of long duration, and its fierceness can be imagined, if we read I-74, where the last line says that "the barbarians will roast like on a spit" (Barbe d'aerain se rostira en broche). "Barbe d'aerain" (Bronze-beard) is here taken as a paragram. Further battles are described in VI-21 and X-86 and will be fought already under the leadership of a "king of Europe." It is impossible to ascertain if he will be a member of the Bonaparte or of the Orléans family. Later the Mohammedans will be pursued in their own countries (III-97).

The long occupation of Europe, which will continue for 150-200 years, will have brought about deep convulsions in all strata of society and all branches of culture. Nostradamus especially mentions changes in the religious life and, as we have seen, foretells the ruin of Catholicism and, at the same time, the birth of a new faith. Protestantism will be consolidated and renovated and will come into close union with the new religion, absorbing it. This religion will find adherents among both Christians and Islamites and, although arisen among the Mohammedan occupants (V-53), will have preserved the essential content of the Christian faith and cult (X-31) and, in reality, will be identical with the spiritual Christianity of the first centuries. Hence, it can be described as a new and at the same time as an ancient form of the Christian faith. Catholicism will strive against the new religious school, sensing in it a rival and competitor in the contest for human souls, but the new faith will soon gain ground (VIII-69) and find many adherents especially in Germany, where the spiritual situation will be extremely favorable for such a profound, religious revolution. Simultaneously with the regeneration of primitive Christianity, a great prophet and law-giver will appear in Asia, probably in the Near East, whither the European Christian churches will send their representatives to take part in theological councils, to determine what is to be rejected, what retained. It can be assumed that the new faith will be based upon some newly found or, rather, recovered documents, which today still remain unknown, although they originate in the times of early Christianity (VII-36). It will be a new, final reformation of the Christian faith.

Under the guidance of this new faith, after the long racial and religious wars, the world will finally, about the year 2800, obtain real peace, which is called "the great millennium" by Nostradamus, and which is identical with the milennium described by the Book of Revelation and long awaited by many Christians (III-92 and I-48).

Gustafsson's commentaries on Nostradamus' epistles:

A.5: "Climates of the world" are geographical zones, calculated according to the astrological geography, as found in Agrippa's book *De occulta philosophia.*

B.9: On April 24 of the mentioned year 1585, Pope Sixtus V was elected. Nostradamus had foretold it to him already, when he was still a monk named Peretti. The other mentioned year, 1606, was astrologically important and is in detail described in B.88-89. "The seventh millenary" began in 1828, since the initial point of the reckoning is year 4173 B.C. (cf.B.86).

B.17-23: The computation of the years does not agree with B.86.

B.30: "The great dame"—France. "Two children"—brothers Louis VIII (1815-1824) and Charles X (1824-1830). "The eighteenth year"—Louis Philipp reigned for eighteen years, from 1830 until 1848. "Thirty six"—thirty-six years from the fall of Napoleon I to the coup d'état of Napoleon III in 1851. During this time France has had three kings and one republican government ("three sons and one daughter"). "Three brothers"—Prussia (Germany), Austro-Hungary and Italy. "Europe will tremble"—war during the 1850s and 1860s.

B.31: "The youngest"—Italy.

B.32: "The first," i.e. the oldest one, is Prussia. Prussia in 1864 had war with Denmark, whose coat of arms of that time did contain three blue lions, in exactly the position as described.

B.33: "The second one"—Austro-Hungary, with dependencies Venice and Lombardy, was in a state of war with Italy in 1848, 1859 and 1866. "Mountain of Jupiter"—the Alps. "Pyrenees"—an error, since the Apennines was meant.

B.34: "Daughter"—France.

B.35: "Faithful child"—the empire of Napoleon III. "Infidel child"—the Third Republic. "Will want to ruin her"—atheists will want to ruin the church.

B.36: "50°–52°"—Holland and Belgium, which were granted permanent neutrality by the treaty of 1839.

B.37: "48°"—Austro-Hungary. "Warlike conquests"—the politics of equilibrium.

B.38: "Faith"—political conviction.

B.39: "The sterile dame"—the Third French Republic. "The second"—the Second Republic. "The first nation"—Russia in 1891. "The second nation"—England in 1904. "The third nation"—Italy in 1914. "Pannonia"—Hungary. "Adriatic Trinacria"—Island Corfu in 1923. "Myrmidons"—the Greeks. "Will succumb wholly"—the Germans will succumb in 1918. "The barbarian sect"—Islam.

B.40: "Empire of the Antechrist"—communism in 1918. Nostradamus has foretold many periods when Christians will be persecuted, and has labeled three of them as "Antechrists." Here he mentions the first Antechrist. "Attila and Xerxes"—southeastern Europe. The domain of Attila, as is well known, comprised especially Hungary, Romania and southern Russia. The Persian ruler Xerxes invaded the Balkan peninsula between the Danube and Greece. "48°"—Austria, among others.

B.41: "Eclipse"—the First World War, described by Nostradamus as the most dark and gloomy since the creation of the world. "In the month of October"—the Bolshevist revolution in Russia on October 25-26, 1917, according to the old style calendar, which was in use in Nostradamus' time and also in Russia at the time of the revolution. Communists themselves call it "the great October revolution," although they celebrate it on November 7-8, according to the new style. This revolution was a signal and prelude for a change of the regime in southern and southeastern Europe, among other places in the territory of "Attila and Xerxes"

(Hungary, Bulgaria, Romania).

B.42: "Springtime"—the February revolution in Russia.

B.43: "Mighty earthquakes"—these phenomena, like the ones mentioned in the previous paragraph of the epistle, are no astronomical or geological catastrophes, but only symbolical denominations for mighty upheavals of a political, social or religious nature, including the revolutions, which took place in 1918 in Germany, Austro-Hungary and elsewhere. "Daughter of Babylon"—communism.

B.44: "Seventy-three years and seven months" may mean the duration of the communistic regime in Russia.

B.45: "50°"—among others, France, Belgium, Germany, Czechoslovakia.

B.46: "Some of the children"—one of them will certainly be France. "Children of misguided ranks"—Russia and countries with similar ideology.

B.48: "Will have enslaved themselves still more profoundly"—satellites of Russia, after they have been "liberated" in 1944.

B.50: "The great dog"—Wilhelm II. "The biggest of mastiffs"—Adolph Hitler, who between 1940 and 1944 destroyed everything that had been constructed in the period between both world wars.

B.51: "Jupiter"—the highest Roman god, here representing Italy. "Tiny Mesopotamia"—Northern Italy.

B.56: "The middle sect"—Protestantism.

B.57: "The first"—Catholicism. "The third"—Islam.

B.58: "Weakened by Easterners"—battles for predominance in the Middle East.

B.61: "City of the Sun"—Rome. "The marine ox"—Bosporus.

B.62:—"Castulum"—Castulona, Roman name for Spain.

B.64: "Achem"—probably Mecca (if we read "Achem" backwards).

B.70: Words of the "Royal Prophet"—Psalm 102:21.

B.72: "The renown of this new sect"—the new faith.

B.82: "130 years" in reality, the age of Jacob, when he entered Egypt (Gen. 47:9).

B.86: "More or less"—the total is wrong, because, adding up all mentioned figures, the result is 4092 years, 2 months.

B.89: "Year without an eclipse"—the astronomical data of B.88 indicate year 1606, except that the Dragon's Head had a different position.

B.90: "Renewal of an epoch"—the new calendar, introduced during the French Revolution, from September 22, 1792.

B.91: "Continual changes"—Italy's unification.

B.92: "Ancient Rome"—Italy as a modern first-rate colonial power.

B.93: "Two Cretans"—naval demonstrations in Canea (Crete) in 1909.

B.94: "The arks built by the ancient Martians will join the waves of Neptune"—Greece has been allied with England during both world wars, Italy during the First World War and again at the end of the Second World War. Both countries are members of NATO.

B.95: "House"—Italy. "45°"—Northern Italy. "41°, 42°, 47°"—Naples, Rome, Brenner Pass (northern boundary of Italy).

B.96: "Second Antechrist"—communist dictatorship in Italy.

B.98: "Mountain of Jupiter"—the Alps.

B.99: "Ogmios"—Gallic god, here representing France.

B.102: "Universal peace"—millennium, but this peace will be disturbed by "Azotians" (from Greek *a zoe*, "without life," namely, persons without spiritual life, consequently, atheists, or people who deny God).

B.103: "Seventh millenary" began in 1797 or in 1827. "Who come from Aquilon"—Russian communists, coming from the north.

THREE VIEWS OF THE FUTURE / 345

B.106: "Kings of Aquilon"—Mohammedan rulers in France, the third Antechrist, whose activities are described in B.106-113.

B.110: "Third king of Aquilon"—this third northern king is a king of Denmark. He will assemble an army not only from Denmark, but from all northern countries. Nostradamus' quatrains often mention the northern kings and their military expeditions. One of these enterprises is described here (cf. also VI-41). "People of the principal title"—Italians. "Straits"—mountain passes in the Alps, leading to Italy. "His ancestors"—the northern or Danish king will have descended from an Italian royal family, married into the Danish dynasty.

B.111: "Vicar of the hood"—the pope. The gist of this relation about the military expedition of the northerners is that the dismissed pope will again be reinstated, but soon after nevertheless ousted permanently. The complainants will be the Italians. Perhaps, the 100,000 marks (VI-41) will be the ransom money for the pope, but the pope will still be "desolated and abandoned," and the related military expedition will prove to have been of no avail. The whole event is only an episode during the final struggle for the existence of the papal church.

B.115: "Golden age"—millennium from 2797 until 3797.

* * * * *

The two last books by E. Ruir, published in 1947 and 1953, contain gloomy predictions about the future of the world and especially of Europe. Contrary to most interpreters of Nostradamus, he does not believe that the prophecies extend until the year 3797. This figure, mentioned in the letter to César, he interprets differently; he expects the realization of all events, foretold by Nostradamus, before the year 2023. He is deeply convinced that the year 2023 is, as it were, the final year in the history of the world or, at least, of Europe, as we know it. Such a commentary by Ruir should not be dismissed with a smile, since Ruir can boast of having in his book *Le grand carnage*, published in 1938, precisely and correctly predicted the Second World War between 1938 and 1947. In this book he has also predicted the course of the war and the total defeat of Italian and German armies. His book was confiscated and included in the list of prohibited books by the German occupational authorities in France.

Ruir maintains that most of the events, foretold by Nostradamus and still to be accomplished, will take place already before the year 1999. Is it possible? Why not? Within 30 years (1914-1944) we have experienced two horrible world wars. A lot can happen during the next 30 years, considering the fact that man now has hydrogen bombs and all kinds of chemical and bacteriological means of annihilation at his disposal.

Ruir's conviction is based upon interesting calculations and considerations, which are here related in a condensed form:

First of all, quite conspicuous is the circumstance that the chronologies of the world, mentioned in Nostradamus' epistle (B.17-23 and B.76-86) are not in accord one with the other. The first one, which extends from Adam to Jesus, comprises 4757 years; the other one, which begins earlier with the creation of the world and should therefore be longer, only 4092 years. Furthermore, Nostradamus has erred in adding the figures up: he quotes 4173 years and 8 months, "more or less," as his total. Nostradamus was a far too competent mathematician to have made such gross errors. It must be assumed that these are intentional errors and have some purpose. Further, Nostradamus in his epistle defines two precise dates of the future: 1585 and 1606 (B.9). Again it would seem that he has made an error, because these are years without any events that were in any way conspicuous or significant for the future of France or of Europe. And how do we reconcile these two fixed figures (1585 and 1606) with the fact that in the text of the epistle (B.90) the year 1789, the year of the great French Revolution, has been unmistakably registered as the beginning for the predictions, which are included in the epistle? Consequently, Nostradamus must have given us these two figures, 1585 and 1606, as aids for the disentanglement of his prophetic riddles. It is remarkable that Nostradamus has expressed them, like the number 3797, not in letters, but in numeral characters. Therefore, they are not to be interpreted "literally" and they don't correspond to any dates of our calendar. In the letter to César he says that his prophecies extend until the year 3797 (A.29), i.e. until the last prophesied event which is the "anaragonic revolution" (A.39), the dislocation of our solar system. This planetary revolution will take place when we will "approach the eighth millenary" (A.41). By inverting the cipher 3797, we get 7973, which quite well corresponds to the year sought for, since it is near the end of the seventh millenary, only a few years before the beginning of the eighth millenary. In dealing likewise with the two other ciphers, 1585 and 1606, we get 5851 and 6061. The balance of both figures (the beginning and the end of the predictions, included in the epistle to Henry the Second) is 210 years. But Nostradamus already has given the year 1789 as the beginning of his predictions of the epistle (B.90). Therefore, if 5851 corresponds to the beginning (year 1789), the other figure (the end) corresponds to the year 1999 (1789+210). The first of these two years, i.e. 1789, is mentioned in B.90 with the words: "Beginning with this year." Note also the introductory words of the previous paragraph (end of B.89): "It will be the commencement, comprising all that will continue to happen." The year 1999 has been also "literally" mentioned in X-72. In such a way Nostradamus has permitted us to find three data of his chronology (5851,

6061, 7973). If we wish to find out the initial point of his chronology, we have to deduct 1789 from 5851, and we get the year 4062 B.C., which is approximately the total of B.76-86. But Nostradamus illogically has mentioned 4173 years and 8 months as the sum total. We have to retain it, since it has been expressed with letters, instead of figures. Adding 3797 A.D. to 4173 B.C., we get 7970 years, a figure, which differs from 7973 by only three years. Presumably, Nostradamus has quoted the year 3797 only to make it possible for us, with the aid of the "literally-stated 4173 years," to find the duration of his chronology, i.e. 7973 years. To the objection that in such a case he should have mentioned 4176 years instead of 4173 years, my reply is that the difference of three years corresponds either to the three years which separate 1789 from 1792 (B.90), or to the three years and eight months which passed from the beginning of the reign of Solomon until the construction of the temple. It has to be taken into account that correct calculations are impeded by the fact that Jesus was not actually born in the year with which we begin our calendar.[4] But it is not at all essential to know if "the translation of the terrestrial globe" will occur exactly in 2023 or a few years sooner or later.

Ruir claims to have found in Nostradamus' texts no fewer than eight Antechrists mentioned. The last two are supposedly represented by the barbarian invasions (Arab and Asian), which he envisages as following each other in two

4. The "star," seen by the three Oriental astrologers, was either 1) a conjunction of Mars and Saturn in 353° (in the constellation of Pisces, i.e. the Fishes) on February 22, 6 B.C. (or, as there is no "zero" year, in the year -5, i.e. minus 5), when Jupiter's position was in 359°, also in Pisces, or 2) the threefold conjunction of Jupiter and Saturn in 7 B.C. (year -6) on September 27, October 4 and December 10, in 348.3°, 347.7° and 346.3°, all three times in the constellation of Pisces, i.e. the Fishes. Fish as a symbol of Christianity has been drawn on the walls of the catacombs in Rome, sometimes even in the form of a dolphin. In antiquity, dolphin was the symbol of soul's survival after death. The word "Messiah" in ancient Hebrew has an additional meaning of "fish." The hat of a Christian bishop, seen from the side, reminds us of a fish's head.

separate waves or onslaughts. Only the future will disclose if it is right to consider the Arab and Asian invasions as two separate, isolated events. In Nostradamus' quatrains it is very difficult to distinguish one from the other.

Another very important point: Ruir is convinced that even in the epistle dedicated to Henry the Second, Nostradamus has changed the order of the predicted events, shuffling the predictions the same way as he has done it with the quatrains. According to Ruir, the epistle has to be read in the following order:

Introduction: 1-16. First chronology: 17-23. Second chronology: 76-87. Then 24-29, 104-105 and 75. Follow the predictions in this order: 89-91, 30-38, 92-95, 39, 96-97, 48-49, 51-53, 43-47, 54, 99, 98, 100, 58, 50, 59-62, 55-57, 63-68, 103, 113-114, 88, 106-107, 112, 110-111, 108-109, 69-72, 74, 73, 40-42, 101-102. The conclusion: 115-119.

We invite the reader to read the epistle once more in the above order, with the aid of Ruir's commentaries, which follow. Here is Ruir's analysis of the epistle and his view of the future, in a condensed form:

B.89-90: The year 1789 was the commencement of a revolutionary period on the European continent. The Catholic church was persecuted, and the persecutions continued through the year 1792 which, by the introduction of the Republican calendar, was believed to be the initiation of a new epoch.

B.30: The great dame, long sterile (the First Republic), conceived two children (two regimes of republican form): the Directorate and the Consulate. From the Consulate, by means of a coup d'état, arose the emperor Napoleon I. Napoleon III too was proclaimed emperor. They did not have the same father; i.e. they did not come into power by succession. Between them both they ruled for almost 36 years. In the interval which separates them, three sons (Louis XVIII, Charles X, Louis-Philippe I) and a daughter (the

Second Republic from 1848 until 1852) were ruling. The three brothers were differing in the domestic policies, but in foreign affairs they had only one goal: to revive and to augment the power of France.

B.32: Louis-Philippe did occupy Belgium (the coat of arms of which country is described by Nostradamus).

B.33: The second Napoleon invaded Italy, but lost power during the war of 1870/71. The Third Republic followed, and during its rule the two first world wars took place.

B.34: New atheistic pagan sects arose: nazism and communism.

B.35: The world split into two groups: believers and unbelievers (atheists). One of the infidel children (nazism or fascism) established its power in three regions without common boundaries: Germany, Italy and Spain. Nostradamus mentions all three by name.

B.36: These countries abandoned the principles of democracy, which are observed by the country between 50° and 52° (England).

B.37: Germany, whose nazi-mysticism was born on the 48th degree (Munich), was the first to tremble. Afterwards trembled countries to the west (Norway, Holland, Belgium, France, England), the south (Czechoslovakia, Yugoslavia, Greece) and the east (Poland, Soviet Russia); so great was the power of Germany and Italy. They were not united spiritually (B.38), but only militarily and by common designs of conquest.

B.92: Fascist Italy occupied Ethiopia and deemed herself already similar to ancient Rome in power and glory. All fell to dust during the Second World War (B.93-94).

B.95: Italy lost Albania, in the Adriatic the great Italian cities suffered from air raids during the war, and the magnitude of all Italy (from 37° to 45°) was shattered.

Ruir's opinion about B.95 has changed since 1947. Then he interpreted this paragraph as a prediction about the future revolution in Italy and Italy's splintering into several parts, because "that which will have been united will be separated" and Rome "which was, and is, a great city, will be reduced to a house." Rome will be devastated, either during the revolution, or during the later war of liberation by France. Be that as it may, the contents of the prophecy do not change, because Ruir considers Italy, in any case, to be one of the countries which are mentioned in B.39 as visited by revolution. But Ruir's opinion about which will be the other country is unsettled and wavering.

B.39: After World War II, revolution (the sterile dame), bloodier than the second (the first was French, the second, Russian), will occur in two nations. Which will be these nations? Ruir is not fully enlightened about it. In 1947 he was convinced that the one which has had "power over all" is England, and that the other one is Italy. Nostradamus has foreseen social revolutionary movements and revolutions in many European countries. The collapse of Great Britain's power and a revolution in that country has been unmistakably prophesied in many quatrains. One of the sixains (sixain 50) relates that after the death of the wolf (Germany), England will see fire which resists water and will be relighting it (i.e. the revolution) with immense force. Human cruelty will spill blood, there will be scarcity of bread, but abundance of knife. Even Spain will experience a new revolution (sixain 46), when Mars will be in Aries, in conjunction with Saturn and the moon (1996-1999 is the nearest date) and Nostradamus advises France not to listen to offers made by Spain or Russia. In France too (sixain 37) government will be taken over by popular front. Each of the parties, which constitute the front, will want to rule alone. The radicals will be forced to submit to the communists, and the communists will finally usurp power. The parties of the right "will pass away," not being able to defend themselves, when the time was still opportune. All these quotations from the sixains have to be taken with a grain of salt, because the authorship of Nostradamus is not certain. They have been quoted here only because they substantiate what has already been predicted in authentic texts of Nostradamus. Let us return now to B.39, which declares that communistic revolutions will break out in two great European nations. Americans will then have withdrawn from Europe, concentrating their political interest more towards Asia. Germany will have become the power nucleus of Europe. Russia will assemble her armies "towards the circuit of the East of Europe," on the iron curtain, where they once stopped at the end of the Second World War. It is a significant circumstance that Nostradamus here specially mentions Hungary (Pannonia), which nation in 1956 cast off the yoke of Bolshevism, but then, having hoped for some helping gesture from the West in vain, had again to yield before the superior force of the Russian army. Russian naval squadrons will pass through the Dardanelles and enter the Adriatic Sea, in order to give support to the revolution in Italy. The Italians (Myrmidons) and the Germans will succumb wholly before the might of the Soviets. After that, all Latin nations of Europe will revolt against the theory of communism, will reject it and drive the barbarian sect out.

B.96: But, before it happens, infernal powers will be active in Italy, deceiving people with propaganda ("seduced by tongues"). The church will suffer persecution, and the pope will be forced to leave Rome.

B.97: This reign of the Antechrist will last until the appearance of a ruler who was born near the seventh millenary, and of the other one (the pope), who either was born or was elected in the city founded by the Roman general Plancus, i.e. Lyons. Possibly, not only the new king, but also the pope, will be descendants of former kings of France. Although communists will have gained power in France and Paris will be their citadel, a new French government will be organized in Avignon ("lieu bien infime, d'exigue comté," I-32). Consequently, in France will arise forces which will revolt against the power of communism in Europe. At the head of this movement will be a person with direct line of succession from a French royal dynasty. Under his leadership all Italy, including Sicily, will be recaptured. He will conquer also Spain, which will again become a monarchy.

B.48-49: The inhabitants of countries, towns, cities, realms and provinces who will have abandoned their ancient religions and social traditions, will acknowledge their mistake when they will be deprived of their liberty and when the cult of Christian religion will be prohibited. Yet what has been possible in Russia, will not be possible in Latin countries and especially not in France. The people will revolt against the tyranny of communism and will re-establish religious freedom.

B.51: The lead in the liberation movement will be taken by someone of the family of Capets, which for a long time had no representative on the throne of France. He will be proclaimed king of France. The royal residence will be a "tiny Mesopotamia," namely, Avignon (I-32 and VIII-38). About the future king of France Nostradamus says (sixain 4) that he will be either born, or will appear, when Saturn is in Libra in exaltation (1921-24, 1951-53, 1980-83, 2009-12), will reign in all Spain, will be the most famous of all kings of France and will be also (sixain 48) the last one of his family (house of Capets). Loved by everybody, he will reign in splendor, and his greatness will be unforgettable.

B.52: The chief of the communistic government will be "cast out" of power, when he will least expect it. The plot against him will be directed by one who will be similar to Thrasibulus, the liberator of Athens.

B.53: Insurrections and revolts will take place in all Europe. The abominations of the communist regime will be brought out everywhere and people will again see things in the right light, but (B.43) it will not happen without great convulsions and upheavals.

B.44: Russia too will be shaken by domestic unrest, but the life span of Russian communism will be seventy-three years and seven months. Only then the new Babylon, the capital of the atheists, will be devastated.

B.45-47: The new king of France will proceed from the 50th degree of latitude. He will renew the unity and concord between nations and with his prestige will ensure peace for many years between most of the European countries. He will be anointed at Reims and will be proclaimed "prince of peace" and emperor of Spain and Italy at Aix-la-Chapelle (IV-86). A general peace will have been established between men, and the church of Christ will be free from afflictions and persecutions, but

B.54: after the death of the "king of Europe" the condition of peace will come to an end and anarchy will again reign in the world.

B.99: A new leader of the atheists will arise, and it does not matter if his movement will be of the extreme right or extreme left, or whether it can be called red fascism or black communism, it will be a worthy successor of both nazism and communism and will call forth new revolutions in Europe.

B.98: His movement will pass the Alps, and Italy again will become a martyr of political terrorism.

B.100, and 58: Great persecutions of the Christian church will again commence, and both monarchists and republicans, weak and disorganized, will become enslaved. Europe will sink into the mire of anarchy and will become easy prey for Mohammedan invasion. The seventh Antechrist, the leader of the Mohammedan hordes, will be like "the great Dog," but Gog of Magog, who will later come from Asia, will be the eighth Antechrist.

B.50: The seventh Antechrist, the leader of the

Mohammedan hordes, will invade Europe from the south (after having the Jews chased out of Palestine). The military engagements between Jews and Arabs in Palestine will become more desperate, and the Jews will be the losers. They will be captured and scattered. The holy sepulchre will be desecrated. This Arab victory will greatly facilitate their preparations for the invasion of Europe and for a concentrated attack against the Christians. After having captured the Holy Land and North Africa, the Arabs will march against Europe, which will be splintered in political factions. The revolutions, instigated by extremists, will have disorganized the armed forces and the navy of France and Italy. England too will be in the power of the revolution. Nothing will hinder the Mohammedans from crossing the Meditteranean Sea and from the conquest of Spain. After that, they will cross the Pyrenees, will attack the French and will become intrenched on the Provençal coast. The Mediterranean coastal areas will be devastated (IX-60). It will happen under the leadership of an Arab chief from Libya. Simultaneously, an Arab commander with his army will invade Italy through Sicily, Sardinia, the Adriatic Sea. Pagan temples will again be set up in the occupied regions, priests will become renegades and will serve the new religion. In the pages of Nostradamus' texts we find a clearly designed picture of the decadence of the Roman church, with anti-popes at the head of it and many priests renouncing the faith (VI-100, X-65, VIII-98). At the end of the 20th century the Roman church will suffer a well-earned retribution for the iniquities of many of her priests. Although the satanic powers of evil will avail nothing against the intrinsic virtue and essence of the church, her visible representatives will undergo deserved punishment. This has been foretold by Nostradamus' prophecies, in complete accord with the book of St. John, the seer of Patmos. Whoever reads it, whoever considers and weighs it and compares it with the devices of

St. Malachi (cf. the last part of this book), will comprehend that these events have now drawn very near us, and that they are not, by any means, a matter of the distant future.

B.59: A period of Christian martyrdom will commence again.

B.60: Plague will arise in three parts of the world. Mortality will be so great that fields and houses will lose their owners and occupants, and weeds will be growing in the streets of the empty cities, higher than the knees.

B.55-57: Of the three religions the middle one (Christian) will be thrown into decadence, since many of the Catholic priests will apostatize from the faith, but the first one (Judaism) will be exterminated in Europe and Africa by the third one (Mohammedanism), which will triumph.

B.62-67: After Arabs will have taken Rome and Venice and, coming from the Adriatic Sea, will have invaded Hungary, France will join forces with England for common defense. The counter-offensive will take place from the side of Portugal (IX-60) and America will give assistance to Europe (I-28). The naval and air forces of the United States, Canada and South America will arrive in the Mediterranean, to save Europe and to liberate Palestine. Hebron, the ancient domicile of Abraham and Jerusalem will be assailed from all sides. Palestine will be visited by the calamities of war. The holy sepulchre, desecrated by the Mohammedans, will yet, for a long time, remain exposed to the sight of the heavens, the sun and the moon.

When will this Arab invasion occur? E. Ruir maintains that the first signs of Mongol expansion in Asia will appear already in 1972, and that at the same time, between 1972 and 1974, Arabs will occupy Palestine. Nostradamus asserts that all this will happen before the end of the reign of the moon, consequently, before 1980-2000. Soon afterwards the Arabs will march against Europe. It will happen when, in Rome, the seat of Peter will be taken by a pope who corresponds to St. Malachi's device "De medietate lunae," and who will be taken prisoner by the Arabs. Possibly, it will be the pope of Capetian descent. He will have a big part in all these events, but he will be abandoned and persecuted. After these Arab victories, the seer of Salon foresees a new European alliance and American assistance in the liberation of Europe. The counter-offensive (V-47) will succeed, and even Constantinople will be captured (VI-85). The defeated Arabs will seek refuge in Tunis (IX-42). Palestine too will be recaptured and will become a new seat of Christianity, because the church will return to Jerusalem.

And yet, there will be no peace. E. Ruir is of the opinion that between 1970 and 1999 the world will be continuously visited by great trials and afflictions, by catastrophes, bloody persecutions and miseries of war. The events, especially after 1975, will follow one another in quick succession, with a culmination in Europe between 1980 and 1988.

B.113-114: Then will come the eighth Antechrist, the infernal prince, i.e. the expansion of the yellow race. In Asia the yellow race will already have begun military aggressions simultaneously with the previously mentioned Arab invasion of Europe and will continue them for twenty-five years (1974-1999). Nostradamus does not emphasize the fact, merely because the Asians will reach Europe much later. It will be the last great war which the humanity will experience before the millennium. No continent, no nation will escape the dire consequences of this cataclysm. Not only all the kingdoms of Christianity will tremble, but also the infidels (i.e. Mohammedans). Constantinople and Egypt will fall between 1994 and 1996. Europe will be attacked and laid waste by the last Antechrist, Gog of Magog, between 1996 and July, 1999. "And power was given unto him to continue (to wage war) forty and two months" (Apocalypse 13:5). Europe will be sinking in wreckage and blood. Japan then will have regained her power and will take part in the Asiatic enterprise of world conquest. This invasion will be more serious, dangerous, bloody and destructive than any of the previous ones. The attacking armies will be better equipped and will number more men than ever before. They will have at their disposal also a powerful airforce, including stratospheric missiles and spaceships. "Strange birds will cry in the air." The Mongol invasion will stop at the Rhine, but their air squadrons will fly over the Alpine snows and will sow death and destruction in all of France. The Mongols will have come through southern Russia and Armenia, along the Black Sea, will capture Trebizond and Constantinople and will proceed to Croatia, in the direction of the Danube (V-54, VI-49) and still farther to the west. They will occupy and pillage the Grecian archipelago, will murder Christians and Mohammedans on the island Pharos, near Alexandria, and on the Greek islands. Their southern columns from Egypt will expand over all North Africa and will easily occupy all Spain. The headquarters of the leader of the invasion will be on the island Corfu (the great Ionian port, III-64).

B.88: Nostradamus here describes the planetary positions on January 1, 1606. The figure 1606 represents the year 6061 according to the chronology of Nostradamus and corresponds to the year 1999 of our calendar. Nostradamus adds that the announced events will take place before and during the year 1999.

B.110: Then the ruler of a great, powerful northern nation (America) will hear the lament of the oppressed people. The United States of America then will have replaced England as the country having paramount influence in the world (IV-50). Its army will pass the straits through which their predecessors and ancestors have traversed on their way to the New World, and they "will put almost everything back in its place." Great battles between the forces of good and evil (Gog) will commence in the spring of 1996.

B.108: The greatest naval battle of all times will take place between American and Asiatic squadrons on March 29, 1998 (III-1).

B.40: During this period will reign the last pope, "Petrus Romanum," Peter II, who will terminate the long line of Roman popes, as prophesied by St. Malachi.

B.41: Decisive battles will take place on the day of lunar eclipse, July 28, 1999. The Mongols will be finally defeated before the solar eclipse of August 11, 1999. This eclipse will be more dark and gloomy than any since the death and passion of Jesus Christ. War will then have reached its culmination point, but fate will favor the arms of the westerners. Mercury will eclipse the sun on November 24, 1999 (IV-29).

During all these long years, the world will be visited, in addition to the calamities of war, also by seismic cataclysms and other natural catastrophes. They all will be connected with the approach of an immense cosmic catastrophe. Human barbarism and collective madness will be joined by raging elements. This dreadful period with manifold planetary convulsions will last for forty years (I-17), from 1983 until 2023. It is very likely, that all these perturbations will be caused by the arrival in our solar system of a new celestial body. If so, this body will be discovered by astronomers already in 1980-83. Many comets also will be seen. Halley's comet will appear already in 1986. It will announce the Mongol invasion, but some other great comet will announce the approach of the final catastrophe, the catastrophe of the end. First will come a long, horrid period of drought, then a period of intense rainfall and floods. Fire will fall from the sky. The whole earth will be enveloped by vapor. The decisive principal phase of the terrestrial translation and the last hecatomb will occur in 2003, but a final planetary equilibrium and the respective rearrangement of the solar system will be attained only in October, 2023. Then there will be a new heaven and earth (Apoc. 21:1), and a new humanity.

B.42: It all will happen before the beginning of the age of the Urn (Aquarius). In Nostradamus' book some unintelligent corrector has changed the word "Vrnal" (Urnal) to "Vernal."

B.101-102: Satan at last will be bound. Peace will be established between God and men, and the millennium will begin under the sign of Aquarius, with spiritual forces as the leaders and rulers of humanity. And everything that has been prophesied, will be accomplished.

* * * * *

Three different views of the future. Although many separate sections are identical, the chronological order differs with each of these commentators of Nostradamus' texts. Nothing keeps the reader of this book from forming his own, different, independent interpretation of Nostradamus' texts. Such is also the intent of this book, and the extensive amplitude of the material, provided by it, is for such a purpose more than adequate.

9
PREDICTIONS OTHER THAN BY NOSTRADAMUS

In this last chapter are compiled famous prophecies other than by Nostradamus. I present them in a condensed form, deeming a literal translation unnecessary. Numerous prophecies exist about the religious persecutions and the great changes which Christianity, and especially the Catholic Church, will have to undergo. Most of the prophecies foretell the pope's flight from Rome and a schism in the Roman church. Almost all of them are essentially in accordance with Nostradamus. For us, who are familiar with Nostradamus' texts, the greatest interest is awakened by prophecies which have origin in times antecedent to Nostradamus.

The prophecy of St. Malachi

The most famous of these prophecies is the one by St. Malachi, an Irishman with the family name of O'Morger. He was born in Armagh (Ireland) in 1094, was ordained priest at the age of 25 and became bishop at the age of 30. In 1139 he betook himself to Rome, but on his way, spent some time in Clairvaux (France) and formed a lasting friendship with St. Bernard. After his arrival in Rome, he asked Pope Innocent II for permission to retire in Bernard's monastery, but the pope preferred to see him continue his mission in Ireland. Shortly before his death he once more went to Clairvaux, but directly became ill, predicted the day of his own death and died on November 2, 1148 at the age of 54. St. Bernard de Clairvaux became his first biographer. In his *Vita Sancti Malachie* he does not mention the "prophecy of popes" among the writings of St. Malachi, but reports a number of his accomplished predictions.

His prediction about the future popes St. Malachi supposedly composed in 1139, when in Rome, and presented them to Pope Innocent II. Arnold de Wion, a Benedictine monk, found the original manuscript in the archives of Vatican and included it in his book *Lignum Vitae* which was published in 1595.

The prophecy of St. Malachi enumerates, under the form of legends or devices, 112 popes between 1143 and the "end of time." Each legend characterizes either the pope himself or the nature of the principle events of his reign. Since 1143 already 109 popes have reigned. After the 110th pope (the present John Paul II) only two more legends remain. The "end of time" approaching, it is possible, that the line of popes will be broken by anti-popes, renegades who, supported by revolutionary forces or by foreign armies, will expel the pope and usurp religious power, with the intent to use it for the advantage of communism or some other political ideology. Although St. Malachi has invented a legend for each of the anti-popes as well, E. Ruir is of the opinion, that he cannot have included usurpators, who are atheists, and act in complete contradiction to all Catholic dogmas. E. Ruir, therefore, according to his interpretation of Nostradamus' prophecies, believes that three such anti-popes will reign during the end time.

Let me enumerate the last popes, beginning with the 106th, who was Pius XII, elected in 1939 and reigning until 1958. His legend, assigned by St. Malachi, is "pastor angelicus" (angelic pastor). The next one, 107th, was "pastor et nauta" (pastor and pilot), John XXIII (1958-1963).

Although John XXIII has known how to pilot Peter's vessel past all dangers and obstacles, great pilot, navigator and traveller was also his successor, pope Paul VI (1963-1978), the 108th pope in the line by St. Malachi. His legend was "flos florum" (the flower of flowers). With the end of his reign supposedly came also end to the era of peace. The 109th pope, with the legend "de medietate lunae" (of the crescent moon), was John Paul I (1978). He had served as patriarch in Venice, a lagoon city of half-moon shape. The length of his short reign was that of only one lunar cycle, with the day of the full moon falling exactly in the middle of his pontificate (see X 12, p. 117). The present, 110th pope, is John Paul II with the device "de labore solis ' (of sun's labor).

According to E. Ruir's interpretation, the period between the 109th and the 111th pope will be at some point interrupted by a schism and three anti-popes, subservient to either communism or some other political ideology. Papacy in the "end time" will suffer attacks not only from outside, but also within the communion of the church by renegades who will cause painful divisions. Aided by revolutionary forces or foreign armies, they will cause schisms and usurp religious power. St. Malachy's prophecy does not include devices for apostates, i.e. popes, who are not legally elected by a conclave of cardinals.

About the next pope E. Ruir comments:

111. De gloria olivae. The olive in the Holy Scriptures symbolizes the Jewish people. This pontificate will see the conversion and christianization of the Jewish nation (Deuteronomy 4:30).

112. Petrus Romanus. To this legend St. Malachi himself has added this commentary: "In persecutione extrema sacrae Romanae Ecclesiae, sedebit Petrus Romanus, qui pascet oves in multis tribulationibus; quibus transactis, civitas septicollis diruetur; et Judex tremendus judicabit populum." (During the last persecution of the holy Roman Church will reign Peter, the Roman, who will tend his sheep amidst numerous tribulations; these having passed, the city of seven hills will be destroyed, and the stern Judge will judge his people). This pope will reign during the eighth Antechrist i.e. during the invasion by Asiatics.

Sundry prophecies about the future of the Christian world

Saint-Cesario, born in 470, became the bishop of Arles. He died in 542. He is the author of "Mirabilis liber qui prophecias revelationes que necron res mirandas praeteritas, praesentes uc futuras aperte demonstrat." His predictions are in accord with the prophecies of Nostradamus. Among other things, he predicted the great French Revolution. In days to come, he foresees a pope, who through his sanctity will lead the church back to the ancient mode of life of the disciples of Christ and will convert all infidels, especially the Jews. He will be seconded by a victorious emperor, a descendant of the great kings of the Franks (the French). But the world will return to the old iniquities and still worse crimes, and then will come the end. La Tour de Noé in 1885 expressed his conviction that the monarch, referred to by St. Cesario, will be the "king of Aquilon" (Henry V), whose reign is predicted by Nostradamus.

Gil de Santarem of the Order of Predicants, lived in the 12th century. His manuscript with predictions, written in Latin, can be found in the Santa Cruz convent of Coimbra (Portugal). It contains the prediction that Lusitania (Portugal), the orphan of royal blood (proclamation of the republic in 1910) will weep for a long time and will suffer in many ways, but God will be propitious and will unexpectedly save her through an unexpected one (ab insperato). Africa will be conquered, and the Ottoman empire ruined. The church will be crowned by martyrs, Constantinople will be destroyed, God's house recovered, and all things changed and transformed.

Pierre d'Ailly, born 1350 in Compiègne, doctor of Sorbonne, confessor of Charles VI, chancellor of Paris University, treasurer of Sainte-Chappelle, bishop of Puy and Cambrai, papal cardinal-legate, "eagle of the doctors of France and hammer of heretics," was one of the great astronomers of his time. He predicted that 1789, being under the influence of Saturn, will be a fatidical year, "with many great and extraordinary events and perturbations in the world, principally respecting the institutions." He affirmed that from that year on the world will live under the regime of the Antechrist. He died in 1425, but his book *Tractatus de concordantia astronomica veritatis cum narratione historica,* which contains these predictions, was published in Louvain and Paris in 1490.

Kelner in his book *De fluctibus mistica envius,* published in 1623, predicted: In the 19th century seditionary forces will arise in all Europe, principally in Gaul (France), Italy and Helvetia (Switzerland). New republics will take birth, kings and clergymen will be assassinated, and nuns will leave their convents. Rome will lose her sceptre, because of her obsession with pesudophilosophers. Then famine, pestilence and earthquakes; many cities devastated. The pope will become captive and the church put under tribute, despoiled of all her temporal goods. For some time there will be no pope. Then a northern king will traverse all Europe, will destroy the republics and exterminate the rebels. He will defend the faith and subjugate the Mohammedan empire. A new pastor of the church will come, according to celestial signs; by his simple heart and the doctrine of Christ, peace will be restituted.

João de Vatiguerro (1524): "All public cult will be interrupted. A terrible and cruel famine will commence in the whole world and principally in western regions, such as has never occurred since the world's beginning."

From an old Italian prophecy: "Famine will have many innumerable victims. Vultures will emerge from their hiding-places to feast on the flesh of corpses."

Helena Walraff (1790): "The pope will be forced to flee, followed by four cardinals. He will find refuge in Cologne."

Mathias Lang, died in 1820: "After the purification of the world, men will again love each other, as they have previously hated each other. It will be a glorious age. Great preachers and holy men will appear and perform miracles.

The prophecy of Saint-Rémy: In Nostradamus' native place circulated the so-called prophecy of Saint-Rémy. Its contents are in accord with Nostradamus' quatrain IV-86: A new king will rule over the whole ancient Roman empire. He will be one of the greatest kings of France and the last of his line, the ancient Capetian dynasty, and his throne will be in southern France (Nostradamus pinpoints Avignon).

Abbot Genet of the convent of Clarisses in Fonjéres

(Bretagne) drew up prophecies before 1798, which were published in 1819 by Baucé in Paris. He depicts the end of the world with the following words: "The 20th century will not pass before the beginning of the Judgment. I have seen it in the light of God."

The archbishop of Tours predicted in 1827: "The archbishop of Paris will have to die. At a moment when peace will seem near and when it will be least expected, great events will take place. It will be the king of France, who will liberate the church and re-establish the pope in his rights."

Vauclin: "The churches will be closed by force if they will not close voluntarily."

Rosa Asdente: "Revolution will expand over all Europe, and there will be no peace, until after the pope will have regained his throne."

Marie de Terreaux of Lyons (1843): "These events will be preceded by a bad year. But, on the contrary, the year of the events will be an exceptionally fertile year, yet too few people will have remained on the earth to consume this abundance."

Ravignan, a Jesuit priest (1847): "The church will suffer great ills; a torrent of evil will open a breach on her, but the first attack will be against her fortune and her riches."

Palma Martarelli (1854): "Republic will be proclaimed in Italy and will be followed by a civil war."

Don Bosco, an Italian priest, the founder of the Salesian order, lived from 1815 until 1888, was canonized in 1933. He left a prophecy, which was published 1911 in the book

L'écho du merveilleux. The authenticity of his prophecy has been documentary proven: "Four hundred days after the month of flowers, which will have had two new moons, revolution will be proclaimed in Italy. Two hundred days later the pope will be forced to leave Rome and will be wandering for one hundred days, then will return to his capital city, to sing Te Deum in St. Peter's church."

Anne de la Foi (1879): "A great nation will be conducted by the spirit of error to the brink of abyss and in a few days will be exterminated."

Marie Julie (1880): "The earth will be like a vast cemetery. Corpses of the impious and of the just will cover it. The earth will tremble to its fundaments, then great waves will agitate the sea and invade the continents."

Pope Pius X, who died in 1914, fell in sleep or trance during an audience in 1909 and, awakening, exclaimed: "I had a horrible vision. Was it of me or one of my successors? I saw the pope leaving Rome and, to get out of Vatican, he had to step over the corpses of his priests."

C. Billenstein, a Danish engineer, in a book, which he published in 1920, prophesied Asian invasion of Europe in the year 2009.

The seer of the Black Forest (Germany) admonished and warned America (in a vision of 1928): "Greetings to the brethren across the great water. Powerful have I cultivated the land and abundantly filled its chambers and granaries. That land has my blessing, since it keeps open its gates for the fallen and has become a home for the ejected. But now mark: the time of the visitation of Europe will become a time of trial for you. Take care not to become tempted to fall to false greediness. Render help to the oppressed without business considerations, because thereafter will come a time when even you will be in need of assistance. Keep your house clean of the disputes of the old world, since it is of no use. Shun the war which is on your doorstep and, because it will come nevertheless, conduct it as men and not as brigands. Then will I remove from over your heads the threatening clouds and you will be a land of power, and the equilibrium of the world will rest in your hands."

Georges Barbarin in his book *Le Secret de la Grande Pyramide*, (Paris, 1936) records the last dates of the underground chamber of the pyramid: "Humanity will enter the Hall of Resurrection and of the Judgment of Nations on the 15th or 16th of September, 1936, and will run against the wall in December 1992."

The prophecy of St. Odile

In the Vosges mountains of Alsace (France), between Colmar and Saverne, lies the monastery of St. Odile. Among the treasures of this old monastery are some documents, containing the last writings of St. Odile, the former abbess of the monastery. They are composed in prophetic style and their principal sections, as far as they refer to our times, are worded as follows:

"Hear, oh, hear, my sisters and brothers: I saw forests and mountains tremble. There will come a time, when war will break out, more terrible than all other wars combined, which have ever visited mankind. A horrible warrior will unleash it, and his adversaries will call him Antichrist. All nations of the earth will fight each other in this war. The fighters will rise up in the heavens to take the stars and will throw them on the cities, to set ablaze the buildings and to cause immense devastations. Oceans will lie between the great warriors, and the monsters of the sea, terrified by everything that happens on \or under the sea, will flee to the deep. Battles of the past will be only skirmishes compared to the battles that will take place, because the earth will be red, and even the sky, the water and the air, since blood will flow in all directions. The earth will shake from the violent fighting. Famine and pestilence will join the war. The nations will then cry "peace, peace," but there will be no peace. Thrice will the sun rise over the heads of the combattants, without having been seen by them. But afterwards there will be peace, and all who have broken peace will have lost their lives. On a single day more men will be killed than the catacombs of Rome have ever held. Pyres will be erected greater than the greatest city, and people will ascend the highest mountains to praise God, and nobody will want to make war any more. Strange signs will appear in the skies: both horns of the moon will join the cross. Happy will be those who will have survived the war, since the pleasures of life will begin again and the sun will have a new brilliancy."

The prophecies of the monastery of Marienthal

Near Haguenau in Alsace, north of Strassburg, lies the famous Alsatian place of pilgrimage, the monastery of Marienthal. Its first beginnings reach back into the 13th century. It has an extremely vicissitudinary history to record. In many wars it has been the refuge of expelled populace and soldiers. It has been repeatedly damaged and ravaged, but has always risen again, thanks to a strange legend that whoever visits this place will never be hard besett by his destiny.

The treasures of this monastery of Marienthal include its famous "book of pilgrimage," printed 1749 in Haguenau. Among other things, it contains a very remarkable prophecy about "coming events of the 20th century." It is composed in the form of post-medieval verses. Translated into the language of our days, its essential part reads as follows:

"A war will come, before which all previous wars will fade. Streams of fire will come from clouds, where are no clouds. And in the middle will be the great water. Big eagles will fly in the skies and moles will be the models for soldiers under the earth to the depth of 300 feet. Great armies with iron horses and dragons will be seen, and everything will be different than it has ever been. Battles will rage on and within the earth and in the air, and whole cities on this side and across the great water will be destroyed. All capital cities on both sides of the water will be buried under rubbish and ashes, and it will be a great groaning and moaning. The horrors of war will be also on and over the water, and the enemy will be smitten on the head with many casualties, and tears will flow and much blood, and then everything will be over. Victory will be sounded through the clouds in all countries, to be heard by the armies which fight for freedom, and they will be victorious after great ills and sufferings. And the whole world will jubilate, because great love is with the countries of freedom and with the great light, which will have been darkened, but will again shine forth brighter than ever. Blessed who reads and hears the words of this prophecy and retains what has been written. Blessed who survives these times, because they will be succeeded by times of great peace."

The prophecy of Stormberger

Stormberger lived in the 18th century. He was born in Rabenstein, in the Bavarian forest region of Germany, not far from the present border of Czechoslovakia. Almost all his life he was a cowherd, living in solitude and close union with nature. Whoever met him and saw him, was astonished by his frequent visions and significant predictions, many had superstitious dread of him, others felt even hostility. That was little to be wondered at, because Stormberger predicted things that in his time i.e. 200 years ago, in every respect had to be considered products of a morbid fantasy. His predictions extended over three great periods. The first period comprised the second half of the 19th century, the second period the first half of the 20th century, and the third the years between 1950 and 2000. For the first period he predicted the invention of the locomotive, the automobile and the airplane, in his time things of impossibility:

"Iron roads will be built, and iron monsters will bark through the wilderness. Cars without horse and shaft will come, and men will fly through the air like birds."

In similar picturesque manner he predicted the First World War:

"When in the outskirts of the forest the iron road will be finished, and there the iron horse will be seen, a war will begin, to last for twice two years. It will be fought with iron fortresses that move without horses, and with powers that come from the earth and fall from the sky."

This prophecy was accomplished in all exactitude. The iron road was the railway section from Kalteneck to Deggendorf, which leads through the outskirts of the Bavarian Forest and which was officially opened for traffic—take notice—of all days, on August 1, 1914. Stormberger had exactly predicted the day of the outbreak of the First World War, and also the tanks, mines, and air raids, all of which were for the first time employed in the war of 1914/18.

He continued his prophecy with the words:

"Right after this horrible war there will come a time when money will have no value. For two hundred guilders not even a loaf of bread will be available, and yet there will be no famine. Money will be made of iron, and gold will become so valuable that for a few gold coins a small farm could be bought."

With this prediction Stormberger strikingly describes the inflation in Austria and Germany. In fact, a loaf of bread did cost at that time in Germany two billion marks. For fifty gold coins of twenty crowns each you could then buy in Austria a small farm. In Germany and Austria money then was coined of iron and aluminum. But the predictions of Stormberger include also the story of two other wars:

"Two or three decades after the first great war will come a second, still greater war. Almost all nations of the world will be involved. Millions of men will die, without being soldiers. Fire will fall from the sky and many great cities will be destroyed. Nobody will endure his fellowman any more. Even the Lord, our God, will be dragged out of his corner. Everybody will have his own, different mind. The little ones will become great and the great ones small. Laws will be made that nobody will keep, and taxes announced that nobody will be able to pay. Nothing will be holy anymore. Everything will be upset. The great clearance will commence. All states will be pitted against each other. The free life and thought will be imprisoned and banished. Severe masters will rule and will try to get everything under their discipline. It will be a terrible time. Whoever flees, should not look back. Whoever has two loafs of bread, will come through. After the great clearance, during which pestilence will tarry in the air and in the cellars and on the roof, millions of men will have no free ground any more, no country and no home, because many cities will be no more and the frontiers of many states will be fixed anew. And after the second great struggle between the nations will come a third universal conflagration, which will determine everything. There will be entirely new weapons. In one day more men will die than in all previous wars combined. Battles will be fought with artificial guns.

Gigantic catastrophes will occur. With open eyes will the nations of the earth enter into these catastrophes. They will not be aware of what is happening, and those who will know and tell, will be silenced. Every thing will become different than before, and in many places the earth will be only just a great cemetery. The third great, great war will be the end for many nations."

Stormberger's predictions are in exact conformity with the visions of the famous seeress St. Katharina (of Emmerich). Stormberger's prophecies have been historically verified by several Bavarian and Austrian writers. In compiled form they have been published also in a book, but after the National-socialists came to power in Germany and in 1934 organized the great auto-da-fé of all disagreeable books, propaganda minister Dr. Goebbels included in the list also the documents, pamphlets and books referring to the prophecies of Stormberger. The dead letters have been burned, and only a very few copies remained intact. But the spirit of prophecy cannot be silenced and unflinchingly continues to warn mankind.

The prophecy of Wismar (1761)

When pulling down an old wall of the Holy Ghost monastery in Wismar (Germany) in 1761, an old Bible was found with an inserted manuscript on parchment, containing predictions. In the form of copies this prediction now circulates in several differing versions. One of them, in a condensed form, is as follows:

"The day will come when a new great war will begin between the East and the West. Mankind will suffer great loss through new weapons. Cars will run without horses, and fiery dragons will fly in the air and spit sulphur and fire, destroying many cities and towns. There will be other forces, taken from the bowels of the earth. Such a time it will be that there will be no buying or selling because nobody will own anything. The quarters of sky and water will be tinted. This terrible period will last for three years and five months. The nation of Pleiades will intervene and will attack the bearded nation from the rear. Thus all nations will get involved in the quarrel. The great struggle will begin when ears of corn will bow down, being full; it will reach its acme when the cherry trees will bloom for the third time, and will end when the shadow of the sun slides down. But there will be no victor, since the victor himself will have been vanquished. Only death will be content, having had such a harvest as never before. God bless the nations, which still survive, since they will be the grain that will make new ears of corn grow."

Another version has instead of "three" years "four" years. The nation of Pleiades will defeat "the country of the seas" and will thus implicate all other nations, including the bearded nation, which will suffer an attack from the rear but which, nevertheless, will survive and continue to exist for a long time. The war will reach its acme when cherry trees will bloom for the "fourth" time. Peace will be concluded at Christmas time.

The miracle of Fatima

Occasionally people appear claiming to have seen Mary, the mother of Jesus, or even Jesus Christ himself. Such a vision is often combined with a supposedly heard or otherwise received message, pertaining to the future. More often as not, such prophecies are only the effects of a hysterical fantasy. They should be received extremely critically. Such is also the practice of the Catholic church, since many sick, religious fanatics with similar assertions only cause confusion in the minds of simple people and inflict injury to their true, genuine religiosity. Nevertheless, some reports of such visions are so exceptional that they cannot but arouse our earnest attention.

The most famous of such phenomenons is the so-called miracle of Fatima. Many books have been written about it, and an American full length movie has been made about this occurrence. During the First World War, on May 13, 1917, near the hamlet Fatima (in Portugal), three Portuguese shepherd children, ten-year-old Lucia, nine-year-old Francisco and seven-year-old Jacinta, were tending their sheep. Francisco and Jacinta were brother and sister, but Lucia belonged to another family. On the aforementioned day they had seen a beautiful lady, who had told them that she has come from heaven. The children had conversed with her, and the lady had promised to return on the 13th day of each month until October, when she promised to perform a miracle. During the third vision, on July 13, 1917, the lady disclosed that she was Mary, the mother of Jesus; among many other things, she spoke the following words: "The war (the First World War) will soon end, but if men will not cease to offend the Lord, a new, much more wicked war will shortly break out. When you then at night will see a strange, unfamiliar light,[1] then know that it is a sign from God, that punishment for the many crimes the world has committed is near: there will be war, famine and persecution of the church and the Holy Father. To prevent it, I will ask that Russia is dedicated to my immaculate heart and that a communion of atonement on the first Saturday of the month is introduced. If my request is granted, Russia will again be converted, and there will be peace. If not, Russia will continue to spread her errors throughout the world, wars and persecutions of the church will be provoked, good people will be tortured, the

1. During the night between January 24 and 25, 1938, an extraordinary bright aurora borealis could be seen in all Europe, including Portugal.

Holy Father will have to suffer greatly, and many nations will be exterminated. Finally, my immaculate heart will yet triumph, the Holy Father will dedicate Russia to me, Russia will be converted and the world will be given peace for a considerable time. Portugal will keep the true faith always."

These words and everything else, that the children had heard, was written down, as related by Lucia, by the bishop of Leiria. The document is kept in the archieves of the bishopry of Leiria and a part of the contents have never been disclosed.[2] It is of interest to note that this document contains a report on visions seen before the October revolution of Russia, including a prediction about the victory of atheism in Russia and about Russia's negative rôle in the history of Europe and the world. Anyway, even after October 1917, very few, if any, of the simple people of Fatima, much less the ten-year-old Lucia, could have any notion about the importance of recent events in Russia.

On the occasion of the last vision, on October 13, 1917, thousands of spectators were crowding Fatima, to witness the promised miracle. The testimonies of numerous eye witnesses have been preserved about "the phenomenon of the dancing sun," which occurred on that day. Among the witnesses were the bishop of Leiria, several newspaper editors and reporters, as well as a professor of the University of Coimbra, Mr. A. Garrete. They all confirm having seen the sun, at noon, dancing and spinning around, throwing yellow, green, red, blue and violet cones of light about him.

Now Fatima is one of the most frequented places of pilgrimage. It has to be noted, that the pope still has not

2. When pope Paul VI on May 13, 1967, arrived in Fatima, to take part in the festivities of the 50th anniversary of the miracle of Fatima, everybody expected the final disclosure of the remainder of the prophecy, which up to now had been kept secret. But it did not happen. A few months later a German newspaper reported from allegedly informed Vatican sources, that the undisclosed part of the message of Fatima contains predictions about horrible events during the Third World War including the complete destruction of Rome and of the Vatican.

...sh of Mary and has not dedicated Russia to her
...n the winter of 1942, when the Second World
...ing at full extent, the pope declared the prophecy
... as authentic and on December 8, in an official
ceremony, dedicated the world and all mankind (which, of
course, includes the Russian nation) to Mary's "immaculate
heart." A separate dedication of Russia has not taken place
to this day.

*   *   *   *   *

The message of Heede. A girl of Heede (village in North
Germany) on November 1, 1937, alleged having seen Christ,
who supposedly told her: "Since nobody has listened to my
mother in Fatima, I am coming now myself, at the last hour,
to warn humanity."

Maria Taigi in 1835 supposedly saw Christ in a vision. He
told her: "At first will come several terrestrial scourges, as
great wars, through which many millions will run into
destruction. After that will come the celestial scourge in full
severity, such as has never been. It will be short, but will cut
off the greater part of mankind. Yet, before that, five big
trees have to be felled." What these trees are, was not
explained.

Maria and Elsa (of Voltago, upper Italy) received stigmata[3]
on December 10, 1937, and, supposedly on Christ's order,
prophesied: "I saw a wide meadow, over which the sky
suddenly reddened. Red rain began to fall. Under it a great
number of people died. Before a great cross in the sky, they
lacerated their own faces and tore their hair. I saw flames of
devastated cities, others completely covered by flood; only a

3. Marks on palms and feet, believed to be supernaturally impressed, in imitation
of the wounds of Christ.

few roofs, chimneys and tree tops were protruding. Still other cities were completely devoured by the earth, while the red of the sky persisted. I saw also many cradles with children swing on the water. I understood it as a sign that only children will be saved from the general destruction."

Emelda Scochy, a twelve-year-old girl in Ham (Belgium) in 1933 declared having seen Christ who told her: "I have come to warn. Hard times will soon arrive although many will doubt it and smile. Earth will shake, seas will overflow the banks, mountains will move, famines and pestilence will arise, all in a short while. Who doubts, will not be saved. Pray to God, because the time is near. Shortly the kingdom of Christ will be founded on this earth, but in the meantime, the prince of this world has been permitted to found a kingdom of his own, which will be only an empty mold of the undivided kingdom of Christ. Many members of the church will not see the difference, because even they seek the temporal, and they will be deceived by the prince of this world."

* * * * *

Many old prophecies circulate in Europe in form of manuscript copies, the origin of which, for the most part, cannot be ascertained. I am quoting here parts of some of the more remarkable ones:

1. In a prophecy, the origin of which has been traced to Palestine, we read, among other things: "The prince of this world will celebrate victory, and the heart of Jesus will bleed. But then God will chastise his people and strike hard. Whoever survives, will owe it to the mercy of God. The times will get more and more confused. Only whoever already now takes precaution, will keep his conception clear, because

many will ask for light in vain, and even the righteous and the chosen will tremble and fear. Whoever through prayers prepares himself for these things, will feel my blessing in the time of the great confusion.

2. "I have told you not to follow false Christs; whoever transforms my teachings according to his desires, in order to gain the favour of the people will be erased from the Book of Life. Beware, you profaners, of feigning piety and faith, and of scorning me. Most frightfully I shall avenge the sin against the Spirit, since whole nations can be led astray through it and innumerable souls pulled into abyss. Beware of imposing your will upon people, with the pretense of making them happy. The hell will help you, but not my blessing."

3. "Write: I shall come over the sinful world with the rumbling of thunder at a cold winter night. The storm will be preceded by a hot south wind, and hailstones of hundredweight will batter the earth. Destructive lightnings will flash through burning red cloud masses, setting everything on fire. The air will become full of poisonous gas, sulphur and a smothering vapour. Tornados will smash all the proud buildings, erected in the frenzy of your sense of power. Then you will recognize that there is a will which prevails over the will of man."

4. "Persevere for three days and three nights. Then the horror will pass. The sign that the judgment has begun will come in a cold winter night with the rumbling of thunder and the trembling of mountains. Fasten the windows and doors, cover all look-outs. Your eyes should not see the most terrible of all happenings, because God's wrath is holy. He will purify the earth for you, the small number of the faithful. Convene in prayer before my crucifix and invoke the guardians of your soul."

5. A similar prophecy has been guarded by a family in Passau (Germany) for more than a century. Its contents have been published in a pamphlet. It is written in the form of verses, in archaic style. Its contents are: "A winter will come, darkness for three days, lightning, thunder and cleft in the earth. Stay at home and pray to God, do not go outside. Do not dare to even look through the window. A poisonous breath will fill the night with dust. Black pestilence, the worst human battle. But the faithful will stay free and unharmed by suffocation and death."

6. In about the year 1800 in Mayence (Germany) was published a prophecy, which came true during the Second World War: "Great misfortune will come over our city. It will be destroyed by iron and fire, and great many of the inhabitants will be killed. But at the last hour relief will come from the west, consisting of seven nations, fighting against three nations. Sanguinary battles will take place on the Rhine and near Hamm. The seventh generation of the German people will be made responsible for its evil-doers. Germany will be heavy afflicted." As is well known, Mayence was reduced to ashes during the Second World War, in which seven allied nations were actively pitted against the Axis: Germany, Italy and Japan.

Shortly before *mahatma Gandhi* was assassinated by a fanatic, he made the following forecast in the circle of friends and co-workers: "Mankind is approaching hard times, because as soon as the measure of its sins will be full, it will be called to account by the superior power above us. You may call this event as you wish: "judgment day," "final settlement" or "doomsday." It will come, most likely, very soon. Whoever will survive this settlement, will see an entirely new earthly existence manifested. For a long, very long time the word "war" will be crossed out from the dictionary of mankind, perhaps even for all times. Christmas, the festival of Christianity, will be accepted by all religions as the true festival of peace. Blessed he, who will live to see this epoch!"

The visions of Madame Sylvia

The most famous European clairvoyant, countess Bianca von Beck-Rzikowsky of Vienna, called "Madame Sylvia," died soon after the Second World War. Among her clients had been many persons of noble rank, including kings, as well as many highly placed politicians and diplomats. She has left a number of predictions, the realization of which still belong to the future. A European diplomat, who had corresponded with the countess, published in 1950 exerpts from her letters. Highly interesting are the following fragments, all written in 1931:

1. I see barbed wire fences in Mongolia and far into Russia. After that a man will appear in the East with a face like carved of stone. The hilt of his sword he always has in his hands.

2. Germany will have two governments. One will come into existence locally, within the territory of the country, and will mean guilt and expiation. The other one will be imposed on Germany from the outside.

3. The fate of the world will be decided by "a man with a pen" and "a man with a sword." France will temporarily lose her prestige through her own fault. One of her statesmen will die at a wrong time, and the situation of France will thereby worsen. Negotiations between France and England will begin, but will fail because of the German question. Austria will at that time be small and calm. Poland will try to meddle into matters of high politics, although not of her own accord, but she will fail.

4. Inclement winters will arise, with unprecedented

frigidity at places. Finally two great, colossal states will collapse, and as a consequence the political structure of governments will change everywhere. But still I see great danger for the Christian states and Christian nations.

Shortly before her death in 1948, Sylvia made the following statement: "During the next twenty years there will be no world war." Dr. F. R. Liesche compiled many of her visions in a book. From it I have borrowed the following fragments:

1. With flying colors the East will draw up against the West. The West will be pushed back at exposed points, but will stand its ground at others or even gain better positions. Yet what follows, is not clear, especially for Europe. Great agitation, many conferences, sensations in all newspapers. What nobody held possible, will yet happen, and will happen unexpectedly, after one side had already deemed having won victory. The masses will turn the scale. The earth shakes and bursts in all junctures, and a time will come, when people will moan and groan in distress, pain and agony. Animals will flee and try to hide themselves, mountains will reel and forests will tumble. Waters will overflow, and eternity will set in. Nothing but death and destruction. Our forces of light are not sufficient for the battle with the powers of darkness. The sublime lies in dust, because men are deaf and blind, they don't want to hear nor to see. Frenzy, folly and madness. I see Rome on fire. Oh, what ruins! Only two tablets of law still erect, wrapped in clouds. Two corpses by the roadside, two fallen colossi; terrible struggle, lament, wreck, ruin and smoke. Where is the sun? Where is day? Where is God and his help? Everything is dark on earth. Hell has opened its gates. The world is without support. The heart of the world is broken, and yet it rises anew—I cannot understand it . . . The earth breathes, whirls around, in terrible catastrophes continents crumble and are washed away, but other continents and islands appear again.

2. In Europe very much will be written, heap and mess of bureaucracy, mountains of documents. Little clerks upon them, pretending to have overcome stupidity with documents. Poor masses, you cannot love, your wretched little souls can only hate. As soon as it will be generally recognized that Germany, like Siegfried, with sword in hand, takes the field against the dragon, all Europe will be in agreement and even England will be on the side of Germany. Europe will become a unity of one nation, not many nations any more. There will be different people and different souls, but not nations. I see one banner—white. In the middle of Europe—a tower. The map of Europe white, not bloody any more.

3. There is one alone, who is great and magnificent. He comes from the mountains, of a nation which once, a long long time ago, disappeared. O, mountains of Asia, upon you already flares the torch, by which the universal conflagration will once be kindled. The South will strike out, far over Europe. The East, turning itself in reverse, will whet the sword in three directions. A new England will be created. A new universal language will be brought forth, which by a magic stroke will make everybody understand other languages. It will be like a bridge, after the sudden perception that in all languages of the earth lies a root of affinity on magical elements. O, what a wonderful secret, unraveled by the great, lonely philosopher, south of those mountains. The new epoch will deliver you from speech, because you will be able to feel what is in the thoughts of other men. You have to comprehend: in those far mountains of the east rests the secret power. It will inexorably extend over the whole earth and will tower toward the sky. Everything that recalls the old times will collapse. Soon you will face a new world, new conceptions of the world, new organizations, new laws.

The prediction of Warsaw: A Polish prophecy, made by a monk in 1790, tells about future events and the end of the world in a wonderfully lucid style, in sharp contrast with the dark, ambiguous Nostradamus:

"Prussia and Russia will divide Poland among themselves (it happened in 1793). In 1805 a war will break out between France and Austria, and if Austria will not make peace, she will lose everything (Austria, as everybody knows, concluded a timely peace in Bratislava). A year later, in 1806, war between Prussia and France will begin (it came true). In 1807 another war, this time between France and Russia, will break out (this prediction was accomplished only in 1812). In 1848 a terrible revolution will spread over all Europe. Kings and emperors will descend from their thrones. The 20th century will be a most remarkable one, and I can see beforehand all the ordeals and afflictions, which will befall the inhabitants of the earth at that time. In many countries the citizens will rebel against their government, children against their parents and the whole mankind against each other. In 1938 the world will be threatened by an universal war and all creatures by annihilation. Whole countries will be devastated, and the greatest and most distinguished cities will be demolished and will become desolate and deserted. Peace will come only in 1986."

Lord Roslin, "the patron of the freemasons," prophesied in 1601 in a stylish manner: "Ten decades after the times of the cross and the sword, the heathen will rise up anew and burn the gates of the temple, the pillars of which are resting in all Christian kingdoms. Then the knights will leave their vaults, will break the rose from the stone and fasten it at their breast, alongside the cross. After desperate battles, they will again build up the eternally ancient temple of wisdom."

Heckenstaller published in the 1923 edition of the Farmer's calendar of Salzburg (Austria) several predictions, which, he declares, will all be fulfilled in the future: 1. Bavaria will detach itself from Germany and form a new monarchy, in confederation with Austria, 2. France will have a different form of government, 3. the submerged continent Atlantis will rise up again, 4. England will vanish in the sea, 5. Germany and Italy will experience changes of climate, 6. the centre of earth gravity will be shifting.

The prediction of pastor Bartholomaeus Holzhauser: It was in 1642, when Bartholomaeus Holzhauser (of Swabia) obtained the pastorate of St. Johann in Tyrol (Austria). Already as a fourteen-year-old boy he had holy visions and had discussed religious problems in a manner prodigious for his age. As a professor of theology, he later, because of his bright intellect, was highly esteemed by princes and kings, especially by elector Johann Philipp of Mayence, who repeatedly invited him to his court. In the eyes of common people he was held in high repute as a holy man. He was often fasting and liked to live in strict seclusion for long periods of time. He depicted the time before the coming of Antechrist as follows:

"At about 1800 A.D. great tribulations will come. Arrogance and vanity will rule the world. Cocks will arise in France, and they will break the lilies,[4] kill monarchs and oppress the Christian faith and the church. Priests and servants of the church will be reduced to misery, the youth led to atheism, and republics will be established in the whole world. And everything will be destroyed by wars.

"In the second period will be peace, but only by name, not in reality. The tribulations will be as great as during a war. The new rulers of Germany will stand up against authorities. God will pour out the spirit of deception over them, and they

4. Lily is the symbol of French monarchy.

will want what they don't want, will not want what they do want, and their actions will become so preposterous, that they will not be able to do what they are able to do. At noonday they will grope about like in darkness.

"And then, under the sign of the eagle, will come a time when the empire will be ruled by terror and cruelty. The ruler will avail himself of the spirit of discord and will enter other countries by force, to govern over them. Exceedingly great will be the misery in the countries devastated by him, and signs will hurry on and new signs will arise, and he himself will be punished for all the punishments, inflicted by him on others. He will not reign for long. As he had come, he will go, leaving the world in chaos.

"And then will come a new period, in which two mighty ones will face each other, and each of them will want to be the most mighty one and to rule over the other. The wrangle between these two will begin in the second half of the twentieth century. It will overthrow mountains and silt up rivers. A great change will come to pass, such as no mortal man will have expected. Heaven and hell will confront each other in this struggle. Old states will perish and light and darkness will be pitted against each other with swords, but it will be swords of a different fashion. With these swords it will be possible to cut up the skies and to split the earth. A great lament will come over all mankind and only a small batch will survive the storm, the pestilence and the horror. And neither of the two adversaries will conquer nor be vanquished. Both mighty ones will lie on the ground, and a new mankind will come into existence. God possesses the key to everything. Blessed who will then be still able to praise him, having obeyed all his commandments. And the great monarch of the world will create new laws for the new mankind and will cause a new age to begin, in which there will be only one flock and one shepherd, and peace will be of long, long duration, for the glory of God in heaven and on earth."

The vision of Billante, princess of Savoy: "Great afflictions will come. I see yellow and red warriors setting out for Europe, which will lie in a yellow vapour. It will kill all cattle on pasture. Nations will end in flames, and famine will annihilate millions."

Prophecy from the monastery Maria Laach (16th century): "The twentieth century will bring death and destruction, apostasy from the church, discord in families, cities and governments. It will be the century of three great wars with intervals of a few decades. They will become evermore devastating and bloody and will lay in ruins not only Germany, but finally all countries of East and West. After a terrible defeat of Germany will follow the next great war. Then there will be no bread for people any more and no fodder for animals. Poisonous clouds, made by human hands, will sink down and exterminate everything. The human mind will be seized by insanity."

The prophecy of La-Salette: La-Salette is a small village in the south of France. There, in the year 1846, two children, Maximin Giraud and Melanie Calvat, declared having seen "the holy Virgin," while they were tending cattle in pasture. The Virgin, according to the childrens' report, had disclosed to them the future. The bishop of Grenoble gave credence to their story and sent Melanie Calvat to the pope to relate everything that they had seen and heard. Many books have been published about the revelations of the children of La-Salette. Among other things Melanie Calvat predicted: "Germans will invade France twice, the first time through Belgium, the second time through Switzerland. The first time they will behave like barbarians, the second time like beasts." Germany during both world wars indeed invaded France, but on both occasions her armies came through Belgium. The predictions include the following words: "Because of the attempt to shake off the yoke of the Lord, Italy will be punished. Italy will have war. Blood will be spilt on the streets. Italians will fight against Italians." About religious persecutions and the fate of the church: "Before the victory of the church will come a year of water, a year of fire and a year of blood."

Quite interesting is the prophecy about the last days of the world: "The peace among men, which will set in after the great visitation, will be only an ostensible peace. During this period the earth will shake because of manifold concussions and convulsions. Mankind will experience continuous wars, which finally will lead to the last great war. The aim of the belligerents will be to rule over the world. During the period of the hollow peace, the seasons will change and stars will deviate from their habitual course. The earth will quake and from the elements water and fire a new destructive force will spring, which will call forth great concussions of the earth. This new force will devour mountains, cities and even whole territories. The evil spirits of air will call forth strange things upon the earth and will throw men into destruction. The glory of the church will be temporarily diminished, and the whole world will be seized by anguish. Woe to the inhabitants of earth! Sanguinary wars will break out, a killing rain will pour down and even the birds will fall from the sky. Thunder and lightning will destroy cities. All universe will be seized by terror. But God will let himself be reconciled with mankind by the blood, the tears and the prayers of the righteous. Thereupon water and fire will purify the earth and the period of true peace will begin."

In Montreal (Canada) the following prophecy was published in 1888: "A time will come that will have nothing in common with the present. Everything will be different. Horses as servants of man will lose their value. They will be supplanted by horses of steel, fed with coal. Finally will come carriages that can move without horses, even carriages that can fly in the air. Men of those times will live like in a fairy tale. But they will make also such wars as never before. All manmade progress will be enlisted for destruction. However, the great fate will raise her hand in warning and will command to stop. If men will listen to the judicious ones among them and stop, it will be to their advantage, if not, it will be their misfortune, and a great calamity will follow."

The prophecy of Johann Friede: Johann Friede (1204-1257), an Austrian monk of the order of St. John, was one of the greatest seers of his time. Here follows an excerpt from one of his many revelations that refer to our present time and our nearest future:

"When the great time will come, in which mankind will face its last, hard trial, it will be foreshadowed by striking changes in nature. The alternation between cold and heat will become more intensive, storms will have more catastrophic effects, earthquakes will destroy greater regions and the seas will overflow many lowlands. Not all of it will be the result of natural causes, but mankind will penetrate into the bowels of the earth and will reach into the clouds, gambling with its own existence. Before the powers of destruction will succeed in their design, the universe will be thrown into disorder, and the age of iron will plunge into nothingness.

"When nights will be filled with more intensive cold and days with heat, a new life will begin in nature. The heat means radiation from the earth, the cold the waning light of the sun. Only a few years more and you will become aware that sunlight has grown perceptibly weaker. When even your artificial light will cease to give service, the great event in the firmament will be near. The nebula of the Greater Bear will have arrived in the vicinity of the earth and finally will fill the space of five hundred suns at the horizon. It will more and more cover up the light of the sun until the days will be like nights at full moon. The illumination will not come from the moon, but from Orion, which constellation, by the light of Jupiter, will send forth its rays on the Greater Bear and will dissolve its nebula with the force of light.

"By this time mankind and the animal kingdom will have been stricken with terror. Birds will be like reptiles and will not use their wings. Animals of the ground, in fear and alarm, will raise such a clamour that it will make human hearts tremble. Men will flee into their abodes in order not to see the weird occurrence. Finally complete darkness will set in and last for three days and three nights.

"During this time men, deprived of the power of light, will fall into a slumberlike sleep, from which many will not awaken, especially those who have had no spark of spiritual life. When the sun will again rise and emerge, earth will be covered by a blanket of ashes like snow in winter, except that the ashes will have the color of sulphur. Damp fog will ascend from the ground, illuminated by igneous gases. Of mankind there will be more dead than there had been casualties in world wars. In the abodes of the children of light the Book of Revelation will be read, and in the palaces of the church servants of the spiritual doctrine will explain the coming and the arrival of the great comet. On the seventh day after the return of light earth will have absorbed the ashes and formed such a fertility as has not been experienced ever before. But Orion will cast down its rays on the earth and show a path toward the last resting place of the greatest and most eminent man who had ever lived on earth. The survivors will proclaim his ancient doctrine in peace and will institute the millennium, announced by the Messiah, in the light of true brotherly and sisterly love, for the glory of the Creator and for the blessedness of all mankind."

Seeress Regina, the German Cassandra: Regina was a very famous German prophetess, who had foreseen, many years before, the coming of the First and Second World War as well as their duration. Most of her prophecies are written in a poetical form. Of those that refer to the present and future time, let me quote the following, condensed from her verses: "We are living now in an age of ill-will, error, and decay. Whoever survives, without losing his moral qualities, has stood his fiery ordeal. The world awaits the Saviour, but before his coming a great catastrophe is threatening. Fires burn at a distance, weapons rattle and bells sound alarm. We have to be vigilant and strong! Afar and near, friends and foes, men who speak in all tongues, will dash against each other. The earth itself will writhe in agony. Mankind will be decimated by epidemics, famines and poison. After the catastrophe they will emerge from their caves and assemble and only a few will have been left to build the new world. The future is approaching at a quick pace. The world will be destroyed in many quarters and will never be the same as before."

About Germany's fate she prophesied: "King and emperor will disappear, and another will lash the whip. An iron crown is for thee, German nation, and it will press and weigh heavily upon thee for many years to come. Only long after will arise a new crown, not of iron, nor gold or silver, but of rays of light. And a man is holding it, of supreme power, and then the German nation will be standing the test, not with weapons or iron or brass, but with deeds high and lofty."

Shortly before the Second World War Regina had a vision, in which she spoke the following words: "A peculiar generation now exists on this earth, which does not carry an inner growth but only death for the whole race. And some day, at some future time, people will say: there lived a clan and here and there again. Germans, Britons or Franks, the old, eternal law induced them to dig their own graves. They are digging graves also for their own souls. Britons, Franks or Germans or whatever the country, where they live: they are all united by an old law, which provides that they wither and die. When the sun will again rise over the graves in golden glory, a new generation will arise in the course of time and a new mankind."

Clairvoyant *Irlmaier* of Freilassing (Bavaria) predicts: "The Third World War will come, but I cannot predict the year. It will be preceded by signs in the skies, which will be seen by millions of people. War will begin on a rainy night, shortly before harvest time, when the ears are full. War will begin after the assassination of an eminent politician in Czechoslovakia or in Yugoslavia. An invasion from the east will follow in three columns. Thousands of airplanes, coming from the direction of Africa, will fly over Germany, but will not drop any bombs. However, east of us everything will be reduced to cinders. Not even grass will grow there, and most men and animals will be killed. The eastern army will be stopped, but will not be able to return home. There will be some trouble in Munich. Three other great cities will be destroyed. The city with the iron tower will be devastated by its own citizens. Southern England will be ruined, because enemy's airplanes will drop a destructive bomb into the sea, which will be followed by an earthquake and tidal waves. Czechoslovakia and Poland will be laid waste. Blood will flow in Italy. Many priests will be killed. The pope will escape and will return after the war, to crown kings in Hungary, Austria and Bavaria. The war will last for three units of time (days, weeks, months or years). Unexpectedly, a great man will die, and then will come peace. The climate of Europe will change, it will become warmer."

American seers and prophets

Since my purpose has been to provide the reader with material not easily accessible, there is no need to dwell in detail on predictions by American prophets. Their prophecies are well known and available in many recently published books.

Many of the earlier American prophets have been founders or followers of religious sects or movements. Their predictions, for the most part, have been commentaries on the prophetic passages of the Bible. So, for instance, the *Jehovah's Witnesses,* an American sect with many followers throughout the world, are expecting the battle of Armageddon to take place before the year 1984 is over.

Many have been also the prophets of harm, woe and bane for the great American cities. Let me mention the long forgotten *"Father Divine,"* the founder of a famous sect in New York. In one of his poems, he called New York "a doomed city" and prophesied its destruction.

On the other hand, the prophecies of *Edgar Cayce* (1876-1945) are far better known today than in his lifetime. Numerous books have been published about him in recent years. Strictly speaking, Cayce was no prophet. He was a psychic healer who, while in hypnotic trance, gave "readings" about absent patients and prescribed medicine for their ailments. Nevertheless, many prophetic messages can be found scattered in his "readings." The most original and remarkable one among them is that, still in the course of the present century, a part of Atlantis will emerge again, and that in the great pyramid of Egypt a new chamber will be discovered with prophecies for the next era.

The most widely known American visionary of our time is

Mrs. Jeane Dixon of Washington, D.C. The most important of her prophecies is the vision which she saw on February 5, 1962, and which lends a prophetic significance to the extraordinary planetary configuration of that same day. First of all, many planets had then assembled in the constellation Aquarius. Furthermore, all planets of our solar system, including the sun, had adapted their course in such a way that on February 5, 1962, they might form an almost straight line, with Uranus and the earth at one end and all other planets (except Pluto and Neptune) at the other end of the line. Finally, during the night of February 5, the moon too moved into the line as the ninth luminary, calling forth a solar eclipse. It was evident to all astrologers that such an extraordinary event cannot remain without consequences on the earth, but nobody could say what such a configuration meant, because there had been no precedent. Some astrologers predicted wars and earthquakes, others even the judgment day and the end of the world. But it seems that this configuration had a much deeper meaning, announcing the beginning of a new era, and that concrete events will become evident only much later.

Such interpretation is confirmed by the vision Mrs. Jeane Dixon had on the morning of February 5, 1962. Her vision can be interpreted thus: On February 5, 1962, a child was born in Egypt to a descendant of the Egyptian queen Nefertiti. This child, grown to a man, will unite people of all races and religions in a new faith, a new form of Christianity.

According to Jeane Dixon's visions, a prelude to the third world war will be enacted in the year 1980 with a battle over Israel. Until 1980 America will continue to live in a false sense of security, but in 1980 this delusive notion will collapse, and the true situation will be revealed to everybody's eyes. During the years 1980-1999 America will have to pay for all previous mistakes and omissions. This great calamitious period will begin with a heavy earthquake in the Middle East, which will serve as a signal for Arab invasion of Israel. The hostilities will continue for eight years and will exhaust the military power of both sides. In 1988 the Soviet Union will openly interfere and militarily occupy the whole region of Mid-East, including Israel. But there will be no peace. Warfare, conflicts, massacres, misery and epidemics will continue to ravage the region until 1995, with a period of precarious peace until 1999.

During all these years America will be economically and militarily too weak to give effective assistance to Israel. But USA will strengthen ties with the European allies. In 1999 the Western armies will be ready to invade the Near East. This will call forth a nuclear assault of Soviet rockets on European and American cities, to which the Western world will answer in kind. The survival of humanity will be at stake. After this war, in 2004, both Soviet Union and USA will have lost their status as super-powers. The third super-power, China, will use this opportunity for a further consolidation and expansion of its influence. China will start the fourth world war in 2005, attaching and overrunning the Soviet Union and later seeking in the Near East to engage in a decisive battle with the USA and their allies. This war will last for 19 years. Then the remnant of the Jewish nation will convert to Christ, giving birth to a new Judeo-Christian religion. This religion will dominate far into the millenium, which will begin around the year 2037.

Mrs. Irene F. Hughes of Chicago, a well-known star among the present-day American clairvoyants, in a personal interview kindly submitted the following of her visions for inclusion in this book:

1. As the sun rose, a huge black cloud enveloped it, and I felt the heavy mist and stifling fog engulf us. As I tried to perceive what the heaviness and darkness meant, I saw flames eating up dollar bills. I realized, with some terror, that it meant the devaluation of the dollar and a sizeable depression. The numerals of the year in which this would take place were

forming like a rainbow above me: 1976-1979. Then I saw the cloud of fog lifting, and the sky became an unbelievable shade of blue. A great calm came over our land.

2. In the year 1982 a different monetary system for the United States will come into being. It will be a much simpler system, but the United States will not be the only country that will undergo a complete change in its financial structure. In that year, many nations will be operating on a similar basis, which will tend to become, in another twenty years, a world monetary system.

3. Somewhere between 1975 and 1985, after major changes in the monarchical type of government, England will revert to the love of pomp and splendor it has enjoyed in the past. This will be an age of discovery, of great painters and musicians and singers.

4. The conflict between China and Russia will continue until friendship between them is totally lost, and China becomes the principal threat to the Western world. Russia will not be an ally to the United States until the middle and late 1980's.

5. In the years 1986-1998 great famine will prevail not only in the United States, but in France, Japan, India and China as well. At that time, I predict that in many areas of the world great turbulence in nature, such as earthquakes, changes in the geographical location of lakes, streams and mountains, will begin and continue through 2003. At intervals, this will happen with increasing intensity during those years.

6. In the years 1989-91, the United States will suffer the beginning of a civil war.

7. It was July, 1993, and I was viewing a phenomenon of pipes. they were enormous like mammoth tunnels, and through They was flowing crystal clear water. Conservation of water was our great need, and the shortage of water had been in the news for several years now. The tunnels or pipes

led to the Pacific Ocean. It had been decided to distill and purify water from that ocean, since the state of New York was having tremendous changes in earth structure and was not conducive to water conservation there at this time.

8. Many new chemicals, helpful in healing cancerous diseases, were being discussed at great length in this year of 1993. It was amazing to see one of the "brain" ships that explored the bottoms of the seas. What a fascinating and interesting era in which to be alive and sharing in these discoveries! The "brain" ships and their crews brought forth the materials for the new chemicals. Hundreds of young women and young men formed the special oceanochemist crews. And to think that the first study for this career started in a big way already in 1972!

9. In the year 2026 the constitution of the United States will be no more. In its place will be an entirely different document, and an entirely new way of governmental rule. I predict that man will live in greater trust and love of his fellowman at that time.

Prophecy of Pastor C. A. Chader

Pastor Carl A. Chader had for many years been missionary and preacher in India, America, Canada and Scandinavia. In 1934 he published a book, called *God's Plan Throughout the Ages,* which was followed in 1941 by *The Portent of World Events* and in 1942 by *The End of the Present World Order.* In all these books Chader maintains the point of view that God has a plan for mankind, and that indications of this plan and of coming historical events, as far as they refer to the future of the Jewish nation and of Christian civilization, can be found in the Bible. The assertions by Old Testament prophets, according to Chader, are God's revelations, directly addressed to the present time and to the future. He contends that almost every Bible prophecy has a double meaning and a double fulfillment. One fulfillment lies near the prophet's own time and the second one in a remote future and under different conditions. The first meaning and first fulfillment is preparatory, and only the second brings the final accomplishment.

In his second book, published in February, 1941, when Hitler's army had marched from victory to victory, and when it seemed that Germany would determine the fate of Europe, Chader wrote:

"The Second World War is only a preparatory war for the final great war which will bring the end of the present world order. In this present world war the chessmen on the political chessboard will gradually take the positions which are prescribed by the Scriptures for the final great affliction."

Chader then gives an interpretation of the eighth chapter of prophet Daniel's book and predicts the following result of the Second World War: "The victory by the Allies will be so complete that not only Italy but even Germany will suffer a great humiliating defeat. Nazi tyranny and Prussian militarism will be eradicated. In connection with the indubitable and definitive victory of the Allies over the block of the Axis, the balance of power will be shifting. During the "time of the end" leadership will belong to Russia; therefore, it is clear that Russia will come out of this war as the real victor and in the near future will conduct her power politics with the obvious design to obtain hegemony over vast parts of European territory. That will be in accord with Bible prophecy, and from that fact we will be able to recognize that "the latter time" has indubitably arrived. Another sign of the "end time," according to the Scriptures, will be the solution of the Palestine question and the return of the Jewish nation to Palestine."

Take note of the fact that Chader's book was published in 1941, when Hitler's power had reached the highest apogee.

So far all these mentioned predictions have come true. The rest still awaits fulfillment. Chader predicts the establishment of two powerful military blocks and the preparation for a dramatic conclusion: "I believe that the present political world order is in its final stage. It will disintegrate and come to an end. In one of the two powerful political confederations, which in Ezekiel's thirty-eighth chapter is comprehensively named "Rosh, Meshech and Tubal," military leadership will belong to Moscow. Russian bolshevistic union will comprise not only "the kings of East" (perhaps India, Iraq, Afganistan, Japan and China?) but also southeastern, central, northern and northwestern Europe. Read Ezekiel's thirty-eighth and thirty-ninth chapter, Daniel's seventh chapter, Joel's second chapter and many others, and it will become evident to you, that it will be a powerful union of many nations."

According to Chader, the other powerful alliance that will come into existence will consist of ten nations and will comprise approximately the same territory that belonged to ancient Rome, in which Italy had the leading rôle, or it will be similar to the "Holy Roman Empire," over which Germany had the decisive influence. Chader is convinced that a ten-state union will finally be formed, but he is uncertain about its political boundary.

Then Chader speaks about Antechrist and says: "He will come forward from the bolshevism. No other interpretation can satisfy the accounts of the Scriptures. This movement, revolution, ideology and view of the world comprises all the elements that make me confident that Russia and the atheistic bolshevism will be the earthly place from which Antechrist will come forth (2 Thess. 2:6-8)."

The next event, according to Chader, will be a clash between both power blocks and the Third World War, which will last for three-and-one-half-years. Three nations of the ten-nation block will be conquered, the rest will capitulate, and Russia will be victorious: "in the 'latter time' an atheistic, anti-Christian earthly power, with origin in Moscow, will expand and finally rule over the whole world."

"But the final scene of this drama will be enacted in Palestine. Antechrist, the leader of the new temporal, political and military power, in his endeavour to annihilate all religions, will arrive in the newly rebuilt Jewish temple of Jerusalem, and will proclaim his own divinity, elevating himself over everything that theretofore had been considered as holy. That will call forth a cry of indignation from the Jews. Enraged and embittered, they will rise up and in a well-planned effort they will succeed in casting out their enemies from Israel. The atheistic world power, naturally, will not tolerate it. For reasons of prestige and also in fear that similar uprisings could occur in other occupied countries, they will strike out hard. The great final 'day of God' will begin:

"Mighty armies from the northwest will disembark in Haifa, and other armies from the north and northeast (Asia Minor, Caucasus, and 'kings from the sunrise' over Euphrates) will assemble in the valley of Armageddon and will start moving southward. The Jewish army will desperately defend itself but, unable to resist the onslaught, will fall back towards Jerusalem. The atheist army will storm the city and set it on fire. A slaughtering of the Jews will begin, and the streets will be full of dead bodies. But then, at noon, the sky will darken. A horrible, unforeseen eclipse of the sun will take place, from the bowels of the earth heavy rumbling will be heard. A queer astronomical phenomenon will occur. The sun, although in the sky, will not give forth any light. Semidarkness will continue, an earthquake will follow, and all nature will be in turbulence. From the bowels of earth will rise fire and sulphur. At the moment when the atheistic dictator will think he has won the battle, a new adversary will appear on the scene. It will be Christ himself (Rev.

19:14), and Antechrist's victory will be turned into a defeat. His army will be routed. Soldiers, not killed by weapons, will become victims of a ravaging pestilence. The whole anti-Christian world will collapse in blood and death. In such a way mankind's greatest and maddest attempt to defeat God will end and a new age, the millennium, will begin."

At this point it is necessary to note, that not all interpreters of Bible prophecies are in accord with Chader's version. Many are of the opinion that Antechrist will not be represented by the Russian block but, on the contrary, by the union of ten nations, and that the political structure of this union will be fascistic and chauvinistic, that within it the Catholic church will experience her last revival and expansion, that a hypocritical, adulterated Christianity will then be dominant and that it will be the pope himself who will want to act God's part on this earth.

Among the exponents of a version which in many points differs from that of Chader, is an American religious organization, represented by *The Ambassador College* and affiliated with the Church of God. It is a serious, respectable organization, which lately has become very active and with daily radio broadcasts and the publication of its magazine "Plain Truth" (circulation over two million copies) disseminates its point of view all over the world.

Anton Johansson's prophecies

One of the greatest and most trustworthy prophets of this century has been a simple, pious Norwegian fisherman, Anton Johansson. He was born in 1858, in Sweden, but at the age of sixteen he moved to Norway and made a living by fishing. In later years he became surveyor of land. Already since 1884 he had begun to see visions and to hear voices, which bade him to pray on behalf of men who were to be shortly carried off by death. His predictions always came true. At night he often woke up, hearing the command to pray on behalf of fishermen who were at sea, of seamen whose ship was endangered by a tornado in the Carribean Sea, of people who were imperiled during the earthquakes of Messina and San Francisco. He later related how he had to pray also on behalf of the Titanic's passengers on the night of the shipwreck.

This simple man in December, 1913, left his village. He had saved 200 crowns for the journey to Kristiania (now called Oslo), the capital of Norway. In Kristiania he called on Keilhaug, the minister of war, and asked him to inform all other members of the cabinet, that in the next year, 1914, a great war would flare up. He implored the government of Norway to do everything in its power to prevent the war. He informed the Norwegian authorities of his intent to go to Stockholm and then to Berlin, in the hope that he would able to persuade Kaiser Wilhelm to abstain from intervening in the coming war.

After his arrival in Stockholm, Johansson called on Emil Melander, colonel of the Swedish general staff. Melander received him in his office, conversed with him and then took him home, where Johansson revealed to him all his prophecies, which Melander wrote down as dictated by Johansson. Melander dissuaded Johansson from journeying to Berlin and assured him that his message of war could as well be made known to the world through the medium of newspapers. Melander kept his promise and published Johansson's message in the March 4, 1914, issue of Stockholm's daily "Svenska Morgonbladet." Johansson's predictions aroused enormous attention, and when a few months later war broke out, interest in this strange man grew even greater. His visions and revelations were published in book form in 1918 and have been repeatedly reprinted. Translated into German, they were published in 1953. It is impossible to relate here in detail all his predictions, but I shall attempt to render the most important ones in a condensed form, in his own words:

"I had my greatest vision in 1907, during the night of November 13. On that day I felt very tired and went to bed early. In the middle of night I was awakened by a voice which said: 'Thou will be given to know the secrets of heaven.' My room was filled with so bright a light that it dazzled me. I wanted to look up towards from where I had heard the voice, but felt myself unworthy and bowed down in prayer. My soul was filled with overwhelming heavenly bliss, and I understood that my Saviour himself had awakened me.

"Then I was led in spirit to a place from where I could see everything that will happen to the world and especially to my homeland Norway. I was shown the greatest misfortune that will afflict the world—a great war. In spirit I saw the officers under whom I will have to work as a surveyor in Finnmarken during the next seven years. I was told their names, and for each name a year was mentioned. This revelation I understood as a sign that the great war will come after the seven years will have passed. I saw and heard that the war will break out between Austro-Hungary and Serbia. Then I saw the German eastern front with trenches full of men and weapons. The front was stretching from the Black Sea to the Baltic Sea, and over the whole front great noise was reigning. I saw how the Russians in great masses overflowed great regions of German land, and how great clouds of smoke were rolling forward, together with the front. Great fires could be seen in many places. Then the voice said: 'The war will come because of the wickedness of men, but thou shall warn the Norwegian government and shall go also to Stockholm and Berlin. Thou shall be my witness.' I answered: 'I am unworthy of being thy witness before these high lords. I have not attended school, I can write only with difficulty and I do not speak German.' The voice said for the second time:

'Thou shall be my witness!' I answered: 'I shall try.' "

About the postwar period Johansson predicted the spreading of frightful diseases. It came true in the form of influenza epidemics, which took the lives of several hundred thousand men. He further predicted that socialism and its varieties would grow immensely throughout the world and cause revolutions and upheavals in Russia, Germany, Austro-Hungary, England, Italy and also in America, Canada, India and China. In Russia war, revolutions and diseases will carry away so many victims that nobody will ever know the number of people that will perish there. Finland too will have a revolution and will liberate itself from the clutches of Russia, but only for a short while. She will become enslaved by Russia again, and will be oppressed more than ever, and much blood will be spilt in that land. Johansson urged the Finnish nation to turn to God in prayer, in order that it should not remain oppressed forever. Germany will be long tormented by revolutionary movements, especially in her southwestern part. In England the worst disturbances will be in the southern part of Wales and the surrounding country. In this connection the voice said, "England stands on the brink of a precipice." Disturbances and rebellion, war in the colonies, war in Ireland and natural catastrophes will be among the misfortunes that will befall that land. Heavy fighting will take place in India: "It will begin with a great rebellion in northern India, where I heard the name of Delhi mentioned as a city greatly visited by war. After that, rebellion will break out also in central and southern India. I heard also the name of Calcutta mentioned. The war will end with India's complete deliverance from England, but will be followed by dreadful epidemics and unprecedented famine and other afflictions. War and its consequences will kill twenty-five million Indians."

"About America I heard our Lord say that five great wars are to be expected for that land in the future, whereof two will be violent civil wars ending with America's division into four or five smaller confederations. In one of the great wars America will be drawn into a conflict with Canada. That was all I heard about America, but as the events of that land interest us less, I did not try to bear them in mind. I also cannot recollect any time or period being mentioned in this connection. Nor do I remember anything about Japan, but about China I heard that there will be immense revolutions, and more to come.

"I saw two natural catastrophes, one was an unheard of hurricane, raging over two continents, and the other an immense earthquake, connected with the eruption of a volcano in the North Sea. I was led in spirit to the great cities on England's east coast. I saw ships thrown on the shore, many collapsed buildings, and much wreckage floating on water. At sea many ships were wrecked. Then I was shown Holland, Belgium and the German coast of the North Sea, which all were heavy visited. Among the most afflicted cities I heard the names of Antwerp and Hamburg mentioned. There great warehouses were flooded and all merchandise lost. Even Denmark's western and northern coast and Sweden's western coast had suffered." This prediction came true in February, 1953, with an unprecedented flood catastrophe in northern Europe. Everything took place exactly as described by Johansson. Whoever has forgotten these events, should re-read news dispatches of those days. When this prediction in 1953 came to be accomplished, great excitement and anxiety arose in Sweden, since everybody began to fear that the rest of Johansson's predictions and especially the predicted Swedish-Russian war (which is described further on) might be imminent.

About natural catastrophes and epidemic diseases Johansson predicted: "Natural catastrophes will occur in many parts of the world, and a turbulent activity will begin within the womb of the earth. Great tremors of earth and vehement eruptions of volcanos will afflict the world and partly also such regions which hitherto have been spared. In Italy they will be more destructive than ever. Great many people there will save only the clothing on their bare backs. There will be a new eruption of the Vesuvius. Hurricanes of great violence will afflict not only America, but also Europe, especially England. I saw not less than five great hurricanes. Thunderstorms too will in those years be devastating and will occur in Denmark, North Germany and southern Sweden. Simultaneously with these trials by nature, great epidemics will roam about the world, carrying off many victims. They will come in three periods, whereof the first will begin already during the last part of the world war and will continue for several years after the war will have ended.[5] The next period will come after the English-Indian war, when two new, unknown diseases will spring into existence. They will be more dangerous than all others and will spread over the whole world, claiming an immense number of victims. In Russia they will be especially intense, and the voice told me that these and other diseases would visit Russia because of her great impiety. If I remember correctly, a fourth part of her people will perish through these diseases. One of the most dangerous diseases will consist of people becoming blind and losing their mind. For those afflicted by this disease, it will be very dangerous to drink alcohol. The third great period of epidemics will come after the Spanish-French war. Mostly it will be a serious pulmonary disease, but there will be also other unknown maladies, one such that people will become utterly emaciated, another one similar to leprosy, because the flesh of the afflicted persons will start to peel off. Both belligerents will be the first to become acquainted with these maladies, but they will later spread over all Europe and over great parts of other continents. France will suffer most and will lose almost all her young men and women.

5. This was fulfilled during the great influenza epidemic after the First World War.

"The last great calamity, seen by me that night of 1907, was Sweden's and Norway's war against Russians and Frenchmen. Socialism will at that time have gained power in both northern countries, and in Sweden socialists will have the reins of government in their hands. They will do what they will and by their actions will be partly responsible for the war and its unfortunate result. Socialists will have drawn a great part of the Swedish nation into atheism. Sweden will be forced to prepare for war in great haste. Yet, during the war, it will turn out that Sweden also has new weapons and inventions, unheard of by the people and kept secret by the government. One of these will be an electrical invention, owned only by Sweden and unknown in the whole world. Because of it, Frenchmen will perish in great numbers near Göteborg. Little would be needed, and Swedes would have won the war. Had not other means of resistance been so deficient, the French or the Russians would have come to terms with Sweden. The voice told me: 'If the Swedes could hold out only fourteen days more, the French army would have capitulated, and had Frenchmen known that the Swedes have weapons so formidable they would never have dared to attack.' "

Then Johansson relates in detail the course of the war, mentioning cities and other place-names. Heavy fighting will take place around Göteborg, which city will almost entirely be reduced to a heap of rubble. Frenchmen will there suffer great losses, but will put to shore always new troops and reinforcements. French resources will be nearly exhausted when the Swedes will suddenly capitulate. Hälsingborg, Malmö and Lund also will be among the heavily devastated cities, but Stockholm will suffer less because of better organized and more effective air defense. Among the heavily bombarded cities of the west coast, Johansson mentions also Falkenberg. He reports on having seen there immense shipmasts, imbedded in the ground, and says that he cannot understand what it means, because the sea is still quite remote from that place. The interpreters of Johansson's predictions attach to these sentences great importance, since it is clear that Johansson has seen the present antenna masts of the great Grimeton radio transmitting station. The fact that Johansson has seen them at a time when they had not yet been built and when such radio transmitting stations did not yet exist at all, can be considered as a proof that Johansson's visions of the future are true and authentic.

The further course of the war: "Russians will invade North Sweden partly through Torneå, partly over Kvarken. Heavy fighting will take place north of Stockholm, with great bravery on the Swedish side. Russians will lose men in great numbers, but it will be of no avail since they will come on in ever new masses. They will conquer all northern Sweden, and as one of the most afflicted and plundered cities I heard Gävle mentioned. Boden will have surrendered without having offered resistance. South of Stockholm the Russians will first take the islands Gotland and Öland. Then they will disembark on Sweden's soil near Västervik and will proceed partly towards Stockholm, partly in the direction of Göteborg, to aid the Frenchmen. But they will not get far, before the Swedes in Göteborg will have capitulated.

"In Norway the Russians will invade Finnmarken. The Norwegians will repel the first attack, but will finally be defeated and will retreat southward to the Porsanger Fjord. In southern Norway, south of Kristiania (Oslo), near the Swedish border, Swedes and Norwegians will fight shoulder to shoulder. French airplanes will bombard the whole coast up to Trondhjem. As the most afflicted cities were mentioned Bergen, Drammen and Kristiania, but none of the Norwegian cities will be so totally destroyed as Kristiansand.

"Norway's defeat will be sealed simultaneously with the defeat of Sweden. Norway will have to cede to Russia all land north and east of Lyngenfjord. Sweden will cede a part of its northern region and the island Gotland. Europe will be astonished seeing that the Russians do not keep all of the occupied northern half of the Scandinavian peninsula. When I anxiously asked the Lord if both our lands will indeed become oppressed and pillaged, the Lord pointed towards Lyngenfjord and said: 'So far they will come but not farther.' The war will be short. It will break out in summer and will end when the autumn will have hardly begun. It will be caused by a conflict at Norway's northern frontier. Hostilities will be opened by the Russians, whereafter the French will help them. Nobody will come to help Sweden. The Germans will be in disagreement, England will have war in Ireland, in southern Europe heavy earthquakes will take place, Belgium will have the same frontier as the military frontier of April 1918. The Finns will take no part in the war. They will be heavily oppressed, will have no access to weapons, and after the war they will be oppressed more than ever. The Balkan states will be in a deplorable situation at that time, especially Romania and Serbia. Even Greece will then be helpless. As for Turkey, I want to warn its citizens not to persecute Christians, but to become devoted to Jesus lest they get effaced from among the number of independent countries. The Jews will at that time have returned in great crowds to Jerusalem.

"Having seen and heard all this, I prayed in spirit to God and said: 'I know that no man shall be informed of the day of Thy coming, but tell me how far or near we then will be from the tribulations of the Book of Revelation?' The Lord answered: 'Before many more tribulations will come, other men will appear who will prophesy and warn mankind of what will happen.' "

Anton Johansson died in 1929. At the beginning, many had scoffed at his predictions, calling them hallucinations. Especially before the outbreak of the First World War, every sensible Swede was of the opinion that the progress of civilization had so far advanced that world war was made impossible. Johansson's warning was of no avail, and war broke out. Some more of his predictions have now been accomplished. How about those which are still under a question mark? Be it as it may, all who have known Johansson personally, have affirmed that he was a sincere, honest man, who himself did not for a moment doubt that God has sent him to warn the world about coming calamities and tribulations. Swedish archbishop Nathan Söderblom, after having met Johansson, pronounced the following opinion: "Anton Johansson made on me the impression of a man who is deeply religious. He also possesses a clear, lively intelligence."

Johansson's predictions include many sentences that are hard to interpret. The sequence of the predicted events also leaves much to wish for. For instance: "England will not be able to separate Belgium from Germany." What does it mean? Two northern countries will undergo peaceful revolutions, the lesser one will be the first of both. Has Sweden, Norway or Denmark been meant? Perhaps England, since in another place he, along with Canada, unmistakably mentions England as a country which will undergo a revolution or at least great disturbancies and riots. Only after these upheavals in two northern countries will follow the Spanish-French war. Will it take place as part of the Third World War? Will the predicted epidemics be caused by bacteriological warfare? Russia during and after a war will lose her extended territory. The Baltic provinces, Poland and Ukraine are mentioned as within German territory. Did this not come true already during the Second World War? Denmark will never be actively involved in a war. And those earthquakes in the Northern Sea that call forth catastrophal flooding in Scotland, Iceland and the coastal region of Norway at a time when there has not yet been snowfall on the mountains of Norway? Could not this all be the result of the explosion of atomic bombs? Johansson predicts that in the Polar Sea a new land will appear, which will connect Norway with Spitzbergen, whereas a part of Scotland will become submerged and disappear. One more thing to be noted: the British-Indian war will break out first, and only then, after a short interval, the French-Spanish war.

A. Gustafsson has dedicated a whole book to Johansson's predictions and makes in it the effort to do away with all this confusion. The more important details of his interpretation are as follows:

"Our planet will be visited by not less than three great hurricanes, two of them before the French-Spanish war." Johansson then with full particulars describes the damage, caused by the hurricanes. Gustafsson doubts that here we have to deal with genuine, natural hurricanes. He expresses the suspicion that here may be described the consequences of atomic explosions or of some other horrible weapons. Johansson relates that a hurricane will develop near the Panama canal and then move in northern and northeastern direction over the continent of North America. Many regions will be flooded, and Americans will not be able to restore what has been damaged and destroyed. Navigation and commerce will come to a halt. Virginia will suffer most, but all Gulf states and Florida will also be among the affected. The hurricane will move in a wide belt along the Mississippi valley northwards and will gather strength near the Canadian lakes. Chicago, Minneapolis, Washington and especially New York will suffer. Skyscrapers will rock and collapse. (Could a hurricane, however huge, have such an impact?) Smoke and fire everywhere. Canadian forests will be set ablaze. The surrounding country of New York will be like a sea of fire. The region of the Great Lakes greatly devastated, Quebec wrecked. From Canada the hurricane will cross the Atlantic ocean to Europe's western and southwestern countries France, Spain, Morocco, then along the Mediterranean to the

Black Sea, Crimea and southern Russia. In Italy Sicily will suffer most, in France it will be Marseilles and Rouen. Austria and Vienna will suffer only minor damage. Johansson relates that another hurricane will devastate northern Europe, especially England which after the catastrophe for several days will not be able to send telegraphic messages. Even after this calamity England will again be visited by other trials. The hurricane will then follow the coast of Germany to the Baltic Sea, then will change the course towards the north and traverse the gulf of Bothnia, crossing Aland islands, then eastward across Finland, between Vaasa and Helsinki. Finland will suffer more than Sweden. Then the hurricane will take its course over northern Russia (Murmansk) to Siberia. Lakes Ladoga and Onega also have been mentioned. Does this narrative remind you of havoc caused by hurricanes? If this prediction is to be accomplished literally, some future hurricanes will be of a dimension, multiple times exceeding that of all previous hurricanes. Gustafsson is convinced that the related scenes are the effects of warfare, and that Johansson has not had a correct comprehension of what he has seen.

Gustafsson is just as firmly convinced that the scenes of war in India, described by Johansson, have been considered by him to be a combat between Indians and the English only because at the time of the vision India had been a British colony, and Johansson has not known to interpret the vision in any other way than as a revolt of Indians against the British. In Gustafsson's opinion the least clearly expressed part of Johansson's predictions is to be interpreted as follows:

1. India will be conquered by China through Tibet and Pakistan. The first skirmishes will take place in northwest India, but the focus of the war will be centered around Delhi. The front will extend from Delhi to Calcutta. Bacteriological warfare, which will claim the lives of twenty-five million

men. New dreadful diseases will spring into existence and through Russia spread into Europe.

2. Persia and Turkey will be conquered by communism, since "Turkey will perish unless she embraces the Christian faith."

3. War will break out in the Balkans, with Greece as a participant. Serbia will suffer most.

4. Italy will be involved in a war and become oppressed and plundered. Great damage, due to war and earthquakes.

5. The armies of communists will invade western Europe in a wide stream that will run through Austro-Hungary and northern Italy to Switzerland and France. Bloody engagements near Basel, northwest and west of that city.

6. The question remains open if red Italy and red France will not annex part of southern Switzerland and if the northern part will not join Germany, after that country has been liberated from communism.

7. France will be conquered by communism. Paris will be set on fire. All country will be ravaged and plundered. Afterwards, red France will start military campaigns against England, Spain and Scandinavia.

8. The war between France and Spain will endanger the whole world, causing the outbreak of new, unheard of diseases. France will be defeated, and America, allied with Spain, will win, since Johansson says that "France will suffer most from the diseases."

9. Germany will be attacked from the west and east. One column of Russian tanks will advance through Vienna and Passau to Nuremberg, another through Prague to Hannover, a third from Berlin to Hamburg. Many concentrated attacks in the Ruhr region. The hostilities will be opened on an autumn night, quite unexpectedly. Germany will be laid waste, but will be liberated by Americans.

10. The Third World War will destroy Finland's future.

11. The United Nations will come asunder.

12. Scandinavia, Germany and England will suffer from bacteriological warfare, since "water will have to be boiled."

13. England will run into debts and will collapse economically. Communists will create in England a sanguinary political explosion. England will lose her great power status forever. A sanguinary war in Ireland. (Either the Irish will rebel against England in North Ireland, or communists will invade Ireland from France.)

14. America will be involved in a war with Canada. Does it mean that communism then will have gained power in Canada? In any case, because of this conflict, America will not be able to render aid to Europe.

15. Even Portugal will be drawn into a military conflict. There will be a sanguinary internal strife in Portugal.

16. All huricanes and damage by hurricanes, as predicted by Johansson, may mean radioactive whirlwinds, called forth by the explosion of atomic bombs.

The prophecy of Pastor Birger Claesson

Swedish Pastor Birger Claesson, together with some other persons, in January, 1951, paid a visit to Swedish Admiral Ekstrand to inform him of the substance of a vision he had had on December 12, 1950. He himself has described it in the following way: "I have the habit to pray to God before four and six o'clock every morning and after that to rest in bed for a while. I always am waking up at the usual hour, and so I did on December 12, ready to get up, when I saw a great, white figure standing near the bed. It was an impressive vision, and I became frightened, but the white figure reassured me, saying: 'Be not afraid thou that art highly gifted in thy poverty of spirit, and I shall show thee what will happen to the northern people in the latter days.' Everything became dark for a moment, and then it was as if I was in a movie theatre. I saw hostile armies invading Sweden at five different places. I saw Swedish cities and heard their names mentioned. Umeå was raided by airplanes and bombarded from the sea by a naval squadron. Then a landing was effected, and troops were disembarking. The whole city was in flames. Near Stockholm a great naval battle took place. A great many of the attacking ships were sinking. Then Stockholm was exposed to frightful air raids. A great part of the city was reduced to ruins. Västervik was attacked from the sea and set on fire whereafter the enemies' army effected a landing and began to advance in the direction of Stockholm."

Claesson describes in detail the further course of the invasion, which in the main is in accord with Johansson's vision. He concludes his narrative as follows:

"The last thing I saw of the military actions was an air raid against Borlänge. Then everything became dark again for a moment, and I heard a voice call out: 'Darkness over the world.' I heard a cry of distress among the people. Above the darkness I saw a streak of light toward which whiteclad figures began to rise from the darkness. At the same time I heard a wonderful song about the lamb who has redeemed us all with his blood. Then I cried out: 'Dear Jesus, why shall all this happen to my people?' The voice answered: 'Read the forty-first Psalm, verses one through four. Thy people were all a people of great compassion. They had rendered help to foreign people in adversity. But now I cannot save them. They don't even pray any more. Only distress can make them humble again, and into distress they are now bound to fall. But many are those who will be saved.' " This prophecy of pastor Claesson was published in Swedish periodicals and also in a separate book.

* * * * *

French poet Paul Valery has said: "Prognostication is one of the fundamental elements of civilization." He is right, since prognostication is no exclusive privilege of prophets and diviners. All men have intuitions, projects and plans, and each such intention or plan is connected with a previous forecasting of the course of actions and of the expected result of each separate action. The word "project" itself means "to cast forward." If this forecast comes true, the plan or project has been successful. Such forecasting or prognostication takes place in connection with every scientific experiment, every commercial enterprise, yes, even with every singular action of man. Meterological stations publish forecasts of weather, and physicians in each separate case of sickness make first a diagnosis and then a prognosis (a forecast) from which depends their course of actions, i.e. the therapy or application of remedies, as prescribed by them. In the same manner, each diplomatic action is preceded by a prognosis. Many books could be written about the prophecies or forecasts made by scientists, politicians, diplomats, poets and writers. For instance, the Spanish statesman Donoso Cortes in the last century has very correctly prophesied about the rôle which Russia at present plays in world politics. Writers have in their novels "invented" all machines, engines and instruments long before they were actually invented by scientists. Their novels, therefore, can be described as prophecies. And many of today's fantastic stories may still come true in some distant future.

In concluding the long line of prophecies, I shall quote here the forecasts by two important writers. Their prospects differ one from the other. Which one is the correct one?

Ernst Jünger, a well-known German writer, looks forward to the future with great hopes: "We are about to enter into a new, changed world, a world quite different from what it was yesterday and what it is today. We will cross a line from which we all will recognize that our thoughts of yesterday have been small thoughts and that progress and evolution of the future will give us great opportunities of compensation. We exist today in an epoch of transition. To many it has become already evident, but many will recognize it only after the future will have again become the past."

The autobiography of the French writer *Georges Bernanos,* does not manifest such an optimism. But his lines too deserve to be read, if we want to grasp the tendency of mankind's fate. Here is an excerpt: "I have lost all hope to be ever able to live in a free world. I am most anxious about freedom. All of the Christian world is now threatened by a terrible crisis. The peculiarity of the present time is that totalitarism by no means is yielding to a process of democratization, but that, on the contrary, all democrats, by degrees, are accepting totalitarian philosophy. Should it become impossible for me in my native country to freely write about what I think—and I reckon that it may come to that—I shall retire somewhere to a quiet corner, far from the cities. I shall write there in the expectation that my books some day yet will accomplish the object for which I have sacrificed my whole life."

CONCLUSION

German writer Dr. Max Kemmerich has written a book about modern prophecy, in which he declares: "I am fully enlightened about the prospect that the overwhelming majority of my contemporary fellowmen will reject the subject of my book as well as the way I have dealt with it, and they will do it with that enviable positiveness which is conferred only by an absolute ignorance. But nobody will be able to deprive me of the assurance that the time will come, when the unthinking multitude, under the influence of my thoughts and without even testing them, will reject in the bulk all that it now, likewise without critical examination, worships, and will worship, what it now condemns."

When I, many years ago, began to make a study of Nostradamus' texts, in order to write a book about them, I expected to be able to prove that they were little more than a residue of the medieval way of thinking. After a thorough study of astrology, prophecy and related subjects in general and of Nostradamus, his critics and interpreters in particular, my point of view underwent a complete change. Today I subscribe to the opinion expressed by M. Kemmerich.

Whoever, with an open mind, will read and peruse Nostradamus and will compare his quatrains with Bible prophecies, modern predictions and the present condition of the world and of mankind, will feel convinced that these old predictions may still have some connection with the present,

419

heretofore never experienced historical situation. It must be clear to everybody that some extremely serious, important, unique and inevitable world events are on the verge of becoming realized facts.

But is it so important to know the exact point of time when this or that detached, isolated or local political or military event will take place? Far more important is to be able to discern the general trend or direction the movement of history is taking. If this trend is in accord with the one announced by prophecy, prophecy has been justified. There is no particular need to fix points of time for each one of Nostradamus' prophecies. His calculations follow a certain system, which as yet remains unexposed. Only after the key will be found, positive calculations will become possible. Without such a key all assertions by commentators are subject to errors, and the reader of such interpretations often cannot help smiling about the prophetic pretensions of the authors.

My advice to the readers of this book is: before you form an opinion about it, attentively reflect about what you have read, confront the quoted authors, consider everything that in the course of history has happened and what is happening today, and then appraise the sincerity and authenticity of these prophecies and the degree of potentiality of their being eventually realized. In other words, do as apostle Paul has said in 1 Thess. 5:20-21: "Despise not prophesyings. Prove all things; hold fast that which is good." This book will have been fully justified, if the reader will watch the future course of historical world events with greater attention, and if he will refuse to participate in gamboling on the brink of precipice, which pastime seems to be the most popular among the majority of people.

For all that, there surely is no need to be a clairvoyant to realize that mankind today indeed is on the brink of a precipice. Wars have always been and will always be; all newly invented weapons have always been used in warfare, and there is not the least reason to suppose that in the future it will be different. An atomic bomb is no evil by itself, but it becomes an evil in the hands of man. And the man himself, in the course of thousands of years, has not become neither more virtuous nor in any other sense any better. For that reason, all his new inventions, although seemingly promising an easier and more comfortable life, on the other hand, warrant more and more destructive wars and perpetually greater fears and calamities. Besides, world population now increases at the rate of a geometrical progression and has led to the so-called "population explosion." According to the opinions and forecasts (i.e. predictions) by leading scientists and experts, the consequences of this explosion in the very near future can be only famine, epidemics and migration of people, called forth by the famine. The production of food is limited, but the increase of population, regardless of the effort by some governments to limit it, can and will be limited only by wars, famine and disease.

Such is the natural solution of this problem, and such answer is given also by prophets and clairvoyants. In the mind of a cool, logical scientist the expected wars and epidemics may seem only a historical necessity and a natural demographic process. For all these mentioned reasons, I consider E. Ruir's interpretation of Nostradamus' texts the most credible one, especially because he expects all the decisive events to take place in the nearest future. The pace of history has become so impetuous and rapid, that we will not have to wait long for the solution. We are indeed living in the "latter time."

Regrettably, scientists have handed to mankind such destructive weapons that now it not only can commit suicide, but also can drag along, into the abyss, all living creatures, turning our planet into a debris of rock and ashes, devoid of life and breath. Even if it comes to the worst, I still hope that some sparks of life will be preserved, and that the earth will revive and will again blossom and breathe, green, living, rejuvenated. Is it really worthwhile to supplement my hopes with the thought that perhaps also a couple of human creatures will survive the holocaust and will be able to resume the same old game of life and death?

LIST OF WORKS CONSULTED

Abellio, Raymond. *Vers un nouveau prophétisme: Essai sur le rôle politique du sacré et la situation de Lucifer dans le monde moderne.* Geneva, 1947.

Agrippa von Nettesheim, Heinrich. *De occulta philosophia libri tres.* Coloniae, 1533.

Anquetil, Georges. *L'anti-Nostradamus ou vrais et faux prophètes.* Paris, 1940.

Barbarin, Georges. *Le secret de la grande pyramide ou la fin du monde adamique.* Paris: Adyar, 1936.

Bareste, Eugène. *Nostradamus.* Paris: Maillet, 1840.

Bauder, H. *Schicksal der Fürsten und Völker, 1945 bis 3797: Prophetische Weltgeschichte nach Nostradamu.* Basel: Neuzeit, 1944-45.

Bible, the Holy. (Oxford, 1923)

Billenstein, Carl Soelberg. *Opklaringen af Nostradamus profetier.* Hillerød, 1920.

Boswell, Rolfe Edmund. *Nostradamus Speaks.* New York: Crowell, 1941.

Boulenger, Jacques R. *Nostradamus.* Paris: Excelsior, 1933.

Chader, C. A. *Den nuvarande världsordningens undergång.* Stockholm: Harrier, 1942.

——————— *Guds plan genom tidsåldrarna* ... Stockholm: Harrier, 1934.

——————— *Vad varsla världshändelserna?* Stockholm: Harrier, 1941.

Chavigny, Jean Aimes de. *Le premier face du Ianus françois, contenant sommairement les troubles, guerres ciuiles & autres choses memorables aduenuës en la France & ailleurs* ... Lyon: les heritiers de P. Roussin, 1594.

Claesson, Birger. *Ny uppenbarelse om Sveriges ödestimme.* Stockholm: Filadelfia, 1952.

Colin de Larmor, A. *Les merveilleux quatrains de Nostradamus.* Nantes, 1925.

Dixon, Jeane. *My Life and Prophecies.* New York, 1969.

Forman, Henry James. *The Story of Prophecy in the Life of Mankind from Early Times to the Present Day.* New York: Farrar & Rinehart, 1936.

Fontbrune, Dr. de. *Les propheties de Maistre Nostradamus.* Paris, 1947.

——————— *Les Propheties de Nostradamus devoilées.* Paris: Adyar, 1937.

——————— *L'étrange XXe siècle vu par Nostradamus.* Paris: Adyar, 1951.

Freire, João Paulo. *O que vai ser o mundo de 1950 ao ano 2000, segundo Nostradamus.* Lisbon: Fr. Franco, 1949.

——————— *Profetas e profecias; Nostradamus prevê em 1555 todos os grandes acontecimentos do mundo até 1999.* Lisbon, 1939.

Gonzaga da Fonseca, Luigi. *Le meraviglie di Fàtima.* Casale Monferrato: G. Lavagno, 1931.

Gustafsson, A. *Den svensk-norske fiskarens Anton Johansen från Finnmarken märkliga syner och förutsägelser om världskriget och folkens kommande öden.* Stockholm, 1918.

——————— *Merkwürdige Gesichte! Die Zukunft der Völker, gesehen von Eismeerfischer Anton Johansson aus Lebesby.* Stockholm: Sverigefonden, 1954.

——————— *Nya syner om världens framtid av den svensk-norske fiskarbonden Anton Johansen* ... Stockholm, 1920.

Gustafsson, G. *Europas framtid enligt Nostradamus.* Härnösand, 1956.

Guynaud, B. *La concordance des propheties de Nostradamus avec l'histoire, depuis Henry II jusqu'a Louis le Grand* ... Paris: J. Morel, 1693.

Hermes Trismegiste. *Traduction complète, précédée d'une étude sur l'origine des livres hermetiques, par Louis Ménard.* Paris, 1866.

Hohlenberg, Johannes E. *Michel de Nostredame, kaldet Nostradamus: En undersøgelse af hans profetiers indhold og overenstemmelse med historien* ... Copenhagen, 1918.

Kemmerich, Max. *Prophezeiungen: Alter Aberglaube oder neue Wahrheit?* Munich: A. Langen, 1911.

Krafft, Karl E. *Nostradamus predice el porvenir de Europe.* Madrid, 1941.

Le Pelletier, Anatole. *Les oracles de Michel de Nostradame, astrologue, medecin et conseiller ordinaire des rois Henri II, François II et Charles IX.* Paris, 1867.

Leoni, Edgar. *Nostradamus: Life and Literature.* New York: Exposition Press, 1961.

Le Roux, Jean. *La clef de Nostradamus, isagoge ou introduction au véritable sens des prophéties de ce fameux auteur* ... Paris: P. Giffard, 1710.

Liesche, F.R. *Sylvia. Trance-Gesichte über die politische, religiöse und wirtschaftliche Zukunft der Welt.* Strassburg: Heitz, 1936.

Ljungström, Georg. *Nostradamus och Anton Johanssons profetior om nu stundande världshändelser.* Stockholm, 1932.

Loog, C. *Die Weissagungen des Nostradamus: Erstmalige Auffindung des Chiffreschlüssels und Enthüllung der Prophezeiungen über Europas Zukunft und Frankreichs Glück und Niedergang, 1555-2200.* Pfullingen: J. Baum, 1921.

McCann, Lee. *Nostradamus, the Man Who Saw Through Time.* New York: Creative Age, 1941.

Menestrier, Claude François. *La philosophe des images enigmatiques, ou il est traité des enigmes, hieroglyphiques, oracles, propheties, sorts, divinations, loteries, talismans, songes, Centuries de Nostradamus, de la baguette.* Lyon: H. Baritel, 1694.

Monterey, Jean. *Nostradamus, prophète du XXe siècle.* Paris: Nef de Paris, 1963.

Moura, Jean and Paul Louvet. *La vie de Nostradamus.* Paris: Gallimard, 1930.

Nicoullaud, Charles. *Nostradamus, ses prophéties.* Paris: Perrin, 1914.

Nostredame, Michel de. *Les prophéties de m. Michel Nostradamvs.* Lyon: P. Rigavd, 1568.

——————— *Les vrayes centuries et prophéties de Maistre Michel Nostradamus.* Amsterdam: I. Ianszon, 1668.

——————— *Les vrayes centuries et prophéties* ... Rouen, 1689.

Piobb, Pierre Vincenti. *Le secret de Nostradamus et de ses célèbres prophéties du XVIe siècle* ... Paris: Adyar, 1927.

Privat, Maurice. *La fin de notre siècle et la vie du futur grand monarque prophetisée par Nostradamus et exposée d'après les Centuries* ... Paris: Floury, 1939.

Rahner, Karl. *Visionen und Prophezeiungen.* Innsbruck: Tyrolia, 1952.

Roberts, Henry C. *The Complete Prophecies of Nostradamus.* New York: Crown, 1947.

Rochetaillée, P. *Prophéties de Nostradamus, clef des centuries, son application à l'histoire* ... Paris: Adyar, 1939.

Ruir, Emile. *Le grand carnage d'après les prophéties de Nostradamus de 1938 à 1947.* Paris: Médicis, 1938.

_____ *L'écroulement de l'Europe d'après des prophéties de Nostradamus; les invasions, la conversion d'Israel, le règne de Dieu et de l'église du Christ, la fin du monde.* Paris: Médicis, 1939.

_____ *Nostradamus, les proches et derniers événements.* Paris: Médicis, 1953.

_____ *Nostradamus, ses prophéties de nos jours à l'an 2023.* Paris: Médicis, 1947.

Sugrue, Thomas. *There Is a River: The Story of Edgar Cayce.* New York: Holt, 1942.

Varena, Marcus. *Gesammelte Prophezeiungen.* Freiburg: Bauer, 1959.

Wohl, Louis de. *Sterne, Krieg und Frieden.* Olten: O. Walter, 1951.